Inside the Ropes with Jesse Ventura

Inside the Ropes with Jesse Ventura

Tom Hauser

University of Minnesota Press
Minneapolis • London

MINNESOTA

Published by the University of Minnesota Press
111 Third Avenue South, Suite 290
Minneapolis, MN 55401-2520
http://www.upress.umn.edu

Printed in the United States of America on acid-free paper

Library of Congress Cataloging-in-Publication Data

Hauser, Tom.
  Inside the ropes with Jesse Ventura / Tom Hauser.
    p. cm.
Includes index.
  ISBN 0-8166-4187-0 (HC/J : alk. paper)
  1. Ventura, Jesse. 2. Governors—Minnesota—Biography. 3.
Minnesota—Politics and government—1951– I. Title.
  F610.3.V46 H38 2002
  977.6′053′092—dc21
                                    2002005963

The University of Minnesota is an equal-opportunity educator and employer.

12 11 10 09 08 07 06 05 04 03 02   10 9 8 7 6 5 4 3 2 1

For Nancy, Hobey, Abigail, Nicklaus, and Caroline

Contents

Preface

The annual holiday party hosted by Hubbard Broadcasting in the Twin Cities is known to be a lavish affair. The cocktail and hors d'oeuvres hour is always followed by a sit-down dinner for hundreds of employees. A celebrity from one of the company's many broadcast holdings is usually tabbed to be master of ceremonies. On December 17, 1994, that celebrity is former professional wrestler Jesse "the Body" Ventura, a controversial but entertaining morning talk-show host on KSTP-AM. He also happens to be completing a four-year term as mayor of Brooklyn Park, Minnesota.

As master of ceremonies Ventura welcomes the crowd, tells a few jokes, and presides over the much anticipated drawing for fabulous door prizes. The first prize of the night is not only fabulous—a new mini-satellite-television system—it serves as a rather remarkable bit of foreshadowing. The next thing I know, Ventura pulls a name out of a box and reads, "Tom Hauser, KSTP-TV." As I went up to shake Ventura's hand and thank him, neither of us had an inkling I was going to need that satellite dish to keep track of his worldwide fame four years later.

I'd only met Ventura one other time, when I interviewed him for a story while he was mayor of Brooklyn Park. Now, seven years later, I've traveled the country and the world for KSTP-TV, covering his exploits as Minnesota's governor. From Los Angeles to Washington, D.C., from New York City to Boston, from Tokyo to Mexico City, I've witnessed one of the most amazing political stories in U.S. history. From Letterman to Leno to Regis to Larry King, it's hard to turn the channel without bumping into Governor Jesse Ventura.

You'd be hard-pressed to name another politician anywhere in the country who came from as improbable a background as Ventura's to win election to a major political office. Even Ronald Reagan's ascendancy was not nearly so remarkable. It's not much of a stretch to imagine a Hollywood actor becoming governor of a state like California, and once Reagan became a successful governor of the biggest state in the nation, it wasn't much of a leap for him to become president.

If you're looking for a true example of a quantum leap from impossibility to reality, Jesse Ventura is your man. This book is the story of that leap. This is not an academic work that delves into the minutiae of the political science of Ventura's election as governor of Minnesota, nor is it a historical or critical analysis of his accomplishments in office or the impact of his policies. Such books will be written after he leaves office and the passage of time gives us better perspective from which to assess his governing abilities. I don't pass judgment on his policies or performance, although I do occasionally take him on when it comes to his criticism of the media.

Much of this story is told in the words of Governor Ventura, legislators, media members, and others who have observed him while in office. All the quotes are verbatim, taken directly from videotaped news conferences, interviews, and impromptu news events involving the governor. I've personally attended most of the major events during Ventura's term. When I or another reporter can't attend an event, KSTP-TV makes it a priority to at least have a photographer cover the governor's public appearances. You just never know what he might say or do next.

This is a chronicle of Jesse Ventura's freewheeling rise from former professional wrestler and local talk-radio obscurity to the most powerful political office in Minnesota. (Vice President Al Gore and Governor George W. Bush even sought his support during the 2000 presidential campaign.) It shows Ventura's transformation from B-movie actor to a man President Bill Clinton asked to help pave the way for free trade with China. It follows Ventura's ascent from U.S. Navy SEAL to a politician who oversees one of the most dramatic tax-reform initiatives in Minnesota history. As I said, it's a book about the transformation from impossibility to reality.

There is no single explanation for Ventura's rise to political prominence. Some suggest Jesse Ventura was elected to amuse. In 1998 life was good for Minnesotans, riding the wave of economic prosperity with no end in sight. When the election came around, maybe voters thought, "Hey, this looks like fun. Let's give Jesse a try. How badly could he screw up with billions of dollars in surplus revenue piling up?" Of course, it could have been the frustration of seeing the state pile up surplus after surplus while still maintaining some of the highest tax rates in the country that turned voters toward Ventura and his fiscal conservatism.

Or maybe he's further evidence of Minnesota's ongoing fascination with quirky politicians. Sure, Minnesota is known for serious statesmen like Walter Mondale and Hubert H. Humphrey. But we twice elected Rudy Perpich as governor, a man nicknamed "Governor Goofy" by his detractors. There's no question Perpich was a dedicated public servant and tireless promoter of the state, but he'll long be remembered for trying to bring a chopsticks factory to Minnesota's Iron Range and traveling to Europe to buy a castle for the University of Minnesota. And let's not forget Rudy Boschwitz. Before Minnesotans elected him to the U.S. Senate in 1978, he was best known for his plaid shirts and hokey television commercials for his company, Plywood Minnesota. After two terms, voters replaced Boschwitz with a little-known, hyperactive college professor who traveled the state campaigning in an ugly green bus. Paul Wellstone is still in the U.S. Senate.

In 1970 Minnesotans even elected one other celebrity governor: a thirty-seven-year-old former Olympic hockey player named Wendell Anderson. Until Ventura came along, Anderson was the only Minnesota governor to grace the cover of *Time* magazine.

Despite the reputation of Minnesotans as stodgy, frostbitten, stoic Scandinavians and Germans, we obviously like to have fun with our politics. The election of Jesse Ventura, however, goes a bit deeper than just having some fun. In Ventura's brand of populist politics, the "pop" stands for "pop culture." He is the embodiment of a culture that consumes sports, movies, and talk radio in mass quantities. Throw in his Navy SEAL career and you've got a living, breathing action figure. A guy like that entering politics is going to draw attention. He might even get some votes.

Ultimately, I think, Ventura became the antidote to all that voters perceived to be wrong with "career politicians." Just take a look at the headlines from Washington, D.C., the week Ventura was elected in 1998. President Clinton, a Democrat, is on the verge of impeachment for lying to Congress about his affair with a White House intern. Newt Gingrich, a Republican, abruptly resigns as Speaker of the House after his polarizing brand of mean-spirited politics finally catches up with him.

Back in Minnesota, Ventura tags his two opponents, Republican Norm Coleman and Democrat Hubert "Skip" Humphrey, with the same negative label of "career politician" that Clinton and Gingrich epitomize at the national level. Humphrey, the son of a career politician, and Coleman, who switched from the Democratic Party to the Republican Party while mayor of St. Paul, made easy targets. When those two began their campaigns by bashing each other at every turn, the door swung wide open for Ventura.

For many voters, Ventura seemed to be a palatable, if risky, remedy to politics-as-usual. He couldn't possibly be worse than Clinton, Gingrich, and their ilk. His blunt talk and refreshing candor resonated with voters. He energized young people and other politically apathetic segments of the population to go to the polls. He could quote Abraham Lincoln and the movie *Animal House* in the same campaign stop. He had name recognition, and, after years of professional wrestling, he knew how to draw a crowd. Ventura called himself "socially liberal" and "fiscally conservative," and suddenly "pop-culture-ism" was born.

The question now is, did voters get what they bargained for? Has he met the expectations of the people who put him in office after he promised less government and lower taxes? Minnesotans seemed to hold their collective breath when Ventura was declared the winner in 1998. They were deluged with e-mails and phone calls from friends around the country, all beginning with the same two words: "What the ...!" Many people who voted for him had no idea what to expect. They hoped he would shake things up, reform government, make it more responsive, lean, and accountable to the people. Still, there were fears that Minnesota's state government was in for unprecedented turmoil. Those fears initially proved unfounded as Ventura quickly surrounded himself with very talented people.

There were also concerns about whether Ventura would respect the dignity of the governor's office. Would he become a serious, button-down, no-nonsense governor who sheds his wrestling past in favor of more serious pursuits? Or would he cross the line separating dignity and buffoonery? It was a legitimate concern. After all, the image of a man in earrings and a brightly colored feather boa was still fresh in the minds of most Minnesotans.

We got some answers to the direction Ventura would go during a remarkable impromptu question-and-answer session with capitol press-corps reporters in December 1998. The governor-elect confirmed he had just signed a book deal with a six-figure advance. He didn't rule out possible movie roles or endorsement deals. When pressed on what guidelines he would follow for accepting private moneymaking deals while in office, he replied, "My guidelines will probably be, first of all, that I'm not like every other governor."

It was on that day the idea for this book was born. In that meeting he made it abundantly clear that most of the old, unwritten rules about what a governor can and cannot do while in office wouldn't necessarily apply to him. I realized then and there I would have to start taking careful notes because this story would one day have to be told. It's the story of a governor who, despite lavishly positive press coverage from the day of his election, immediately identified the media as Public

Acknowledgments

Although I spent countless hours compiling notes, transcribing interviews, and writing *Inside the Ropes with Jesse Ventura* over three years, it truly was a collaborative effort involving many talented people. Most of them had no idea I was writing this book, but without their help it would not have been possible.

At times the "Jesse beat" at KSTP-TV has seemed like a twenty-four-hours-a-day, seven-days-a-week operation. Even though I tried, I couldn't possibly be there for every milestone in this remarkable political odyssey. Whether I was there or not, I relied heavily on the work of an outstanding team of photojournalists. There's a reason that team, led by chief photographer Mark Anderson and assistant chief photographer Dave Wertheimer, was named "Station of the Year" in 1999 by the National Press Photographers Association: they managed to get their cameras and microphones in all the right places at all the right times.

Each contributed in ways large and small, but in particular I'd like to thank Dan Dwyer, Denny DeGriselles, Al Carlson, Jason Hanson, Lee Zwiefelhofer, Tyler Damerville, Dave Ogle, Joe Caffrey, Mark Garvey, and Mike Paidar, all of whom have either traveled extensively nationwide and worldwide with me while covering Governor Ventura or camped out in the KSTP-TV State Capitol Bureau for our ringside seat to his frequent matches with the Minnesota legislature.

Others have been there to cover the vast number of Ventura news conferences and public appearances, including Brad Jacobs, Phil Engelstad, Monty Stuempert, Jeff Ganahl, Greg Schulzetenberg, Phil Thiesse, Russ Brown, Dave Peterson, Joe Kaczynski, Lorri Burchett, Marlon Hall, and John Elliott. And there's Steve Walker and Al Sanders, who each has a talent for tracking down videotape of Ventura via satellite, no matter where in the world the governor might be. It's always perilous to begin naming people you want to thank because inevitably names are missed, but let me just say that photojournalists are among the hardest-working people in television news and deserve all the recognition they can get. The same goes for assignment-desk editors like Margaret Hart, Andrea Melberg, and Mike Caputa, who often arranged coverage of as many as five or six Ventura appearances in a single day.

I'd also like to thank KSTP-TV news director Scott Libin, assistant news director Mark Ginther, and general manager Ed Piette for recognizing that, when one of the greatest political stories of all time lands in your lap, you commit the resources necessary to cover it no matter where it takes you, whether it's Royalton, Minnesota, or Tokyo, Japan. The same goes for the Hubbard family, owners of KSTP-TV and one of the nation's great broadcasting families. Of course, I'd be remiss if I didn't thank Georgia Walesheck, whose tenacity at making newsroom travel arrangements is matched only by her zeal to make sure expense reports are turned in and properly documented.

At the State Capitol, producer Kristin Fischer helped me keep track of the legislature while I was often on some far-flung adventure, trying to keep up with the governor. I've been covering the Minnesota legislature for five years now, but I'm still one of the "new guys." So I'm indebted to many capitol press-corps colleagues who often shared their vast insight and experiences with me, including Eric Eskola of WCCO Radio; Dane Smith, Patricia Lopez, and Robert Whereatt of the *Star Tribune;* Jim Ragsdale, Patrick Sweeney, and Bill Salisbury of the *St. Paul Pioneer Press;* Brian Bakst, Ashley Grant, and Patrick Howe at the Associated Press; and, yes, even my "archenemy" television competitors, Pat Kessler of WCCO-TV and Kerri Miller of KARE-TV.

I also couldn't have kept up with Governor Ventura without the help of his communications staff. John Wodele, Janet Hafner, Paul Moore, David Ruth, Samantha Massagalia, and Steve Lebeau always tried to be helpful, even when it seemed every political reporter in the country was making some kind of unreasonable demand, sometimes all at once.

Although I've taken my lumps along with the rest of the "media jackals," I'd also like to thank Governor Jesse Ventura. When he isn't too busy bashing us, he does take time to accommodate some of our many requests for interviews. While he often displays all the tact of a charging bull at a news conference, he can be quite gracious and disarming one-on-one. I know because I've sat across from him for more than a dozen one-on-one interviews.

To Todd Orjala at the University of Minnesota Press, thanks for taking an interest in this book, guiding it to publication, and trying to make sense of my 3:00 A.M. e-mails.

To my wife, Nancy, and my kids, Hobey, Abigail, Nicklaus, and Caroline, thanks for putting up with me during this project. Your love and support is dearly appreciated. Nothing throws off a household schedule like someone working all day and writing all night. Your willingness to endure that means everything to me.

Last, to my late parents, Don and Mary Hauser, you will always be my inspiration.

CHAPTER 1

"We Shocked the World"
Jesse Ventura's Unlikely Path
to the Governor's Mansion

This story seems like a real loser. It's July 21, 1998, one of those hot, sticky Minnesota summer days when you can see the heat rising off the asphalt. I know this all too well because I'm sitting in the parking lot of KFAN Radio in the Minneapolis suburb of Bloomington, staking out a wrestler-turned-actor-turned-radio-talk-show-host who may or may not run for governor. Does anyone else smell radio-station publicity stunt? I do. But it's a slow news day, and our threshold for what constitutes news is lowered significantly.

Never mind the polls that say he doesn't have a chance to win. I can't believe what this guy's saying on the radio. In his latest bit of political bluster he just said, "In my first act as governor I'll eliminate every county assessor's office in the state." He then goes on a familiar rant about how his property taxes are too high and stops just short of saying Minnesota is in the grips of Communism.

My story assignment for KSTP-TV on this hot, miserable day is to find out if Jesse "the Body" Ventura is actually going to run for governor. He first announced his candidacy in January on the steps of the State Capitol, but few take it as anything more than shameless promotion for his radio show. Today is the deadline to file the official paperwork if he plans to run.

My photographer and I park outside KFAN a few parking stalls away from Ventura's car. My story assignment isn't quite Watergate, so it doesn't take Woodward and Bernstein to find his car. It's the only light blue Porsche with vanity plates that read "NAVY SEAL." If there's one thing Ventura knows, it's how to draw attention.

We're sitting in our news van, ears glued to our cheap speakers, listening to Ventura bluster away on KFAN. If he does officially register for the governor's race, this is expected to be his last day on the air until after the election. KFAN's general manager, Mick Anselmo, has hinted publicly that Ventura will be taken off the air without pay so the station doesn't run afoul of campaign rules that might force it to give equal time to other candidates. We're hoping Ventura will announce his intentions on his show. We're not allowed in the studio to shoot video or to do an interview with him. So, out of desperation to make this a news story, we're shooting video of KFAN's "1130" on our digital AM dial and recording the show in case Ventura stops bad-mouthing politicians long enough to announce he wants to become one himself.

Our intrepid efforts are wasted when Ventura goes off the air with barely a hint of his gubernatorial intentions. "Isn't that amazing," he says as he concludes his broadcast. "I may have to give up my job. Yet all the career politicians who have been elected sit at public jobs that get paid with our tax dollars and *they* don't have to."

My backup plan is to do an ambush interview with Ventura when he leaves the radio station and heads to his car. It's not as if I've never had to resort to this before in my quest for the truth. However, this is my first ambush of a man who stands six feet, four inches tall, weighs 245 pounds, and once uttered the words "I ain't got time to bleed." He's also got a reputation for being a bit surly. Not to mention he's probably bent about 613 metal folding chairs over the heads of opponents much larger than I. Ignoring my impulse to go to plan C and ambush by e-mail instead, photographer Mike Paidar and I climb out of the news van and get in position between the radio-station door and Ventura's Porsche.

It's important to note here that Paidar stands six feet, nine inches tall and weighs 260 pounds. That affords me some level of comfort until it dawns on me that he'll be too busy videotaping my inevitable pulverization by "the Body" to come to my aid. OK, I'm exaggerating the danger. I've interviewed Ventura once before. It was in 1994 when, as mayor of Brooklyn Park, he moved to Maple Grove. Some of his political opponents said he couldn't be mayor of one Twin Cities suburb if he lived in another and that he should resign. I had to ask some tough questions then and lived to tell about it, so why not now?

Ventura emerges from the KFAN studios about an hour after his show. He's wearing a white T-shirt, blue jeans, and cowboy boots. He's carrying a briefcase as he briskly walks across the lot toward his car. Paidar and I approach, camera rolling. "Hey, Jesse, Tom Hauser from Channel Five. Can you tell us if you're going to run for governor?" No response. He keeps walking. "Are you going to file for the election today?"

"It's none of your business," he growls.

Hey, it's not much but it's a start. And I'm not bleeding. "Can't you just tell us that?"

"No," he replies.

"Why not?" I ask.

"Because it's my business, not yours."

Clearly, I'm not dealing with a career politician, because no career politician would turn down the kind of free media exposure we're trying to hand him. I take one more stab at it. "Why can't you just tell us if you're going to run or not?" Once again he responds, "It's none of your business."

He opens his car door, throws his briefcase on the seat, climbs in, and drives off. So far, I don't have much of a story. But I do have my health.

Ventura doesn't keep us in suspense too long. Within an hour he shows up at the Minnesota secretary of state's office accompanied by Doug Friedline, a Reform Party activist and now Ventura's campaign manager. This unlikely tag team arrives to file the papers necessary for Ventura to run for governor of Minnesota. All of a sudden, it *is* our business.

"We're all done?" Ventura asks the clerk after signing the election forms. "Time to go to work." Moments later his menacing scowl of an hour ago is replaced by a look of determination. "It's a much anticipated day. Naturally, we've been doing a lot of work before this day, so it isn't like it's just begun at this point in time."

July 21, 1998, is a milestone day in Minnesota history.

The next day, Ventura's so-called "Bod Squad" radio show is off the air. "Effective today, Jesse has been removed from his air shift until after the election in early November," fill-in host Paul Allen says, reading a prepared statement to listeners from KFAN Radio management. Allen also announces the "temporary" show that will fill Ventura's time slot. "Paul Allen, Jeff Dubay, David Ruth—now known as the 'Odd Squad.'"

Ventura tells me he finds the move more than odd. He says it's unfair. He agrees to meet me for an interview about his campaign and his radio show. As if to illustrate the apparent absurdity of his long-shot candidacy, he wants to do the interview in the parking lot of a car wash in St. Louis Park, a few miles from downtown Minneapolis. A car wash, it turns out, managed by Dean Barkley, another Reform Party activist and Ventura's chief political strategist.

Ventura arrives in his Porsche, wearing an athletic warm-up and tennis shoes. He's ready to vent about anything and everything. "I was led to believe by KFAN management that, as long as I had no opponent against me, there would be no FCC problems," Ventura says on his first day as an unemployed radio talk-show host. "They said I would still be able to stay on the air and do my show until September 15."

He hoped to at least keep his radio show (and its high-profile forum for his candidacy) until after the primary elections because he would be running unopposed in the Reform Party. But KFAN general manager Mick Anselmo has other ideas. "This is just really a proper course of action to ensure fairness in the election process," Anselmo says. "It's a judgment call."

Anselmo makes that decision despite some questionable maneuvering by Ventura and Barkley the day before in an effort to head off Ventura's removal from the airwaves. The two men went to the home of

Bill Dahn, a would-be Reform Party candidate for governor. Dahn has already filed as a Reform Party candidate, and Ventura fears having a challenger will dismiss any chance he has of keeping his radio job until the primary election in September. Ventura and Barkley persuade Dahn to refile as a Republican candidate. Dahn's principal motivation to run for office is a long-standing and bizarre feud with St. Paul's Republican mayor, Norm Coleman, who also is running for governor. Dahn holds Coleman responsible for physical problems caused by what he calls "formaldehyde poisoning" that resulted from a government program that provided insulation and heating assistance for low-income homeowners.

Into this mess step Ventura and Barkley, who convince Dahn he'd be better off running against Coleman in the primary. They even offer to pay the $600 filing fee. Dahn agrees. Ventura defends the action by telling me that Dahn didn't realize he could file to run against Coleman in the primary and that, once it was explained to him, Dahn decided that's what he wanted to do.

Despite those election-law gymnastics, Ventura still loses his job. His KFAN contract allows the station to take him off the air without pay if he runs for public office. It's tough on both Ventura and KFAN. After a year in the 10:00 A.M. to 1:00 P.M. slot, mixing sports talk with renegade political views, Ventura is a hit with his target audience of men ages twenty-five to fifty-four. In fact, he claims to have the highest rating on the station. But now Ventura is free to aim his political vitriol at his archenemies: career politicians. He uses the loss of his radio job and his estimated $50,000 salary to launch his campaign against the half-dozen Democratic and Republican candidates running for governor.

As we stand in the car-wash parking lot, Ventura issues his first campaign ultimatum. "I challenge each and every one of them to prove how bad they want to be governor," he says of his opponents like Mayor Coleman and Minnesota attorney general Hubert H. "Skip" Humphrey III, a Democrat. Glaring into the camera and pointing his finger, Ventura adds, "Take a leave of absence without pay and you'd see them all heading for the hills." He then leans over to me and laughs, "That was a good one. You'll wanna use that!"

Suddenly, two things occur to me. One, I'm being used as Ventura's foil like a two-bit wrestling announcer. And two, he still doesn't have a chance to become governor—but this will be fun.

Among Minnesotans it's long been known as the "Great Minnesota Get-Together." In 1998, the Minnesota State Fair could be known as the "Great Jesse Ventura Love-in." Politicians have used the State Fair to meet voters and get their message out for as long as people have eaten hot dogs off sticks. But the combination of Pronto Pups and populism is either turning Ventura into a bona fide contender or a novelty candidate with amazing drawing power.

It's Wednesday, September 2, and I've just arrived at the Ventura campaign booth near the corner of Nelson Street and Judson Avenue at the fairgrounds in St. Paul. I'm scheduled to meet him at 1:00 P.M. for a candidate-profile story. I quickly realize I'm going to have to wait. Sandwiched between "Monty's Traveling Reptile Show" and the "Pork Chops on a Stick" booth is a big, bald political sideshow.

The Ventura for Governor campaign booth is decorated with "Retaliate in '98" T-shirts, bumper stickers, and signs. At least fifty people crowd around the booth, listening to Ventura while he autographs fake dollar bills adorned with his picture and campaign slogans. Another one hundred or so people stand around the periphery, trying to get a look at him. All those within earshot are getting a crash course in life and politics according to Ventura. It's Jesse on a shtick.

"You a Harley rider?" Ventura asks one man dressed in a Harley-Davidson T-shirt and holding his young daughter. "You bet," the man replies. "I'll tell you this," Ventura says. "With me as governor, rest assured I'll veto any helmet law." He's just warming up. There's a one-liner for every question or comment he hears. About politics: "I don't believe in politics. I believe in results." About whether he's smart enough to be governor: "They automatically assume that to be intelligent you have to have gone to college." About Democrats and Republicans: "I don't want a Democrat in the boardroom and I don't want a Republican in the bedroom." About taxes: "I will veto any new tax that comes on my desk. There's not an excuse they can give me for it." About wrestling: "Win if you can, lose if you must, but always cheat. That's right, but that's only in wrestling." All the while he's signing autographs and shaking hands.

We manage to get a microphone on him during all of this, but he's too busy to stop for an interview just yet. On one side of the booth, campaign workers are selling Ventura T-shirts. On the other, there's a clipboard with a sign-up sheet for people who want Ventura yard signs. People are actually signing up to have campaign signs in their yards! Ventura, dressed in a black Navy SEAL T-shirt, sits in the middle, part circus ringmaster and part carnival barker.

"I'm a Navy SEAL. I don't get mad, I get even," he tells anyone who will listen. "I don't care if a bill is Democrat or Republican. If it's good for Minnesota, I'll sign it. If it's bad, I'll veto it." If his opponents don't take him seriously, he says, they better watch out. "I wouldn't run if I couldn't win," he says. "You hear candidates say, oh, I'm a wasted vote. I find that to be utterly pompous, arrogant."

It's become obvious we don't really need to interview Ventura. We just need to listen. There's no way to tell how many of these people are just stopping by to meet a celebrity and how many take him seriously as a candidate for governor. Day after day he shows up at the fair, meeting people, repeating his plainspoken stands on issues, making connections. Someone asks about the state budget surplus. "You give money back to the people," he says. "Let the people spend their own money and make their own decisions rather than relying on government to do it for them." On education, he's against vouchers for private schools. "My view is simple: We're here to provide a public education by the Constitution, K through 12. If you choose not to use it, that's your business."

Although he's serious about the issues, Ventura can't escape being the celebrity candidate. The people surrounding his booth are young and old, male and female, white collar and blue collar (one guy even wears a dog collar). And, of course, the State Fair draws its share of wrestling fans, and many visitors to the Ventura booth want to talk about his former career. He even attracts a gaggle of screaming teenage girls who couldn't possibly have been alive when Ventura was at the height of his wrestling career.

"I was screaming," one of them blurts out to us as she describes their encounter with Ventura. "And then we came and saw this guy and I said, ooooh, I know, Jesse 'the Body.' And it was really cool!" I ask Ventura if that bothers him now that he's trying to be taken seriously as a candidate. His response is a classic: "I make my living with my mind now instead of my body. So I'm Jesse 'the Mind.'"

"Does that disappoint some of your fans?" I ask. A wry smile appears on his face that usually signals a punch line. "I don't think so, because I still got eighteen-inch pipes." His fans around the booth howl with laughter as Ventura's head starts bobbing with self-satisfaction. He knows he's delivering what the people want to hear.

The Commando Candidate

On primary election day, September 15, Ventura easily wins the Minnesota Reform Party nomination for governor as he runs unopposed. He's automatically a huge underdog to the primary winners in the Democratic and Republican parties. Hubert H. "Skip" Humphrey III wins the Democratic race (in Minnesota it's called the Democratic-Farmer-Labor Party, or DFL). Yes, it's *that* Humphrey family. His dad once served as vice president and U.S. senator, and Skip Humphrey is currently Minnesota's attorney general. The Republican nominee is Norm Coleman, the longtime mayor of St. Paul who not so long ago was a Democrat himself. Ventura's opponents are traditional politicians in every way.

Three days later Ventura marches uninvited into a candidate forum, dressed in combat fatigues, boots, and a camouflage Australian-outback hat he once wore in the movie *Predator*. There's a smattering of applause and some not-so-subtle chuckling. Ventura is anything but traditional. The lunchtime forum is called the "Governor's Economic Summit," and organizers of the event invited only the candidates with the top two vote totals in the primary elections, Humphrey and Coleman. Humphrey received 182,562 votes in the Democratic primary, Coleman got 127,957 Republican votes, and Ventura received just 17,169 votes in the Reform Party primary.

Looking very much the part of a commando candidate, Ventura takes a seat at one of the tables adorned with white linen tablecloths and floral centerpieces. This luncheon crowd of men in suits and ties and women in business suits and dresses doesn't quite know what to make of this interloper. He's *Predator* come to life.

"Minnesota's a great state, and it's a great state because of all of you," state Senator Roger Moe tells the audience. Moe is Humphrey's lieutenant-governor running mate filling in at this forum because Humphrey is in California on a fund-raising trip. "We're blessed," Moe tells the crowd in a rather dull speech he's reading from a podium. "We have abundant natural resources, economic diversity, homegrown sense of community, and as a state we are one in spirit." It's all standard politic-speak. But Moe surprises the crowd about ten minutes into his speech. "There are three [political] parties in this state," he says. "All of them ought to have the opportunity to address you, and so I yield the rest of my time to Jesse Ventura."

The crowd offers polite applause as Ventura makes his way to the podium, stopping along the way to shake hands with Moe. "Good afternoon," Ventura says as he looks out over the tables, sizing up the crowd. "The first thing I'll say to you is you're going to find me a little bit different," he continues, drawing some laughter. "You can open your eyes and probably see that. Go ahead, you can laugh." He pulls off his hat and gets down to business.

"We're here to talk economics today, and I'm going to talk economics," Ventura tells the audience, watching and listening now with rapt attention, probably thankful this won't be just another boring political speech. But first, he has a few pointed remarks about not being invited to this event. "I was very disappointed that I was not allowed to come here and speak to you, because I'm going to take you for a moment back in history and I want you to think very seriously about that. If the thought process were the same as it is today 150 years ago in this country, you would not have had Abraham Lincoln up here to talk to you," Ventura tells them, giving a history lesson of all things. "Because Abraham Lincoln was a third-party candidate. At that point in time the Republicans were the growing, new party." He says having just two choices in most American elections is "ridiculous." He says we need "maybe four or five because we come from a very diverse nation."

Ventura delivers a seven-minute speech about how the state's economic situation compelled him to run for governor. He points out that he watched a $4 billion budget surplus disappear while his property taxes went up an average of $460 a year five years in a row. "That was beyond belief to me," he says.

Ventura then sets his sights on his two opponents in the upcoming general election and their promises of tax cuts and rebates of surplus money. "They're going to cut your taxes?" he asks with a hint of sarcasm. "Well, what this is going to boil down to is, who do you trust is going to come through with what they say? I am the only major-party candidate who stood on the steps of the State Capitol and said, 'Give the surplus back!' And I laugh now. 'Oh, it's an election year, *now* we're going to cut taxes.' Are they really? That's the judgment you have to make."

He concludes his speech by taking a shot at legislators, including Senator Moe, who gave Ventura the platform to speak and is still sitting in the audience. "You have people voting to get reelected, not voting for what necessarily is right, and I want you to remember this when they tell you voting for a third party is a wasted vote," he says, as Moe smiles in amusement. "Remember, the only wasted vote is walking into that voting booth and not voting your conscience. That is a wasted vote! Thank you." Ventura gets much more applause than before. He begins to walk off the stage but returns to the microphone to thank Moe for giving him the time to speak "in the interest of fair play."

Afterward, Ventura is still angry he wasn't invited to speak in the first place. "I thought that was a huge disservice to the people of Minnesota and almost a slap in the face to freedom and what the election system is all about," he says. "I am a major-party candidate. I'm playing a major role in this election no matter what happens."

Ventura also admits it wasn't his idea to attend the luncheon. "We did not seek out anything to be involved in this. It was the Humphrey campaign. When they found out I was not invited, they graciously—and Roger Moe graciously—cut his speech down to ten minutes, rewrote it, and said he would give up ten minutes of his time to allow me to go out there, and I commend him for that."

Moe later acknowledges that, by allowing Ventura time to speak at the luncheon, the Humphrey-Moe campaign is "serving notice" it won't appear at any debates or forums unless Ventura gets equal time. "We're doing this in the interest of fairness," Moe says minutes after the luncheon. "His party has earned major-party status, and he deserves as much a chance to speak as any of us."

Moe's benevolence might seem out of place in the cutthroat world of politics. In fact, the stance taken by Humphrey and Moe is laced with cunning strategy.

Most political observers expect the fiscally conservative Ventura to pull far more votes from the Republican Coleman than from the Democrat Humphrey, possibly enough to provide the margin of victory for Humphrey. By insisting that Ventura take part in every debate and forum, the Humphrey campaign aims to set up a classic divide-and-conquer strategy. Humphrey builds up Ventura's political stature in hopes of taking down Coleman. Coleman sees what's happening and does just what you'd expect him to do: He tries to minimize Ventura's candidacy. Coleman won't rule out debate appearances with Ventura but makes it clear he thinks Ventura's participation would be a waste of time. "We haven't precluded Jesse," Coleman tells the Minneapolis-based *Star Tribune*. "But we have said to debate organizers, 'It's your preference. If you want to hear from one of the two candidates who will become governor, you want me and Skip [Humphrey].'"

The first major three-way gubernatorial debate is set for October 1 in the northern-Minnesota city of Brainerd, and by mutual agreement all three major-party candidates will be present. Anyone expecting

Ventura to show up at Central Lakes College in military fatigues or a feather boa and wrestling tights is in for a surprise. He arrives dressed in a navy blue suit, a blue diamond-patterned tie, and a starched white button-down shirt. Ventura strikes an imposing figure and exudes power and confidence. His opponents also appear in navy blue pinstripe suits, but somehow these two men, slouched and looking uncomfortable in their chairs, seem out of place next to the media-savvy Jesse "the Body" Ventura. It soon becomes apparent Coleman and Humphrey have as much a chance to beat Ventura in this debate as they would in a wrestling ring.

The debate picks up steam when the topic turns to negative campaign advertising. The candidates are asked to comment on a negative ad the Humphrey campaign is running about remarks Coleman reportedly made about the family farm becoming a thing of the past. The following exchange sets the tone for the rest of the campaign:

HUMPHREY: You want to know who's been hit hardest with negative ads that have come from Norm Coleman's campaign? It's Skip Humphrey. Just go and ask the citizens. They come up to me every day and say, "My goodness, listen to that kind of crud that's on television." I want to see us talk specifically and expressly about the truth.

COLEMAN: Let me just jump in. This campaign should be on the record, on what we've done and our capacity to deliver on what we're going to do. The fact is, Skip, you didn't quote what was in the paper [about Coleman's comments on the family farm]. You got up there on TV and said, "I heard Norm Coleman say!" And you *didn't* hear me say. And the fact is, if we're going to do this, let's be fair, let's be straightforward, let's be honest, let's look at the record. Let's fight about our different views on the family!

(By this time Humphrey and Coleman seem to have forgotten there's a third candidate in the debate. They'll soon be reminded.)

HUMPHREY: The reality here is, it's not about what we say, it's what are we going to do for family farmers? That's the bottom line. And frankly,

Norm, if you don't know what the family farm's all about, you ought to admit it and go find out about it. I can tell you this: They're not cash-flowing anything today. They're going down the tubes and we need to make ... changes, and governors ought to be involved directly in that effort!

COLEMAN: They want free and fair trade, which you oppose. They don't want moratoriums on [feedlots] and they don't want you to roll back workers' comp reform, because that kills Main Street!

(Suddenly, all three candidates start talking at once and the moderator intervenes.)

MODERATOR: Mr. Ventura deserves to get in on this match!

VENTURA: I think it shows obviously who's above all of this, doesn't it? And I think that right now, if you want to look at fair and good campaigning, I will just state this. I'm embarrassed as a United States citizen and as a veteran to what both of these two premier parties, the Democrats and Republicans, are sinking to today, from Washington right on down here locally. I noticed a cartoon the other day in the *Star Tribune* newspaper that kind of took a shot and said, "Amazing—the only candidate that's campaigning on the issues and not slinging mud is the former pro wrestler, actor, and talk-show host."

In that one exchange, Ventura epitomizes the campaign for governor. The two career politicians go for each other's throats while Ventura looks on in amusement. Humphrey and Coleman become political caricatures showing just how absurd the election process has become. Ventura knows it and can't wait to pounce every time they talk, usually with a roar of approval from the audience. But the other two candidates, who've all but dismissed Ventura as a threat, continually ignore him and take jabs at each other.

It is remarkable to watch the two traditional party candidates show a nearly total disregard for the Reform Party candidate as the series of debates continues. It's as if Humphrey and Coleman are happy just to have Ventura in the debates as window dressing to show how generous they can be to the underdog candidate. Little do they know, Ventura is scoring big with undecided voters. In fact, he seems to look better and better every time his opponents open their mouths.

This is never more abundantly clear than during the final major debate of the campaign, on October 30, just four days before the election. The debate is televised statewide from the studios of KTCA-TV, the public-television station in downtown St. Paul. Ken Stone of KTCA is the moderator with three news anchors from Twin Cities network television affiliates as panelists. Citizens will be asking questions via a microwave hookup from the Mall of America in Bloomington.

"No stopwatches here," Stone tells the candidates. "We want to keep this loose and informal." He should be careful what he wishes for.

The first significant skirmish of the debate comes after a seemingly innocuous question about how to reduce health-care costs for low-income senior citizens. In the following exchange, notice Humphrey's confusing answer, Coleman's fiery retort, and finally, Ventura's zinger:

HUMPHREY: We can cut down those costs up to 70 percent. What I've proposed is an initiative that will provide for no more than $200 per year for those that are near or just above the poverty line, and for every senior citizen that has a Medicare card I'm going to be working with pharmacies, and we are going to pull a pool together and we will have a lower cost area and that will complement what the state is already doing with regard to their own formularies.

COLEMAN: Skip ran for the U.S. Senate ten years ago, and ten years ago he said the same thing! That he was going to be pounding on the table to equalize those costs, those Medicare costs, because we are—we are losing. You've been attorney general for ten years during that period, and in that period nothing's been done. And here we are again—the same promise is being made. Go back, play the tape. Ten years ago he said it was a terrible situation. "Seniors in Minnesota are being overcharged, I'm going to pound away at it ..."

VENTURA: Ten years ago Norm was a Democrat.

HUMPHREY: And working in my office!

And just like that, Coleman and Humphrey start bickering at each other while Ventura sits between them, chuckling. He listens politely and intently, allowing Coleman to let out enough rope to hang himself, then simply reminds Coleman and the audience watching on television that Coleman once switched political parties. For a guy who once made a living as a bad guy in the professional wrestling ring, Ventura is coming across as a hero in the political ring.

A few minutes later he manages to take a question about the price of turkey and turn it into an assault on career politicians. As a means of determining whether the candidates are in touch with average citizens, a panelist asks them if they know the price of a pound of turkey. After they all admit they don't know, Ventura turns the question around and says that's not a good way to determine if someone's in touch with the people. He says working in the private sector is the way to keep in touch.

VENTURA: It's pretty hard to get fired when you work for the government. You pretty well have to commit a felony to get fired, and then maybe you still don't do it. I'm the only candidate who spent his whole career literally working in the private sector. Even while I was mayor I was required to hold a full-time job in the private sector. My two opponents, they've been cashing government checks for well over twenty years!

COLEMAN: Jesse, that's an absurd proposition. It really is!

It might be absurd, but it also clearly underscores the differences between Ventura and his opponents. And for one of the few times in the debate, Humphrey and Coleman actually pay attention to him. It wouldn't be long before Ventura turns his opponents against each other again by challenging their budget and tax-cut plans. Moderator Ken Stone has finally heard enough and tries to cut off a verbal skirmish between Humphrey and Coleman.

STONE: *Stop! Stop! Stop! Whoa, whoa. OK! Let's stop it right now!*

(Ventura clearly relishes the political mayhem he's witnessing—and has sparked—and pretends to physically hold the two men apart.)

STONE: *OK! Stop! Stop! Stop! Stop! Stop! Stop! Stop!*

Ventura is the clear winner because the unseemly bickering between Humphrey and Coleman during this final debate is replayed many times on Twin Cities television newscasts. In fact, Ventura wins every debate simply because he doesn't sound like a politician. He says out loud to the career politicians the same things many voters want to say themselves. The only thing voters can do when they get tired of listening to politicians is throw shoes at the TV. Ventura goes on TV, sticks his fingers in their eyes, pulls their hair, and challenges them. Who says professional wrestling isn't a suitable background for politics?

Man of Action

With Ventura scoring so well in the debates, his opponents are taking significant body blows. They still don't seem to be taking him seriously, despite evidence he's coming on strong. A Minnesota Poll published by the *Star Tribune* on September 23 shows Humphrey leading Coleman 49 to 29 percent with Ventura at 10 percent. On October 20 another Minnesota Poll shows Humphrey at 35 percent, Coleman at 34 percent, and Ventura doubling his support to 21 percent. There's little doubt Humphrey's free fall and Ventura's stunning rise are the result of their debate performances.

You'd expect Ventura to come off the top rope now and body-slam his opponents with a decisive move. His campaign staff comes up with one. In late October they unveil a secret weapon. At a State Capitol news conference to preview new Ventura TV ads, Bill Hillsman of North Woods Advertising also introduces the Jesse Ventura "action figure."

"The other candidates have complained that Jesse's a larger-than-life character," Hillsman tells a roomful of chuckling reporters. "We've decided to bring him back down in stature to their level."

He holds up a doll that, surprisingly, looks a lot like Ventura. Especially surprising when you hear how they built the action figure using parts of other action figures. The body comes from Batman and the head belongs to General Omar Bradley, with the addition of a tiny mustache to make him look like Ventura. The business suit came from a Ken doll. This clever creation is the star of a campaign commercial that is later credited with playing a major role in putting Ventura over the top.

Hillsman gives reporters a sneak preview of the thirty-second spot. It shows one boy holding the Ventura action figure and mimicking Ventura, saying, "I don't want your stupid money!" Another boy holds the Special Interest Man action figure and says, "We politicians have special powers the average man can't comprehend!" A narrator concludes the ad with the theme of the Ventura campaign: "Don't waste your vote on politics-as-usual. Vote Reform Party candidate Jesse Ventura for governor!"

The ad draws laughter from reporters, but also some pointed questions. One reporter asks campaign strategist Dean Barkley if the tone of the ad is demeaning the office of governor. "No, I don't think we are," Barkley responds. "I think the other two are the way they're behaving." Barkley is a lawyer and an experienced hand at running for major elective office. He helped put the Reform Party on the map with U.S. Senate campaigns in 1994 and 1996. He didn't win, but he gained enough votes to earn the Reform Party major-party status in Minnesota, which gives it access to public campaign funds. Now the party needed a strong candidate. Realizing his own limitations as a candidate with low name recognition in a fledgling party, Barkley is the one who sensed Ventura might have some magic on the campaign trail.

There's plenty of magic, but also a pratfall or two along the way. As he's rising in the polls and connecting with voters, Ventura nearly fumbles away his newfound success. At an October 21 appearance before a business association in Forest Lake, north of St. Paul, he hints that prostitution should be legalized. He only briefly mentions the issue in his speech to the association but is questioned about it by reporters afterward.

"It's a lot easier to control something when it's legal than when it's illegal," Ventura tells reporters, citing legalized prostitution in Nevada and Amsterdam as examples of where it seems to work in controlled areas. He goes on to say he doesn't necessarily plan to push for legalization, but says it shouldn't be ruled out. "I don't know that I'd support it," Ventura tells the Associated Press. "But I think it's something we certainly should look at … in the aspect of getting [prostitutes] out of the neighborhoods."

The reaction from his opponents is immediate and scathing. After consciously refraining from attacking Ventura for months so as not to offend Ventura supporters who may still be sitting on the fence, they hold nothing back on this issue. "That is one of the most absurd and outrageous propositions I have heard in the entire course of this campaign," Norm Coleman tells the *Star Tribune*. "The people of Minnesota should be outraged. They should be frightened." Skip Humphrey also comes off the top rope to take a shot. "We've seen Jesse go down these risky roads.... It's bad, terrible public policy, a terrible message to women young and old, and to children." With Ventura gaining in the polls, his opponents see a chance to take him down a peg. It doesn't work.

One week before the election, Barkley seems to think the Ventura campaign can do no wrong. In fact, the Forest Lake flap is quickly forgotten. "We firmly believe this campaign is poised to rewrite some political history," he says. "A little over a year ago, when I was out in Jesse Ventura's horse barn with his wife, trying to convince him to run for office, it took about four hours of persuasion. I let them know what they were in for, what they had to do to win this race."

First, Barkley says, he told Ventura he would have to be in all the debates and do well. So far, Barkley says, he's succeeded. Second, he said Ventura would have to be at 20 to 24 percent in the polls of the "likely voters." That's roughly the percentage of votes Reform Party presidential candidate Ross Perot received in Minnesota in 1992. Again, Barkley says the campaign is right on track. "Last week we were at 21 percent. Some other polls are putting us at 24 percent. Again, of 'likely voters.'"

So, Barkley says, the battle zone for the Ventura campaign will be in the sea of "unlikely voters" who make up nearly half the Minnesota electorate. "Our strategy now is . . . to be able to do an ad campaign the last two weeks of this campaign to convince the unlikely voter or the nonmotivated voter or the turned-off voter that this is the chance to get back in the political process and make a difference."

Of course, that takes money. Just one week earlier that piece of the puzzle also fell into place. After weeks of frustration, the campaign finally found a bank willing to lend $310,000. "We got our money last week after umpteen denials by banks," Barkley says. With another $150,000 to $200,000 in campaign contributions that poured in during recent weeks, Ventura now has enough money to get TV ads on across the state. "We'll be pretty competitive with the other guys in the last week," says Bill Hillsman of North Woods Advertising. "A statewide buy, all over the place. You'll have a hard time escaping us."

Which is exactly Barkley's strategy to reach the unlikely voters. "They've gotta see us on television," he says. "Whether that's right or wrong, or sad commentary on the political process, I've learned from three campaigns that, if you're not on the TV screen, that people will discount you and don't think you have a chance."

Even with the TV ads, most people still don't believe Ventura has a chance. While he is getting more television and newspaper coverage than any other third-party candidate in history, most of it is still the "isn't that a cute little campaign" variety. Ventura's ads and antics are a pleasant diversion from the traditional campaign tactics of Coleman and Humphrey, but no one seems to be taking him too seriously. My time and attention, and that of most other political reporters, remains focused on the front-runners in the polls, Humphrey and Coleman. That will turn out to be a monumental mistake.

So what else would a nontraditional, break-all-the-rules candidate do next? How about a madcap, seventy-two-hour statewide campaign blitz in a recreational vehicle, followed by a convoy of campaign supporters? Barkley says it's the jolt of electricity needed to energize a growing legion of Ventura supporters begging to help out. "Quite frankly, we have been swamped," Barkley tells reporters at another State Capitol news conference. "We're all out of T-shirts. We're all out of bumper stickers. We're all out of everything, and they're clamoring for something to do. So I said, what better way of doing it than to give everyone in the state of Minnesota who wants to see Jesse Ventura, our next governor, a chance to participate in the last seventy-two hours of the campaign?"

The plan is as simple as the name Ventura's camp has dreamed up: "Drive to Victory Tour." They'll go nearly nonstop for three straight days up until election day, visiting every region of the state. "And our message is going to be simple," Barkley says. "If you want this man to be your next governor, we need you to do your part. We need you to get out and vote. If you haven't registered, we'll have materials along that will tell you how to register at the polls."

Barkley also says this won't be a haphazard statewide hopscotch. "It's been targeted. We know where our people are that we have to get out to vote, and we're going to them. . . . If they stay home, we'll lose. We know that. This is a horse race. Nobody knows who's going to win. Whichever camp can get the votes out is going to be the one that's going to win on Tuesday."

New polling data shows Ventura now trailing Humphrey and Coleman by just five or six percentage points. The chances of winning this race are now so tangible the Ventura campaign decides it's time to add a new dimension to the candidate. For the first time, his wife, son, and daughter are about to become publicly involved in the campaign by taking part in the "Drive to Victory." "Jesse's been very, very protective of his family and his privacy," Barkley says. "He finally decided the state of Minnesota deserves to know what Jesse Ventura's family is like and what his wife is like, so here's your chance to find out."

The "Drive to Victory" is actually part of a two-pronged campaign attack plan. While Ventura's victory tour is really a throwback to the whistle-stop train tours by candidates of years past, it will be accompanied by a decidedly cutting-edge, off-the-wall multimedia campaign that will become the talk of the nation. There are the television ads, including a hilarious spot geared to run during the "Drive to Victory." It features the Ventura action figure driving a huge recreational vehicle down the highway. The campaign also introduces two new radio ads comparing Ventura's third-party candidacy with that of Abraham Lincoln's presidential campaign. Here's the text of one of those ads, narrated by Ventura to the tune of "I'm a Yankee Doodle Dandy":

Once upon a time in America, there was a third-party candidate running for major office. He was a big man, six feet, four inches tall. He used to wrestle in his younger days, and the people voted for him because they believed in what he stood for. So in 1860 Republican candidate Abraham Lincoln was elected president of the United States. I'm Jesse Ventura. I'm six-foot-four, I used to wrestle a bit in my younger days, and, like the Republican Party, which was America's third party in 1860, I'm a third-party candidate too! I'm running as the Reform Party candidate for governor. So when Norm Coleman or Skip Humphrey tell you you're wasting your vote on a third-party candidate, remind them it was those wasted third-party votes that elected the father of the Republican Party and perhaps our greatest president ever, Abe Lincoln. By the way, old Abe and I have something else in common. We're both honest!

"They're not attack ads," declares Bill Hillsman. "They're a call to arms. We're trying to get people out to vote."

But the unique media aspect of the upcoming RV tour is using the Internet to communicate with voters. Ventura's campaign Web site is already wildly popular. A month before the election, the site was getting 50,000 hits a week; a week before the election, Barkley says, the number jumped to 121,000 hits. "What we want to do is exploit as much as possible all of the capabilities of the Internet," he says. "And already the Internet community worldwide is beginning to take an interest in the 'Jesse Ventura Show' that's going to be occurring on this 'Drive to Victory' tour over the weekend."

The campaign plans to constantly update the Web site with news of Ventura's whereabouts. When he's heading for a particular town, the Web site will alert voters in that area exactly where and what time he'll be there. Phil Madsen, Ventura's Internet coordinator, says volunteers are coming forward to donate the necessary equipment, such as digital cameras, laptops, and modems. "During the tour the Jesse Ventura Web site, www.jesseventura.org, is going to be live, highly interactive, twenty-four hours a day," according to Madsen. "We're going to have ongoing discussion sites going on so people can interact with the tour.... We'll go to a city, let's say Austin, and people can get a group picture taken with Jesse in that town. And if it works the way we're planning it to work, by the time they get home they'll be able to see that photo on the Internet." Madsen and Barkley say they plan to have two carloads of volunteers running the roaming Internet operation. They call them Jesse's "Geek Squad."

"Drive to Victory"

On November 1, 1998, the victory tour drives into Hastings, a town just south of the Twin Cities, under gray skies for an early breakfast stop at a Perkins restaurant. Ventura's RV, plastered with huge, green campaign signs that simply say "Jesse!", pulls into the parking lot. Ventura emerges from the RV wearing a leather Timberwolves NBA jacket and blue jeans. The crowd of about fifty people that awaits him is a diverse group. It's an unseasonably warm November day in Minnesota, and many in the crowd are wearing Ventura's "Retaliate in '98" T-shirts. There are a few gray-haired retirees, a young woman holding a baby, and a couple of biker-types wearing bandannas. Ventura obviously appeals to a cross-section of generations.

A reporter informs Ventura that a new poll shows he's closing the gap, with Humphrey at 35 percent, Coleman at 30 percent, and Ventura at 27 percent. "You're right there," the reporter says. Ventura is aware he's closing fast. "I just saw one that says 32, 32, 28," he replies. "With hard-core registered voters we're right in the hunt, and we're even-up, but that's not taking into consideration all the people I'm seeing out there. . . . People come up to me saying, 'Jesse, I haven't voted in twenty-five years. Jesse, I've never voted and we're coming out to vote for you.' And those people are not polled. And that's what's gonna carry us over the top. The disenchanted voters that have been driven away by the Republicans and Democrats."

Another reporter asks him about Hillary Rodham Clinton's remark at a Humphrey campaign appearance the day before about Ventura's campaign being nothing but a "sideshow." It's like a fastball down the middle. "Well, Mrs. Clinton, if I were her, I'd be more concerned about leaving Bill alone at the White House," Ventura deadpans as the crowd erupts with laughter.

Later in the day Ventura is holding court at a table near the bay window in his RV. Still wearing his Timberwolves jacket, he's got a cigar in one hand, a Pepsi in another, and a bucket of Halloween candy on the table. "That looks like a Jesse sign up there," he says as he glances out his window. "Yes, it is!" He takes a big puff of what's left of his cigar and blows some smoke. "Yes, it does, that looks like a Jesse sign," he says, still seemingly amazed himself by his newfound political popularity.

The Ventura caravan is on its way to a couple of southern-Minnesota college towns, St. Peter and Mankato. Ventura is joking with some campaign aides and a few reporters along for the ride. Every now and then the RV rocks with laughter. "Now, are we having more fun than the other campaigns?" Ventura asks no one in particular.

"Hell, yeah," is the response from a television reporter.

"I like that, 'Hell, yes' from a reporter, all right," Ventura responds. "I betcha no other reporters are saying that in them other campaigns." One last puff from his cigar. "We're just lucky we don't have no liquor!"

"We are here, Jesse. Here we go, people!" barks a campaign worker when the tour reaches St. Peter. "No feedlots. No feedlots here," an adviser tells Ventura while prepping him about the message to deliver. It's a college crowd, and agricultural issues regarding hog feedlots won't play well here. Ventura steps out the door of his RV, twirling his fist above his head and whipping hundreds of cheering students into a frenzy at Gustavus Adolphus College.

"This is a lot like *National Lampoon's Animal House*," Ventura says, joking about his raucous campaign road trip. "In fact, you can just call us the Deltas!" He climbs into the back of a pickup to address the crowd. "It's kind of like going back up to that top rope again," he says, alluding to his wrestling days. "It's been a while since I did that."

Campaign volunteers are working the crowd, handing out green and black "Jesse!" signs, while Ventura rattles off the towns the tour has already visited: Hastings, Rochester, Austin, Albert Lea, Blue Earth, Vernon Center. Then, he strays from the advice he received just minutes ago. "I don't want no feedlots around here." The students give him a big cheer. "The air smells just fine!" Ventura exclaims after drawing a deep breath. So much for the advice. Ventura, it seems, can do no wrong.

"We're calling it the 'Victory Tour,'" he tells the students, getting back to his primary message. "But even more so than the 'Victory Tour,' I personally call it the 'Get Out the Vote Tour.' There's an old saying: if you don't vote, don't bitch! They don't poll the young people, because you people normally don't vote. But this time the young people are going to vote. You've heard all this stuff about voting for Jesse's a wasted vote. Rest assured, voting for Jesse is just that, a vote for Jesse and nobody else!" The crowd roars with approval. "It's sending a clear message not only to Minnesota but to the world. They better start paying attention to the voter again!"

These kids are so charged up they're ready to vote right now. "I think Jesse Ventura's a great guy and we need a change," says student Mary Balmes. "We'd be lucky to have him as governor of Minnesota." Freshman political-science major Nick Chirhirt is also ready for change. "He's not bowing down to all the partisan pressure that's out there," Chirhirt says. "He's not bought off by special interests. He's actually trying to do what's best for the state, not what's best for partisan politics.

His heart is with the people and not some party." With dusk approaching, Ventura climbs back aboard his RV with a final wave to the cheering throng. With the sun setting, the caravan drives past a sign painted on a bed sheet in big orange letters: "Ventura: Highway to the Future."

The final day of the campaign—November 2, 1998—finds the "Victory Tour" snaking its way through the picturesque Minnesota north woods. The sky is big and blue and dotted with puffy white clouds as the caravan winds its way amid the jack pines and working-class homes of Cloquet, 150 miles north of the Twin Cities. Ventura arrives at the sprawling Potlatch Paper plant, where light snow flurries somehow fall from the nearly clear sky. He aims his message here squarely at the men and women toiling for an hourly wage.

"I've worked in the private sector my whole life," Ventura says to a small sea of orange hard hats while a volunteer hands out campaign buttons. "I have two opponents that have been working for the government their whole life. I don't knock government employees. But the point is, with the government you always know you're going to get a paycheck, don't ya? Unless you commit a felony they can't fire you, can they? Us in the private sector know what it's like to get hired and fired. We know what it's like to lose a job, and I know what it's like to be suspended without pay from July 21 to today."

By bashing his two career-politician opponents, Ventura finds a friendly audience among the hard hats. He reminds them that he's not only going unpaid, he also doesn't accept any campaign money from lobbyists or political action committees. "Those two guys are traveling around right now, campaigning as hard as I am, sixteen hours a day, and we're paying for it. Now, aren't they supposed to be the attorney general and the mayor? Who's doing that job while they're campaigning? I want to make it illegal [to campaign] between the hours of eight and four-thirty for career politicians. Do the job we're paying you to do, then campaign like we have to in the private sector. Let's make it a level playing field."

In his Timberwolves jacket, baseball cap, and jeans, Ventura looks more like one of the employees reporting for work than a candidate for governor. And he knows it. "I had a kid say to me last night in Willmar—he made the most simple statement—he said, 'Jesse, you are us.' And I can't add nothing more than that."

Not all those assembled are Ventura fans. One man comes out of the crowd and takes the candidate by surprise, barking, "Why do you believe in drugs and butchering babies?" He then starts handing out flyers with a list of reasons not to vote for Ventura. "You know, you can't please everyone," Ventura responds. "I learned that as mayor. No matter how you vote, somebody's going to get angry."

For most, his message hits home. "He's down to earth," says Dean Halberson, who just listened to Ventura. "That's the kind of guy I want representing me. He's not a politician. He's not for abortion one year and against it the next." Before boarding his RV for the trip back to the Twin Cities, Ventura takes a parting shot at his opponents that draws uproarious applause. "They told me before I can't win, and isn't that remarkable, the word 'can't.' I can't win. And now all of a sudden the question has changed to, can he govern? Well, I'll tell you something. I've jumped out of thirty-four airplanes in my life. I've dove 212 feet under the water. I've swam with sharks before. I've did things that would make Skip and Norm wet their pants." When the laughter subsides, he turns serious and determined. "This is simply governing and common sense and logic. Nothing more. Nothing less. I can do the job."

The three candidates wrap up a final day of campaign barnstorming around the state with an appearance at KSTP-TV for a last chance to speak to voters. Coleman spent the day flying to several cities in southern and northern Minnesota. Humphrey concentrated on the north, with a rally at a state university in Moorhead and a news conference in Duluth. Unlike Ventura's crowds that seemed to spontaneously appear for his campaign stops, the Coleman and Humphrey crowds appeared to be largely staged events organized by the Republican and Democratic Party machines.

Ventura arrives at the television studios hoarse and exhausted from his nearly nonstop, seventy-two-hour "Drive to Victory." Dressed in a dark blue suit and tie, he plops down in a chair to have makeup applied to hide the dark clouds under his eyes.

KSTP-TV is giving each candidate exactly two minutes on its 6:30 P.M. newscast to speak directly to viewers. No questions and no TelePrompTers. Ventura and Humphrey are already seated in the studio by the time Coleman arrives. Coleman gets a quick makeup job while standing just off the studio set. The three men exchange cool, yet cordial greetings.

News anchor Chris Conangla introduces the candidates, then Ventura leads off. "A vote for Jesse Ventura is just that, a vote for Jesse Ventura," he says. After assuring viewers a vote for him wouldn't be a wasted vote, he repeats the story he told on his RV tour. "A young, first-time voter in Willmar, Minnesota, looked at me and said, 'Jesse, you are us.'"

Next up is Norm Coleman. "You've told me, 'Mayor, don't tax us to death. Don't regulate us to death. Make sure our streets are safe and our kids go to the best schools.' And I can deliver on that. I've delivered on that for your capital city, and I'll deliver on that for Minnesota."

While Ventura and Coleman deliver direct and concise messages, Humphrey rambles on a bit and promises just about everything to everyone. He talks about making sure parents pay child support, promises to bust up street gangs, and says he'll provide world-class public education and affordable health care. "But most importantly," Humphrey says, "I want to return tax dollars. A billion dollars' worth of income-tax cuts. Permanent. Three hundred and forty million dollars' worth of permanent property-tax relief for our working families."

When the red camera light blinks off, the three candidates shake hands and even manage weak smiles. Surprisingly, one of Coleman's top campaign advisers, Cyndy Brucato (a former communications director for outgoing Republican governor Arne Carlson), seeks out Ventura to shake his hand and quietly tells him, "I have to say, I do like what you say too." The two share a laugh. But only one will be laughing on election day.

Election Day

On election day, November 3, Ventura walks into his polling place in Maple Grove, a suburb just northwest of Minneapolis. He's wearing a leather jacket with fringe hanging off each sleeve. Blue pants and tennis shoes complete the unusual ensemble. A campaign aide asks Ventura if he'll do some interviews with the media assembled to cover his vote. He promises he'll talk after he votes but warns, "We'll do 'em quick. I want to see *Young and the Restless* too. It's my favorite TV show." Clearly he's not buckling under the stress of election day. "I feel a lot more rested today and very relaxed. I mean, what the heck—there's no reason to get tense now. It's up to the voters, and the voters will make a choice and life will go on for all of us."

While standing just outside his own polling precinct after voting, Ventura laments that so few people even bother to vote. He blames career politicians for the apathy. "I mean, 50 percent of Minnesotans have quit voting. That's terrible. I won't make promises I can't keep. I'm not going to make promises, promises, promises just to get elected. If I don't get elected, rest assured, Jesse Ventura's life goes on. No matter what happens, I'm gonna have fun. You can be serious, but you still have to have a sense of humor about it all, because life's too short not to have a laugh now and then."

He then tells probably one of the funniest stories of his campaign. It involves his lieutenant-governor running mate, Mae Schunk. The sixty-four-year old Schunk is a gray-haired, grandmotherly, sweet little old schoolteacher involved in her first political campaign. She is the exact opposite of Ventura in every way, providing nice balance to the ticket. Among other things, her place on the ticket is supposed to send a message to voters he's serious about education.

It also helps send the message he won't turn the State Capitol into a frat house. But the story he tells makes you wonder if she thinks that might be what he *does* have in mind. "We were riding in the RV yesterday and Mae Schunk . . . God bless her! We're having fun talking about 'what if,' and what are we gonna do at the inauguration and who are we going to get for music, and somebody suggested the band Barenaked

Ladies. And Mae heard it and spins around and goes, 'You can't have that at an inauguration!' Mae had no idea this was the name of a band. She thought all of a sudden we're talking about bringing in bare-naked ladies for an inauguration!"

What's funnier still is that she actually thought Ventura might consider it.

Ventura arrives at his election-night headquarters in a black sedan with his wife, Terry, and two children, nineteen-year-old Tyrel and fifteen-year-old Jade. Hundreds of supporters are gathered at Canterbury Park, a horse-racing track in Shakopee, where, as Ventura notes, long shots often win. A pack of reporters and cameras surrounds him as he arrives. He's asked what kind of mood he's in. "My mood is actually kind of laid-back," he says. "I'm excited a little bit, but it's out of my hands. It's up to the voters." Ventura says he hasn't been watching the early evening newscasts to keep tabs on exit polls. "I watched *JFK* all day. It's one of my favorite movies."

A reporter tells him of the latest exit-poll numbers showing Coleman and Humphrey both at 34 percent and Ventura at 31 percent, with a 5 percent margin of error. Ventura quickly dismisses those numbers, even though they're a huge jump from the late summer and early fall, when he was usually in the 10 to 15 percent range. "We've changed politics in Minnesota no matter what happens," Ventura says. "I've never been in the lead in any of these polls. What are those, exit polls? Ah, they don't mean nothing." He relishes the underdog role and won't give it up now.

Buried in the fine print at the end of most previous polls is the fact that results are weighted toward "likely voters," even though Minnesota is one of the few states that allow voter registration on election day. That can make it difficult to pinpoint likely voters. The exit polls of people who actually voted make it apparent "unlikely voters" will carry the day in the most stunning Minnesota election night in history.

After making his way past reporters, Ventura enters Canterbury

Park to the cheers of his supporters. Unlike the suit-and-tie crowd at the Humphrey and Coleman election-night headquarters, this is a tap-beer and blue-jean bunch. There are so many baseball caps and unshaven faces at this campaign party it looks more like a rock concert or monster-truck pull. They're mostly young and enthusiastic, and seem to have absolutely no experience at attending an election-night party.

Within an hour of the 8:00 P.M. poll closing, the first vote totals begin trickling in. With the first 1 percent of the precincts reporting, Humphrey, as expected, has a slight lead over Coleman and Ventura. Within minutes, however, there's a sudden shift: with fewer than 10 percent of the precincts reporting, Ventura is in the lead! Ventura supporters at Canterbury Park begin wondering if there's something funny in their beer. These latest numbers draw chuckles at the Coleman and Humphrey camps, where nearly everyone thinks it's far too early for the numbers to mean anything.

And let's be real: Who thinks an ex-professional wrestler can be elected governor in a state that has produced statesmen like Hubert Humphrey and Walter Mondale? Certainly I don't. I'm covering election night from the Coleman campaign headquarters at the Radisson Hotel in St. Paul because I have a hunch Coleman is going to be the one to upset Humphrey. In fact, none of the main political reporters for the local television stations is covering the election from Ventura's headquarters. Most are at Humphrey's headquarters.

So naturally Ventura's lead grows through the night and the excitement builds with each passing minute. At 10:00 P.M., with 27 percent of the precincts reporting, Ventura has an astounding lead. Ventura is at 37 percent (236,735 votes); Coleman is at 31 percent (199,489), just ahead of Humphrey, also at 31 percent (197,304). "I think it's going to be a late, late night," Secretary of State Joan Growe tells KSTP-TV as she oversees her final election before stepping down from office. "I don't see how we could get a closer race. I think it's very hard to predict or even look at exit polls when you've got three candidates in the race. This is a new phenomenon for us in Minnesota, and I don't think we quite know how to handle it."

The Ventura campaign knows how to handle it. They've got Rolling Stones music blaring as supporters sense a colossal upset. With 30 percent of the vote in at 10:05 P.M. and Ventura holding his lead, the boisterous crowd starts chanting "Jesse! Jesse! Jesse!" to draw him out of a private room where he's watching the results. He doesn't disappoint. To thunderous applause he makes his way to the stage in front of the room.

"Let's be excited, because no matter what, we're leading!" he bellows to the crowd and to a live television audience. The crowd roars. Even though a third of the precinct results are in, he's leading by 5 percent, and everything from exit polls to the actual polls are trending his way, Ventura isn't ready to claim victory. "As you look up there, you see that's still 70 percent of the precincts to go yet," he says. "We're a third of the way around the racetrack out here! I bet they're never going to take the people lightly again, are they?"

Again, the crowd erupts with cheers and chants of "You da man!"

"What is so gratifying about this is being able to prove the experts wrong," Ventura says. "They kept saying, 'He can't, he can't, he can't. Spoiler, spoiler, this and that.' Well, we are and we did!"

Now that he's got everyone lathered up, Ventura urges the crowd to keep partying and says he hopes to be back out soon with a victory speech. So the crowd turns its attention to his running mate. "Mae! Mae! Mae!" they shout to Mae Schunk as Ventura grabs her hand and they raise their arms together. Schunk has kept a low profile during the campaign, but she's fired up now.

"He *can* govern and he *will* govern!" she yells. The Ventura headquarters is now truly beginning to look like a rock concert. "Landslide! Landslide! Landslide!" goes the chant. Next thing you know, people are being lifted off their feet and passed through the crowd. "Keep partying and having fun!" Ventura shouts. "We'll be back ..."

By 10:08, Humphrey and his running mate, Roger Moe, appear on stage to rally the spirits of their own troops at the Minneapolis Hilton. With 30 percent of the vote now counted, Humphrey is actually in third place (Ventura 37 percent, Coleman 32 percent, Humphrey 30 percent).

"I don't know about you, but I believe in Minnesota and I believe in the voters of Minnesota, and I believe that we're going to have a victory," Humphrey says in a halfhearted attempt to light a fire at DFL election headquarters. The crowd responds with halfhearted applause and cheers. "Keep the faith and keep the spirit up," Humphrey tells them.

His words say he believes, his voice and body language say he's lost. By 10:30, with Humphrey still mired in third place, his senior campaign adviser, Eric Johnson, appears on KSTP-TV, trying to sound optimistic, saying votes from northern Minnesota might still turn the tide for his candidate. Johnson's also coming to grips with reality. "We gotta admit Jesse Ventura brought a lot of new people into the process," he says. "Jesse was not a candidate with an agenda. He was a candidate with an attitude, and he delivered it in a very entertaining way and brought in people who hadn't been involved in politics before."

He admits the Humphrey campaign grossly underestimated Ventura. "I'm sure in hindsight we'd think of other strategies, but he was very unconventional," Johnson says. "He frankly didn't show up much in the polls early on, and we've had to react very late in the campaign to a guy who has really soared in the polls. Jesse's judged by a different standard. He talks about abolishing child-care subsidies. If Skip Humphrey or Norm Coleman had said that, they would have been run out of town on a rail. But Jesse Ventura can say things like that and . . . somehow he doesn't pay a price."

At 10:40 the news gets even worse for Humphrey. With 39 percent of votes tallied, Ventura remains at 37 percent, with Coleman rising to 33 percent and Humphrey dropping to 29 percent. Democrats, like Mayor Sharon Sayles Belton of Minneapolis, appear on television and refuse to concede their candidate is out of the picture. "There's a lot of people that believe in the thirty-second sound bites that sound good," Sayles Belton says. "But the bottom line is, very often there's nothing behind them. Jesse Ventura is going to have to show the people of Minnesota that he knows how to run a state government, knows how to put a budget together. He was not held to that standard during the debates. This vote is all about some gut reactions to Jesse Ventura. I was surprised. I was campaigning all over the city of Minneapolis today, and I was really blown away by the number of people I came in contact with on the streets of our city [who] said, 'I voted for Jesse.' And I asked them why and they weren't sure why, but they did vote for Jesse."

At 10:43 Norm Coleman begins wading through a sea of supporters in the St. Paul Radisson Grand Ballroom. "Norm! Norm! Norm!" they chant in unison as a surge of excitement sweeps the Republican faithful. "I gotta make up about three points, which is better than the seven I had to make up earlier. The night's still young," Coleman tells reporters on his way to the stage. Actually, with 44 percent of the precincts now reporting, he is four points behind Ventura. But Coleman is cutting into Ventura's lead and Humphrey is dropping and nearly out of the picture.

"The good news is there's no doubt our message got out," Coleman shouts from the stage adorned in red, white, and blue. "Our message of cutting taxes and making government work for you and not against you! Now, the bad news is you're going to have to be patient," he says to a crowd desperate for anything to cheer about. "About 60 percent of the state hasn't been heard from. . . . Keep the faith! Keep the faith!"

Two minutes later in a live television interview, Coleman tells me he's still got a chance. But just as he did during the debates, he seems programmed to ignore Ventura and focus on Humphrey, even while Humphrey is clearly going down the tubes and Ventura is on the verge of victory. "The early returns were certainly the metro area where the DFL and Skip do well, but now we're moving into other parts of the state," Coleman says, refusing to acknowledge what's obvious to everyone else.

"Did you ever in your imagination believe Jesse Ventura could become governor of this state?" I ask Coleman, trying to snap him back into reality. "I can't tell you I conceived of it before, but clearly he's tapped into something," he replies.

By 10:50, we get one of the first predictions that Ventura is going to win. It comes from D. J. Leary, a veteran political analyst and co-editor of the *Politics in Minnesota* newsletter. Working as an analyst for

KSTP-TV on election night, Leary sees Ventura's numbers holding steady with the precincts now reporting well over 40 percent. Finally, he says, "Folks, it's going to happen." He follows that up with another prediction. KSTP-TV news anchor Randy Meier asks Leary and another analyst on the broadcast, KSTP Radio talk-show host Jason Lewis, "If Jesse Ventura were to win this election, who would work better with him, Democrats or Republicans?" Without missing a beat, Leary responds, "Probably wrestling promoters. Everybody's going to have to get used to Jesse as governor.... People are going to wake up tomorrow in some kind of shock!"

Lewis isn't quite ready to call the race for Ventura. "If it happens—*if* it happens—our state motto is going to be, 'Governor Ventura: Get Over It!'"

While Lewis seems to fear the prospect of a "Governor Ventura," Leary relishes the idea. "This guy's going to be great to write about the next four years," he says, making both another accurate prediction and huge understatement.

At 11:05 the race shows signs of tightening a bit. With 49 percent of the precincts now counted, Ventura leads Coleman by just 3 percent, 37 to 34. Although Humphrey is still languishing at 29 percent, some staunch Democrats refuse to believe their eyes. "It's a little early yet," according to Representative Phil Carruthers, Speaker of the House in the Minnesota legislature. "As we get into more of the rural parts of the state, I think we'll know more. Humphrey is building momentum, so it's too early to say who's going to be the next governor."

Appearing minutes later on KSTP-TV, Democratic state senator John Marty brings some sanity to the discussion. Marty was crushed in the 1994 gubernatorial race by Republican governor Arne Carlson and knows a thing or two about when to throw in the towel, which he now thinks Humphrey should. "An 80,000-vote margin or whatever it is now—it's not likely to change. I would guess where things stand now, Jesse Ventura's in pretty good shape."

Republicans, on the other hand, have some reason for tepid optimism. Vin Weber, a former Republican congressman from Minnesota's

Second District and now a prominent national-party strategist, is impressed by Ventura's performance but still not convinced he can win. "We all knew there was a Jesse thing happening out there; we didn't know it was a phenomenon of this strength," Weber tells me in a live interview at 11:14 P.M. "I do not think he's going to win. I think Norm Coleman is going to win. I think it's going to be a late victory tonight."

At 11:24 Coleman makes another appearance onstage at Republican headquarters. This time he's accompanied by Governor Arne Carlson, and the two are intent on firing up supporters now that Coleman is closing the gap on Ventura. "This is the time of the evening when we get serious about our politics," Carlson tells Republicans, who for the first time in hours seem to think Coleman has a chance to pull out a victory. "We've heard from the metropolitan area, and now we're going out and counting votes in Coleman country. We may have to serve breakfast here, but for a Coleman victory it's well worth it!"

A few minutes later the vote totals include 55 percent of precincts in the state, with Ventura maintaining a three-percentage point lead over Coleman, 37 to 34. Humphrey has dropped to 28 percent, a whopping 105,000 votes behind Ventura.

"We're not really shocked," Governor Carlson tells me after he leaves the stage. "I think a lot of people felt the surge for Ventura last week, so it's not a shock, it's not a stunner. But I think the media's making a big mistake tonight. I'd be very careful about calling this one until all the votes are in." Coleman trails Ventura by 35,000 votes, and Carlson says that, with 45 percent of the votes yet to be tallied, Coleman can catch Ventura.

But did Carlson ever imagine a Ventura victory? "We speculated on it, yes. It isn't a complete shock, because what was happening was kind of strange. One [thing] is, Humphrey was dropping, and we knew from the internal polls that the Humphrey drop could go as low as the high twenties, which appears to be happening tonight. On the other hand, we didn't know how high Coleman could go, and we certainly didn't know how high Ventura could go."

Less than ten minutes after Carlson says the media is making a big mistake, we find out just how high Ventura can go. At 11:45 KSTP-TV is running through a series of results in the Minnesota legislative races when news anchor Colleen Needles pauses to listen to her producer speaking in her earphone.

"We have just heard," she says, speaking slowly and deliberately to make sure she's hearing it correctly, "Jesse Ventura has just been projected the winner in the race for governor in the state of Minnesota—a result that is going to send shock waves through the state for those folks who have perhaps gone to bed tonight before this moment."

As you'd imagine, bedlam ensues at Ventura's election headquarters. "Jesse! Jesse! Jesse!" goes the chant as his beer-splashed supporters exchange hugs and high fives. They see the big red check mark next to his name on the television screens, projecting Ventura the winner. Soon, they start to sound like hockey fans taunting the opposing team: "Na-na-na-na, na-na-na-na, hey, hey, good-bye ..."

Within minutes Ventura returns to the podium, surrounded by men in black T-shirts and baseball caps that read "Ventura Security" in bright green letters. But several Minnesota state troopers now also accompany him. As he arrives onstage, he holds both hands over his head with his index fingers pointed skyward. He's number one!

Just as Ventura is about to address the crowd, an aide whispers that he's needed elsewhere for a short time. Ventura looks to the crowd and says, "Hold it down just for a moment, if you will. We have to go national on NBC right now."

After telling NBC's Tom Brokaw and the nation that he's Jesse "the Mind" now, not Jesse "the Body," Ventura returns to the stage with Mae Schunk. He steps to the microphone to deliver what his supporters dreamed they'd one day hear.

"Thank you for renewing my faith that the American dream still lives," Ventura says, drowned out by raucous applause and cheers. "It was back in '64 that a hero and idol of mine named Muhammad Ali beat Sonny Liston. And I remember in those days you listened on the radio. And I remember my dad and my brother and I listening on the radio and he did it! He won! He shocked the world! No one said he could do it. Then, in later years, I think it was 1980, we sent a hockey team to the Olympics, a bunch of amateur kids who weren't given a chance. They had to face the Russians, who were like professionals. No one gave 'em a chance and what happened? They shocked the world!"

The cheers are building to a crescendo. "Well, now it's 1998 and the American dream lives on in Minnesota, 'cause we shocked the world!" Ventura pumps a fist in the air and the crowd explodes. "Jesse! Jesse! Jesse! Jesse! Jesse!"

"It's kind of ironic," Ventura continues as the crowd quiets to listen to their new governor. "I believe it was 1981 that Adrian [Adonis, his former tag-team wrestling partner] and I first sold out the Civic Center in St. Paul, and you're still cheering me—only in '81 it was 'Jesse sucks!'"

The room is now giddy with laughter and celebration. "I don't know what else to say. We've shocked the world. Minnesota leads the way! We lead the way in setting the example for the rest of the country that hopefully the Democrats and Republicans will take notice now. They will stop their partisan party politics and start doing what's right for the people.... During this campaign I didn't make a lot of promises, because I'm a person who believes I don't want to make promises I can't keep. But I'm going to make you one simple promise tonight. I promise you I will do the best job I can do!"

Then Ventura all but admits he never thought he'd see this day. "This is just so remarkable it's truly mind-boggling. But the one thing, you know, I never gave up the faith. When all the experts said he can't win, he's the spoiler, he's this, he's that, I kept thinking, no, that's not true. We can win and we have won! Let them say a vote for Jesse's a wasted vote, because there were more wasted votes than there were for anybody else. In fact, we wasted them with wasted votes!"

Now there's a new chant. "President! President! President!"

Ventura shakes his head and smiles. Eventually, the tough guy turns emotional when talking about his family. "I want to thank my wife, Terry, who, about a year ago, said to me, 'Are you nuts?'" He thanks his son, Tyrel, and his daughter, Jade, for putting up with their dad's latest escapade. "And I want to thank my mom and dad," he says, as his voice begins to crack. "They're not far from here. They're in Fort Snelling [National Cemetery], but thank you." He looks to the heavens with tears in his eyes and embraces his wife and kids.

After Schunk delivers her own short victory speech, Ventura still seems to harbor a bit of distrust at the experts now projecting him the winner. "I want you to remember something," he says. "These are still just numbers and we haven't received phone calls yet. That's the thing that has to happen.... If the numbers hold as they are, I want to congratulate Mr. Humphrey and Mr. Coleman for the hard job they did, because they worked extremely hard. They wanted the job very badly, and we owe them a round of applause for the effort that they gave."

Jesse "the Body" Ventura has come a long way from his bad-guy wrestling days when his shtick was being a poor loser and ungrateful winner. Yet, even in his reluctance to officially accept victory, he is already spontaneously planning his inauguration party. "Everybody knows I love music and everybody knows you have an inaugural ball, and so I want to put it out now: Jonny Lang, if you're out there listening, Jesse 'the Body' wants a phone call, Jonny! If Jonny wants to call, I'll be happy to entertain that call, because that young man can play the blues!" With that, Ventura disappears from the stage again, saying, "Party on, we're going to watch the final numbers come in."

Beer flows at Ventura headquarters while tears flow at the Humphrey and Coleman camps. There's also more than a little bitterness. Democrats and Republicans both begin bashing the media for not challenging Ventura during the campaign and not forcing him to take positions on key issues. Bill Cooper, the state chair of the Republican Party, is openly rancorous shortly after Ventura is projected the winner. But he refuses to concede, even though 63 percent of the vote is now in and Ventura's lead over Coleman has expanded to 40,000 votes.

"It doesn't look good but I don't think it's over yet," Cooper tells me during a live interview at Republican headquarters.

"Are you stunned by what's happening?" I ask.

"I just can't wait until we appoint Hulk Hogan as the commissioner of education," he fires back. Clearly, he's not impressed by the prospects of a Ventura administration or the ability of Minnesotans to choose a governor.

Over at Democratic headquarters in Minneapolis, where much of the crowd headed for the doors hours earlier, Humphrey campaign volunteer Julie Regina struggles to explain what happened. "I think it was the novelty," she says of Ventura's candidacy. "I think it was the fact of an ordinary man getting into the [governor's office]. Somebody that was like them. Just an ordinary guy."

It's still amazing how so many people refer to a former Navy SEAL, pro wrestler, Hollywood movie actor, NFL football announcer, and radio talk-show host as just an ordinary guy. Ventura is both wealthy and flamboyant. He drives a Porsche and lives in a $500,000 house on a horse ranch. Yet he has that rare ability to come across as a man of the people. Whatever he is, Regina doesn't think Ventura will make much of a governor. "I think it's going to be a little chaotic, and I wonder how things are going to get done in the legislature," she says.

Coleman is the first candidate to offer a concession speech at 12:40 A.M., nearly an hour after the first projections of Ventura as the winner. "Let me first say to Jesse that I pledge my commitment to work with you," Coleman tells the crowd at Republican headquarters in St. Paul.

At Humphrey headquarters in Minneapolis, both Humphrey and his running mate, Senate Majority Leader Roger Moe, deliver concession speeches just after 12:45 A.M. "Roger and I have had a chance to speak with Jesse Ventura, and we have congratulated him personally," Humphrey tells his Democratic Party faithful. "The people have spoken, and we believe and trust in the people. So we congratulate you, Jesse and Mae, on a campaign well run."

Moe not only congratulates the winners but also acknowledges there's a deeper meaning to their victory. "Obviously, there was a message sent in this vote tonight and we have to listen to the voters," he says. "Obviously, all of the great pundits will give us a lot of advice on that, but no question about it—we have to listen to what the voters say, even when it hurts. No question about it, it hurts tonight. I think it's very safe to say we've been body-slammed!"

The pundits are already at work analyzing this race. KSTP-TV analysts D. J. Leary and Jason Lewis agree the Republicans and Democrats have serious problems. "The Republican and DFL parties of this state will have to ask the most important question," Leary says. "What in the world did we do wrong or are we doing wrong that the people of Minnesota no longer trust us?" Lewis isn't sure what message Ventura sent to voters, but it worked. "The two major parties have to define themselves, and right now, in Minnesota, anyway, Jesse Ventura defined them and he defined them first," Lewis says. "That's what killed them."

Over at Ventura headquarters a "Ventura Kicks Ass" sign bobs up and down in the crowd as they cheer the concession speeches. "This is a dream," says Dean Barkley, the man who talked Ventura into running. "And I just thank Jesse Ventura for making it happen. The guy's incredible. He's gonna be the most incredible governor. It tells that the political center, the commonsense, everyday people out there, finally have risen up and said enough is enough of partisan bickering. Enough of liberal-conservative! It's time we have some commonsense, decent, honest people go in and give it a shot. That's what it says."

When all the votes are counted, Ventura wins with 37 percent (773,713 votes); Coleman has 34 percent (717,350) and Humphrey 28 percent (587,528). The preelection polls have been turned upside down. It's a result no one saw coming. Even Ventura and his closest aides are stunned. It defies all conventional wisdom. Ventura pinned his long-shot hopes on getting first-time voters to the polls, and a whopping 332,720 voters registered on election day. It turns out the Ventura votes weren't wasted, but they were inexpensive. Ventura spent just $626,067 to get elected, or about $.81 per vote. Coleman spent $2,168,393, or $3.02 per vote. Humphrey spent $2,125,465, or $3.62 per vote.

Just after 1:00 A.M. following election night, Ventura, the bargain-vote shopper, makes a final encore appearance onstage. "You have a resolve to outlast me tonight, don't ya," he says as the now hoarse and exhausted crowd musters another cheer. "I've gotten both the phone calls from the other two opponents. I very much accept to be your next governor of the state of Minnesota!"

CHAPTER 2

"I Can Kick Your Ass!"
The Quotable Ventura Becomes
a Media Sensation

A sleep-deprived Jesse Ventura spends the first morning of his remarkable new life fending off the effects of a long night of celebrating with champagne. There's no time to sleep it off. After going from long-shot former pro wrestler to governor-elect of Minnesota, he's the hottest news flash in the country. He's conducting dozens of interviews with national and local news organizations and making headlines around the world.

CNN conducts a quick and unscientific Internet poll about Ventura's election. Nearly forty thousand people respond, with 51 percent saying his election is a "refreshing change." However, 36 percent say his election win is a "joke." The remaining 13 percent call it a "watershed" event in American politics.

Governor-elect Ventura finally escapes the media for a quick trip to the State Capitol in St. Paul for a tour of his transition offices and a meeting with Governor Arne Carlson. The offices will sit empty for a few days yet. Ventura's campaign operated by cell phone, laptop computer, and shoestring. Now it's scrambling to organize a transition no one expected. What once seemed unthinkable is now reality. He will soon become Jesse "the Governor" Ventura. As he ascends the steps of the State Capitol he's surrounded again, this time by a dozen television and newspaper photographers along with a pack of reporters and security guards. Jesse Ventura will no longer walk alone.

With flashbulbs popping and television cameras capturing every step, the governor-elect heads into the ornate governor's reception room. Huge paintings show scenes of Minnesota's Civil War infantrymen at Little Rock and Gettysburg doing battle with the Confederacy. In the center of the room is an oval-shaped table with a sign on top reading, "Please do not touch or lean on historic table." Someone may want to move that table. A former pro wrestler with a penchant for breaking furniture is about to become governor.

The room is packed with reporters and curious capitol staffers for Ventura's joint appearance with Governor Carlson. Carlson hands Ventura a stack of booklets outlining basic information about every state department and agency. But when asked what Ventura's greatest challenge will be, Carlson says it isn't learning how state government works. Instead, he jokes, it's "probably to get some sleep."

As for his thoughts on Ventura's stunning victory, the Republican Carlson chooses his words carefully and politically. "I think if you take a very broad view of it, Governor-elect Ventura is moderate on his social positions and conservative on the fiscal, and that's clearly where our administration has been," Carlson says. "I think it's abundantly clear that's where the people of Minnesota are at. I think that's a good vantage point from which to govern."

The vantage point from which Ventura will govern is that of a Reform Party governor squaring off with a Senate controlled by Democrats and Republicans newly in control of the House of Representatives. It will be a daunting challenge because Ventura will become the first governor in Minnesota history with no member of his political party in either the House or Senate.

Carlson reminds Ventura and the media that the governor-elect will be handed the keys to a government that is running at peak economic efficiency. He says the state has $2 billion in reserves and is among a handful of states with a triple-A bond rating. "In the end we do want the people of Minnesota to win," Carlson says. "And the way to make them win is to make sure this governor succeeds."

After his quick tour of the State Capitol, Ventura heads to a sports bar in Bloomington. What could be more fitting for Minnesota's unconventional governor-elect? He's scheduled to return to the radio airwaves to host a show on KFAN for the first time since being forced off the air in July. Outside Joe Senser's Bar and Grill just off Interstate 494 a sign blinks "Have Lunch with Jesse Ventura Today" and flashes the forty-degree temperature. A Bloomington cop is on duty, directing a traffic jam as cars try to get into the parking lot. If you elect him, they will come.

The place is jammed with Ventura supporters. Some look like they were up partying with the governor-elect all night. "Jesse's a real person," says Rick Gatlin, eagerly awaiting the arrival of his lunch and Ventura. "Right from the start it was his honesty. He didn't come out and promise us the world. He said he was going to try, and that's all we can ask of him." Another young male who says he voted for Ventura is still stunned that his vote actually counted. "It's kind of like Christmas Day. You're so excited. You have so much nervous energy you don't know what to do with it. It's a great, great thing, and there's so much anticipation for what's going to happen the next four years."

When Ventura arrives around noon, he's overwhelmed by a raucous reception in the standing-room-only sports bar. When he gets in front of the radio microphone, he thanks his supporters, cracks a few jokes, and settles a score or two from the campaign. His most stinging remark is reserved for a competing radio talk-show host, conservative Jason Lewis of KSTP, who calls himself "Minnesota's Mr. Right." Lewis is among those who said Ventura couldn't win.

"I've got news for you, buddy boy, and I hope you're listening out there ...," Ventura bellows, slipping almost too comfortably back into his pro-wrestling persona. "I'm renaming you Mr. Minnesota Wrong.... Well, Mr. Wrong, stick it where the sun don't shine!"

Ventura takes several phone calls from notables like Minnesota Vikings owner Red McCombs. "Jesse, you're the governor!" McCombs drawls into the phone in Texas-sized amazement.

"You mean that means I get out of the nosebleed seats?" Ventura fires back.

"Oh yeah, come sit with me!" McCombs replies to loud cheers.

The ink isn't even dry on Ventura's election returns and McCombs is on the phone from Texas, beginning a subtle lobbying effort for a new football stadium. Ventura also takes a call from Vikings long snapper Mike Morris (this is a sports radio station, after all). Morris calls to tell Ventura he sincerely respects him for what he's accomplished and that he contributed to his campaign. Ventura isn't ready for sincerity. "Now tell 'em the real reason you look up to me," he deadpans. "Because I can kick your ass!" Clearly, there will be no shortage of quotes in the Ventura administration.

A couple of hours later the cyclone of attention around Ventura sweeps onto the Champlin Park High School football practice fields. "I've gotta coach!" Ventura barks. "I want the press off on the sideline." Never mind that he "shocked the world" the night before. Ventura is the team's volunteer conditioning coach and he's made a commitment to be here at this Twin Cities–area high school. He's surrounded by state troopers and at least a half-dozen television camera crews and reporters. Boom microphones with big, furry wind socks hang above his head. Smaller microphones are attached to his warm-up suit. His players greet him with cheers and high fives.

In an interview before practice, head coach Tim Hermann marvels at the example Ventura sets for his team. "He's been excited about being with the kids and trying to inspire them to do things that maybe were above and beyond what they thought they could do.... Everything he says he's going to do he works very hard to get accomplished. If that carries from the football team to the state of Minnesota, I think it will be great."

After football practice the governor-elect returns to his Maple Grove home for dinner and some rest. He goes to bed by ten o'clock, so he is likely sleeping when David Letterman caps off the first full day since Ventura's election with a "Top 10 List." According to Letterman, the following are the "Top 10 Jesse 'the Body' Ventura campaign slogans":

10. He's already used to deceiving the public.

9. Let's get ready to legislate.

8. Building a steroid-enhanced bridge to the twenty-first century.

7. A man in tights has nothing to hide.

6. C'mon, don't you want to see Newt Gingrich in a chokehold?

5. I'm the only candidate endorsed by Bobby "the Brain" Heenan.

4. Finally, a governor whose shorts glitter.

3. Combining the wise economic stewardship of Hulk Hogan and the progressive policies of Jimmy "Superfly" Snuka.

2. Vote for me or, so help me God, I'll pile-drive you.

1. It's the stupidity, stupid!

Later that night another late-night comic has some fun with Ventura's election. "That is a sign of the state of politics when the voting public is so fed up with phoniness and theatrics they'll go for a professional wrestler," jokes Bill Maher, host of *Politically Incorrect* on ABC. "Who, by the way, said today in his first official act he will annihilate Wisconsin."

"Morning, people! Welcome to Fantasy Island," bellows Doug Friedline, Ventura's campaign manager. He's greeting television and newspaper reporters camped outside Ventura's thirty-two-acre Maple Grove horse ranch two days after Ventura's shocking victory. Television live trucks and news vans line Brockton Lane at the entrance to the property, where a sign reads "Jesters' Falling Tree Ranch."

Friedline tells the media it's uncertain if Ventura will be available for local-media interviews. He says a *Newsweek* photographer is at the ranch for a photo shoot with Ventura. A *Time* reporter is waiting to do an interview and the magazine has a photo shoot scheduled for later. The phone is ringing nonstop with more requests for interviews and photo shoots.

From the fence, reporters eventually get a glimpse of the governor-elect. He's walking along the driveway, wearing a suit and tie with his shirt hanging out over blue jeans and athletic shoes. He's also chomping on a cigar. Among the local and national reporters waiting outside the ranch to cover Ventura's election is Steve Rubenstein of the *San Francisco Chronicle*. "The editor said, 'We got a little money left in the kitty this year,'" Rubenstein explains. "'Go out to Minnesota and find out what they did out there and how come.' It's very different than what all the smart guys thought was going to happen out here."

Ventura is eventually persuaded to come to the ranch entrance to speak with reporters. Just this morning he's had interviews with *Newsweek*, *Time*, MSNBC, and CNN. *Time* and *Newsweek* both are considering him for cover stories. "I basically will allow and focus on the media through Sunday," Ventura tells reporters, desperate for any quotes from the hottest political figure in the country. "I have people working on the transition, but I am not being able to focus on it, because of the media and the overwhelming national media. But I figure something will happen between now and Sunday that will take the spotlight off of me. And when that happens, we'll go real hard on the transition."

He laughs when asked how his wife and kids are dealing with all the attention. "Remember, the kids have been with Jesse 'the Body' for a number of years, and it's not exactly a normal lifestyle with me anyway." On other topics, he reveals that he will take the oath of office under his wrestling name, Jesse Ventura, rather than his real name, James Janos. He also says his public request on election night to have Jonny Lang perform at his inaugural party might just pay off. Negotiations with Lang's promoters are under way.

A couple of hours later Ventura arrives at Icehouse Productions' Minneapolis studios for a *Time* magazine photo shoot and an ESPN interview. ESPN's Roy Firestone, regarded as one of the best interviewers in broadcasting, can't wait to get a crack at Ventura. "Anything that shakes up the status quo is interesting to me and I'll cover it," Firestone says. "I think this is a great story. I think it's great to be around something that puts the whole status quo on its ear."

Firestone figures Minnesotans finally did what many people in the country have wanted to do but didn't have the right candidate to rally around. "Maybe that's what they're trying to say. We don't want a professional politician. We don't want somebody who's done it the way everybody else has done it since the beginning of this century. He'll step on some toes. He'll offend some people along the way. But I think he's going to galvanize the public. I think it's a great story for this state, and this state has a rich tradition in politics."

On Friday, November 6, Ventura spends most of the day doing media interviews in his transition office in the capitol basement. But the primary item on his agenda is the Champlin Park football team's play-off game tonight against arch rival Blaine. The game isn't until 7:30, but Ventura gets a good excuse to leave the office a little early: there's a bomb threat at the capitol. It's a fitting way to end one of the wackiest weeks in Minnesota political history.

At about three o'clock several state troopers and capitol security officers whisk the governor-elect out of his office. There's a paper bag duct-taped to a tree on the capitol's front lawn near a row of parked cars. A veiled threat about a bomb is scribbled on the bag. It doesn't specifically mention Ventura, but no one's taking chances. The entire building is evacuated. Ironically, in their zeal to evacuate the governor-elect, the escorts take him out the front of the capitol directly toward the suspicious package, which is only fifty feet from where his white Lincoln Town Car is waiting. He's whisked away unharmed, as the threat turns out to be a hoax.

After that shot of adrenaline Ventura is ready for more traditional excitement. It's finally game time, and despite his hectic schedule the governor-elect is on the sidelines for Champlin Park's play-off game. It's probably the only high-school football game in the country that CNN is covering. In fact, there's probably more media covering this game than all the other high-school games in the state combined. Ventura is wearing at least a half-dozen wireless microphones and isn't exactly thrilled. "I'm so wired up now they're probably all going to break," he complains to one photographer as he adds yet another microphone. "I'm not going to be responsible if the damn things break! And if I swear, you better bleep it out!"

Just minutes before kickoff, the Champlin Park players gather around the volunteer conditioning coach/governor-elect/worldwide celebrity for a pregame pep talk. "Every play tonight you play it like your last play," Ventura says, crouched in the middle of the huddle. "We don't have to fear these guys.... I shocked the world on Tuesday! Nobody gave us a chance. Nobody's giving us a chance tonight. We prove 'em wrong! Let's do it!"

On his way to the sideline someone stops Ventura and asks him to autograph a campaign sign. "Hold on to 'em. It might be worth something someday," the governor-elect tells the fan. Although Ventura seems annoyed by all the microphones he's wearing, he also still seems more than a little impressed by some of the media attention. "You know who we got here tonight," he tells head coach Tim Hermann. "The damn *New York Times!*"

Eventually the game, like the recent election, is too close to call with just eleven seconds to play. Champlin Park leads 25–22, but Blaine has the ball. The Blaine quarterback throws a Hail Mary to the end zone. Champlin Park intercepts and the stadium erupts. Ventura jumps up and down with his teenage players, everyone screaming, "Interception! Interception! Interception!" He slaps high fives with the other coaches and players before walking toward the Champlin Park cheering section with his fists over his head. As reporters swarm him on the field moments later he's too emotional to say much. "I'll tell you it's been a hell of a week for me," he says, stopping as tears come to his eyes and his voice begins to crack. "It's been great ..." His voice trails off as he turns to join the rest of the team in celebration. His remarkable string of good fortune continues.

"Next up: Is this how you train to be governor?" asks Tim Russert, as video appears on the television screen showing Jesse "the Body" coming off the top rope and ramming his knee into an opponent's back. "It is if you're Jesse Ventura, the next governor of Minnesota. One of a kind with us, right after this."

It's Sunday, November 8, and Ventura is about to make a political rite of passage. He's a featured interview on NBC's *Meet the Press*. After four days of mostly favorable, gee-whiz-how-did-you-get-elected coverage, the theme of Russert's interview is "Now what?" Talking with Ventura via a satellite link from the Twin Cities, Russert asks him about the centerpiece of his campaign: a promise to return budget surpluses to taxpayers.

"There was a $4 billion surplus being held hostage at the State Capitol as you described it," Russert says, "and ... you wanted to give that surplus back to the people of Minnesota in the form of about $1,000 for every man, woman, and child in Minnesota. Will they be getting a check soon after you become governor?"

"No, because that money's been spent," Ventura responds. "The Democrats and Republicans with great bipartisan support jumped in with both feet and they spent that surplus. Now, there may be future surpluses that come to the state of Minnesota, which is an obvious sign that we're being overtaxed here. You know, they call us the 'Land of 10,000 Lakes.' I call us the 'Land of 10,000 Taxes.' If a new surplus does rear its head, I would like to have a trigger mechanism put in that when a certain percentage of that gets above the budget.... It would automatically go back to the taxpayer rather than being allowed to get to the legislature."

Russert listens to the explanation but seems intent on exposing Ventura for backtracking on a campaign promise. "I've talked to some people who are already saying, 'Uh, oh, Jesse Ventura's starting to sound like a politician.' Let me show you what you said during the campaign and get you to reconcile it."

Russert shows one graphic that quotes a Ventura radio campaign ad pledging "to return the entire $4 billion tax surplus back to you, the taxpayers—about $1,000 for every man, woman, and child in Minnesota." Another says, "If everybody who wants their $1,000 back sends us $50 or more, we'll have the resources to make it happen."

"And now," Russert continues, "the governor-elect says, 'Well, gee, I didn't know the surplus was already spent.'"

"Oh, no, no, no, no. I knew it," Ventura says. "I just anticipate that there will be more surpluses because nobody's cut any taxes, so the rate of that tax money coming in could very well stay the same. But you can't give back something you don't have.... I knew very well the surplus was already dealt with and that was the reason it was a campaign issue."

Russert presses Ventura on comments he's made about legalizing marijuana and about the "war on drugs" being a failed policy. "Fifty percent of the people under the age of thirty who voted Tuesday voted for Jesse Ventura. Are you concerned and will you take a new, fresh attitude in your thoughts and discussion of drugs and alcohol, knowing full well people are now looking at you as the governor and if you say, 'I got wasted' or 'I did this,' they may get the wrong message?"

"Well, I'm going to keep dignity in the office and I'm not sending any wrong message out there at all," Ventura insists. "I'm sending a message: be smart, be responsible for yourself, and be intelligent, and take it as a personal thing."

Russert then turns the interview to national politics and the two easiest targets in the world: Bill and Hillary Clinton. Russert clearly knows what buttons to push with Ventura. "Hillary Clinton came to Minnesota and called your campaign a 'sideshow,'" Russert says, not really asking a question but rather throwing a fastball down the middle of the plate for Ventura to knock out of the park.

"Well, first of all, I think that she maybe oughta not leave the White House as often as she used to," Ventura says. "You know, there's other work for her to do, I think. Bad things seem to happen when she leaves, so she'd be better off staying back at the White House and taking care of business there rather than worrying about politics in Minnesota."

Russert moves on to President Clinton. "Do you think his personal behavior is fair game to be discussed and analyzed by the media and to be dealt with in the House of Representatives for impeachment hearings?"

Ventura's answer isn't what we've come to expect from the dry politicians who usually appear on Sunday-morning talk shows. "I think it's one thing if you want to dally outside your marriage if you go to a motel room. But I have a big problem when it's being done right in the White House, which belongs to us. That's our house, that's not his house. He is just occupying it. We're the owners, he's the renter. And I think he needs to abide by those rules and show more dignity."

Ventura was elected governor just five days ago, yet there are persistent questions about his own aspirations for the White House. "The *New York Times* says that your old buddy Hulk Hogan says Jesse Ventura is going to run for president," Russert tells Ventura.

"First of all, he's not my old buddy," Ventura says, alluding to his longtime feud with Hogan from their World Wrestling Federation days. "And second of all, no, I don't think so, because I've made a commitment to the state of Minnesota.... In order for me to run for president in 2000, I'd have to start campaigning now. I've got too much business to do here in the state of Minnesota, and I will fulfill my commitment to the state of Minnesota for the next four years. I have no intention of running for president."

Russert can't resist the next question. "If I call you Jesse 'the Mind' Ventura, will you call me Tim 'the Body' Russert?"

Ventura doesn't miss a beat. "Take your shirt off right now, Tim, let's see what you got!" Russert and his studio crew crack up. Ventura is going to be a talk-show star.

The Transition Begins

On Monday, November 9, Ventura conducts his first formal news conference at the State Capitol. It's scheduled to start at 10:30 A.M., but by 10:23 Room 181 in the State Office Building across from the capitol is jammed with reporters, legislators, and capitol staffers, so he starts the news conference seven minutes early. One more example of why he's not a typical politician.

Six days after his election, Ventura is finally ready to announce his choice for chief of staff to lead his transition into office. He introduces Steven Bosacker, the executive director of the University of Minnesota board of regents and former chief of staff for former Minnesota representative Tim Penny. Bosacker and Ventura appear to be as opposite as two people can be. Ventura is big and brusque and at times outlandish. Bosacker is slight of build, reserved, and button-down. He's exactly what Ventura needs to assure the public he's serious about governing. Bosacker will immediately begin focusing on the budget, communications, legislative relations, and cabinet appointments.

The news conference turns into a freewheeling exchange with reporters eager to hear more about how Ventura plans to govern. "Is there a plan to reach out to the 60 percent that didn't vote for you, Governor-elect? Make them feel a part of this administration?" a reporter asks.

"We're all part of it in our own way," Ventura responds. "This is what's best for the state of Minnesota, and if they have that same attitude we're not going to have any problems."

Bosacker and Ventura say hundreds of people are coming forward, looking for jobs in the new administration. Ventura is amazed. "My first day at home [after the election] I had 120 phone calls—and I have an unlisted phone number."

"How important is it for you to build up the Reform Party?" another reporter asks.

"It's not going to be me necessarily out there putting hammerlocks on people, saying, 'Join the Reform Party.' I think it's more an opportunity for people out there who truly believe in a third party, especially here in Minnesota.... We always have a twelve-step program for all recovering Democrats and Republicans."

Then a reporter actually leaves Ventura speechless after he does a little bragging about his recent *Meet the Press* appearance. "Actually, the *Meet the Press* people called after and were so excited and said they want me after the inauguration for a full hour," Ventura proudly reveals.

"Really?" a reporter asks, her voice dripping with incredulity. "To do what?" The room erupts in laughter for a full ten seconds as Ventura leans back, seemingly amazed anyone would question why he'd be in demand on national television.

Someone asks Ventura if he's disappointed that House Speaker Newt Gingrich's resignation knocked him out as a possible cover story for *Time* and *Newsweek* magazines. "No, I think they're going to see the results in a loss of revenue," he says in a cocky tone that draws more laughter. "My mom and dad are up there looking down, and believe me, there's no way in their life they thought they'd see their son on the cover of *Time* magazine. And like I said, that's *Time*'s loss, because I guarantee you they would have sold more with me on there."

He's probably right. Both *Time* and *Newsweek* hit newsstands with Newt Gingrich on the covers. However, the savvy publishers of *Time* put out a rare special Minnesota edition of their magazine that features Ventura on the cover. Instead of the frowning face of Gingrich, the Minnesota edition of *Time* shows the smiling, bald Ventura with the caption, "Body Slam! America sends its leaders a message: Get a life—we've got one!" Inside, there's a three-page story headlined, "Everyone laughed. Then everyone gasped. Now it's time to take Jesse Ventura seriously. Here's why he's a populist hero."

Naturally, the article is accompanied by photos featuring Ventura's wrestling days, his term as mayor of Brooklyn Park, and a new photo of the governor-elect in a leather-fringed jacket. A sidebar essay by fellow Minnesotan Garrison Keillor tries to explain Ventura's ascendancy in the land of Lake Wobegon.

"He was the protest candidate, a chance to throw toilet paper in the trees and piss off Dad, nobody dreaming he would actually be elected," Keillor writes. "All across Minnesota, the quiet, decent people who believe in Good Government and Working Together to Resolve Differences are leaning forward in disbelief at the thought that the next Governor of their state might be THIS GREAT BIG HONKING BULLET-HEADED SHOVEL-FACED MUTHA WHO TALKS IN A STEROID GROWL AND DOESN'T STOP. And then he won."

Although he isn't on the cover, *Newsweek* does its part to add to the legend-in-the-making. "Jesse Ventura's 'Body' Politics," blares the headline. A four-page spread includes a full-page photo of Ventura in a size-fifty business suit with his fists clenched. It's a kind of half-governor, half-wrestler pose. "Out of nowhere," the *Newsweek* piece begins, "'The Body' Ventura puts politics-as-usual in a headlock with a victory as

Minnesota Governor: The voters' message to Washington? If you act like pro wrestlers, we'll give you pro wrestlers."

In addition to photos from his wrestling, political, movie, and Navy SEAL careers, there's also a Q & A with the governor-elect that includes a quote regarding fears some Minnesotans have about whether he'll serve with dignity. Ventura responds this way: "I'll do some fun things, but I don't want to cheapen the office. It's a very dignified honor. I'm not about to turn it into some dog-and-pony show. I'm an honorable person."

With flattering coverage from the nation's top news magazines and almost daily reports of his activities on CNN and other network news shows, Ventura is off on his first road trip as governor-elect. He's headed to the National Governors Conference in Wilmington, Delaware. The November conference is typically a sleepy event that serves as an orientation for new governors. Not exactly your high-profile political get-together reporters clamor to cover. Until now.

Governor-elect Ventura's scheduled appearance at the conference swamps the National Governors Association with requests for media credentials. In an average year this conference draws about a dozen or so journalists. This time they expect nearly one hundred. Anyone hoping to cover a story about how politics-as-usual has bitten the dust will not be disappointed.

Ventura pulls up to the posh Hotel du Pont in a silver Lincoln Continental. He steps out of the car wearing his fringed leather jacket, a white golf shirt, and cowboy boots. The moment he enters the hotel, a phalanx of security guards supplied by the Delaware state police surrounds him while he makes a roughly thirty-foot walk to an elevator. About fifteen minutes later, when he comes back down to the lobby, the guards pounce on him again. Thirteen security guards wearing earphones and carrying mysterious black bags surround Ventura and keep reporters and others away. Meanwhile, governors and governors-elect from most of the other forty-nine states walk virtually unnoticed (and mostly unguarded) through the hotel.

Ventura is on his way to a CNN interview in a park across the street. He steps out the front door and is quickly surrounded by the security platoon and a squad of reporters and photographers. He does his best to ignore our questions. "How have the other governors welcomed you today, Mr. Ventura?" a television reporter asks, seemingly oblivious to the fact he's only been in town about a half-hour.

"I haven't met any of them yet," he responds.

"What are you going to say to them when you do?" the reporter asks, probing ever deeper.

"'Hello, how are you,'" Ventura says. Clearly, the guards aren't protecting him from stupid questions.

In fact, it's unclear what they're protecting him from. The streets of Wilmington have pretty much rolled up for the night. Ventura's walking across a mostly empty street to a mostly empty park, except for the CNN crew. They're set up for Ventura to be interviewed via satellite by Bernard Shaw on *Inside Politics*. It's a comical scene as the security guards and news crews literally trip over each other along the way.

It's November 12, nine days since the election, but Shaw and most members of the national media still can't comprehend what happened in Minnesota. Shaw begins his interview by saying even an electrician who worked on his house earlier in the day is a Ventura fan.

"I told him I was going to be interviewing you on *Inside Politics*," Shaw tells Ventura. "And he said, 'I like that guy because he doesn't pull punches. He tells you what he thinks. He tells the truth.' And this electrician said of you, 'When he doesn't know something, he says he doesn't know.' My question to you is, are Minnesotans ready for you?"

Ventura has no doubts. "They're ready for me, Bernie. I'm a Minnesotan. How can they not be ready for a fellow Minnesotan?... They are more familiar with me in Minnesota in government than the rest of the nation is at this time because I did govern for four years as mayor and Brooklyn Park is the sixth-largest city in the state." Ventura says he was elected because voters want less government and lower taxes, and he plans to deliver both.

In a brief news conference with the Minnesota media after the

CNN interview, Ventura is asked if he's surprised he was greeted in Delaware by the national media and so much security. "Well, I guess I know what it's like to be Mick Jagger now. I'm flattered. There's a lot of great governors here; I just happen to be one that comes from a more different life, and, like I said, I shocked the world when I won in the first place. So naturally the media jumps onboard and likes to talk to Rocky Balboa ... because no one gave Rocky a chance and nobody gave Jesse Ventura a chance."

Will the other governors resent all the attention he's getting? "I hope not. We're all here to do the same thing and that's govern our states." Moments later his thirteen security guards escort him back to the hotel.

Governor Parris Glendening of Maryland tells me Ventura's appeal to younger voters is obvious and enviable. "My son came home from college all excited election night," Glendening says. "'Dad! Dad! You didn't tell me 'the Body' was elected.' And I said, 'Yeah, but I was too!' And he says, 'Yeah, but *the Body!*' All the fun and the puns and the media hype notwithstanding, I really wish him well. There's only fifty of us in the whole country. He deserves the respect he's earned."

Ventura's voice is raspy after nine days of nearly nonstop interviews, news conferences, and public appearances. Before he can get to bed on the first night of the governors conference, he holds one more news conference with the insatiable national media. A reporter asks if he's overwhelmed.

"I sold out Madison Square Garden three times," Ventura says, alluding to his wrestling career. "There's a little pressure there to perform. Also in my military career I was a demolition expert. That's pressure. You connect the wrong wire, that's pressure! Jump out of an airplane, that's pressure. Dive 200 feet under the water, that's literally pressure." In other words, no, he's not overwhelmed.

Someone asks if a former pro wrestler can be taken seriously while espousing out-of-the-mainstream views such as legalizing marijuana and prostitution. "Why would I not be taken seriously? I'm a governor-elect.

Why would I be taken any different than any other governor-elect? I won. I'm the next governor of the state of Minnesota.... I wish the press would look at wrestling in a new light. It's ballet with violence. Nobody makes fun of Nureyev. Don't make fun of us either. We're great athletes and we do entertain people. Take a look at the rating points. Obviously the public likes it."

The next morning Governor-elect Ventura attends orientation meetings designed to help new governors deal with transitions and budgets. Thirty-six governors are here, thirteen rookies and twenty-three veterans. Ventura also spends time getting acquainted with fellow governors like Florida's Jeb Bush and Wisconsin's Tommy Thompson. "I think he's a wonderful guy," Thompson tells me after his first meeting with Ventura. "He's a delight. A breath of fresh air for the political process, and I think he's going to be a star."

Ventura has to leave the conference Friday afternoon less than twenty-four hours after his arrival because of a commitment to coach his high-school football team. It seems he's spent most of his twenty-four hours holding news conferences or giving interviews. He spends his last twenty minutes giving the media one more crack at him.

What did you and Governor Thompson talk about? "We talked about how the Vikings kicked [the Green Bay Packers'] ass on Monday night." What did you tell the other governors about your election victory? "I reminded them I'm a fiscal conservative, and I think it showed in my campaign, where we spent around $600,000 to get elected. And I told them, 'You can do it too. Just wrestle for twelve years.'"

What's going to be your first act as governor? "My first act? Kick my feet up on a chair and smoke a stogie." What did you and Jeb Bush talk about? "He told me his brother [Texas governor George W. Bush] said he could kick my butt, and I said I ain't met a Texican yet that can shade me!" What message does your election send to America? "I come from a blue collar [background]. Yeah, I own a Porsche. Yeah, I own a thirty-two-acre horse ranch. But when I left to start my wrestling career, I had a beat-up Chevy, two hundred bucks, and I lived in a $22.50

a week hotel room.... What that means is that the American dream exists. If you work hard, you can become anything. If Jesse Ventura can become governor, you can become anything too. The doors are open and the American dream lives on."

His wife, Terry Ventura, is asked what it feels like to go from having a relatively private family life to life in a fishbowl. She grew up on a farm in Vernon Center, Minnesota, and has been married to Ventura for twenty-four years, including the ups and downs of his wrestling and movie careers. In recent years they've devoted much of their time to raising their two children and breeding horses at their ranch.

"Just remember, three weeks ago we were still cleaning the barns and spreading manure behind the John Deere," she says. "And four years or eight years from now, we'll be doing the same thing." The governor-elect can't resist chiming in. "The sign is still up at my property, you know. I have that carved-out wooden pistol and it says, 'We don't call 911.' You all just remember that." Moments later his phalanx of Delaware state police follows him to his car and escorts him to the airport.

Coast-to-Coast Ventura

"My next guest is an old buddy and one of the most exciting things to happen in politics in years, the former professional wrestler known as 'the Body.' He ran as an independent candidate for governor of Minnesota, and, to everybody's surprise, he won. I want to show you one of his campaign commercials before we bring him out. Take a look at this."

Across the nation flashes one of Ventura's now-famous action-figure campaign ads as Jay Leno introduces Minnesota's governor-elect on NBC's *Tonight Show* in Los Angeles. "Please welcome Governor-elect Jesse Ventura!" The band strikes up the music and from around the corner walks Ventura in a navy blue double-breasted suit. He hugs Leno and shakes hands with another guest, Garry Shandling, before sitting down for his first late-night talk-show appearance since his election.

"You're not using Jesse 'the Body' anymore," Leno says. "What do you want to be called now?"

"Governor," Ventura deadpans as the audience roars with approval.

Leno then holds up an old World Wrestling Federation action figure of Jesse "the Body" Ventura wearing a bandanna and pink tights.

"Did you ever think you'd go literally from ... this to the governor's mansion?" Leno asks.

"Actually, the royalties from that got me my first Porsche," Ventura tells him.

Ventura spends the next eight minutes on the *Tonight Show* sparking many funny exchanges with Leno. He reveals that he changed his name from James Janos to Jesse Ventura by looking at a map of California. He tells Leno he always liked the name "Jesse" and when he saw Ventura, California, on a map, it seemed like a great name for the wrestling image he wanted to create. Using the persona of a bleach-blond bad guy from California, he became one of the hottest stars in professional wrestling.

After his guest spot is over, Ventura stays on the set for the remainder of the show. And why not? The final guest is supermodel Stephanie Seymour. "You're certainly the prettiest person on our panel tonight," Leno tells her, looking over at Ventura and Shandling. Leno attempts to interview Seymour about a book she's written on beauty tips when Shandling and Ventura upstage her.

SHANDLING: Jay, may I ask you something?

LENO: Yes?

SHANDLING: Why am I suddenly on a loveseat with Jesse "the Body" Ventura?

LENO: I think it's pretty self-explanatory, isn't it?

SHANDLING: I don't know. I'm very uncomfortable. I just had to say ...

VENTURA: Aw, relax. (Ventura starts to put his arm around Shandling, who then jumps out of his seat.)

SHANDLING: Don't you touch me ... you're a dead man! (The audience is howling as Seymour then turns her attention to Ventura.)

SEYMOUR: I didn't realize how good-looking you are!

LENO: It's starting, Governor! Women love power!

SEYMOUR: No, no, no ... I love bald heads!

After taping the *Tonight Show*, Ventura heads over to the CBS Studios in Los Angeles to tape an appearance on the *Late, Late Show with Tom Snyder*. Leno went for the slapstick; Snyder goes for the substance. He asks Ventura to expand on what he meant during the campaign when he said, "You can't legislate against stupidity."

Ventura tells him it's a pretty simple concept: You can't make laws to stop every stupid thing people are going to do. He says nature has a way of "weeding out the stupid" without government getting involved.

Of course, it's only a matter of time before any interviewer gets around to Ventura's wrestling career. Snyder asks why he wanted to be a bad guy.

"The good guy, that's Mom, apple pie," Ventura tells him. "You can't be creative. A bad guy, you can insult everyone. It's expected of you. It was great. Nobody realizes what it's like to have nineteen thousand people in the palm of your hand, on your every move. The first time I sold out my hometown of St. Paul [actually, he's from Minneapolis], the Civic Center, of course, they billed me from San Diego. They didn't tell them I was from there. And as I went to the ring nineteen thousand people were chanting in unison, "Jesse sucks!" What better compliment. I mean, I did my job!"

Snyder and his studio crew roar with laughter.

After taping the shows with Leno and Snyder, Ventura wraps up his trip to Los Angeles by having dinner with Arnold Schwarzenegger at Spago. Ventura and Schwarzenegger first met when they shot the movie *Predator* together in 1986. Ventura later appeared with Schwarzenegger in *The Running Man* and a *Batman* movie. Over dinner the two men celebrate Ventura's latest career move and all its plot twists. It all seems to be the work of some Hollywood screenwriter.

When he arrives back in Minnesota, Ventura sets out on an ambitious and possibly unprecedented tour of every state department that will soon be under his authority. From the Department of Natural Resources to the Planning Office, he wants to see all of the state's twenty-five major departments firsthand. Ventura says he wants to meet and shake hands with as many state workers as he can.

He's treated like a rock star during just about every visit. On November 25, the day before Thanksgiving, he walks into the new Department of Revenue building near downtown St. Paul and is greeted by hundreds of cheering employees. They're packed on two floors overlooking the lobby, cheering wildly and taking pictures and video. "Now I know where my taxes are going!" he jokes.

That draws another big laugh and round of applause. Before continuing his tour with department administrators, Ventura is swarmed by employees seeking autographs and snapshots. "Can you sign these?" one woman asks before shoving a few old wrestling cards at him that feature Ventura from his wrestling days. "They're for my dad," she assures him. Ventura laughs and starts signing. "Geez, look at these old things! When I had hair!"

Although Ventura enjoys overwhelmingly positive media coverage during the first month after his election victory, his critics do start taking some shots. Before November is over, a Minnesota military veteran openly questions Ventura's Vietnam service record and a newspaper editor claims Ventura has a hot temper and a "darker side." The veteran is Dick Franson, a retired first sergeant in the U.S. Army who served in both the Korean and Vietnam wars. He's also a perennial political candidate in Minnesota who seems to relish being called a "gadfly."

In an interview with the tabloid *Globe* newspaper, Franson claims Ventura is misleading the public about how much combat action he saw in Vietnam. "I think Jesse inflated his war record to pump up his tough-guy image," Franson tells the *Globe*. "I knew cooks who saw more action." Military records do show Ventura served as a "storekeeper/ supply clerk" at the U.S. Navy base in the Philippines. He was sent there in 1972 after completing Navy SEAL training in California. Ventura won't say publicly how much time he actually spent in Vietnam or what, if any, action he saw there, but he did receive a Vietnam Service Medal. Franson dismisses the significance of that medal. "If he cruised past the Vietnam coastline one day, he was eligible for that award," Franson says.

Later a writer in California would question whether Ventura was even a real Navy SEAL. Bill Salisbury, a San Diego attorney and former SEAL, wrote an article for the *San Diego Reader*, questioning Ventura's credentials. Ventura went through SEAL training, but actually served with an underwater demolition team, or UDT. SEALs (Sea, Air, and Land units) conducted combat and clandestine operations during the Vietnam War. UDTs performed, as their name implies, underwater demolition operations and reconnaissance missions. "No one from UDT during the Vietnam War would dare represent himself as a SEAL," Salisbury wrote, claiming SEALs always faced more danger.

Ventura wouldn't comment publicly about Salisbury's claims, but, as he's often fond of saying, it turns out to be "much ado about nothing." In 1983 UDTs merged with the SEAL teams and there is now considered little distinction between the two. Most UDT members from Ventura's era now consider themselves SEALs with the Navy's blessing.

One of the few other negative items to find its way into print during the early Ventura honeymoon period is a guest column in the *St. Paul Pioneer Press* written by the editor of a suburban newspaper. Harvey Rockwood claims he witnessed Ventura's "darker side" on a few occasions, including episodes of losing his temper and physical intimidation of his critics while Ventura was mayor of Brooklyn Park, Minnesota.

Rockwood was editor of the weekly *Sun Post* newspaper when Ventura was mayor from 1990 to 1994. Rockwood says Ventura's mayoral term was rife with conflict.

"As in the governor's race, Ventura managed to tap into a disaffected group of citizens who were tired of business-as-usual," Rockwood writes. "The honeymoon was remarkably short: It turned out the new mayor was petulant, short-tempered and self-centered, and, by his own admission, out to entertain." Rockwood cites examples of when Ventura would quote professional wrestlers to make his point during city-council meetings or to intimidate council members. One time Ventura confronted a council member who was considering running for mayor. In doing so, Ventura quoted "Nature Boy" Ric Flair, telling the council member, "If you want to be the man, you got to beat the man!"

Rockwood claims that a week after that exchange, a writer for his newspaper wrote an editorial criticizing Ventura for his council-meeting theatrics. Rockwood says Ventura showed up at the newspaper office to complain. When he invited Ventura in to discuss the matter, Rockwood quickly had second thoughts.

"This was a mistake," he writes. "He wagged his index finger in my face and advanced toward me. I honestly thought he might punch me. Don't get me wrong—I'm not fainthearted. I've been pestering politicians for years and I don't worry about making them mad. This was different. He took a step forward. I took a step backward."

Neither of these stories gets much play in either the local or national media. The fact is, there's little room for these stories amid the lavish praise being heaped on a man who single-handedly seems to be shaking up the political status quo. They're little more than bumps in the road on Ventura's highway to national political superstardom.

CHAPTER 3

"Hooyah!"
Governor Ventura Takes the Oath

The days since Jesse Ventura's election have been filled with a seemingly nonstop string of speaking engagements. The speeches all give glimpses of why voters found Ventura so refreshing. After being introduced by Minnesota's Supreme Court chief justice, Kathleen Blatz, Ventura points out to a convention of judges assembled at the Minneapolis Airport Marriott that, although he's never had a day of law school, he's probably the only unbeaten lawyer in the state. He tells the story about when the city of Brooklyn Park sued him when he was its mayor, claiming he was no longer a city resident and should be thrown out of office.

Ventura explains that in 1994 he purchased a home in neighboring Maple Grove with about five or six months left in his term (he had already announced he wasn't running for reelection) so that he would have a bigger house in which to take care of his elderly mother. He also maintained his Brooklyn Park residence. But his political opponents in the city filed a lawsuit, and Brooklyn Park, by law, had to provide Ventura, its mayor, with a private attorney.

"This whole thing is absurd," he tells the judges. "I said, I'm not going to spend people's hard-earned tax dollars on something as ridiculous as this. I said, I'll defend myself, because it all came down to I knew I was right." That elicits laughter from the judges, who've probably heard that from more than one defendant. Ventura got the last laugh in his case because he won.

He says that's an example of how he's lived his life: living and learning. "I'm very much, if you want to call it, street smart. I'm very much OJT—on-the-job-training." He says in most aspects of his diverse career, he's had to start from scratch and build himself up. His race for governor was no different.

"I'm proud to say no one gave me a chance," Ventura tells the judges. "All the experts were wrong, and to me that's refreshing to know they can be wrong. And the other remarkable thing is, I'm going to ask for a recount. You wanna know why? Because if everybody that's told me they voted for me *did* vote for me, it would have been 75 [percent] to 15 to 10!"

The governor closes his remarks with a funny story about a congratulatory phone call he got from Governor Angus King of Maine. "Angus called up and was thrilled and he said, 'Governor-elect, I'm so happy.' And I said, 'Why?' And he said, 'What a remarkable place this United States of America is. In one election we've doubled our party!'"

That brings laughter from the judges and an explanation from Ventura. "For those that don't know, of course, Angus belongs to no party. Which is kind of the same as being in the Reform Party!" This draws the biggest laugh yet. "I hope they're not here," Ventura says facetiously as he looks around the room for Reform Party officials.

On December 3, exactly one month after his election, Ventura is handed a gift any incoming governor would relish. The Minnesota Department of Finance says the state has another $1.5 billion budget surplus through 1999. "I think it's going to be a nice Christmas season for the people of Minnesota," Governor Carlson says as he makes the official announcement.

It's the state's seventh straight year of budget surpluses. Carlson already has a proposal for what to do with most of the money: return $1 billion directly back to taxpayers. He's got a plan for so-called instant income-tax rebates that would average $516 per tax filer or family. That's the equivalent of a 22 percent income-tax rebate. Sounds like a no-brainer of a proposal for Ventura to embrace, in principle at least, if not in detail. After all, he was elected on a campaign pledge to return all future budget surpluses to the taxpayers. But one thing we've already learned about the governor-elect is to expect the unexpected. Ventura doesn't bite on the Carlson tax-rebate idea. Not yet, anyway.

"The governor's leaving in three weeks, so it's easy for him to say that as he's heading off into the sunset," Ventura tells reporters, reminding us this is a "projected" budget surplus, not money in the bank. "There wasn't one person in this state projecting I'd be governor. So projections can be wrong."

The state of Minnesota isn't alone in hitting the jackpot. It now appears Ventura will cash in big-time on his stunning election victory. On December 8, the day before taking off for his first vacation since beginning his campaign in July, the governor-elect sits down with several members of the capitol press corps for an informal (but on-the-record) briefing in the conference room of his transition offices.

Ventura speaks with remarkable candor about some untraditional activities he might pursue after taking office. During this meeting he confirms he's been offered a book deal for a substantial amount of money. "I've just agreed to it," he says. "Nothing more than that. A writer hasn't been picked yet. It will be done on my own time, and at this point I have nothing more to say [about it]."

That pledge lasts about ten seconds. "Will you tell us what the deal is worth?" a reporter asks.

"No," Ventura responds.

"Mid-six figures?" the reporter presses.

"Six figures," Ventura says matter-of-factly. "That's just up-front money. You can do a book deal with no front money and it can still make a ton of money. If it doesn't sell, then you don't make money on it."

I ask Ventura if there are any other private deals in the works to cash in on his "celebrity governor" status. He doesn't rule out anything, from appearing in ads to taking on movie roles. "If I do any types of deals, they'll be deals the same as I was doing before I was elected. I've done advertising before. I've used my name as such. It's copyrighted to me."

Ventura also reveals that his agent in Los Angeles is letting it be known he'd be open to a movie based on his book. He's already fuming about reports that NBC is working on an unauthorized made-for-TV movie about his life. "I disagree with the laws that when you become, quote-unquote, a 'public figure,' that all of a sudden you lose all your rights. They can do it without my permission, but it won't be authorized." They can also do it without paying him a dime.

"I don't like that," Ventura continues. "I don't think anyone would. Your life is pretty important to you, and I think you'd at least like the ability to have some hand in what's said and how it's portrayed. And for them not to give that to you, and for them to have the right to do it that way, is kind of disturbing."

With Ventura's potential moneymaking ventures in the offing, a reporter asks him if, for ethical reasons, he should reveal his sources of income and the amounts he's earning outside the office of governor. "No, I don't think I necessarily need to, because, you know, this is how I earned my living before I got elected, and this whole book thing is based on up to the election. It's not based on anything beyond that. The book will not go into anything beyond the election." Ventura also says he's not concerned about possible appearances he's "trading" on his position of governor or demeaning the office.

His musings about the potential for profit while in office seem to run counter to the spirit of ethics laws enacted by the Minnesota legislature in recent years. In 1994 the legislature passed and Governor Carlson signed a tough new ethics law for most elected officials in the state. It prohibits them from accepting meals or gifts from lobbyists or others with business pending before them. The law is so strict it even outlaws elected officials from accepting wedding gifts from lobbyists. The goal of such legislation is to restore public trust in state government, where the practice of lobbyists' gifts, meals, and entertainment had gone on virtually unchecked for years before 1994. Ventura isn't proposing to violate any of these specific rules, but he is flirting with violating the spirit of the law.

"My guidelines will probably be, first of all, that I'm not like every other governor," he tells reporters in a laughable understatement. "I think we can all agree on that. Where I come from and how I got here is far different than any other governor ever has, so maybe that allows me a little more leeway. I'm not doing anything I haven't done before in my career. You know, I've licensed my name before in my career. The key for me is that I will not license it with 'Governor' attached to it. I will not allow them to say 'Governor Jesse Ventura' in an ad. I would allow them to use Jesse 'the Body' because I do have that copyrighted."

We continue to press him on the issue of devoting time to private moneymaking projects while holding public office. He doesn't back down, reminding us that he hasn't had a paycheck since July 21 and that he was a public figure before he was elected governor.

"But these things [book deals and other possible offers] wouldn't have happened if you hadn't been elected," a reporter responds.

"Oh, baloney!" Ventura snaps back. "Maybe, maybe not. But I've done twelve movies prior to ever getting elected, and they didn't hire me to do movies because I was mayor of Brooklyn Park. And I did those while I was mayor of Brooklyn Park, so it's not like I'm creating some new ground here.... Is there time to have the weekends off? As long as I'm doing it at home on my own time and I'm not on government business. I'll be very careful about that. This is my main job, rest assured of that. Governor comes first. Anything else will come secondary."

After a five-day vacation in Florida, Ventura returns to the Twin Cities. His absence left a serious void on Minnesota television stations and in newspapers. After six weeks of nonstop saturation coverage of the Ventura phenomenon, all of a sudden there was nothing. He changes that when he sets off on a whirlwind three-city tour of southern Minnesota. Call it a victory lap.

Among his stops is a Rochester shopping mall just a few blocks from the Mayo Clinic. When he steps from his car outside the Centerplace Galleria Mall, even Ventura isn't prepared for the reception he's about to receive. There's a mob of people waiting for him on the sidewalk.

"I'm from Hawaii—can I get my picture taken with you?" a woman in a red jacket yells to him. He obliges. The mayor of Rochester then greets him and walks him to the main door of the mall. Inside, the scene is almost surreal.

Hundreds of people are packed in the food-court area of the mall, hanging over the railings three stories up. Surrounded by state troopers and television cameras, the governor-elect makes his way to a podium while being bombarded by cheers and screams. Rock stars or teen heartthrobs get receptions like this, not politicians!

"You're stuck with me for four years!" Ventura shouts to the crowd when they finally settle down. That sets off another long round of applause and cheers. He then jokes that one of his first acts as governor will be to increase tourism promotion in Minnesota. "But I want to warn you, if you're walking around and people are staring at you, relax. It's probably just a tourist. They've told me they're all coming to Minnesota because they want to look at who voted me in! So don't feel bad if you feel like you're at the zoo or something."

He tells them he'll propose that every June 30, when the fiscal year ends, the state should "settle up" with taxpayers and keep the surplus money out of the hands of legislators. Another huge cheer. At this point he could mandate a sharp stick in the eye for every Minnesotan and still get a cheer.

"I've been in Florida where a governor who was supposed to be highly respected only drew, like, twenty people," says Joe Towne, a Florida native working temporarily at the Mayo Clinic. "[Ventura's] got this place packed." Rochester resident Ben Riley is also amazed by what he's witnessing. "I think it's great," he says. "It's nice to see all the people behind him, and if we can get the state of Minnesota behind him as a whole, maybe we can get a lot of things done."

From Rochester the Ventura road show moves to Austin, Minnesota, about thirty miles west along Interstate-90. It's the same town that once vilified another governor, Rudy Perpich, in 1986 when he sent the National Guard to Austin to quell a union uprising at the Hormel meatpacking plant. In contrast, Governor-elect Ventura arrives like a conquering hero. He walks into Austin High School and signs a few copies of his *Time* magazine cover for some school staff members. Moments later he's introduced to an audience packed into the school's auditorium.

"Please welcome Governor-elect Jesse Ventura!" Ventura pulls aside a curtain and appears onstage to a standing ovation. While students scream and cheer in the lower level and from a large balcony, the governor-elect basks in the glory. He's the "rock star" governor.

Then it's time for a civics lesson the students probably never heard in government class. "The thing I want you to remember about government is this: Government doesn't create one dollar of money. So when someone gets a dollar from the government, they took that dollar from someone else. And the chances are they took two dollars. They kept one for carrying charges, you know. So the thing I would like to see out of your generation is not to be reliant upon the government. You can do it, believe me you can. The American dream is still out there. You can be anything you want to be."

As an example of the dream he's living, Ventura reminds them he'll be sworn in as governor in a few weeks. He really impresses them when he reveals that one of Hollywood's biggest stars—Arnold Schwarzenegger—will be there to witness the event. "The Terminator's coming in. Ahhhnold . . . he'll be in Minnesota. He said he wouldn't miss it for the world."

Then he opens up for questions. As usual, questions from kids tend to bring out some of the governor-elect's most provocative and amusing quotes.

He's asked if it bothers him that the media always brings up his wrestling career. "No, I'm very proud of my wrestling past. I would rather be a wrestler than a career politician." That comment brings thunderous applause. "I don't hide from it at all. It made me a lot of money. It got me much of the notoriety that I have today and it led to a film career. And after all, what guy can walk around in pink tights and a feathered boa and still be tough?"

Keep in mind this December 17 appearance in Austin comes as

President Clinton's impeachment hearings are beginning in Washington, D.C., and the United States is beginning new air attacks on Iraq. A student asks Ventura if he thinks Clinton ordered the attacks to divert attention from the Monica Lewinsky scandal and his impeachment.

"It's serious in the fact—not whether the president cheated on his wife, that's between he and his wife—but the fact that he lied to me when he came out on TV. He lied [by saying he didn't have sex with Lewinsky]. We all remember that. Well, now he's sending our young people to war and I question in the back of my mind, can I trust him? Can I trust his judgment? If I were president, and this is only me and my opinion, if I were the president and I had done what he had done in misleading the people of Minnesota—I'll put it to you as governor: I would resign."

10,000 Lakes, One Navy SEAL

On December 23, at a Mall of America gift shop, Ventura campaign manager Doug Friedline announces that a new nonprofit corporation will license and market a line of Jesse Ventura merchandise. Friedline says all money raised by VMI—Ventura for Minnesota, Inc.—through sales of the merchandise will go to various charities to be designated by Ventura and his wife. Ventura, he says, will not personally profit. The corporation plans to put the Ventura image on everything imaginable, including T-shirts, hats, mugs, shot glasses, key chains, and kid's clothing.

But the biggest-selling item is expected to be the Jesse Ventura action figure. You remember him from the campaign, driving the RV and fighting Special Interest Man. Now the twelve-inch action figure is going to be mass-produced and on store shelves by April or May with a $15 to $20 price tag. Preliminary plans call for an initial production order of one hundred thousand action figures from a plant in China.

All the new, authorized merchandise will carry a VMI logo to show it's approved by Ventura for Minnesota, Inc., with the proceeds going to charity. That means the new organization will begin forcing unauthorized products off store shelves. Friedline holds up several

T-shirts that have been in stores during the Christmas season that will no longer be allowed. This includes a line of popular shirts and bumper stickers that say, "My governor can beat up your governor." Friedline says Ventura doesn't think those items send the right message to kids. He drops them in a nearby waste can to illustrate for the cameras that those items must go.

"Jesse does now and always has owned the right to his own name and likeness, as do other famous people," says David Bradley Olsen, Ventura's private attorney. "In the past he's made a living off licensing the rights to his name and likeness. We're asking the people that are producing the unauthorized merchandise to stop." Olsen points out that Ventura once successfully took the World Wrestling Federation all the way to the U.S. Supreme Court to establish the right to his name and likeness.

Friedline and Olsen say several retailers will sell the merchandise in Minnesota and nationally. Friedline shows off several authorized versions of T-shirts and hats. There's one featuring Ventura's bald head with the caption "Head of State," and another with the caption "Jesse Ventura: America's Governing Body." Two other shirts seem destined to become top sellers. One includes an image of the action figure with the caption "Minnesota's Man of Action." The other features Ventura's face and the caption "10,000 Lakes, One Navy SEAL."

The idea of marketing a political figure through merchandise that anyone would actually *want* to buy is clearly a groundbreaking event. Friedline says all proceeds will go into an escrow account until a foundation can be established to distribute the money to charities. He also says it's possible some money could go toward Ventura's campaign committee.

Olsen says they'll move ahead cautiously, making sure they get approval from the Minnesota Campaign Finance and Public Disclosure Board. Olsen also says VMI will license only those products that are "strictly limited" to Ventura's "public persona" as the governor. Ventura will retain his personal right to market the name and likeness of "Jesse 'the Body' Ventura" that he developed as a wrestler and movie actor.

A reporter asks Olsen if it's actually possible to stop people from selling things with the Ventura image, now that he's a public figure and a public official. Olsen admits that's unclear, but he's confident Ventura will prevail. "We're operating in somewhat of a gray area because no one's ever done this before," Olsen responds. "No other elected official has had this kind of marketability. But to the extent that people are unfairly profiting by selling their products solely through the use of Jesse Ventura's name and likeness, as opposed to making some kind of political statement, we think the law's going to be on our side when it finally shakes out."

Jesse and Terry Ventura get their first tour of the official governor's residence in December just a few weeks before inauguration day. The twenty-room mansion on St. Paul's historic Summit Avenue is just a few minutes' drive from the State Capitol. After touring the house, Ventura hints that it's unlikely his family will move in on a full-time basis. He prefers the privacy of his thirty-two-acre ranch in the western suburb of Maple Grove. Instead, the governor-elect says, he'll probably spend many weeknights at the mansion because it's so close to the capitol.

This isn't as unorthodox as it might sound, because Governor Carlson isn't living at the mansion now either. His family did live there during his first term, but they've since moved to a new home in Forest Lake, north of St. Paul. The mansion is mostly just used for official state functions and meetings.

What is unorthodox is an idea the governor-elect floats in an interview with the *Star Tribune* at the end of December. He says his wife should be paid a salary to assume the duties of First Lady, possibly as much as $25,000. "It's a bit sexist that the First Lady is not paid for what she does," Ventura tells reporters Patricia Lopez and Robert Whereatt. "She's working for the government, she has a specific role, and she's required to do that." He says his wife has had to hire outside help to run her horse-breeding operation and that it might go out of business if she can't devote more time to it. "[Voters] elect both of you," Ventura says. "With my job automatically comes her job. She can't turn it down and say, 'No, I don't want to be First Lady.'"

Technically, that's not correct. State law doesn't require a governor's spouse to do anything. Politically, however, he might be right. The First Lady does usually oversee the governor's residence staff and is expected to make possibly hundreds of personal appearances for charity and fund-raising. "They're asked to do all this work for virtually no compensation," Ventura says. "It's not because it's my wife. Sometime in the future we will have a female governor. Will a man then have to leave his job to fulfill for free the job of being First Man?"

In just a few days Ventura will begin drawing a $120,303 annual salary as governor. He says a salary for his wife could come from state money used to operate the governor's residence or from private donations. But one of Ventura's harshest critics, Darrell McKigney of the Taxpayers League of Minnesota, comes out swinging. He calls the idea of paying Terry Ventura $25,000 a year "as outrageous as some of [Ventura's] old wrestling costumes. If he believes she deserves to be paid for helping him do his job, why doesn't he pay her out of his own salary? It's ridiculous that this 'man of the people' isn't satisfied with a $120,000 salary and a free mansion. Now he wants his wife to be paid to oversee the servants."

The governor-elect kicks off a week of inaugural events on January 2, 1999, by releasing a bald eagle back into the wild at the Izaak Walton League nature shelter in Brooklyn Park—the same place that served as his election headquarters the night he was elected mayor of that city in 1990. It's a fitting place to begin the week's celebrations, but it's not the inaugural event that sets the tone for his administration.

That comes later in the day when Ventura and his wife board a horse-drawn wagon in Hastings, about forty-five minutes south of St. Paul. They ride along a gravel driveway to a family farm, passing a sign along the way that says "Ventura Highway." The Venturas are here to enjoy a potluck lunch with several farm families and listen to their concerns about the ailing farm economy. Farmers are among the few not enjoying the fruits of the state's robust economy. So, after a big midwestern spread of roast beef, meatballs, potatoes, beans, and salads, Ventura spends a half-hour listening to the farmers.

One farmer stands up to complain about hog prices. "Today's price for pork is seventeen cents a pound, which is the same that it was in 1955," he tells Ventura. "That isn't very good." Others complain about low dairy prices and difficulty in getting their grain to market. Yet another laments the loss of good quality farmland to out-of-control urban sprawl. Terry Ventura is taking notes while her husband listens.

After the last farmer speaks, it's time for Ventura to get up and respond. He'll be the first to admit he doesn't know much detail about agriculture policy and he's about to show it. "A lot of what you spoke about, you're speaking to the—how does the term go?" Ventura asks. "You're preaching to the choir, in a way. My wife and I haven't been getting paid either." He is about to get away with something no ordinary politician could. Instead of responding in any meaningful way to their concerns or suggesting ways his administration can help farmers, he launches into his own complaint about how his wife won't get paid to be First Lady.

"She's burying her head already because she knows where I'm going," Ventura jokes. "What has jumped out at me is the sexist thing we have called the First Lady, who doesn't get paid. Let's say Mae [Schunk, his lieutenant governor] becomes the governor. Does that mean her husband has to leave his job to go do this other one for free? Do you think that would happen? Because we will have a female governor some day, rest assured that will happen. And when that does happen, will the male First Man or First Person be required to leave his job and go perform these duties?"

Ventura tells the farmers both he and his wife have put in twelve hours a day without pay during the transition. Which brings him to another sore subject (but again, one that has nothing to do with farmers). "Imagine if one of my opponents had won, shall we for a moment? They would have been paid through the entire transition period because they would still be holding their former career-politician jobs as attorney general or mayor, even though they wouldn't have been working on them, because I just went through a transition. I know how many hours I put in every day. They would have been paid by your tax dollars and my tax dollars to do a job they were not doing. So you can see there are some changes that need to take place one way or the other, and I will introduce legislation as such."

That elicits a hearty round of applause from the farmers, whose own concerns about farm income have just been all but ignored. Like everyone else, they seem happy just to have this celebrity governor-elect spending some time with them, even if his primary concern seemed to be his own ability to earn money. "Let's have a blessed, prosperous, go-get-'em 1999," Ventura tells the farmers as he concludes. "We gotta do the best we can because you're stuck with me for the next four years." He gets yet another rousing round of applause from a group thrilled by that prospect.

The Inauguration

Two months after his shocking election victory, it's finally time for Governor-elect Ventura to become Governor Ventura. After several minor roles in Hollywood, he's about to get top billing on January 4, 1999. Only one hundred invited guests are allowed on the ground floor of the State Capitol rotunda, where the swearing-in is about to take place. Those guests include Ventura's family, former governors, members of the Minnesota Supreme Court, and other newly elected constitutional officers such as the attorney general and secretary of state.

The select audience also includes special guests of the governor-elect's, including Hollywood superstar Arnold Schwarzenegger and several of Ventura's former Navy SEAL buddies (wrestlers are conspicuous by their absence). Several hundred Minnesotans watch from the circular balconies overlooking the rotunda two stories high. While the Sounds of Blackness sings a moving rendition of "America the Beautiful," it occurs to me that Jesse Ventura is starring in a drama no Hollywood writer could come up with and be taken seriously. It appears this production will be short on action-adventure and long on drama and heart. In this drama, even Schwarzenegger is relegated to a bit part.

After Ventura is introduced amid thunderous applause, Minnesota Supreme Court chief justice Kathleen Blatz takes the stage. "As he becomes governor today, Jesse Ventura begins a new chapter in a long and very public career, which is well known not only to Minnesotans but to people throughout the country," Blatz says. She calls Ventura to the stage along with U.S. District Court judge Paul Magnuson, who will swear Ventura into office. The rotunda is now silent as Ventura walks onstage, grinning ear to ear.

Magnuson places a Bible in the hands of Terry Ventura while her husband puts his left hand on the Bible, lifts his right hand in the air, and takes the oath of office.

"Ladies and gentlemen, the governor of the state of Minnesota," Magnuson says as he introduces Ventura after completing the oath. During a ninety-second standing ovation, the governor hugs his wife and two children before turning to the crowd and soaking it all in.

After acknowledging former governor Arne Carlson and his wife and leading a round of applause for the job they did the past eight years, Ventura promises his inauguration speech will come from the heart. He says he didn't use any written speeches during the campaign and doesn't plan to start now.

"For everyone that did work on the campaign, we shocked the world," he says. "We really did. To my wife, Terry; my daughter, Jade; my son, Tyrel—they're riding along on another one of Dad's escapades, and we're not done yet!"

He also thanks his deceased mother and father, both military veterans buried at Fort Snelling National Cemetery. "And I can tell right now the ground's heating up a little bit where they're at," Ventura says, "because I think today, most of all, my mom and dad would look down and say, 'I can't believe it! Look what he's done now!'"

The governor can't let this occasion go by without acknowledging another key part of his past—his Navy SEAL days. "It was a time in my life that created who I am today," he says to the crowd and a statewide television audience. "But, you know, there's a lot of questions that go on. Is Jesse Ventura up to governing? Can Jesse Ventura do the job? Well,

I told you I was going to come here today and I was going to speak from the heart. Well, that's not totally true. I have to read something."

He reaches into the pocket of his suit for his reading glasses. "And, yes, when you get to be forty-seven, these become part of your uniform," he says about the eyewear as he prepares to read a letter. "I received this yesterday and it said, 'I'm sure you must be nervous and apprehensive and maybe a little frightened by such a huge and challenging endeavor. But keep this in mind: You've been there. You've been pushed, tried, and tested by the best and you've passed with flying colors. Keep that 'hooyah' spirit and don't change a thing. I wish you the very best of luck and success. Sincerely, Master Chief Terry 'Mother' Moy.'"

Moy is standing just behind the stage in his full-dress uniform as a sort of Navy SEAL honor guard. Ventura turns and smiles at Moy as the audience applauds. It's a long way from his Navy days when Ventura says Moy was the meanest, toughest man he ever met.

Governor Ventura concludes his ten-minute inaugural address by promising to always be honest. He says focus-group research his administration conducted during the transition indicated that honesty in government should be the top priority. "Let's do what's right for the people of Minnesota. We hold these jobs, state officials, with that in mind. We are here to serve the people and do what's best for the state of Minnesota. We are all Minnesotans. That's the bottom line, whether you're a Democrat, a Republican, or Reform Party, or whatever party you might be. We are all Minnesotans. Now, move forward to do Minnesota's business, and we will do it to the best of our ability. Hooyah!"

With that "hooyah" cry from his Navy days, Ventura throws a fist in the air and marches off the stage to another standing ovation.

While Governor Ventura and his wife stand in a receiving line on the stage, his brother, Jan Janos, looks on with pride. "The whole situation here in the rotunda," he says, "looking up at the people, the performers, the orchestra, the singers, Arnold being here, my old [Navy SEAL] teammates—like I say, it's a very hard experience to realize that it's all happening right now."

Jan and Jim Janos (the governor's real name) couldn't be more different. They did serve in the Navy together, but that's where the similarities end. "He's always in the spotlight and chooses to be so," Jan Janos tells me minutes after his younger brother is sworn in. "I'm just the opposite. To make a long story short, I had great difficulty in high school to even go up in front of the class and give an oral book report. He's just the opposite. He thrives off things like that. You put a microphone in his hand and he's at the top of his game."

But Janos admits he never thought his brother was capable of anything like this. "I'm real proud of him," he says. "Words can hardly describe it. Like I say, thinking back in the service days when we were all together, this is the farthest thing from any of our minds, that someday he would be governor of Minnesota." And just what would his parents say if they were alive? "They would be completely astounded by this whole thing!"

Leaders of the other major political parties in the state have moved past being astounded by Ventura's rapid rise to power. They've moved on to dealing with the political realities of the situation. "I think it's a time of hope," Republican House Speaker Steve Sviggum says after the inauguration. "You enter into a new reign with hope. Everybody has high hopes of what the new governor will bring to Minnesota."

Senate Majority Leader Roger Moe, a powerful member of Minnesota's Democratic-Farmer-Labor party, was Skip Humphrey's running mate in a losing cause against Ventura. He says he's now ready to help the new governor succeed. "I think everybody wants him to be successful," Moe says, noting the electricity Ventura brings to the office. "If he's successful, we'll all be successful. So I think he will have a longer-than-normal honeymoon."

After shaking hands for nearly an hour, Governor Ventura takes a brief break from the receiving line. A half-dozen state troopers escort him to his new office in the capitol. The reception room outside his office is filled with staff members and security, but one visitor stands out in the crowd. "Hey, Jesse," Arnold Schwarzenegger yells across the room, "come over here for a second. We brought a little gift for you."

When the governor walks over, Schwarzenegger hands him a bronze eagle. "Everyone talks about the eagle being the symbol of freedom," Schwarzenegger says. "It's for the governor's desk. On the back it says simply, 'To my friend Jesse, you are a true leader. Arnold. '" Ventura thanks him for the gift and assures him it will be prominently displayed on his desk.

"I'm very excited about Jesse Ventura," Schwarzenegger tells the small group in the reception room (including KSTP-TV photographer Dan Dwyer, who somehow managed to wiggle his way into the room with his camera, much to the dismay of the governor's security people). "I, of course, have worked on many films together with him, and I know what a dedicated man he is, how talented he is, how smart he is, and how much he cares about people. He's always there for the underdog, and he will do a great job for this great state."

That's a great tribute, but I was kind of hoping he'd say something like, "If Jesse screws up, 'I'll be baaack!'"

At noon on January 5 another swearing-in ceremony takes place, this time in the Minnesota House of Representatives, where Republicans have taken control for the first time since 1986. After taking the oath as the new Speaker of the House, Representative Steve Sviggum immediately reveals Republican intentions for this session. "You have my word that this body will permanently and significantly cut your taxes," he pledges to taxpayers, drawing thunderous applause from the Republican majority. "We will ask you to hold us accountable!"

Sviggum also offers an olive branch to Governor Ventura. "You pledge to do your best and you pledged to be honest," Sviggum says to the governor, although he's not in attendance. "Let me assure that as speaker, and, speaking for the House of Representatives, we will do the same."

For the first time in Minnesota there will be a tripartisan government. Ventura, of the Reform Party, heads the executive branch. The Republican Sviggum leads the House, and DFLer Roger Moe leads the Senate. Moe promises a cooperative effort with Ventura and Sviggum to cut taxes. "We will argue over which tax, who's going to benefit, what's the timing of all of this," Moe says. "All of that will come to pass in this session."

Of course, the opening of what promises to be one of the most fascinating legislative sessions in the country couldn't go by without at least one joke about wrestling. As a formality, the House convenes a special ceremonial committee that walks to the governor's office to officially let the governor know the House is in session. This is usually done without fanfare. Unless, it turns out, a former wrestler is governor.

After returning from this duty, Representative Torrey Westrom announces mission accomplished. Sort of. "Mr. Speaker, the five of us that were just appointed to the committee went down to the governor's office and were thankful we came out alive. He threw us in a headlock and said, 'Get back to work!'" That gets the session off to a rollicking start.

The fun and games soon give way to serious business as the three sides start drawing their lines in the sand on tax issues. On the second day of the session, House Republicans unveil plans to cut taxes and return much of the state's budget surplus to taxpayers. They call it the "House Inspection Report," a checklist of tax measures that will return the surplus and lower taxes. "We feel that Minnesota families are overburdened with their taxes," Sviggum tells reporters. He wants Minnesotans to be able to keep more of what they earn rather than have the state continue piling up huge surpluses. He says they'll seek an immediate $1 billion income-tax rebate. It would equal 20 percent of a taxpayer's 1997 state income taxes (an average of $970 per tax filer). They will also seek the largest permanent income-tax rate cut in Minnesota history and property-tax relief for farmers and businesses.

Governor Ventura will wait a week before making his own proposal about what to do with the budget surplus. It will be one of the first major tests of his new administration. But first he has other things to accomplish that will also be watched closely. During his first week in office he appoints two commissioners, Charlie Weaver at the Department of Public Safety and Pam Wheelock at the Department of Finance.

Both have impeccable credentials. Weaver is an assistant county prosecutor and former state representative who ran as a Republican in the attorney general's race in November, losing to Democrat Mike Hatch. Wheelock is the finance director for the city of St. Paul, but has been on leave to help the Ventura transition team put together a state budget plan. There are still two dozen appointments to be made to his cabinet. Everyone is wondering what kind of people Ventura will surround himself with in what many expect to be a maverick administration. So far, he's made a couple of safe and impressive picks.

During his campaign Ventura promised he'd seek new people with new ideas to fill his cabinet positions. He didn't want all of his commissioners to be career politicians. Ideally, he'd find some people from the private sector to answer the call of public service. His first few commissioners are highly qualified but also familiar faces in government. On January 13 he breaks the mold. Ventura announces three new commissioners. One of them is Gene Hugoson, who is being reappointed as agriculture commissioner. The other two are the mold-breakers. They simply sent in letters and résumés and went through a job-interview process like anyone else would do. Neither one has experience in state government.

Christine Jax is the new commissioner of Children, Families, and Learning (previously known as the Department of Education). She's an education professor at a local university who applied for her job after watching Ventura on television after the election. "When he said he was going to be open to new thoughts and new people, I took him at his word and put in my résumé and here I am," she tells reporters at a news conference.

The other new appointee is Alan Horner, who will take over the Department of Natural Resources, a major post in Minnesota, where people take outdoor recreation very seriously. Horner is a businessman and avid outdoorsman and, like Ventura, is a former Navy SEAL. That raises questions about whether that swayed the governor to give Horner the job despite his apparent lack of experience for one of the toughest jobs in Minnesota government.

Horner claims Ventura didn't even know Horner was in the Navy SEALs until the two sat down for a formal interview. "The process had integrity," Horner tells reporters. "I'm here for reasons besides the fact we were both SEALs. I sent out a résumé and a letter with ideas and concepts, and it worked its way through."

Ventura also defends the appointment by saying Horner's SEAL record didn't get him the job, but it didn't hurt him either. "One of the things about Alan that struck home with me is the fact that, truthfully, I knew where he's coming from without knowing him. And I know that this job requires someone with integrity, someone with a never-quit attitude, and someone with an attitude who will succeed. This is probably the most controversial appointment in the state.... I need a guy who I know is tough enough to handle the job."

The next day, Governor Ventura makes the first major tax proposal of his administration. He wants new ideas, and that's just what his new finance commissioner, Pam Wheelock, and her staff came up with. During a news conference in the governor's reception room, Ventura announces a plan to give back more than a billion dollars in surplus tax revenue. Instead of an income-tax rebate, such as the one proposed by the Republicans in the House, he unveils a sales-tax rebate. He says there will be no forms for anyone to fill out. The checks will be mailed August 1, about a month after the end of the fiscal year. "When the state's books are settled up, we'll divide it up and send it back to the citizens," Ventura says, vowing to make good on one of his primary campaign promises.

The checks would amount to an average of $779 for families and $385 for single taxpayers. The amounts would be determined by a formula devised by the Department of Revenue. It boils down to this: the rebate amount would equal 35 percent of the sales tax each tax filer paid over the previous two years based on an average determined by the income earned over those two years.

Republican House Speaker Steve Sviggum gives the proposal a tepid response. "I don't think it's enough of a rebate, and I don't think it's quick enough," he says. "We want this money out the door now." A frequent critic of Ventura, Darrell McKigney of the Taxpayers League of Minnesota calls the governor's rebate plan "a huge rip-off of our state's taxpayers." He points out the proposal returns only $1 billion of the state's $1.5 billion surplus.

"The bottom line is, Governor Ventura's plan comes up far short of his often-repeated promise to return the entire state budget surplus," McKigney says. "The Ventura rebate plan pile-drives taxpayers and rips off their money. It looks like politics-as-usual at the State Capitol."

Ventura says his plan has one major benefit. He says the sales-tax rebate would not likely be subject to a federal tax, meaning taxpayers wouldn't have to declare it as income on their federal tax returns. The income-tax rebate proposed by Republicans would be subject to federal taxes. Ventura also says his plan would benefit middle-class families more than the House plan. Under the Ventura plan a family of four with a $50,000 income would get $764 back, compared with $508 under the House plan. An upper-income family making $500,000 a year would get just $2,000 back under the Ventura plan, compared with $7,600 under the House plan. The sales-tax plan gets generally favorable reviews from just about everyone but the Republicans and the Taxpayers League. Ventura might not look or sound like a traditional governor, but he sure is learning how to act like one. Or is he?

Two days later, January 16, it's time for the much anticipated "People's Celebration" at Target Center in downtown Minneapolis. It's safe to say this is going to be one of the most raucous gubernatorial inaugural parties in our nation's history. You could call it a sort of political Woodstock. Forget black ties and evening gowns. This crowd is dressed mostly in denim and T-shirts. More than fourteen thousand tickets sold out in just over twenty-four hours for $10, $15, and $20. At least a dozen Minnesota bands are scheduled to perform along with several national acts.

At about 8:00 P.M. the lights go down in Target Center and a huge video screen pops on with highlights from Ventura's election campaign accompanied by the song "Power to the People." At the end of the video we see what looks like a motorcycle gang escorting the governor's RV to the arena. Moments later a spotlight shines on a man in the crowd wearing sunglasses, earrings, a leather-fringed jacket, a Jimi Hendrix T-shirt, and a handkerchief wrapped on his head. It's the governor of Minnesota!

Surrounded by state troopers Ventura slowly makes his way to the main stage. He lumbers up onstage to an ovation he probably hasn't heard since his wrestling days. "The 'Body' [is] back for tonight!" he yells into a microphone, punching his fist in the air. "Thank you, everyone! Let's party, Minnesota!" An indoor fireworks display explodes throughout the arena and confetti drops from the ceiling. The crowd cheers wildly while Minnesota's unlikeliest governor stands onstage basking in the spotlight. When the stage clears a couple of minutes later, the governor goes back to his front-row seat to listen to a performance by David Pirner of Minnesota's own Soul Asylum.

After that performance a taped greeting from *Tonight Show* host Jay Leno plays on the giant video screen. "There are some unusual similarities between me and Governor Jesse Ventura," Leno says in the segment taped before one of his live studio audiences. He says they both ride motorcycles and were both born in states that begin with M, Minnesota and Massachusetts.

"But that's not all," Leno continues. "Here are some other eerie similarities between Jesse Ventura and myself. For example, Jesse's nickname was 'the Body.' My nickname, also 'the Body.' Jesse spends an hour every morning shaving his head. I spend an hour every morning shaving my chin. Jesse was a Navy SEAL. I once bought an Easter Seal. You see how eerie this is? Jesse comes from Minnesota, land of lakes. I come from California, land of fakes. Jesse, an expert in delivering head butts. I'm an expert in being a butt head. Finally, Jesse wrestled Hulk Hogan. I wrestled Hulk Hogan ... and won!"

That draws a big laugh from Leno's studio audience and the audience in Target Center. "But Jesse, we're all very proud of you.... Good luck to you, Jesse. All the way to the White House!" Then the camera cuts to show the *Tonight Show* audience in Los Angeles giving Ventura a standing ovation.

The celebration is just picking up steam. The next act to perform live is America, playing its famous "Ventura Highway" song in honor of the governor. To honor Terry Ventura and her love of horses the band also plays its big hit "A Horse with No Name." When they finish she jumps up onstage in her black leather miniskirt and hugs everyone in the band.

The highlight of the night comes a few minutes later with Warren Zevon performing. Governor Ventura gets up onstage now with a feather boa added to his already outrageous outfit to sing along with Zevon on "Werewolves of London."

When Zevon and the governor finish their unlikely duet, Ventura takes the microphone to address the crowd. "Minnesota, this has been the most unique inaugural ball in history. It will be one that will go down in the annals of Minnesota as well as the history of the world. I couldn't be prouder to be a part of it, and I thank you, because you're the ones that made it happen. You're the ones that got out to vote and you're the ones that this party is for. This is a people's celebration!"

When a tremendous ovation dies down, Ventura says it's time for the biggest act of the night. "You know, being governor you pretty much get what you want. And the night that I won I wanted Jonny Lang, and that's what we got! Jonny Lang!" As Lang takes the stage Ventura goes back to his seat and settles in for the featured act. So far, it seems Ventura can do no wrong.

Wrong again. Just two days after his triumphant celebration the governor finds himself in a political minefield. Remember one of the "nontraditional" appointees to his cabinet, Alan Horner, the new commissioner of the Department of Natural Resources? He's resigning just six days after his appointment. Some DNR employees ran a computer check on Horner's fishing and hunting record and found that he'd been issued two fishing-license citations in 1988 and 1990. Horner paid fines in both cases. He also received a warning in 1998 for not being in possession of his hunting license while grouse hunting. The infractions weren't brought to the governor's attention until the day after he appointed Horner to the DNR post. Nevertheless, both Ventura and Horner deemed the citations minor events.

It mushrooms into a major event just two days after Horner's appointment when a deputy DNR commissioner, Ron Nargang, resigns in protest. "I'm concerned about the message going to the sporting public that it's OK not to have a license or that it's OK that you don't have one if you're only going out for a little while," Nargang tells the *St. Paul Pioneer Press.* "If we get that attitude started, it makes it impossible to have any respect for game and fish laws."

Horner calls a meeting of DNR employees at the department headquarters in St. Paul to try to explain how he got the tickets. When he criticizes the conservation officer who issued the citations rather than accept responsibility for them, what little support he has within the department unravels. A few days later another deputy DNR commissioner resigns.

With the Twin Cities media now writing and airing daily stories about the controversy, Horner and Ventura run out of options. On January 19, Horner meets with the governor at 9:00 A.M. and offers his resignation. Horner walks out of Ventura's office and past reporters without answering questions. Two hours later Ventura holds a news conference to announce two other new commissioners, for the state Department of Health and the Department of Labor and Industry. But the only thing reporters want to ask the governor about is Al Horner, his *former* DNR commissioner.

Ventura reluctantly agrees to discuss the matter but refuses to say if he asked for Horner's resignation. Instead, he launches more volleys in an intensifying battle with the media. "What I would rather say is that I think it's very sad ... that people of the private sector are put under extreme scrutiny by the media as well as whoever else. Let's look at it from this aspect: if a police officer got two speeding tickets, would that disqualify him from being a police officer and enforcing speeding and traffic violations later if he got two speeding tickets earlier in life? I just hope the message isn't out there now that stops people from the private sector from stepping forward and serving the public sector."

A reporter asks the governor if he's saying that there doesn't need to be background checks for applicants for public sector jobs. "I'm saying that I don't believe it's fair to go back in someone's life," Ventura responds. "It's like double jeopardy. He made a mistake. He got fined. He paid the fine. Shouldn't it have ended there? If we want to look at it, then why do we rehire criminals? Why do we give second chances to people who go to prison, which I think we all agree happens?"

Ventura then criticizes the media for going beyond just reporting the Horner story, but also publishing editorial cartoons that make Horner look like a buffoon. "That type of unfair publicity to him and his family I thought was outrageous," he says.

He's done talking about the Horner situation, so the governor begins to walk away from the podium in the governor's reception room toward his office door. He's not in a good mood to begin with, and he stops dead in his tracks when he hears a question shouted by a reporter.

"Governor, after singing with Warren Zevon, are you considering singing lessons?" The question comes from Dan Bernard, a reporter for the *Duluth News-Tribune*. Ventura turns around, walks back to the podium, and takes off his glasses while glaring at Bernard. There are nervous chuckles coming from the other reporters in the room.

"That was cute," Ventura responds, slipping momentarily back into his wrestling persona. "I don't know—are you? I was there having fun and that's what it was. You know, if you're going to criticize my singing, feel free. You criticize everything else I do."

Bernard tries to tell the governor he's just kidding. Ventura walks away again while reporters try to ask him more questions about Horner and says, "I have nothing more to say." Then he slips through his office door and disappears, apparently resisting an urge to pile-drive someone. We may have just witnessed the first major volleys in Ventura's media war.

Ventura makes a quick rebound from Horner's resignation and that unpleasant news conference. The next day he scores some major credibility points by appointing David Jennings as the new commissioner of the Department of Commerce. Jennings is a former Republican Speaker of the House. He's been working in the private sector since leaving the legislature in the late 1980s. Jennings says he left because he became disillusioned about state government and the whole political process. So what brings him back? "The election of Jesse Ventura," he says without hesitation. "I probably would not have sought a similar opportunity under other circumstances. His election represents a dramatic change, perhaps a historic change, in Minnesota politics. I went away from here twelve years ago with somewhat of a cynical attitude about whether such change was ever possible. I frankly did not believe Jesse Ventura could beat the entrenched political machines at their own game. Obviously, no one explained that to now Governor Ventura. It restored my faith in the system."

That's high praise from a man of Jennings's political pedigree. Ironically, he admits he didn't vote for Ventura. He says he voted for the Humphrey-Moe ticket because of his high regard for Senate Majority Leader Roger Moe and because "I was dumb enough to think Governor Ventura couldn't win." Jennings says his vote was canceled out anyway because both his sons voted for Ventura.

The appointments of Jennings and Matt Smith as commissioner of revenue are announced at a news conference just twenty-four hours after the governor's testy exchange with reporters. This time Ventura is in a much better mood and even jokes about the Horner situation. "I think my two new commissioners will find out that I asked if they ever fished without a license." This news conference ends with laughter.

Ventura makes sure he doesn't repeat his DNR mistake. He later appoints Allen Garber, a former FBI agent and local police chief, as DNR commissioner. It's a safe pick from one standpoint: Garber rarely fishes and had never hunted.

Packing Heat

One day before he's due to deliver his first state budget, it's learned that Governor Ventura is packing heat. Or, at least, he has a permit to pack heat. Pat Kessler of WCCO-TV reports that sometime after his election on November 3, Ventura applied for and has been granted a permit to carry a concealed handgun. The "conceal and carry" issue was a pet peeve of his during the campaign. He was rejected for a permit in 1990 shortly after his election as mayor of Brooklyn Park. He says that's an example of how the state's current concealed weapons law is too restrictive. State law allows only sheriffs and police chiefs to issue permits to residents in their jurisdictions. Applicants must not have a criminal record and need either to prove a business reason (handling large sums of cash in public) or a personal-safety concern (being the victim of a stalker) to get one. Ventura won't say why he applied for a permit. Concealed-weapons permit information isn't public in Minnesota.

The governor's gun permit becomes endless fodder for critics and columnists. Here's the take on the gun-toting Ventura by *St. Paul Pioneer Press* columnist and KSTP Radio talk-show host Joe Soucheray. "The gun fits," writes Soucheray of the man he calls Governor Turnbuckle. "It's part of the ride. I wouldn't be surprised if, by the end of the four years, Jesse is wearing an eye patch and carrying a sword. We have elected a showman, a former professional wrestler, and talk-show host who, as mayor of Brooklyn Park, once threatened to take the action outside. We have elected a former Navy SEAL, motorcycle-club member, and bar bouncer. Nobody in their right mind should be at all surprised that this fellow packs a sidearm."

Although it's now been nearly three months since his election, doubts remain about Ventura's ability to govern. With so many distractions, like the gun-permit flap, the raucous inaugural celebration, and the Horner resignation, there isn't much focus on his actual job performance. He put together an effective transition team and continues to appoint impressive commissioners to head state departments, but his administration still hasn't faced a major test. That's about to change.

On January 28, Governor Ventura unveils his two-year budget proposal for 2000–2001. As he often says, crafting a state budget is probably the most important thing any governor does. His budget proposal will be a significant milestone. It will indicate whether he's up to the challenge of governing and also show if he plans to keep his campaign promises of lowering taxes, holding the line on new spending, and returning all budget surpluses. If nothing else, the governor will certainly get good marks for timeliness. By law the budget isn't due until mid-February. Ventura's budget proposal is more than two weeks early.

The public announcement of the budget is clearly geared for maximum television coverage. This isn't the sort of thing that generally makes for exciting TV, but everything Ventura does in office tends to get magnified. He is scheduled to deliver his budget speech at 5:00 P.M. The event will be carried live on statewide public television from the World Trade Center in downtown St. Paul. The presentation is scheduled to end just a few minutes before 6:00 P.M. so the governor can be available for live interviews on three local network affiliates during the six o'clock news. Shortly before beginning his budget address, he jokingly opens his suit coat to show he's not packing heat. After that bit of comic relief, he's all business.

Ventura makes it clear what makes him proudest about his two-year, $23 billion budget proposal. "I want to state unequivocally that we spoke to not one lobbyist," he says, highlighting his campaign promise that he would govern with no strings attached. "There was no lobbyist input into this budget whatsoever. They didn't help elect me, so what the heck!"

On the tax side, Ventura recommends $2.5 billion in tax cuts through 2001. This includes establishing a $1.087 billion sales-tax rebate; reducing the motor-vehicle registration tax so that no car owner will pay more than $75 per vehicle; and cutting the lowest of the state's three tax bracket rates from 6 percent to 5.75 percent. The goal, he says, is to "let people keep more of their money, plain and simple."

Ventura also wants a tax system that makes sense to the average person. As an example, he points to the vehicle registration fees that vary depending on how much your car is worth. It's an issue, he says, that came up constantly during the campaign. "I just find it grossly unfair that one car pays more than another car when they all drive the same," he says in his own plainspoken way. "Let me put it to you this way. When you go in for your driver's license, do you have to bring in your W-2? No. You pay a flat rate to purchase a driver's license, which gives you the ability and privilege to drive on our highways. Nothing is based upon your income."

On the spending side, Ventura proposes a budget of $23.35 billion, holding the growth in government spending to an average of 2.9 percent a year (not including another 3 percent increase automatically built into state spending). Of the $1.15 billion in new spending, $561 million is for K–12 education, which includes money to reduce class sizes to no greater than a seventeen-to-one student/teacher ratio in kindergarten through third grade. Ventura also includes $248 million in additional spending for higher education. The governor points out that 70 percent of all new spending will go to education.

"I want to ensure the best public education possible," he says in his televised speech. "I'm not backing away from public education, I'm attacking it. I'm going after it, and I'm going after it with a challenge."

His challenge is for schools to get parents more involved in their children's education. "If parents are involved, the child stands a great chance to succeed. If the parents are not involved, the child stands a great chance not to succeed.... The only place you'll see an increase in spending is in education. But it's a challenge to the educational system. They had better produce."

For taxpayers, Ventura's budget proposal boils down to this: a two-income family earning $70,000 a year, with two kids and two cars, would get an $884 sales-tax rebate and a $413 income-tax cut, and save $286 on car-license registration. That amounts to a total tax savings of $1,583 a year. It sounds impressive, but Republicans say it falls far short of the tax savings Minnesotans deserve after years of overtaxation and a remarkable run of budget surpluses. House Speaker Steve Sviggum says Minnesotans need a much deeper cut in income-tax rates across the board, not just the lowest bracket.

"We applaud the governor for slowing the rate of state spending," House Majority Leader Tim Pawlenty chimes in, "but we feel like we bought a ticket to an overhyped pay-per-view event. We're not getting the Crusher of tax cuts, we're getting Sodbuster Kenny Jay."

It's a funny line, but Republicans walk a thin line when getting into a war of words with a former wrestler and wrestling announcer. When told about Pawlenty's remark, Ventura is ready with a comeback. "I guess I'd say that I didn't realize that Republicans spent so much time watching wrestling. Maybe they oughta spend more time on something else."

CHAPTER 4

"Oh, Am I in Trouble Now!"

Taking on Single Mothers
and Drunken Irishmen

Jesse Ventura continues to take a stand against anyone trying to cash in on his name, whether it's Garrison Keillor of public-radio fame or a sixty-three-year-old secretary in the State Capitol. Keillor runs afoul of the governor when he publishes a satirical novel based on Ventura's unfathomable rise from professional wrestling to the governor's office. The book, *Me, by Jimmy (Big Boy) Valente*, subtly pokes fun at Ventura's emergence from working-class childhood to pro wrestling to ego-driven politics through the fictitious character named in the title. Ventura doesn't seem as upset by the subject matter as he does by someone trying to make money off him. He tells the *St. Paul Pioneer Press* that Keillor is "cheating" him by publishing the book without his permission.

Keillor responds with a statement, issued through his publisher, reminding the governor of a famous legal precedent that gives the press freedom to criticize government. "Freedom of the press is a principle that goes back to the trial of John Peter Zenger in 1735, when he wrote about the British governor of the colony of New York and offended him," Keillor said. It's just the latest volley between Keillor and Ventura, dating to Keillor's biting essay in *Time* magazine shortly after Ventura's election and subsequent proposal to phase out state funding for public radio and television. Ventura eventually backs down and, through his spokesperson John Wodele, sarcastically says he hopes Keillor "makes a bundle."

The governor doesn't let State Capitol secretary Pat Helmberger off so easily. His attorney sent a "cease-and-desist" letter to stop her from selling Valentine's Day cards using the governor's image. Helmberger sold about $200 worth of cards before Ventura's letter arrived. "When I got this letter, I felt very intimidated," she says. "We're just a little tiny company run by two little women in Bloomington." Ventura says he didn't mean to be heavy-handed. "We're writing the letters not to be vindictive or threatening at all," he says. "It's just that we have to be careful what goes out and represents me."

If there's any doubt about the staying power of the Ventura honeymoon with Minnesotans, it's put to rest with publication of a new *Star Tribune*/KMSP-TV Minnesota Poll about his popularity. One month into his term in office and it shows a whopping 72 percent of Minnesotans approve of his job performance. Only 9 percent disapprove, and, somehow, 19 percent have "no opinion" of the lightning-rod governor. The newspaper says the 72-percent approval rating ties Ventura for the highest approval rating measured by the Minnesota Poll since 1947.

And it's not just his politics they like. The poll also asks, "Thinking about Ventura as a person, do you have a favorable or unfavorable impression of him?" In response, 74 percent say "favorable," 12 percent "unfavorable," and 14 percent "don't know." Keep in mind that he received only 37 percent of the vote in the three-way election race. Now, he's getting a vote of confidence from across the political spectrum. Among Republicans polled, 70 percent approve of his performance, along with 74 percent of Democrats and 71 percent of people identified as "independent."

Ventura's newly minted approval ratings will be put to the test because he's making news on every front imaginable. He announces he's seeking a radio station to carry a weekly call-in show, sees his sales-tax rebate plan rejected in the Minnesota House, and gets permission to carry his concealed handgun in the State Capitol and other state buildings.

The gun story makes the biggest splash. Although he has a concealed-weapon permit, he isn't allowed to carry the gun in state buildings without the written authorization of the public-safety commissioner. Public Safety Commissioner Charlie Weaver doesn't hesitate to give permission. "I am not going to second-guess a guy that is a Navy SEAL in his ability to handle a weapon," Weaver says. Although Ventura is always accompanied by security from the Minnesota State Patrol, especially in the State Capitol, critics question the need for the governor to carry a gun in the hallowed halls. Weaver says Ventura isn't like any other Minnesota governor. "Where Governor Carlson blended in, [Ventura] instead attracts people. He attracts people who like to touch him. So it is a much different security issue for him."

At least one state lawmaker doesn't buy that argument. Republican senator Gary Laidig writes a letter to Weaver, demanding revocation of Ventura's capitol gun-toting privileges. "I find it outrageous and offensive that the chief executive, who is not a trained, licensed law enforcement officer, is now carrying a gun in the very corridors that are frequently filled with visiting school children," Laidig writes in his letter. He threatens to author a bill that would change state law to disallow the governor's special privilege. "The governor has an ever-present, professional security team of trained, licensed law enforcement officers. Previous governors have served in times of war, depression and civil unrest. Yet, this particular governor requires a gun? Does Ventura's need for a loaded gun supersede the right to safety of everyone else at the Capitol? I think not."

The governor refuses to comment on the matter. But his spokesperson, John Wodele, says Ventura doesn't plan to carry his gun in the capitol. He wants the authorization only in case he inadvertently carries it in a state building. Weaver declines to revoke Ventura's authorization.

Amid all the hoopla about guns and sky-high approval ratings, one key element of his budget takes a broadside hit in the Minnesota House. The Republican-controlled House votes 93–35 to pass a $1.1 billion income-tax rebate. In doing so, House Speaker Steve Sviggum and his Republican colleagues reject Ventura's plan for a sales tax rebate.

This isn't the final word on the issue, however, as more than three months remain in the legislative session. With Ventura and the DFL-controlled Senate favoring a sales-tax rebate, odds remain in the governor's favor. Ventura knows it. "Maybe Sviggum doesn't like being speaker," he says at a news conference on the day his approval rating is published in the *Star Tribune*. "There's an election in two years. I hope he picked up the paper this morning." It's obvious Ventura plans to use his approval rating to his advantage.

Within a week Ventura puts his approval rating on the line in a way few governors would ever consider. About 150 college students are demonstrating on the steps of the State Capitol on February 10, 1999. Demonstrations of one sort or another happen nearly every day during legislative sessions. Today is no different. What *is* different is that Governor Ventura agrees to come out of the capitol to briefly address the crowd. He's playing this "man of the people" routine to the hilt. He's also playing with political fire.

The Minnesota State College Student Association organized the demonstration. Remember, young voters put Ventura over the top in the election, but he also wasn't bashful about telling college students to quit relying on government to pay for their education. He's about to find out college students aren't bashful about telling him what they think.

"We want Jesse! We want Jesse! We want Jesse!" The chant sounds friendly enough. It's not unlike the chants we heard on the campaign trail or at countless events since his election. When the governor eventually emerges from the capitol, it still appears to be a friendly crowd as they let out a cheer and another chant, "Jesse! Jesse! Jesse!" Someone hands Ventura a bullhorn, and he begins by thanking the young people for voting in the November elections.

"That's the way that government works, and that's the way your voice is best heard is in the voting booth," he says. So far so good, but he will soon find out they want him to hear their voices a little more directly. "The public is always welcome here," says Ventura, dressed in a suit but without an overcoat on this chilly day. "Demonstration is good as long as it's orderly and as long as it's to get a message across . . . and we appreciate it when you come here."

He's doing fine until he starts bragging about how much funding he's proposed for higher education in his budget. His proposal includes a 3 percent increase in the State Grant Program, which provides tuition assistance for students in private and public colleges. "If you're smart enough to be in college, you ought to be smart enough to figure out how to pay for it," Ventura says, repeating a statement he made often during the campaign. "That did not mean you wouldn't get government support. What it meant was, you must be smart enough to find that government support."

Someone in the crowd yells to him that the government doesn't provide enough support. This is when things get ugly in a hurry. "Excuse me?" Ventura barks into the bullhorn. "Who put me through college? The government?"

A protester yells back, "The GI bill!" Ventura is quick with a comeback. "That's right, and that was four years of giving my life, putting it on the line, and earning it!" he says, referring to his service in the Navy that qualified him for the GI bill, which helped pay for his education at a junior college.

Then another protester yells something about the lack of financial aid available for single parents. This is a land mine and the governor steps right on it. "A single parent?" he says to the woman. "I don't want to sound hard core, but why did you become a single parent?"

That draws a cacophony of boos. Ventura is undaunted. "It takes two people to parent. It takes two! You're asking government to make up for mistakes. Is that government's job, to make up for people's mistakes?"

The woman going toe-to-toe with the governor is Robin Melin, a single mother of two boys. She's not backing down from a now rather menacing-looking governor. "How can I [raise my kids and go to school] if I don't have financial assistance?" she asks.

"And you're asking me for that answer?" Ventura says somewhat sarcastically.

The protesters are now grouped closely around the governor while his security officers try to keep them separated. Ventura is clearly frustrated and agitated by not getting his point across. "I'm not going to bother anymore," he says, "I'm not going to bother anymore. I believe in self-sufficiency, and I'm not bothering anymore.... Who gave me anything?"

Melin has her own frustrations to vent. "But you know what?" she says, looking Ventura in the eye with a tinge of desperation in her voice. "I work eighteen hours a day, trying to raise my children, wanting to get an education. I believe in a little bit of sacrifice. But sacrificing what? Raising your children? Falling asleep in class? Our students are working so much they can't even stay awake in class!"

Ventura doesn't offer much sympathy. "I've spent my whole life getting government assistance for me too. Thank you," he says, brusquely handing over the bullhorn and turning back up the capitol steps.

"But we are the future," Melin yells to him. "We are the future!" All the students now start chanting "We are the future!" as Ventura steps into the capitol and disappears.

Of course, the verbal sparring match with the single mother is captured on videotape by all Twin Cities television stations. By that evening, clips of the episode appear on most of the national news networks. Accounts of the incident are also published in newspapers around the country. Next to President Clinton, Ventura is now the most closely watched politician in the country.

When the governor's not sparring with single mothers, he also serves as the state's social director. On February 15, for instance, Ventura declares "Rolling Stones Day" in Minnesota. Among the many things that make the governor's résumé so unique is a stint many years ago as a bodyguard for the Rolling Stones. With the legendary rock band in Minneapolis for a concert, and Ventura being one of the band's biggest fans, it shouldn't come as much of a surprise that he comes up with an official state proclamation for the day:

Whereas: In the world of rock 'n' roll, to last four decades—and surely into the new millennium—is unheard of; and whereas, their music is timeless for many generations of fans; and whereas, Keith Richards was born on December 18, 1943, is now 55, and is still alive; and whereas, the Rolling Stones have performed in Minnesota multiple times and this concert will represent the highest grossing concert of all time at the Target Center; and whereas, the Stones have always employed the best 'Body' guards; now therefore, I, Jesse Ventura, Governor of Minnesota, do hereby proclaim official recognition of February 15, 1999 as Rolling Stones Day.

Ventura invites the Stones to the governor's residence for lunch that day, but their plane doesn't arrive in town until about three o'clock. When Mick Jagger and the rest of the band land at the airport, they're handed a copy of the governor's proclamation. A gaggle of television cameras and reporters greets Jagger as he gets off a private jet. "Rolling Stones Day. It's very amusing," he says in a brief exchange with the media. "What did he say? Something about Keith being alive and music for generations and we've played here many times? Anyway, we're very thankful."

Someone asks Jagger if he plans to invite the governor onstage to sing. "I don't know," he says. "I hope he doesn't want to wrestle." During the concert later that night, the Stones acknowledge the governor, who is at the show with First Lady Terry Ventura. At one point during the show, the band also stops to shake hands with Ventura. Fortunately, considering the performance with Warren Zevon last month, Ventura doesn't get up on stage to sing.

Mr. Ventura Goes to Washington

Four days later Ventura arrives on the biggest political stage of all—Washington, D.C. As always, he knows how to make an entrance. It's February 20, and he's in Washington for the winter meetings of the National Governors Association. There's no trouble picking out Ventura as he walks through the lobby of the J. W. Marriott Hotel. He's the governor wearing the Navy SEAL cap, leather fringed jacket, and cowboy boots. As he makes his way to the front desk to check in, flashbulbs go off and strangers come up to shake his hand. Governor Tom Vilsack of Iowa, dressed in a dark suit and tie, takes one look at Ventura's outfit and tells me he does have one thing in common with the Minnesota governor, and it's not their taste in clothing. "We're both fans of the Rolling Stones," he says, chuckling.

The first meeting Ventura attends at the conference is focused on "Reinventing State Government with Technology." Ventura looks like he's at least trying to reinvent the dress code. The governors are sitting around a large horseshoe-shaped table, listening to a Microsoft executive discuss how state governments can use on-line services to serve the public. Once Ventura arrives, much of the attention shifts to him. He tries to blend in by sitting at his seat, putting on his reading glasses, and looking over some materials he's been handed.

One of the other governors eventually welcomes Ventura to the conference. "You're probably all familiar with his T-shirts, bumper stickers, and coffee cups saying, 'My governor can beat up your governor,'" he says, drawing a big laugh. Ventura counters with a punch line of his own, leaning into his microphone and saying, "I'd like to add they're all probably illegal."

After stopping in his room to change into a business suit, Ventura returns to the lobby to meet the one other governor who isn't a Republican or Democrat. He's Governor Angus King, an independent from Maine. Ventura and King have notified reporters they will walk to Independence Avenue to hold their own caucus.

It's a bright, sunny day in the nation's capital as Ventura and King head out on the four-block walk to the corner of Independence Avenue Southwest and Fourteenth Street. The scene is almost comical as the two men start down the street surrounded by security guards, a half-dozen television cameras, several newspaper photographers, and at least twenty reporters. That's roughly a half-dozen television cameras, several newspaper photographers, and twenty reporters more than are now covering the other forty-eight governors back at the hotel. Once again Ventura is stealing the show and King is along for the ride.

As this walking media circus makes its way along Fourteenth Street, people driving by are honking their car horns and waving. "Jesseeee!" a man yells out his window.

"Yesss!" Ventura says as he pumps his fist in the air and laughs. "It's fun that it happens in some place other than Minnesota," he says. "I get it a lot in Minnesota, and here we are in Washington, making it happen." It's amusing to see even Ventura stunned by his notoriety.

"How important is it that you be perceived as credible here?" a reporter asks him.

"I am credible," Ventura fires back. "I'm the governor of Minnesota. I won, and I've held office now for a month and a half.... I won with 37 percent, but the latest polls, if you believe in them, have me at 72 percent with opposition of only 9. Which makes me the most popular governor in Minnesota history at this point."

King can't resist chiming in. "The real trouble is, he knows the names of that 9 percent."

The two maverick governors draw a crowd at the intersection of Fourteenth and Independence in the shadows of the Washington Monument. A teenage girl with a group from Texas climbs on the shoulders of a friend to take a picture of Ventura. "This is for my friends back home," she says. "They think pro wrestling is so cool. I think it's pathetic, myself."

Ventura is up early the next day for another appearance on NBC's *Meet the Press*. Moderator Tim Russert lines up three governors for the show: Ventura from the Reform Party, Democrat Gray Davis from California, and Republican Christine Todd Whitman from New Jersey. Make no mistake about it: Ventura is the drawing card.

Once again, Ventura says things you'd never expect from a politician. Russert is discussing federal funding for local schools with Governor Davis when Ventura can't resist jumping in. "Why does Washington get the money in the first place?" he asks rhetorically. "My view is, if Washington didn't overtax so much on their end, we would have that much more money to spend as individual states and allow us to take care of our own education system. Why should Washington be involved at all in a state's education? If they didn't tax us so much, we'd have that much more to deal with rather than going in this big circle of us sending our money to Washington and then Washington returning it to us."

Russert challenges the point, but Ventura manages to hold his ground. "So you would cut federal taxes dramatically?" Russert asks.

"I'd love to see it, absolutely," Ventura responds.

"Then you'd have to raise state taxes," Russert says, "to make up for that money that you don't get from the federal government for education."

Ventura is momentarily tripped up before recovering. "No, we wouldn't. Not necessarily.... Well, maybe we would, but we wouldn't have to send as much to the feds. The closer you keep the money to you, Tim, the better the bang for the dollar you get. The farther you send it, the less return you get back on it."

Ventura has this knack for saying things that sound implausible and logical at the same time.

Russert, of course, has far juicier topics he wants to cover with Ventura, like the governor's concealed-weapons permit. Ventura won't talk to the Minnesota media about this, but he can't wait to discuss it on national television. "I'm the head of the state troopers. I'm the top law-enforcement officer in the state of Minnesota. I'm also the commander-in-chief of the National Guard. I'm an ex–Navy SEAL team member. I'm highly qualified and there are times I don't have my protection with me. Now, if I'm not in a position [of danger], why do I have protection? I just had a death threat a week ago."

Ventura says he has a right to carry a concealed weapon just like any other law-abiding Minnesotan. "And yet you find some of the legislators accusing me of putting children in jeopardy at the capitol. I have never once been armed in the capitol, yet I find that very disturbing that they get diarrhea of the mouth when they don't even know what they're talking about."

After that outburst, Russert can't resist the next line. "So you're not packing this morning with me?"

"Not at all," Ventura says. "Just this," as he holds up his clenched fist.

"Thank God," Russert says, laughing.

After the show, the governors walk out the front door of the NBC studios in Washington to face more cameras and reporters waiting outside. Whitman and Davis say Ventura impresses them. "No, he's not hard to take seriously, because he obviously cares a great deal," Governor Whitman says. She also admires Ventura's ability to say just about anything and get away with it. "He has a freedom of expression that many other politicians don't enjoy to the same degree." Governor Davis says despite Ventura's unorthodox style, he shouldn't be taken lightly. "I think he's a very engaging man. You've got to give people credit. When you can expand the electorate as he did, you're a force in politics, and I think he'll do a very good job."

Later in the evening, President and Mrs. Clinton greet all the governors in the State Dining Room at the White House for a formal dinner. With the governors and their spouses in formal evening attire, they mingle at tables set with Franklin Delano Roosevelt china and Kennedy Morgantown crystal. The centerpieces are filled with blue hydrangea and white roses, lilacs, and orchids and surrounded by silver candlesticks and votive candles. Every inch of the room exudes class, dignity, and history.

Before dinner President Clinton addresses the governors briefly, talking about the partnership they've developed during his administration and how together they've fought crime, reduced welfare, and prospered during good economic times. He concludes by leading the governors in a champagne toast. This is as far from the World Wrestling Federation as Governor Ventura could possibly be.

Reporters are able to witness some of what happens during the dinner because one pool camera is allowed in for a live video feed. To find out what went on later in the East Room, we have to rely on Governor Ventura and his wife to fill us in. When they arrive back at the hotel just before midnight, they're more than willing to regale us with tales of their first visit to the White House.

"It was fantastic," Ventura tells a few reporters staking out the hotel lobby, waiting for their return. "The portraits, the books in the library, the dinner was fantastic. The ambience was beyond belief." The governor is in a black tuxedo and Terry Ventura wears a white sequined evening gown and carries an elegant gold purse. They're as giddy as two school kids. "The president and First Lady were dancing, and I grabbed the First Lady and took her out there," Ventura says, then laughs when making a quick clarification. "Not the president's First Lady, my First Lady! I said, we're not going to miss a minute of this, and we went and danced right next to the president and First Lady. And when the dance ended, the president came over and greeted both of us, asked us if we were having a good time. And we talked for probably three to four minutes. We talked about the Rolling Stones and my proclamation. The president thought it was terrific when I said, 'Keith is fifty-five and still alive,' and it was my first proclamation ever. He was very impressed. No shoptalk at all. It was just a good social occasion and a lot of fun."

It's hard to believe this is coming from Ventura. He's the same man who harshly criticized Hillary Clinton during the election when she called the Ventura campaign a "sideshow." The same man who, after his election, told a group of high-school students that he doesn't think Clinton can be trusted and suggested he should resign. The same man who earlier that day told Tim Russert on *Meet the Press* that Hillary Clinton shouldn't "hopscotch" around the country, looking for a state where she can run for the U.S. Senate. Now he's dancing the night away with the two of them.

"I never felt bad about them in the first place," Ventura says now. "I mean, he's my president of the United States of America. He has a remarkable memory. He's very cordial and friendly. I truly believe, yeah, he's the kind of guy that I could go out and smoke a cigar and go fishing with."

So despite all the verbal shots he's taken at the president and his wife in the past, there was no animosity? "Absolutely not," Ventura tells me. "That's politics. This wasn't politics tonight.... I would even go back tomorrow if he asked."

While Governor Ventura is becoming head of President Clinton's fan club, his wife can't believe what a fairy tale her life is becoming. Terry says they split up the governors and their spouses at dinner and put them at different tables so they could meet new people. At one point, after strolling violinists came by her table playing "God Bless America," she says she got up, walked over to her husband, and said, 'Oh my God, do you believe this?'"

Not long ago she was raising horses in a quiet Twin Cities suburb and spreading manure behind a John Deere while her husband spent a few hours a day doing talk radio. Next thing she knows, it's dinner at the White House. "You know," she says as they head off to their hotel room for the night, "this is like living in *Alice in Wonderland*, I swear ..."

The next day, Ventura is the featured attraction at a sold-out luncheon at the National Press Club. The club is famous for its celebrity speakers, but few sell out weeks in advance like Minnesota's new governor. If the audience came hoping to hear an outrageous speech from an outrageous politician, they get their money's worth. They also get a political-science lesson, Ventura-style.

The introduction of Ventura by National Press Club president Larry Lippman sets the tone for what's about to follow. "He showed up at his inaugural ball in leather fringe, a Jimi Hendrix T-shirt, a bandanna, and earrings," Lippman tells the packed luncheon crowd and an audience watching on C-Span and listening on National Public Radio. "His stunning triumph last fall captured the imagination of the country, if not the world. Almost overnight the former professional wrestler has become the most talked-about politician of the day.... He was a U.S. Navy SEAL and then a member of a California motorcycle gang. But he was also a nearly straight-A student at North Hennepin Community College before he used his brawn and machismo to win a role as a bad guy on the pro-wrestling circuit."

It had to be one of the strangest résumés ever recited at such a distinguished club.

More than a dozen television crews are set up in the back of the room. In the front row, sports artist LeRoy Neiman, a St. Paul native, is sketching Ventura's face. "I'm destroying some of the myths that I had about what it's like to serve as governor," Ventura says to begin his speech. "I used to always sit back kind of cynically when [a university] gave an honorary degree to a politician. Well, I've taken it to show you I can handle change. I've changed my mind on that. After the last three months or so I realized, truly, there's no university in our great country that could teach you what I'm learning on the job as the governor of the state of Minnesota. So Harvard and Yale, if you're listening out there [he pauses while the audience laughs] ... when I'm done, I wouldn't mind one."

He admits that even on election night, he didn't think he would win. When he first took the lead with 5 percent of the precincts reporting, he didn't think it would hold. He was just happy he could say he was in first place at least for a short time. "Well, the lead widened and the lead got bigger and bigger until, at 60 percent [of the precincts reporting], they asked me to go out and address the crowd one more time. I'd been out there twice. I said, 'I don't want to do that. I'll be repeating myself.' But the problem was, I had the first campaign in history that had an active mosh pit going."

This implausible yet true story draws howls of laughter from a Washington crowd not used to election-night frat parties. "For those of you that don't know what [a mosh pit] is, that's what young people do when they pick up bodies and pass them around on top at arm's length," Ventura explains by holding his arms over his head. "And we had a pretty good one going out there. They felt I needed to get them under control a little bit."

It didn't work. Ventura says the crowd continued building to a frenzy until it finally happened: he's suddenly projected the winner. "We had the three TVs on in the private room and up came the first check mark. I was declared the winner! I still didn't believe it. Not one expert, not one pundit declared that I could win. Not one poll said I could win, and now, with 40 percent of Minnesotans not even counted, they were declaring me the winner. I didn't believe it. I said, 'I'm not going out there and declaring victory. Look how embarrassed I'll be if 20 percent later I'm back in third.'"

That's when Bill Hillsman, Ventura's advertising guru who came up with the action-figure ads, told him to believe it. "And I said, 'Bill, how could this be? Forty percent is still out there.' He said, 'Trust me, they haven't been wrong since Dewey and Truman.'"

The biggest laugh comes when he tells the audience the kicker to the story. "The day after the election, we all looked at each other and said, 'Oh my God, what do we do now?' We didn't know!"

He also recounts his exploits from the night before when he was dancing at the White House. He admits he considered doing something that probably would have made headlines around the country. "I did have one more little devious idea, and [my wife] said, 'Don't you dare!' I almost went out and tapped on the president's shoulder and cut in!" The press-club crowd is now practically in tears from laughter at the thought of the unlikely dance team of Hillary Clinton and Jesse "the Body" Ventura.

Someone asks if any other "big-name wrestlers" called Ventura to ask for advice about running for public office. "I've spoken to no wrestlers since I won. I'm very disappointed in the world of wrestling and how they treated me during [the campaign], and I say this very seriously because I gave fifteen to twenty years of my life to the business. And they came to Minnesota, the WCW [World Championship Wrestling], the Atlanta group with [Hulk] Hogan last June, and I went down there feeling that if anywhere I could get support, this would be the place to do it. It was sold out at the Target Center. They purposefully would not show me on television. They did not introduce me to the crowd in any manner, and I will tell you very honestly it hurt, personally, because, as I said, I gave my heart and soul to the world of wrestling for a number of years. Because of what happened there, I didn't refer to wrestling at all in my inaugural address. I had no wrestlers or anyone in wrestling at my inauguration. We have a saying in the SEALs: We don't get mad, we get even."

On campaign-finance reform, he's convinced meaningful reform won't happen because career politicians will never vote for it. So he's got his own plan to finance another campaign, using his nonprofit Ventura for Minnesota, Inc. "We're hoping if I run again to totally finance my campaign through merchandising. No one's ever done it before. But think about it. What's a cleaner way to get money? Me turning to you and saying, 'Give me fifty bucks,' or selling you a T-shirt, you buy it, and the profits are used to support my campaign? I will continue to break new ground and set new standards in the political world."

Drunken Irishmen

Later that day Ventura departs the governors conference and boards a plane at Reagan National Airport for the short flight to New York City. He's scheduled to appear on the *Late Show with David Letterman*. The taping is scheduled for 5:00 P.M. By 3:00, the usual assortment of groupies and gawkers are waiting by the stage door of the Ed Sullivan Theater. Many of them are Jesse "the Body" Ventura fans hoping to get a glimpse of their wrestling hero turned governor.

"I liked him in *Predator* and I used to be a wrestling fan," says Nestor Aviles while patiently waiting and hoping to get an autograph. "I figured I'd give it a shot." He's carrying a black-and-white photo of Ventura wearing his outback hat and toting a machine gun in *Predator*. So what does he think his chances are of getting an autograph? "With all the bodyguards, slim to none. There's always a chance. It's a roll of the dice."

Another Ventura fan is holding a bag full of Jesse "the Body" wrestling stuff. "I've been a wrestling fan since I'm a kid," says the man, carrying a Ventura wrestling action-figure from the 1980s, a World Wrestling Federation record album, and a photo of Ventura in the ring at Madison Square Garden with a feather boa around his neck. "Over the years I met a lot of the guys from the Hulk to Macho Man. Jesse's one of the last ones. . . . I'm hoping he's a nice enough guy to take a picture with me. That would be cool."

A few minutes later Ventura suddenly appears on the sidewalk headed toward the side stage door. Instead of hopping out of a car a few feet from the door and darting inside like many of the celebrities who appear on the *Late Show*, Ventura gets out on Broadway and walks half a block along busy West Fifty-third Street, smoking a cigar. The crowd cheers and people shout his name, but there will be no autographs and no posing for pictures. He's surrounded by his contingent of three Minnesota state troopers and a half-dozen other security guards in dark overcoats.

He walks right past the famous Hello Deli shop that's often featured on the *Late Show*. The deli features a David Letterman Sandwich for $4.95. Owner Rupert Jee says most stars arriving at the *Late Show* try to sneak in. "He's a very brave man to walk the streets of New York," Jee says. "I thought it was pretty exciting. . . . I thought they would chauffeur him over to the front entrance, but he just walked right on by. That's very admirable. It just shows he's a very people-type of governor."

When Letterman introduces Ventura, there's a rousing round of applause. Not just because the applause signs are blinking; the crowd is genuinely excited. Minnesota's governor is now in the media capital of the world, and he's the toast of a very large town.

Like everyone else in the world, Letterman is still trying to figure out how Ventura went from pro-wrestling bad guy to the Minnesota governor's office. "People in Minnesota, were they happy about it? Were they stunned? Were they incredulous?" Letterman asks.

"Well, the Democrats and Republicans were stunned," Ventura replies. The conversation quickly turns to his recent standoff with single mothers on the steps of the State Capitol earlier in the month. Some in the audience groan when he again says some harsh things about single mothers and how it's not the government's fault their husbands or boyfriends ran off. The real trouble develops a few minutes later, however, after what seems like a fairly harmless question.

"Which do you like better, Minneapolis or St. Paul?" Letterman asks. Ventura pauses before answering because the crowd is laughing in anticipation of his response to this politically tricky question.

"Ah, Minneapolis," he reluctantly responds. The crowd is laughing again because he answered honestly rather than giving some politically correct answer. "I'm born in Minneapolis, and besides, have you ever been to St. Paul?" Ventura asks Letterman.

Letterman says yes, which sets the table for another public-relations nightmare for the governor. "Whoever designed the streets must have been drunk, because in Minneapolis, you know if you're on Thirty-second Street, Thirty-sixth Street's four blocks away. In St. Paul, there's no rhyme or reason. It's not numerical. It's not alphabetical. You know, I think it was those Irish guys. You know what they like to do over there." As he says this, Ventura holds his thumb up to his mouth like he's drinking booze while Letterman just shakes his head, amused by what he's seeing and hearing. "Oh, am I in trouble now," Ventura says.

The governor's instinct on the "trouble" issue is right on the mark. I'm with a photographer waiting for the governor to come out of the Ed Sullivan Theater. We're elbow-to-elbow with a growing crowd of paparazzi hoping to get photos of Ventura.

About a half-hour after the show ends, he steps out the stage door. "Jesse!" "Mr. Ventura!" "Governor!" Everybody's trying to get his attention. I manage to get the attention of John Wodele, the governor's communications director, who gets Ventura to stop for a question before jumping into his vehicle. I ask him if people in St. Paul will understand he was just joking about the drunken Irishmen designing their streets. "I hope they do, because I'm a Minneapolis kid," he shouts to me. "What do they expect? Absolutely it's in fun. St. Paul's a great city, but I went to Minneapolis Roosevelt. It's just a natural rivalry between the two cities. I mean, I couldn't very well say St. Paul, could I, when I grew up in Minneapolis?"

He hops into his waiting car and heads off to meet NBC's Tom Brokaw at a New York Knicks basketball game with little idea of the controversy he just sparked back home.

Along with St. Paul's German, Swede, and Norwegian cultural connections, there's a strong Irish heritage. Stereotyping all the Irish as drunks is bound to cause trouble for anyone, even a governor who thrives on political incorrectness. "He made some comments that could get some flak," says Lisa Bjelland, a Minnesotan who was in the studio audience after winning a Twin Cities radio-show contest for the trip to New York.

"He's just a shoot-from-the-hip kind of guy," her husband, Bruce Bjelland, tells me while we stand under the *Late Show* marquee on Broadway. "I thought it was pretty entertaining, but a few of the things he said will obviously get people talking at home."

The mayor of St. Paul certainly has plenty to say. The mayor is Norm Coleman, one of Ventura's opponents in the gubernatorial race. "I think you got to watch the ethnic humor," Coleman says in an interview on the KSTP-TV morning news program the day after the Letterman appearance. "He's the governor of the *whole* state, and he's got a very unhappy mayor here."

Coleman says it's not just a matter of political correctness, but rather a case of embarrassing the state. "A little advice to Jesse," Coleman says, "is that you want people laughing with us, not at us."

While the criticism grows at home, Ventura is flying back from New York still unaware of the brewing controversy. He finds out about it the moment he steps off the plane and into the terminal at the Minneapolis–St. Paul International Airport. A half-dozen television crews are waiting for him when he comes through the Northwest Airlines gate, wearing his trademark leather fringed jacket and Navy SEAL hat. Reporters try to ask him about his comments on the *Late Show*, but he's in no mood to talk.

"I had a great time until I get back here," Ventura says. "I'd rather swap the Washington press for you. Geez, I've had enough of this."

The governor tries to make his way through the terminal, but photographers and reporters surround him. Every time he changes direction he bumps into another camera. "He doesn't want to talk to you," says John Wodele, trying to direct the governor through the media maze. A reporter asks Ventura about Coleman's reaction. "I don't care what Mayor Coleman said," he snaps back.

He's peppered with more questions but just keeps walking without response. Finally, he's heard enough and can't resist firing back. "It was a joke. It made people smile. If feathers get ruffled, then obviously people need to take lessons in humor, maybe. When I grew up in the Twin Cities, you were allowed to have a sense of humor. Maybe if the mayor was from the Twin Cities for real, you know, maybe he'd have one. Actually, the mayor is just jealous because I was on *Letterman* and he wasn't."

He walks a little bit more and then gets more off his chest. "If it gets to the point where you can't make fun or say anything, we live in a too politically correct world, and I'm not going to live in a world like that," he says.

"So you're just going to be yourself?" a reporter asks.

"Absolutely," Ventura responds before reporters give up the chase and he leaves the airport.

After twenty-four hours of criticism on television, radio, and in newspapers, Governor Ventura is urged by aides to apologize for his *Letterman*-show remarks. He reluctantly agrees to apologize during a news conference scheduled on February 25 to announce three more commissioner appointments. At 10:00 A.M. Ventura walks out of his office to the podium in the governor's reception room. "I want to make a statement and I'll take no questions on it. When I'm done with the statement, I'm done with the statement." He's clearly not thrilled to be in this position.

"I would just like to say if I offended anyone, I apologize. The *David Letterman* show is a show of comedy. It's a show that has top-ten lists and is generally considered comedic, and that's the light in which I did the show. . . . The city of St. Paul is a tremendous city, and when I talked about the streets, it was simply me remembering back when I used to wrestle at the Civic Center and I would always try to beat the crowd out of the Civic Center if it was possible. And it never failed.

Every three weeks I'd take a wrong turn, and I would spend a great length of time trying to find the freeway."

The apology loses some of its luster when he takes a veiled shot at his critics. "The Minneapolis–St. Paul and Minnesota that I grew up in and spent my life in had a sense of humor, and apparently today the Minneapolis–St. Paul and Minnesota that I live in now does not." He also promises that from now on he'll be more sullen and boring when he appears on late-night talk shows.

Although the governor took some criticism over the *Letterman* comments, he survives the controversy without much lasting damage. A few days later that controversy is pushed out of the headlines, replaced by news of movie stars at the governor's mansion and the state forecast of an even bigger budget surplus.

Ventura hosts a dinner for two of Hollywood's biggest stars, Jack Nicholson and Sean Penn. The two are in Minnesota scouting movie locations in St. Paul, Minneapolis, and Duluth for a police thriller called *The Pledge*. Ventura says he plans to spend a lot of time promoting Minnesota to Hollywood as a movie location, starting with lobbying Nicholson and Penn.

Governor Ventura's run of luck continues to read like a Hollywood script. The state's huge budget surplus is projected to grow by another $732 million over the next three years, bringing the total estimated surplus through 2001 to $4.1 billion.

House Republicans say this bolsters their argument that Minnesotans are overtaxed and deserve across-the-board income-tax cuts. Ventura resists that idea. For all his brashness on other matters, he doesn't trust forecasts any more than election opinion polls. He says he doesn't want to cut taxes too much and then be forced to raise taxes if the economy takes a downturn. "I just saw this surplus now," Ventura says. "I'm not going to give you some knee-jerk reaction."

He'll save those reactions for Letterman.

CHAPTER 5

"We Can't Legislate against Every Stupid Thing"
Ventura's Vision for Minnesota

"I have the honor to announce the arrival of the governor of the great state of Minnesota, the honorable Jesse Ventura," shouts the sergeant-at-arms of the Minnesota House of Representatives.

On March 2, 1999, Governor Ventura is ushered into the ornate House chambers amid much fanfare to deliver his first State of the State address. The ceiling is adorned with the names of four early French explorers in Minnesota, La Salle, Hennepin, Perrot, and Duluth. The House chamber has been in use since 1905, but the most remarkable slice of its history is being written as Ventura walks down the center isle to a sustained standing ovation. He's greeted by 201 state representatives and senators assembled here, along with Minnesota Supreme Court justices, the lieutenant governor, attorney general, secretary of state, and the governor's cabinet.

In the gallery above are members of the public and several invited guests of the governor, including many young, first-time voters he credits with helping him "shock the world." The governor makes his way to the front of the House floor and shakes hands with Speaker of the House Steve Sviggum before turning to bask in the limelight. It's more far-fetched than any plot the World Wrestling Federation's Vince McMahon could dream up.

"The state of the state is great!" Ventura says to begin his speech, drawing another lengthy ovation. There's no denying that simple statement. Minnesota is awash in budget surpluses, unemployment is at or near a record low, and crime is on the decline. Against the backdrop of such prosperity Governor Ventura outlines his three fundamental beliefs that will guide how he will govern. The common thread is this: Don't rely on government to solve all your problems.

"First, said best by Abraham Lincoln, the role of government is to do only what the people cannot do for themselves.... We can't legislate against every stupid thing people will do, and yet the temptation is there to try time and time again.... Second, I believe in personal responsibility and self-sufficiency. The state of the state is jeopardized by this weak notion that taxpayers must step forward to provide nearly unlimited resources to anyone who faces adversity, who lives with circumstances they brought about through their own decisions or who lives with consequences of choices to act illegally. I stand before you as governor willing to say what too many politicians at all levels of government have been scared to say: the free ride is over!"

That brings another big round of applause, primarily from Republican lawmakers who have long advocated smaller government and a reduction in welfare programs. There are 199 Republicans and Democrats, two independents and no Reform Party members in the legislature. Ventura is convinced his election is a sign that Minnesotans want change in the two-party system.

He's about halfway through his thirteen-page, forty-five-minute speech when he outlines some specific goals and proposals for his administration. Most of them are aimed at getting government off the backs of the people and providing them with ways to become self-sufficient.

"As soon as you're ready to send me a sales-tax rebate bill, I'm ready to sign it and get on to permanent income-tax-cut discussions," he says to a standing ovation led by Republican lawmakers, who, ironically, have so far ignored his sales-tax rebate plan.

One of the first issues that spurred Ventura to run for governor was the state's complex property-tax system. He hasn't forgotten that in this speech. Reforming the system will be among the administration's highest priorities. "Let's face it. We've lost any logic to this system. Property taxes no longer are tied to the services that are delivered. We have created a so-called progressive tax based on the value of property. It punishes people for doing the right thing. If I keep up my property, my value and taxes go up even though I don't need as many local services as the property that has been allowed to deteriorate and needs inspections, fire protection, or police patrols."

Ventura addresses another issue that will clearly have a high priority: mass transit. The governor is a major proponent of light-rail transit, an idea that's been studied but ultimately rejected year after year in Minnesota since the last streetcars were taken off the tracks in the 1950s. "I want to stop planning to do something about transit and urban sprawl and get something done. Our roads have grown more congested and the Twin Cities region has become one of the most sprawling in the country. In Minnesota every day an area the size of the Mall of America gets paved over, and we're still 'planning' to do something about transit and sprawl." He ambitiously calls for a light-rail transit system to be up and running by 2002.

The governor concludes by introducing guests in the gallery who are examples of "self-sufficiency." Among them is a fourteen-year-old St. Paul boy, Joe Lynch, who helped build a neighborhood playground after a group of adults backed out. The adults worried that the playground would attract gangs and violence. Instead, four teams of teenagers took it upon themselves to raise money, work on safety issues, and get the playground built. That's an example of what Ventura expects from Minnesotans. "It's been said that the world belongs to those who show up. Thank you for showing up today. I too am very happy to be here. Thank you." He walks off to one more standing ovation.

Ventura gets generally high marks for his speech. He was interrupted by applause thirty-four times, but it wasn't always bipartisan applause. Republicans gave him standing ovations from one side of the room every time he mentioned tax cuts. Democrats stood up on the other side and applauded when he proposed spending the state's huge tobacco-settlement money on social programs. Ventura tells me later it reminded him of one of those old "Tastes great, less filling" beer commercials.

The day after his State of the State address, we get a taste of Ventura's maverick governing style as he attempts to follow through on the goals he outlined in his speech. During a speech at a National Institute of Health Policy meeting at the Radisson Metrodome Hotel in Minneapolis, the governor makes a surprise announcement regarding his position on tax rebates.

The House and Senate have approved differing tax-rebate bills. Both involve rebating $1.1 billion of the budget surplus, but the House approved an income-tax rebate and the Senate supports a sales-tax rebate. The Republican-controlled House sets the maximum rebates at $7,600 for joint tax filers and $3,800 for single filers to allow the wealthiest Minnesotans who paid the most income taxes to get the largest rebates. In the Senate, where Democrats are in control, the maximum sales-tax rebates top out at $2,000 and $1,000, which favors lower- and middle-income taxpayers. The Senate plan is closest to what Governor Ventura has proposed, but so far the two sides are deadlocked. The governor, the House, and the Senate all are taking heat because they can't even agree on how to give money back to the people.

With neither side budging from their position, Governor Ventura takes a step to put a stop to business-as-usual. He chooses to use his speech to the health-policy group to announce a proposal to break the rebate stalemate. "We got the press here?" the governor asks, pushing his reading glasses to the end of his nose and looking across the room for the television cameras. "As I said yesterday in the State of the State, there's been a big elephant standing in the middle of the legislature right now," referring to the rebate standoff. "It's been there for too long, and I guess I'm the only one willing to kick it out." He then announces he'll agree to increase the maximum rebates to $5,000 for joint filers and $2,500 for single taxpayers if the House Republicans will switch to the sales-tax rebate favored by the Senate and the governor.

"I want to get this done," Ventura tells me an hour after the speech during an interview in his office. "I think the ball is in their court now, the House's court, to do a sales-tax rebate. And I don't know what excuses they could come up with this time." The governor says he's tired of being the scapegoat for the legislative stalemate on this issue. "A lot of people are accusing me of not being aggressive enough. This is aggressive. And I think it's part of my leadership role of the governor of the state of Minnesota to get this surplus out the door."

House Majority Leader Tim Pawlenty says he's encouraged that the governor now sees the wisdom in allowing wealthier Minnesotans to get back the fair share of the taxes they've overpaid. "This is a very substantial and welcome jump and somewhat surprising," Pawlenty says. "We are glad the governor has heard our position and is trying to address our concerns, and in that spirit we're going to try to work with them."

President Ventura?

On the night of Ventura's election, speculation had already begun about a possible run for president. In March 1999, KSTP-TV commissions the first national poll of Ventura's viability as a presidential candidate. The numbers show surprising strength for the governor across the country. In a survey of one thousand U.S. citizens conducted by the SurveyUSA polling firm, 34 percent indicate Ventura should run for president. That's a remarkable number when you consider six months ago he was a washed-up wrestler turned radio talk-show host running a long-shot candidacy for governor of Minnesota.

On the flip side, 57 percent of Americans polled say Ventura should not run for president and 9 percent are not sure. Another question asks: "Assume that Jesse Ventura does run as the Reform Party candidate for president in the year 2000, and the other candidates are Democrat Al Gore, the current vice president, and Republican George W. Bush, the current governor of Texas. If the election for president were today and you were standing in the voting booth right now, whom would you vote for?" Framed that way, 45 percent picked Bush, 30 percent chose Gore, and 21 percent selected Ventura. Again, this is remarkable when you consider Ventura is only nine points behind the sitting vice president of the United States.

It's important to point out that the one thousand people polled were randomly chosen in a telephone survey and did not have to be registered voters to participate. In Ventura's case that's significant because he won the Minnesota governor's race by appealing to people who had lost interest in the political process. It was first-time voters who put him over the top.

"I'm flattered," Ventura tells me as I show him the numbers in his office. "But you know, in light of what's gone on with the federal government over the last year, it doesn't surprise me that the American people would want someone like me to run." How does he interpret the numbers? "Looking at these numbers it would tell me I can win, because when I started in Minnesota I was at 10 percent and I won. So here I'm already well above that. You know, 23 percent puts me to where I only have to pick up about 15 percent, and maybe in a way that would be a piece of cake after what I faced here in Minnesota. It tells me I could win if I wanted it."

But will he run for president in 2000? "No," he says flatly. "One of the great criticisms I had for the Republican candidate I opposed was the fact that he just ran for mayor, was reelected, and in less than nine months turns around and runs for governor. I would be a hypocrite if I turned around.... I would have to start running now. I'd have to start now. I don't have time to do that. I have business to take care of in the state of Minnesota. But it does present an interesting thought. Even to be considered at this point in time by 34 percent of the people to run for presidency of the United States is mind-boggling for a kid from south Minneapolis."

One of the biggest college sports scandals in history rocks the University of Minnesota on March 10, 1999. It also sparks an intense feud between Governor Ventura and the *St. Paul Pioneer Press*. The *Pioneer Press* breaks the story about a former tutor in the men's athletic department who wrote hundreds of papers for as many as two dozen players on the Minnesota Golden Gophers basketball team. The tutor, Jan Gangelhoff, tells the newspaper she's been doing the academic work for several years with the knowledge of key members of the basketball program. She even alleges that head coach Clem Haskins has been aware of her activities, including those during the team's Final Four season in 1997.

Gangelhoff gives the newspaper computer disks with copies of most of the papers she's written for the players, including some she's done for players on the current team. The reporter, George Dohrmann, also interviews several former players who admit Gangelhoff wrote papers for them so they could concentrate on basketball. It's about as rock solid and thorough a piece of investigative reporting you could ever hope to read. The story breaks just one day before the Gophers basketball team is supposed to play an opening-round game in the NCAA tournament in Seattle. This is where the story and Governor Ventura collide.

The morning the basketball-scandal story breaks, Ventura attends a news conference at the State Capitol to endorse a Reform Party candidate running for a state Senate seat in a special election. As the news conference winds down, reporters ask the governor for his reaction to the *Pioneer Press* story that is now making national news. "I know nothing about it" is his curt answer. But seconds later, when pressed on the issue, he's suddenly got plenty of opinions.

"It just showed me another example of *Pioneer Press* sensational journalism, of their timing. I think it's despicable in the fact that they would release a story like this that has been going on for, what, a year? They felt the need to release this story the day before the NCAA tournament. It couldn't have waited until after? It's just another example of sensational journalism. That their needs are more important than anyone else's . . . that they could take the pleasure of these young people who have worked so hard to get to that tournament and somehow try to spoil it for them. It somehow doesn't surprise me."

It seems odd that the focus of his concern is the newspaper's reporting of the story rather than on allegations of a major scandal at the state's major university. So, a couple of hours later, I go to a

Chamber of Commerce speech the governor is delivering at the Radisson hotel in downtown St. Paul to ask him more specifically about the allegations. After letting the story sink in for a few hours, maybe he's got a different view. Inexplicably, his focus is still on the media and not the possible NCAA rules violations.

"The only thing I'm angry about is the timing of it. I expect nothing less of the *Pioneer Press* because not only have they now ruined the tournament for those young people playing in it, ruined it for the University of Minnesota, but they've virtually ruined it for all of us Minnesotans who were looking forward to a great NCAA tournament. This was an investigative story that could have been held onto until their participation in the tournament was over. But they chose for their own personal, shall we call it *National Enquirer,* reasons, to break it the day before the tournament started. I thought their timing was despicable."

When I ask him about the specific allegations of academic misconduct, Ventura cuts me off in midquestion. "It doesn't matter. Why would it matter whether you broke it now or after the tournament, whether the allegations are true or not? The point is, if they'd waited a week or two it wouldn't make any difference. The same allegations, if true, would hold true a week or two from now as they would right now. It was just done to put the *Pioneer Press* in the headlines, and that was their motive."

The governor's reaction to the reporting of the basketball scandal puts him at odds not only with the editor of the *Pioneer Press* but also with the university president. "I don't think it was a cheap shot," says University of Minnesota president Mark Yudof. "I accept at face value that these things are going to happen, and I'm not going to blame the *Pioneer Press.*"

Walker Lundy, editor of the *Pioneer Press,* is less charitable in his response to the governor's tirade. "I would have felt a little better if, after calling us 'despicable,' he would have mentioned academic fraud isn't a very good idea either," Lundy says in a live interview on KSTP-TV. "I think he needs to remember the first job the University of Minnesota has is to educate students, not play basketball."

Lundy denies the newspaper timed the story to get maximum attention on the eve of the NCAA tournament. "We don't hold news at the *Pioneer Press*. When it's ready, we put it in the paper."

Lundy says if they held the story until after the tournament, the newspaper would be guilty of the same kind of timing accusation the governor has already leveled at the paper. As it turns out, by publishing the story when the paper did, the university is able to suspend four players from the opening tournament game against Gonzaga University. If they played, the university might have been forced to forfeit the game if the team won (they ended up losing the game) and forced to return any NCAA money they earned for the appearance.

Ultimately, Lundy proves to be a worthy adversary for Ventura in this war of words. "This is the governor who, on his first day as governor, went to the University of Minnesota campus and spoke to a large crowd of students and said, 'Win if you can, lose if you must, but always cheat.'"

Back to Hollywood

When Governor Ventura steps out of a black stretch limousine along Santa Monica Beach on March 20, about one hundred yards from the sun-splashed Pacific Ocean, there's little doubt about his national popularity. A crowd lets out a big cheer as they recognize him in his now trademark leather fringed jacket and Navy SEAL cap.

"Jesse!" "Jesse, you're awesome, Jesse!" "Jesse 'the Man' Ventura!" The screams are coming from a crowd watching celebrities arrive for the Independent Spirit Awards in Santa Monica, California. It's kind of an informal version of the Academy Awards for the makers and stars of independent films. Ventura has been invited to present the Truer Than Fiction Award to the producer of the best documentary film. Although it's not as glamorous as the Academy Awards, scheduled for two days later, there's still plenty of star power at this event. Arriving before Ventura are the likes of Alec Baldwin, Nick Nolte, Jeff Goldblum, Andie MacDowell, Marisa Tomei, Randy Quaid, Lisa Kudrow, and Lara Flynn Boyle.

Ventura draws as big a reaction as any movie star when he steps out of his limousine. "I'm not amazed at all," says one of those cheering loudest for Ventura, Daniel Schainen of Los Angeles. "He's a big name, he's a big figure, and I think people in general really respect who he is.... He's kind of a voice for a lot of people. Even though he's the governor of Minnesota, a lot of people are following him."

Ventura isn't surprised by his reception either. "I've been gone from Hollywood for a little while," he tells me after waving to the crowd outside his limousine, "but with all the press and high profile I've had since the election, it doesn't surprise me. They read papers."

Ventura is combining his appearance at this awards show with a trade mission to Hollywood. He's hoping to lure more feature-film projects to Minnesota, where since 1970 more than eighty feature films have been shot. The list includes *Airport, Slaughterhouse Five*, and *Ice Castles* from the 1970s to *Fargo, The Mighty Ducks*, and *Grumpy Old Men* in the 1990s. The last two movies were so successful they both ended up with sequels shot in Minnesota.

The sixty films shot in the state in the 1990s resulted in $102 million of direct spending in Minnesota. This figure doesn't include broadcast and cable-television projects that get shot in the state every year. Ventura says his own Hollywood career won't hurt Minnesota's efforts to aggressively court the movie industry.

His first movie role, in *Predator*, is also his best known. It was an Arnold Schwarzenegger action flick with Ventura in a supporting role as part of a CIA-hired band of suicidal tough guys sent on a rescue mission to a South American jungle. It's the film where Ventura utters his signature line, "I ain't got time to bleed." It's also the film where he develops a lasting friendship with Schwarzenegger while shooting on location for several weeks in Puerto Vallarta, Mexico.

It's a friendship that leads to a number of other movie roles for Ventura. After *Predator*'s release in 1987, Ventura goes on to appearances in *The Running Man* (1987), *Demolition Man* (1993), *Major League 2* (1994), and *Batman and Robin* (1997).

During a news conference in a media tent after the awards

ceremony, I tell Ventura his critics are already calling his Hollywood trip another self-serving junket. "Who cares?" he responds. "Let 'em criticize. In *Predator* I said, 'I don't have time to bleed.' As governor, I don't have time for criticism."

When Ventura steps out of the tent, he runs into actor Nick Nolte. The two men shake hands as they meet for the first time and Nolte recounts the eight or nine years he spent working in local theater in Minnesota.

"I just gotta tell you, Minnesota is just one of the greatest states I've ever been in," he tells Ventura. Inexplicably, Ventura responds by saying, "I'm excited. I'm the governor there now." He apparently thinks Nolte has no access to television or newspapers way out here in California. "Yeah, I know," Nolte tells him.

Once they clear that up, Ventura the movie buff has a question about a film Nolte made thirteen years ago, *Down and Out in Beverly Hills*. He wants to know if Nolte ate real dog food in the movie. "I ate the dog food," Nolte confirms. "The dog ate vegetarian. He was a vegetarian dog."

Ventura is laughing as he recounts the humor of that scene. "That's one of the greatest scenes, when you're down on the floor showing the dog how to eat." Nolte has made thirty-four feature films in his career, playing many critically acclaimed roles. Ventura manages to reduce that career to a highlight of one scene where Nolte eats dog food.

The next day, March 21, Los Angeles buzzes with excitement about Hollywood's biggest event of the year: the Oscar ceremony. Ventura is staying at the historic Roosevelt Hotel on Hollywood Boulevard, where the first Academy Awards show was held in 1929. He begins the day by heading out for brunch with his Hollywood agent.

Although his movie career is on hold because of politics, he says he keeps in touch with his agent. He tells reporters waiting outside the hotel that he doesn't plan to go to the Oscars, but he'll attend some Oscar parties. "That's how business is conducted out here. Most business deals are made at parties, at brunches, at lunches, and things of that nature. That's just the nature of the business out here and how it's done, so you just have to adapt to the way it's done out here." However, he doesn't want reporters adapting to his way of doing business today. "I'm going to brunch. Don't follow me or we'll lose ya. I got good drivers and the California Highway Patrol."

While Ventura doesn't have much to say on Oscar day, the head of the Minnesota Film Board does. Randy Adamsick is in the parking lot of the Roosevelt Hotel, showing off the front page of that day's metro section of the *Los Angeles Times*. "All the L.A. press told us before we came out here, 'Oh, it's Oscars weekend, don't think you're going to get any press,'" Adamsick tells a group of Minnesota reporters. "And, you know, the governor was on the front page of the *L.A. Times* business section yesterday and the front page of the metro section today."

He holds up the business section with its headline "'The Body' Arrives in Hollywood as 'The Salesman.'" Then he holds up today's headline: "A Blasé Reaction to 'The Body': Head of L.A. film office isn't worried by Minnesota Gov. Jesse Ventura's attempts to lure away productions." Color photos of Ventura accompany both articles.

Although today's article downplays the significance of Ventura's trade mission, Adamsick is clearly in the "any publicity is good publicity" camp. "Our job has always been about visibility and getting the word out about what we have to offer," Adamsick says, "and this is what we really have in Governor Ventura—the ability to get the word out in a way we've never been able to before. Governor [Arne] Carlson did a tremendous job and was very instrumental in bringing *A Simple Plan* to the state. But when you get the kind of publicity you do with Governor Ventura, people catch that out here."

It's not just L.A. newspapers taking notice. KABC-TV, the ABC affiliate in Los Angeles, follows Ventura during his visit. They also track down Los Angeles mayor Richard Riordan at a groundbreaking ceremony to get his reaction to Ventura's visit. "I think Governor Ventura is a great governor," Riordan says diplomatically before taking a tongue-in-cheek shot. "Minnesota's a great state, and if you want to have pictures about the Arctic and people freezing to death, things like that, I think Minnesota's perfect."

On Oscar night Ventura spends a couple of hours at a private party hosted by Arnold Schwarzenegger and a few more hours at the House of Blues nightclub on Sunset Boulevard. Ventura makes plenty of connections along the way, assuring me afterward that "Hollywood knows Minnesota is open for business."

Despite the late night of partying, Ventura is up early the next day, promoting Minnesota at a roundtable discussion with the Minnesota Film Board and several Hollywood producers and writers. The primary focus isn't how Minnesota can lure Hollywood movie producers from California; it's how the state can lure Hollywood movie producers from Canada. The favorable exchange rate in Canada, coupled with government-sponsored subsidies for movie productions, is sending producers north of the border at an alarming rate. Many of those so-called runaway productions that escape the California borders used to go to other states in the United States. Minnesota is trying to fight back with a Minnesota Film Jobs Fund that offers a 5 percent rebate on production expenditures in the state. Ventura wants to make sure Hollywood producers know at least some financial assistance is available in Minnesota.

The annual Minnesota Film Board meeting usually receives zero media coverage. With Ventura in attendance, five Minnesota TV stations, several Los Angeles stations, and the syndicated *Access Hollywood* show are all on hand to cover the event. Many of those same cameras follow Ventura as he later visits a couple of Hollywood movie studios, Disney and Paramount Pictures. At a news conference afterward back at the Roosevelt Hotel, some of the Los Angeles media get on the governor's case about his attempts at "poaching" movie business. Ventura dismisses the criticism.

"We're trying to say rather than going to Toronto or going to Vancouver, consider going to Minnesota," he says. "Keep it within the country. We're all part of the United States. Like I said, this is more national than what was portrayed in the L.A. paper, that I'm somehow trying to undercut Los Angeles. This will always be the mecca of filmmaking. They like the sun too much out here."

His attempts to diffuse the criticism fall on deaf ears. Moments later another Los Angeles television reporter asks, "Before you leave, could you address the folks here in Los Angeles and assure them that you're not trying to rip off our industry?"

Ventura stares him down and shakes his head in disgust. "Well, watch out. I guess when I become president, you better really worry. That's about how much credence I give to that. Come on! In other words, you're telling me you think *Fargo* should have been shot here? Is that what you're telling me? Is that ripping you off? Those are strong terms when you use the words 'rip off.'"

He's still on a roll when he fields the next question about whether he plans a return to the movie business. "No, my full-time job is being governor of the state of Minnesota and attempting not to rip off L.A."

Ventura wraps up his trade mission in whirlwind fashion. After the news conference he visits Schwarzenegger on location at a movie shoot in downtown Los Angeles. He then heads back to a movie theater on Sunset Boulevard in Hollywood for the premiere of an independent film shot in Minnesota, *With or Without You*. After the premiere, it's back to the Roosevelt Hotel for a party with seven hundred native Minnesotans now working in the Hollywood film industry.

For obvious reasons, the annual event is called the "Ice Pack Party." On his way through the hotel Ventura stops outside the ballroom to tape a quick cameo appearance for the HBO television series *Arli$$*. When he finally makes it to the party, actor and comedian Tom Arnold introduces him. Arnold, an Iowa native who spent several years working in Twin Cities comedy clubs, has an interesting spin on how Ventura got elected.

"He had the luxury of having the time to spend in the state not really too incredibly busy with anything," Arnold says jokingly, alluding to Ventura's part-time radio talk show and stalled movie career. "He got to know the people, know what's going on. He definitely believes in himself. I think he's great for the state."

While Ventura makes the rounds in L.A., there's one place he deftly avoids—the set of the late-night ABC talk show *Politically Incorrect*. Host

Bill Maher frequently pokes fun at the governor in his monologues, but he's also one of Ventura's biggest fans. "He doesn't look like the robots that we have running the country, and that's a good thing," Maher tells me in an interview after taping a show the day Ventura leaves town. Maher would love to have the governor on his show, but he has declined several invitations, including one on this trip.

Maher thinks Ventura is gun-shy after the controversy he stirred on the *Late Show with David Letterman* last month. "You know, he made a joke about drunken Irishmen," Maher says. "I'm a proud drunken Irishman! I was disappointed when he apologized for it. Somebody somewhere along the line in politics is going to stand up and say, 'You know what? I don't think this deserves an apology. I'm going to save my apologies for when I really pull a boner. When I really say something wrong, when I really say something stupid. This was just a joke! The rest of you should lighten up. Not me apologize, you lighten up!'"

Maher is fascinated by Ventura's election and sees him as a litmus test for whether a politically incorrect politician can succeed in office. "Voters are hypocritical," Maher says. "As Barney Frank once said on our show, 'Politicians have a lot of faults, but the voters are no prize either.' They say they want straight talk, but very often straight talk gets you thrown out of office. We'll see how far his poll ratings go down when he tells people continually what the truth is, as he sees it.... I don't know if he can last as governor. I'd like to see him stick to his guns, keep saying what he's really thinking and not pander. Then, if he gets thrown out of office, we'll know the people aren't ready for honesty and therefore they don't deserve it."

So does Maher think he deserves a shot at getting Ventura on his show? "If there's one show he should be doing, it's this one," Maher says, adding, "You tell him if he doesn't do it, he's a pussy!"

I'm going to let Maher handle that one himself.

Governor Ventura exercises his veto power for the first time in April 1999. It's not a momentous piece of legislation, but in a microcosm it does indicate the type of government Ventura wants to shape. He vetoes a bill requiring owners of landscape irrigation systems to install rain-fall detectors that would conserve water by preventing the systems from activating after a rainfall. Such a device would cost about $35. In exercising the veto, Ventura says the bill is a "perfect example of un-necessary government regulation." Although the bill sailed through the House and Senate, he says lawmakers are trying to solve a problem that should be left up to individuals, not government.

So far the governor and the legislature also don't agree on what to do with the state's huge budget surplus. They've agreed most of it should go back to the taxpayers, but they can't agree how it should go back. This stalemate over tax rebates and another over income-tax cuts catches the attention of the *Wall Street Journal.*

The newspaper fires a volley over Ventura's bow on, of all days, April Fools' Day. "Just five months ago, a promise to cut income taxes and 'give back' every penny of the $4 billion Minnesota surplus helped to propel wrestler Jesse Ventura into the state governor's office," the newspaper says in an editorial. "Since the Reform Party candidate's surprise victory, that surplus figure has swelled by another billion. Yet when it comes to paring back government, the muscular Mr. Ventura is looking more like Casper Milquetoast.... For starters, he has unfurled a budget that leaves more than half of the state's surplus intact. And the main tax cut he does propose is a sales tax rebate.... Welcome to state tax policy, 1990s-style."

Tax policy isn't the only hotly debated issue on Ventura's plate. Just two weeks after he has been targeted by a pie thrower while speak-ing to a neighborhood group in Minneapolis, the issue of Governor Ventura's security force sparks debate on the House floor. There's a $17.6 million emergency-funding bill on the floor that includes more than $200,000 to pay for extra security the governor has needed since his election in November. The money is mostly to pay for unanticipated overtime costs. With the governor becoming an international celebrity, Public Safety Commissioner Charlie Weaver says Ventura is "more of a security challenge than any other governor in Minnesota history."

Although it's just a fraction of the $17.6 million in the bill, the security money is a lightning rod for the governor's critics. Democratic representative Phyllis Kahn of Minneapolis questions the need for so many guards to be with the governor everywhere he goes and a separate set of guards at his private home and the governor's mansion. "I said there was no objection to the personal guard around the governor," Kahn says. "I think that's appropriate. But the governor's only in one place at any time."

Some Republican lawmakers leap to the governor's defense. "We should provide reasonable protection at the request of the governor, and we certainly wouldn't be doing our duty if we didn't," says Republican representative Dave Bishop of Rochester. Bishop's colleague, Representative Dennis Ozment of Rosemount, takes the argument a step further. "I think we need to have some common sense put into this discussion when we're talking about security for a governor that's an extreme celebrity," Ozment says, possibly coining a new catchphrase for the twenty-first century. "When you talk about somebody who's nationally known—we have a governor that is nationally known—along with that comes considerable risk. We're talking the security of the top official of the state of Minnesota.... For people to indicate or seem to feel that we're paying too much to protect the governor, how much is a life worth?" he asks, raising his voice to make the point.

Despite that impassioned plea, the emergency-spending bill is voted down, seventy-four to forty-nine, by a bipartisan coalition of Democrats and Republicans.

Coincidentally, the same day lawmakers debate the governor's security, Ventura takes delivery of his new official vehicle. It's a red Lincoln Navigator. Not exactly a low-profile vehicle for security reasons, but the price is right. The governor's office says the lease on the luxury sport utility vehicle will cost $643, two dollars less per month than the Lincoln Town Car favored by the previous governor. It's another example of Ventura's effort to reduce the size and cost of government.

Light-rail also sparks debate. In his State of the State address the governor said he wants to "ride a train by 2002." In April, he starts laying some political tracks to make that happen. On April 8 he boards a Metro Transit bus during the morning and afternoon rush hours with several lawmakers, transit officials, and the omnipresent media. The "Ventura Express," as a sign reads on the bus, is aimed at illustrating the need for light-rail and other mass-transit initiatives by taking a bumper-to-bumper ride in traffic.

"We're bumper-to-bumper, stop and start, stop and start," Ventura says as the bus makes it way from his suburban home of Maple Grove to the State Capitol in St. Paul during morning rush hour. The thirty-mile trip takes about one hour, only about fifteen minutes longer than non-rush hour, but the governor says that even in these ideal conditions the traffic is slow and will only get worse in the future.

Despite the publicity stunt, a couple of hours later a House committee votes down the governor's $60 million funding request. "We have problems, but I don't think that's the solution to all the problems," says Representative Carol Molnau, the Republican chairperson of the transportation finance committee. The $60 million in state money is key to getting the federal government to kick in another $250 million. That money will go toward the initial light-rail line that would run from downtown Minneapolis to the Minneapolis–St. Paul International Airport to the Mall of America. The total cost to build the 11.5-mile line is estimated at $446 million.

A few days later the governor's light-rail battle gets back on track in the Senate Transportation Committee, which votes to approve the same $60 million turned down by a House committee. "That's a small contribution when you consider you get $250 million in federal dollars, which will be lost forever if we don't come up with our local share now," says Democratic senator Carol Flynn, the committee chairperson.

The money isn't approved without some vocal dissent. "I call it the half-billion-dollar train to nowhere," says Republican senator Dick Day of Owatonna. "I don't think we've even proved people will get out of cars to ride a bus, let alone a train that will take just as long."

While that vote is taking place at the State Capitol in St. Paul, Governor Ventura is going toe-to-toe with some light-rail opponents at a luncheon across the river in downtown Minneapolis. He's addressing a luncheon organized by a local chapter of the Cato Institute, a public-policy research foundation based in Washington, D.C., that favors a limited role of government in people's lives. Everything is fine as long as Ventura sticks to that notion in his speech. "I feel strongly that government should only do what you can't do yourself," he says. "It's a simple premise."

He's on safe ground until he moves directly from that premise to talking about light-rail transit. "That's why I get a lot of negative on my transportation package. People think it's a waste of money. But think about it. Doesn't transportation fit the role of government?" That sets off a volley from a group of hecklers.

"No! No! No! No!" they yell.

"No?" Ventura responds. "These highways you drive on, who built them, you? Let me finish while you yell your nos. I see ... libertarian, aren't you?" he asks as he recognizes some of his hecklers.

"That's right," one yells back.

The banter between Ventura and the hecklers derails the remainder of the speech. "We'll get you next time, Jesse!" one heckler yells. "You'll what?" he responds.

"We'll come around next time. Beat you next time. You sound like a bureaucrat. A government bureaucrat."

"No, I sound like a realist. I live in the real world," Ventura says. "I'm not a libertarian, I go out and earn money!" Now he's getting booed and hissed by the small band of hecklers. He's back in his element. Jesse "the Mind" might be governor, but Jesse "the Body" still likes to come out and play.

Action Figures Approved

While Ventura pushes his legislative agenda, Ventura for Minnesota, Inc., is quietly going about its final marketing plans for the Jesse Ventura action figures. VMI is awaiting a ruling from the Minnesota Campaign Finance and Public Disclosure Board about how it must handle the money earned through the sale of the figures and other Ventura merchandise.

VMI has requested an opinion from the board that would allow the nonprofit corporation to market action figures, T-shirts, and hats without the same financial reporting requirements that cover campaign committees. Ventura established VMI as a way to protect the rights to his image and likeness while he serves in public office, but he doesn't want VMI to be considered a campaign committee.

The campaign-finance board is leaning toward ruling in VMI's favor, although it's not an easy issue to resolve. "We have the competing interests of the right of the individual to market himself and to protect his image and likeness along with the rights of the public to know what's going on with campaign finance," says Gary Goldsmith, the board's assistant executive director.

In a memorandum to the campaign-finance board David Bradley Olsen, Ventura's private attorney and a board member of VMI, makes the case that VMI is not a political committee. "Jesse Ventura is not currently a candidate for any election, and it is unlikely that he will be for well in excess of three years," Olsen writes. "VMI does not, therefore, exist to influence his nomination or election." Olsen says the sole purpose of VMI is to protect the governor's image and raise money for charity through the sale of licensed products.

The attempt by VMI to avoid the scrutiny of the campaign-finance board is vigorously opposed by the public-interest group Common Cause Minnesota. "Specifically, we believe that permitting VMI to operate and sell Jesse Ventura merchandise may violate several Minnesota and federal laws and serve as a means to circumvent existing campaign-finance laws," Common Cause president David Schultz writes to the campaign-finance board. Schultz argues that every sale of a Jesse Ventura action figure is the same as a contribution to his campaign and should be reported.

By April, the campaign-finance board is poised to rule in VMI's favor. In a working draft of an advisory opinion on the matter, the board concludes that VMI is not a political committee and therefore not required to register with or report its financial activities to the board.

Steven Schier, a political-science professor at Carleton College in Northfield, Minnesota, and KSTP-TV political analyst, sees the proposed ruling as a troubling precedent. "Should it be the case that a celebrity, because of a prior career as a celebrity, gets a political advantage of this sort that other equally capable public servants don't? I think that's a serious question that deserves some consideration."

A few weeks later the campaign-finance board approves VMI's marketing plan for the action figures and other merchandise after clearing up one minor problem: the boxes for seventy thousand action figures include artwork showing a campaign button that reads "Jesse Ventura for Governor." The board says such packaging would constitute campaign activity. After VMI promises to eliminate the design from all future packaging, Jesse "the Governor," Jesse "the Navy SEAL" and Jesse "the Football Coach" action figures will soon be on their way to store shelves. Once again, Governor Ventura is on his way to breaking new ground in the American political system.

With an aide blowing what sounds like a train whistle, Republican House Majority Leader Tim Pawlenty chugs into Governor Ventura's office on April 15, hoping to get him onboard the Republican "Tax Cut Train." Ventura isn't in, so his communications director, John Wodele, is the only one meeting the train.

"We have a ticket for the governor to get aboard the 'Tax Cut Train,'" Pawlenty tells Wodele as he hands him a mock train ticket with the governor's name on it. "And we have a conductor's cap because we really do want him to lead this train. We want tax cuts across the state, and we want him to get in front, take the throttle, and lead us to the promised land."

Just two nights earlier the House passed on a vote of 129 to 1 the largest tax-cut bill in state history, a $3.3 billion package of tax cuts and rebates. It includes $1.7 billion's worth of income-tax cuts and a $1.3 billion sales-tax rebate. Wodele accepts the train ticket and conductor's cap without any promises from the governor. Despite his vow to give back all surplus money and reduce the burden on overtaxed Minnesotans, Governor Ventura is reluctant to endorse the House plan.

The governor is pleased House Republicans have finally embraced his sales-tax rebate proposal, but he's concerned the income-tax cuts are too deep, too fast.

The governor's reluctance to embrace the Republican plan for tax cuts and rebates results in a not-so-friendly visit from thousands of protesting taxpayers. They've come to the State Capitol on a Saturday to demand tax rebates and tax cuts, accusing the governor and Senate Democrats of reneging on campaign promises. One year ago Ventura stood on the same steps with a similar group, demanding a return of the huge budget surplus.

"All through the campaign I listened to Jesse Ventura say, 'I stood on the steps of the capitol and said give it all back,'" says state Senator Gen Olson, who ran as Norm Coleman's Republican running mate in the governor's race. Now she's got a chance to throw it back in Ventura's face. "Jesse, where are you? Where are you?" That sparks an angry chant from the crowd of, "Where is Jesse? Where is Jesse?"

Signs vilifying the governor dot the crowd, many of them with Ventura's picture on them. Some say, "Give Back the Money," "He Promised Smaller Government," "Jesse 'the Weasel'" and "Jesse 'the Liar.'"

Bill Cooper, the state Republican Party chair, fires up the partisan crowd with his own shots at Ventura. "I don't know where Jesse is either," Cooper shouts into a microphone. "I remember what he used to say in all those debates: 'Give it all back! Cut the taxes! Less government!' I don't know where he is now!" Later, more anti-Ventura chants. "Jesse lied! Jesse lied! Jesse lied!"

At a suburban chamber of commerce event a couple of days later, Ventura fires back at the Republicans. "I want to kill this thing that somehow I'm the one responsible for us not getting our rebate," the governor says in an off-the-cuff speech. "Ladies and gentlemen, I submitted my budget two-and-a-half weeks ahead of time at the end of January. It was not due until the middle of February. My budget clearly has every dollar of surplus going back to you in a sales-tax rebate. I cannot give it back until a bill hits my desk. Who's responsible for the rebate not getting to you? The legislature. I can't give it to you until they give me a bill to sign. What they're doing is, they're playing politics. They're playing poker. They won't give back the rebate until they get their tax cuts."

Columbine Controversy

In late April Ventura is on another one of his field trips to learn as much as he can about state government. He's touring the St. Cloud correctional facility, one of Minnesota's maximum-security prisons. It's a gray and foreboding place built in the late 1800s. The thick walls rimmed with razor wire give it the look of a classic prison setting you'd expect to see in an old black-and-white gangster movie.

"I've always driven by those big granite walls along Highway 10 and wondered what it's like on the inside," Ventura tells reporters as he watches prisoners making Minnesota license plates. Sheryl Ramstad Hvass, the commissioner of corrections, later gives him a personalized license plate that reads "The Gov." She also informs him he's the first governor in the 110-year history of this prison to step foot inside the walls. He's about to spark a historic controversy during his historic visit.

Ventura's prison visit is his first public appearance since the Columbine High School massacre the day before that left fifteen people dead and two dozen injured. The shooting rampage by two Columbine students stuns the nation and forces school and government officials around the country to examine their own school security issues.

It's against this backdrop that Governor Ventura is asked about the Columbine incident by reporters while touring the prison. His responses draw some of the most heated criticism he's faced yet and prompt another remarkable public apology. What follows is a word-for-word account of what he said about Columbine and his views on school security and gun control.

"Governor, have some thoughts about school safety crossed your mind since you saw what happened in Colorado yesterday?" asks Kerri Miller of KARE-TV. "What happened there words can't describe, but we still can't make our schools fortresses," Ventura responds. "We still,

I don't believe, cannot declare martial law and have troops in schools. I don't think that's the right thing to do also. If we got to that level, then 'they' win."

Mary Lahammer, a reporter for KTCA-TV, then asks, "But what would be a good role for the state to play in the safety of schools?" Again, Ventura doesn't hesitate to answer.

"A good role for the state to play? Well, now all of a sudden everyone's looking to the state and all I hear is 'local decision-making.' I mean, in the case of schools, you hear a very strong 'We want local control of our schools.' And now, in light of this, is that going to switch it? That we want state operation of schools? I don't think so. I think it'll still come down to local control."

Now it's my turn to follow up, and this is where the governor ends up in trouble. "The Colorado legislature postponed a debate today they were supposed to have on concealed-weapons legislation in light of what happened. After what happened in Colorado, does any of that change your view about the concealed-weapons issue?"

"Not a bit," Ventura quickly responds, "because imagine if someone with a legal concealed weapon happened to have been there. Maybe lives would have been saved. Think about it from that aspect too. These are not legally obtained weapons. And you don't penalize the law-abiding citizen for the act of the criminal or the non-law-abiding citizen. Let's remember that very often, if you were to have someone with a legitimate conceal-and-carry weapon, you can stop crimes like this from happening."

Kerri Miller follows up with, "You mean like one of the teachers?" Ventura almost goes there but then responds, "Well, if there happened to be a … I don't know. I'm not going to make a hypothetical on it. But in the case where crazed gunmen go crazy, when everyone's unarmed, how do you fight him? How do you defend yourself against someone who is armed? You can't very well."

"So it sounds like, if anything, this kind of reinforces your opinion about the concealed weapons," I say to the governor.

"I just feel—again, I'm not going to get into that debate," Ventura says. "And it's really a nonissue because there's not a bill for it. It was a nonissue in the end during the election. It's a media issue and generally raised by the media and all of that. But certainly I still support law-abiding citizens having the right to bear arms. There's a difference between law-abiding and not law-abiding. I oppose vehemently unlawful people from having them, but I certainly support the right for law-abiding citizens to be able to protect themselves. This [Columbine], I think, may be a classic example, again showing that no matter how much police protection we have, and no matter how much protection we try to provide as government, we can't be there all the time. And there are situations where the government can't protect you, and I think this may be an example of it in some ways."

By reading Ventura's words carefully, at no point will you find him advocating the arming of teachers, staff members, or students. After covering Ventura for so long and knowing his stance on the concealed-weapons issue, I found his comments so unremarkable that I made only a brief mention of them in my story on the six o'clock news.

However, an article in the next day's *Star Tribune* is headlined this way: "Ventura sees case for easing gun laws; legislators, educators voiced concern after governor said concealed-carry laws could have spared lives."

The story makes it clear Ventura isn't advocating more guns in schools. "Ventura said he wasn't advocating arming teachers or anyone else in schools," the article says. "At one point, though, he suggested that 'a highly qualified Navy SEAL' with a handgun permit—a description that applies to the governor—could have stopped the carnage in Colorado." The Navy SEAL comment was made in a separate interview with the newspaper after Ventura's remarks at the St. Cloud prison.

The *Star Tribune* article goes on to say, "In Minnesota, legislators, educators and police officials expressed shock and disapproval over Ventura's comments." The quote that follows that statement is the epitome of the overreaction to the governor's comments. "Arming everyone in the schools would make the OK Corral look like a picnic," Representative Matt Entenza, a St. Paul Democrat who opposes conceal-and-carry gun legislation, tells the paper. It's a great quote, but has nothing to do with what Ventura actually said.

The drumbeat continues on Twin Cities talk-radio shows on which Ventura is harshly criticized all day, mostly based on what has appeared in the morning papers. You'd think the governor has authorized the issuance of handguns to every schoolteacher in Minnesota. Phone calls pour into the governor's office, and even some of his closest advisers tell Ventura he needs to apologize for his remarks.

This story takes on a life of its own amid the hysteria of the tragedy at Columbine. The governor has a light afternoon schedule on April 22, the day after his Columbine comments. The only things on his public schedule are a short visit with Miss Minnesota and a photo op to promote "Take Your Child to Work Day." He soon has to squeeze in a third appearance to respond to the criticism he's taking about Columbine.

John Wodele steps into the governor's reception room to address the media first, saying the governor will be out shortly. He won't say if the governor plans to apologize. "You can characterize it however you want to characterize it once the governor makes his statement," Wodele says. He won't say if the governor's statement is prompted by the talk-radio criticism or phone calls he's receiving. "It is a statement born out of our concern and isn't driven by anything else," he says.

Minutes later Ventura steps out of his office to deliver a statement and says he will not take any questions. "Yesterday, in response to questions over the senseless loss of the lives of innocent children, I regret that I responded to questions concerning conceal-and-carry issues in relationship to the tragic situation in Littleton, Colorado. I said that perhaps lives could have been saved if only someone in that school would have been carrying a concealed weapon. I believe that, except for uniformed police officers, a school is no place for weapons and that carrying of concealed weapons in schools is not the answer to this terrible problem. And I regret mixing this incident with the conceal-and-carry issue."

The "apology" does little to stem the tide of criticism. Three days later Doug Grow, a *Star Tribune* columnist, writes a column headlined "Jesse (the Mouth) needs that foot extractor again." Grow, no fan of Ventura to begin with, writes, "Ventura needed less than 24 hours to apologize for a dunderheaded remark he made after the nightmarish school killings in Littleton, Colo. Can any Minnesotan forget Wednesday's comment from our leader? 'To me it justifies conceal and carry more.... It should open people's eyes.... We have the right to protect ourselves from attacks such as this. If we can't protect our schools, how can we protect our citizens on the street?'"

If you read that quote, it really doesn't sound all that shocking. It's the same argument conceal-and-carry proponents have been using forever, except this time it's attached to a specific situation as opposed to a hypothetical situation. Nevertheless, Grow writes, "the Littleton-related comment was, by far, Ventura's most foolish public utterance since becoming governor. But it wasn't the first time the Mouth has roared without engaging the Brain.... How many dumb things can one governor say before he blows up his own credibility?"

This seems to be another example of the Governor Ventura lightning-rod effect. Nearly any public utterance the governor makes on any issue with the slightest potential for controversy will attract attention all out of proportion to what it actually deserves. Consider, for example, what was being said in Colorado by a prominent lawmaker on the same day Ventura made his comments in Minnesota.

In the wake of the Columbine shootings, Colorado's Republican House Majority Leader Doug Dean is asked about the future of a bill he's authored that would allow more law-abiding adults to carry concealed weapons. "I would feel safer knowing that there was a teacher at my kid's school who was a concealed-weapons-permit holder who could intervene in a situation like this," Dean tells the *Denver Post*.

A powerful Colorado lawmaker makes a statement that goes well beyond anything Governor Ventura said in Minnesota. And he says it right in Columbine's backyard! Opponents of Dean's position criticize him and offer their own opposing viewpoints in news coverage of his remarks, but there isn't the outrage or demands for a public apology faced by Ventura. Governor Ventura doesn't go nearly as far as Dean in his comments, but Ventura is clearly held to a different standard in Minnesota, mostly by people who didn't bother to read precisely what he said.

CHAPTER 6

"A Trick and Ten Dollars"
Jesse's Book Tells All

With just twelve days to go in the 1999 legislative session, Jesse Ventura invites the House and Senate leaders to the governor's mansion to break the stalemate over their competing tax bills. Ventura, House Speaker Steve Sviggum, and Senate Majority Leader Roger Moe have virtually nothing in common. Ventura is a forty-seven-year-old ex-professional wrestler from Minneapolis with no prior state-government experience. The Republican Sviggum is a forty-seven-year-old farmer from Kenyon in southeastern Minnesota serving his twelfth term in the House and first as House Speaker. Moe has seen eight House Speakers and three governors come and go since he first became DFL Senate majority leader in 1981. A fifty-four-year-old former teacher from Erskine in northwestern Minnesota, Moe has been in the legislature since 1970 and has served as Senate majority leader longer than anyone in state history.

In an attempt to broker a deal with his two more experienced counterparts, Ventura invites them over for an informal meeting. The House won't budge from its $3.3 billion tax cut and rebate bill and the Senate is sticking to a $2.5 billion tax package. A conference committee (which Ventura intensely dislikes) isn't making any progress on a compromise. So he calls the leaders together for some closed-door meetings (which he also dislikes, or at least claimed to during the campaign). For now, Ventura's willing to play the game their way.

Moe, Sviggum, and a few other lawmakers arrive at the governor's Summit Avenue mansion in a pouring rain. It's only fitting, since the state is floating in surplus revenue for the umpteenth year in a row. So far the only thing they agree on is a $1.3 billion sales-tax rebate.

However, serious differences remain on the level of income-tax cuts and spending on education. After the mansion summit, the only progress to report is that both sides are still talking and Ventura is still refereeing. "Everyone has a position they'd like to keep, but it's not all 'My way or the highway' on anything," Sviggum says, standing on the steps of the mansion, where the rain has given way to partial sunshine.

As the budget negotiations drag on, a confluence of events on May 6, 1999, will always stand out in my mind as the perfect illustration of how little Governor Ventura understands the media in general, and the news media in particular.

It's just before 10:00 A.M. and people are lined up outside a Mall of America gift store, where the first Jesse Ventura action figures are about to go on sale. A trio of Ventura look-alikes inside the store will help with promotion. When the metal gate is finally lifted, customers pour into the store to snatch up the action figures. They're selling for $19.95 apiece, and some people are walking to the sales counter with armfuls of boxes, forking over more than $100 at a time. The "Navy SEAL" and "Volunteer Football Coach" figures quickly become the hottest sellers, with the "Governor" figure being all but ignored. There must be something about an action figure in a business suit that doesn't seem quite right.

More than thirty-two thousand action figures went on sale in Minnesota. Another thirty-eight thousand are on order and will be shipped from the manufacturing plant in China. "We're seeing unbelievable demand," says Pady Regnier of St. Croix Marketing Group, the wholesale distributor of the first thirty-two thousand action figures. She's already nearly sold out the entire first shipment to retail stores, including her own Mall of America gift shops.

Watching this spectacle unfold in America's shopping mecca is Bill Hillsman, the political advertising whiz who dreamed up the Ventura action figure during the campaign. "I am surprised by it," says Hillsman, both about the sales he's witnessing and the whole Ventura phenomenon. "I figured this would be kind of a blip on the radar screen, and the press and the country would pay attention to it for a month or so and then they'd move on. But I guess the idea of Jesse as a personality, and the fact that he's the only third-party governor in America, continues to make news and astound people."

As Hillsman watches sale after sale ring through the cash registers, he reflects on what's transpired from election night to today. "I don't think any of us had an idea this would happen. I don't know how many people really thought that Jesse was going to win, even on election night. But it's been phenomenal."

At the same time the Ventura action figures are disappearing from store shelves on May 6, the governor himself is involved in a considerably more important endeavor. He's assembled a group of state leaders from the late 1970s and early 1980s at the Minnesota History Center in St. Paul to discuss the lessons learned from the state's economic crisis back then.

In 1979, the state cut taxes by more than $1 billion while increasing spending nearly 15 percent. The national economy then went into a long recession and Minnesota started running up budget deficits, resulting in a series of tax increases. The point of this meeting, as envisioned by Ventura, is to get state leaders from yesterday and today in the same room to discuss ways to avoid repeating those mistakes. The event is billed "Learning from History: Lessons from Minnesota Leaders 1980–1981."

In addition to House Speaker Sviggum and Senate Majority Leader Moe, Ventura has invited former Republican governor Al Quie, who served from 1978 to 1982, and several lawmakers and administration officials from that era. Obviously, Ventura has a motive for this event. He's trying to convince skeptics his cautious approach to tax cuts is the right approach. He figures if anyone can illustrate that point it's Quie, who cut taxes early in his administration and then was forced to raise taxes.

Governor Ventura clearly considers his economic-history summit to be the most newsworthy event of the day on May 6. He promoted it heavily to make sure it got maximum media coverage. The problem is he just can't stop making news today. First it's the action figures, then the history lesson, and then a bizarre announcement by Ventura on a talk-radio show a couple of hours later.

Ventura is appearing on Joe Soucheray's afternoon talk-radio show on KSTP-AM. The appearance wasn't included on the governor's original public schedule for the day, but it turns out to be the appearance that makes the biggest news splash. Soucheray, a columnist for the *St. Paul Pioneer Press*, is a frequent and funny critic of Governor Ventura, both in print and on the air.

Soucheray is busy giving Ventura a hard time about his support for light-rail transit. He tells the governor it's just another step toward bigger government and more spending. Somehow out of this discussion about the size of government Ventura decides to drop his bombshell. "June 1 we're cutting government," he says. "The First Lady's retiring. But then again, she don't get paid, so there's really no expenditure cut there. She's retiring."

"Is that an official announcement?" a surprised Soucheray asks. "You're breaking that news here on KSTP. June 1?"

"Yep," Ventura responds.

"So Mrs. Ventura, the First Lady, will no longer be making public appearances then?"

"Yep. Pretty close to that," the governor says. "She's going back to her business."

This announcement is not only broadcast on KSTP's fifty-thousand-watt radio airwaves, it's also being covered by most of the Twin Cities print and broadcast outlets. Within minutes, news of Terry Ventura's "retirement" is on the Associated Press news wire. Less than an hour later, spokesperson John Wodele informs the media that Governor Ventura will soon make a statement in the governor's reception room.

When reporters show up, Wodele hands out a three-paragraph

statement that reads, in part: "On KSTP-AM today Governor Ventura referred to the First Lady's desire to maintain a less rigorous schedule. The Governor's statement was not meant to infer that the First Lady will no longer maintain a public schedule or make personal appearances on behalf of the Governor and the State of Minnesota.... Terry Ventura will in fact maintain her role as First Lady."

The statement is ammunition for a whole new series of questions from reporters, including Rochelle Olson, a State Capitol correspondent for the Associated Press. "So, John, is this a prank?" a clearly annoyed Olson asks. "Is he just having fun? I mean, because there's a story on the wire right now, and I have to explain why the story is no longer accurate."

Wodele chooses his words carefully. "The context in which the governor spoke these words was talk radio, Joe Soucheray. The expression of the First Lady retiring was probably just a tad exaggerated, as often happens on talk radio. It's entertainment, as the governor says. Talk radio is not hard news. What you're reading right now in that statement is hard news."

Wodele's explanation isn't a big hit with the capitol press corps. "Does that mean he misspoke?" a reporter asks. "Is he engaging in hyperbole or sarcasm?" Wodele says he won't speculate about that. In frustration another reporter blurts out, "Will the governor ever take responsibility for what he says?" Wodele doesn't answer.

A few minutes later the governor emerges from his office and steps up to the podium in the reception room. "I brought you all here to make an important announcement," he says, as we all wonder what the hell is coming next. "With eleven days left in the legislative session it's my privilege to sign into law House File 132, Senate File 1138." He's referring to a relatively inconsequential piece of legislation regarding bingo in nursing homes.

The governor continues his sarcastic setup for a not-so-subtle jab at the legislature. "With urgent budget issues before the state, including the future of public-education funding ... the future tobacco endowments, the size of permanent tax cuts, providing a sales-tax rebate to Minnesota citizens and all the other programs that Minnesotans depend upon, the legislature sent me this important legislation to allow senior citizens to play bingo in nursing homes without state regulations.... It is my hope that with this burdensome issue behind them, they can now address other issues that are equally important."

No one knows quite how to respond, because most of us were expecting some kind of clarification about his wife's situation. So that's what we ask him about. "The simple matter is that, due to health concerns, she will fulfill a schedule through June 1, but then she's going back to her private business for at least the length of the summer," Ventura says, referring to his wife's horse-breeding business at their Maple Grove ranch.

Terry Ventura is recovering from a bout with what is believed to be Epstein-Barr syndrome, which zapped her of energy. She came out on the front porch of the governor's mansion a day earlier while reporters were waiting for the budget meeting to conclude, and she said she was feeling much better. She even jokingly flexed her bicep muscles to show how much stronger she's getting. But the governor says she'll devote most of her time to her horse business over the summer, probably until about October 1. After that, he says, "she will be very, very selective about what she does."

When television newscasts hit the air that evening, the stories getting the biggest play about Ventura are about his wife's "retirement" and the sale of his action figures. He doesn't understand why the "Learning from History" budget story ends up as just a brief mention in most newscasts.

The governor later complains to me about the media's handling of the news that day. "I can't control what you deem is newsworthy," he says. "You are out for ratings points, be honest.... You're going to choose what you think is going to give you the best hoorah on getting the most people to watch your news show that night. And so, if the Jesse Ventura action figure is more important than legislative things here in a news hoorah, you make that decision. That's out of my hands. I can't control that." (And I can't control the use of the word "hoorah.")

Actually, he doesn't understand that to a certain extent he *is* in control. If he had simply focused on the budget history event that day, which he clearly hoped would be the focus of the media, it would have been the primary story coming out of the State Capitol. Instead, he trumps the story he wanted to see on the air by putting action figures on sale, announcing his wife's retirement on talk radio and calling a news conference shortly before news time to make fun of bingo legislation. He's a reporter's dream, and his own worst nightmare.

Backroom Deals

Ventura waged his campaign for governor with harsh criticism about conference committees and "backroom deals," where legislation is finalized without public input. Now he's got a front-row seat to the politics-as-usual he's derided for so long. Eventually, his seat will end up smack in the middle of some of those backroom meetings.

On May 7, with the session deadline looming just days away, the House-Senate Tax Conference Committee meets for about four hours without coming close to reconciling significant differences in their two tax bills. So that sends House Speaker Sviggum and Senate Majority Leader Moe behind closed doors with other lawmakers to try to work out major differences about income-tax cuts and education spending, and about how to spend the first installment of a $6 billion state tobacco-lawsuit settlement. The two sides meet in a State Capitol conference room with the governor's representative in the talks, Pam Wheelock, the commissioner of finance. Various aides to all three sides are also in the meetings, sleeves rolled up and crunching numbers.

They work late into that Friday evening without reaching an agreement. Moe walks out of the room, his once crisp, starched shirt now wrinkled and no longer tucked into his pants. "I can't give you anything," a frustrated Moe tells reporters asking for details of where negotiations stand. "All you have to do is dig out all your old notes and clips, because that's what it is."

Sviggum is slightly more optimistic. "It was a very good give-and-take," he says. "You get down to the last issues and it gets tougher. . . .

I think it maybe got tense a couple times where people wanted to get up and walk out." The backroom dealing will continue over the weekend, and this time there will be a surprising participant: Governor Ventura.

On Saturday, several more hours of talks fail to produce an agreement. The key participants are now Ventura, Sviggum, and Moe, sometimes meeting face-to-face. At other times, emissaries from all three sides shuttle back and forth across Constitution Avenue between the State Office Building and the State Capitol with proposals and counterproposals. By Sunday, with still no agreement in sight, Governor Ventura makes a move to break the stalemate. It's Mother's Day, but he is in his office again and notifies the media he'll be making an announcement in the governor's reception room at noon.

At the appointed hour he steps out of his office in a leather bomber jacket and Navy SEAL cap with bright red sunglasses hanging around his neck. He tells reporters and a few legislators attending the news conference it's absolutely essential to reach a budget agreement by Monday so the session can conclude by the deadline of May 17.

To accomplish that, Ventura is prepared to make a major concession. Just as he did with the sales-tax rebate last month, the governor modifies his position on income-tax cuts sought by House Republicans. Ventura says House leaders are coming closer to his position on funding light-rail transit and investing tobacco-lawsuit settlement money in endowments for health care and low-income Minnesota families. So he's ready to compromise. He agrees to expand an income-tax cut to the highest tax bracket as long as the bulk of the tax relief still targets middle-income taxpayers. If the Senate agrees to go along, Ventura says, "we can close the deal and finish the session on time."

This is critical, because it's the first time Ventura agrees to across-the-board income-tax cuts.

Why the sudden change of heart? "I just feel strong enough that an across-the-board equal tax cut in all three tiers is not going to make or break what I consider to be a very sound budget, a terrific budget. And I'm hoping this will break the logjam loose."

Ventura says he's not bluffing about shutting government down at the end of the fiscal year if a budget agreement isn't reached during the regular legislative session. "There's virtually no excuse ... to force us to call a special session. I'm not going to do it." The problem is, his concession to House Republicans complicates his dealings with the Senate. Ventura gave in on the across-the-board tax cuts in exchange for House support on $60 million in light-rail transit funding.

Senate Majority Leader Moe and Senate Democrats are already in line on the light-rail funding, but Moe remains strongly opposed to what he considers a tax cut for the rich. "I just hope the governor and Republicans haven't cut and run on middle-income taxpayers just so they can give tax relief on that upper bracket," Moe tells reporters after we track him down in a hallway outside the Senate chambers.

After making what seemed like two steps forward over the weekend, the negotiations take a step back on Monday. Moe and Sviggum meet behind closed doors again to work out their differences based on the tax-cut offer Ventura made on Sunday. The meeting ends abruptly—and badly. "We just met with the majority leader, and, frankly, it didn't go very well," Sviggum tells reporters waiting in a capitol corridor. Moe is clearly frustrated. "This is a lot different than I've ever seen in the past," he says. "It's going to be a mad crunch at the end, and that's unfortunate." The only way Moe says the Senate will go along with the tax cuts is if Ventura and the House pony up more money for education.

How does the governor respond? He says he's ordered his commissioners and other administration officials to begin preparing contingency plans for a government shutdown.

Ventura summons Moe and Sviggum to his office for another closed-door meeting, but they break it up after only twenty minutes with no progress. Ventura says an extra $100 million the Senate wants for education shouldn't be a deal-breaker. He just can't understand why that request is surfacing now. He calls it the "business-as-usual, typical bipartisan party politics" that has always frustrated Minnesotans.

On Tuesday, Ventura takes the offensive during a live interview on Minnesota Public Radio. The emphasis here is on the word "offensive." He again offers to throw open the doors of the governor's mansion for

Moe and Sviggum to work out their differences, but now he's threatening to lock them in a room with his flatulent bulldog, Franklin. "I think if I put 'em in the library with Franklin, and if I feed him a little bit of hamburger, I gotta feeling we'll get a deal in about a half an hour," he says with a snicker.

While lawmakers keep trying to iron out an agreement, Ventura spends part of his day dealing with a rumor he might make a return to the wrestling ring. He's not totally dismissing the rumor. Several wrestling Web sites are abuzz with word that wrestling promoters are offering him $1 million for a one-time, pay-per-view match.

Verne Gagne, one of Ventura's former wrestling promoters, says he's heard the rumors about a Ventura comeback, including one about an offer from Japan. The now-retired Gagne says it could be a blockbuster event. "If he gets the chance to wrestle again and he does it, I mean, I wouldn't mind promoting it myself."

For now, Ventura is content trying to promote a tax deal. An accord is finally reached May 11, less than a week before the deadline for the session to end. After a two-hour meeting, House and Senate leaders agree to a tax-and-spending deal with the Ventura administration. Senate Democrats get the extra $100 million for education spending, House Republicans get across-the-board income-tax cuts, and Governor Ventura gets the $60 million he wants for light-rail transit funding. Every Minnesotan gets a sales-tax rebate.

Minnesota's unique political system achieves a historic accord. "This is a good day for the people of Minnesota," Ventura says at a news conference with legislative leaders in the governor's reception room. "Tripartisan government works. We can look forward to the largest tax cut in Minnesota history."

The deal provides a tax cut that focuses mostly on the middle class and maintains a balanced budget for four years. In addition to the rebates and tax cuts, nearly $1 billion of tobacco-settlement money will be used for family and health-care endowments.

Ventura managed to broker a historic budget deal near the end of his first legislative session. He didn't do it in some remarkable new way that he seemed to promise during his campaign. Instead, he used the backroom deals and the other politics-as-usual tools to his advantage. He's not letting that ironic twist stand in the way of celebrating his achievement.

"Skivvy Check!"

For the next two days Ventura has a light schedule of public appearances so he can be available to focus on his legislative agenda in the closing days of the session. As always, another major controversy erupts to add another dose of chaos to the usually mundane legislative proceedings. This time it's the release of his autobiography, *I Ain't Got Time to Bleed: Reworking the Body Politic from the Bottom Up.*

The book isn't expected on store shelves until June, but it's already for sale on Amazon.com and Barnes and Noble's Web site. The book's publisher, Villard Books, releases copies to the media on May 12. On May 13, the *Star Tribune* publishes excerpts from the book detailing the governor's revelations about losing his virginity at age sixteen, using drugs, cavorting with a prostitute in a Nevada brothel, drinking heavily as a teenager, and using steroids as a wrestler. He also reveals that he still honors a longtime Navy SEAL tradition of not wearing underwear.

"The day I was sworn in as governor, there was some concern that someone might yell for a skivvy check in the middle of my inaugural speech," he writes in the book. Much of the 208-page book, titled after his famous movie line from *Predator,* outlines his basic political philosophy, covers how he got elected, and recounts amusing stories about his military, wrestling, and Hollywood careers. It's not your typical, ho-hum autobiography by a politician, and it doesn't get a typical, ho-hum reaction.

In fact, the book is denounced on the floor of the Senate. "In today's news there is extensive coverage of Governor Ventura's soon-to-be-released book," Senator Jane Ranum of Minneapolis says to her colleagues. "To my governor and fellow baby-boomer parent, I say, Governor, your bragging is sending very mixed messages to the young people of this state about alcohol and how men should treat women.

On the one hand, you are bragging about your alcohol abuse and sexual exploitation of women. But, on the other hand, you're saying that behavior would not be good enough for your kids. You said, 'If my kids behaved the way I did, there'd be a lot more gray hair on my head.' Governor, the young people of this state are looking to you as their role model. Don't let them down. As you tour this state and country to promote your book, don't send mixed messages. Don't let them down." She gets a round of applause from her fellow senators.

Ventura isn't making any public appearances the day the excerpts are published and he's declining requests for interviews about the book. In his only public comments about the book in a previously scheduled telephone interview with WCCO Radio, he says he's not surprised by the criticism. "Oh, it'll be controversial because I told the truth," he says. "I was just a typical south-side kid in that era of time, doing what all the kids in south Minneapolis did."

The governor's office is taking so many calls about the book his communications staff is forced to send out two separate media advisories. "The autobiographical book, *I Ain't Got Time to Bleed*, by Governor Ventura is not a project of the Office of the Governor and is not available from any government source," the first advisory says. "The Governor will not be available to discuss the book unless an interview has been arranged through Villard Books." The advisory refers all questions about the book to the publisher in New York. The other advisory announces that the governor's office will not return any books or action figures sent for the governor's autograph, because they "are not official projects of the Office of Governor."

The governor's communications director, John Wodele, is clearly in uncharted territory in his battle to separate the "celebrity" governor from the "public servant" governor. Wodele comes to the press-corps offices in the basement of the capitol to respond to the growing number of questions about the book and its possible impact on the end of the legislative session.

"The governor is remaining focused on legislative issues and will remain focused on legislative issues until we get the job done," he says.

Wodele steadfastly assures reporters it wasn't the governor's idea to release the book in the middle of the last week of the session. "Our understanding was that the book would not be available until after the session. That was our desire. That was the understanding we had with the publisher. Unfortunately, it did not work out that way."

Don't be fooled. The book was released at the time of maximum possible exposure. It's true the governor's office had no control over the timing, but a source at Villard Books tells me there was no agreement to hold the book's release until after the session. The publisher paid Ventura as much as a $500,000 advance for the book. For that kind of money the publisher is going to release the book whenever it thinks it can cash in on the maximum publicity. What better time than at the peak of the legislative session, when Ventura is looking his gubernatorial best? The remarkable contrast between Ventura as "statesman" and Ventura as a "brothel-frolicking Navy SEAL" is too good to pass up.

Obviously, that's going to attract national publicity the publishing company simply can't buy. In fact, Senator Ranum's rant on the Senate floor is a dream-come-true for a book publicist. Her criticism alone probably sends thousands of people to bookstores or computer Web sites, looking for the book so they can find out what the hell she's so mad about.

After mostly hearing jeers at the capitol, it's nothing but cheers at a Minnesota Timberwolves play-off basketball game later that night. The public-address announcer at Target Center introduces Ventura to a loud standing ovation from play-off-frenzied fans. He walks out on the floor and rips off his sport coat to reveal a No. 21 Kevin Garnett jersey he's wearing. Someone hands him a microphone and he taunts the opposing team to the delight of the delirious crowd. "Hey! If I could beat the House and the Senate, we sure as heck can beat the Spurs tonight!"

Then he playfully grabs one of the game referees and says, "I'm the governor now, so don't get out of line with me!" The ref laughs and shakes Ventura's hand, knowing it's not the last he's heard from the governor tonight.

Ventura's mood sours at halftime when a television reporter from WCCO-TV approaches him and asks if he's a bad role model for kids. "So, telling the truth is a bad role model?" he responds angrily.

"Are there apologies for some of the behavior or how would you approach children?" the reporter asks.

"I don't have to apologize for my life!" Ventura says before waving her off and walking away.

Reaction among fans to the governor's book is generally favorable, both among young people and adults. Paul Safarz and Josh Fraser, two high-school students from Bloomington, are watching the Wolves game and enjoying Ventura's antics in lower-level seats not far from the court. They're not concerned about the governor's revelations.

"I think he wants to be truthful to the people that he governs," Fraser tells me. "You know, everybody makes mistakes, so I don't hold it against him or anything. I don't think a lot of people do either.... As long as he's changed now and he's not like that now, that's fine." For Safarz, honesty is the best policy. "He reveals a little too much, but if he's honest about it, that's good enough."

Adults in the crowd say pretty much the same. Pete Anderson of Shoreview says it's better for Ventura to reveal details of his past than to have reporters dig it up. "They'll eventually come out anyway so it's probably a good thing to do," Anderson says. "I'm sure we all have things in our past that aren't perfect." What about female fans? "At least he's being honest about it," says Anne Wolf of Northfield, a college town south of the Twin Cities. "I don't know if I applaud him for it, but I'd rather hear that than 'I didn't inhale.'" President Clinton already has the copyright on that one.

It should be pointed out Ventura didn't actually write his autobiography. In January and February he spent about two weeks making an audio recording of his life story and his thoughts on politics in America. A ghostwriter, Julie Ann Mooney, would essentially interview him from 7:00 to 10:00 each weeknight over that two-week period. Her job was to record Ventura and put his life story in words. She then went back to New York and would send him transcripts periodically to be checked for accuracy.

So how much of what's in the book did his wife, Terry, know about? "Everything that was in that book I knew before I married my husband," she says, adding with a laugh, "except that he was going to run for governor. That might have changed my mind!" She also says she read the book's manuscript before publication. "I knew that there would be people that would be very upset, but I also knew my husband. And I knew the context in which everything was written."

She says if the book doesn't bother her, it shouldn't bother others. "My husband's still a darn good governor. No matter what's in the book, he's a good governor. He believes in Minnesota. He cares about the people in this state, and he's an honest person who's doing a great job. So it doesn't really bother me at all."

Even when the governor tries to hang a "Gone Fishin'" sign on his office door, he can't escape questions about his book. On Friday, May 14, the governor flies to Grand Rapids, Minnesota, for the annual governor's fishing opener. Before taking off, Ventura calls a 10:00 A.M. news conference at Holman Field in St. Paul, where a state plane is waiting for him. The news conference was originally called to discuss a piece of pending seat-belt legislation he's threatening to veto. Inevitably, reporters are more interested in talking about his book.

Ventura comes prepared with a written statement. "It accurately and truthfully depicts my life and is written in a style that is characteristic of my personality as a young adult in the late '60s and early '70s," Ventura says, reading from the statement. "If anyone has a problem with that, they shouldn't buy the book." Ventura adamantly refuses to apologize. "My book is the truth. If it offends someone, I can't control that."

Just before ending the news conference, the governor offers a bizarre defense of the revelation about losing his virginity at age sixteen. "There's a reference in the book about the night I lost my virginity," Ventura tells reporters. "The girl was older than me and she wasn't a virgin. So, tell me, who got seduced? Think about it. The shoe can fit on both feet, can't it?"

As he takes off for Grand Rapids, Ventura is taking criticism from some of his usual critics. The Taxpayers League of Minnesota, which calls itself a nonpartisan, nonprofit organization (it's actually heavily funded by Republicans), calls on the governor to cancel an upcoming book tour. "The governor should cancel the book tour and save the people of Minnesota from further embarrassment," the group says in a news release. "We don't need Howard Stern and Jay Leno talking to our governor about prostitutes and his underwear in front of the rest of the country."

This is new territory for the Taxpayers League. It usually just bashes Ventura's fiscal policy. In fact, it does manage to find a negative, albeit far-fetched, fiscal impact from the book. "This state spends millions of dollars promoting a positive image, and our economy benefits from the rest of the country viewing us as a healthy, intelligent state. Ventura's book makes us look like we're just one big Jerry Springer audience."

Ventura's first stop on his fishing-opener weekend will be his first official public appearance since the book's release. It's at Grand Rapids High School, where he finds a friendly audience to strike back at his critics and the media.

The governor and his wife walk hand in hand into a packed gymnasium while the school band plays "Hail to the Chief." Five male students rip off their shirts to reveal their chests, where each of them has painted on a letter to spell J-E-S-S-E. Then they turn around to show their backs where they're supposed to spell R-U-L-E-S, but two of the guys are out of order so it spells R-U-E-L-S. It's a friendly audience, not a brilliant audience.

After giving the students advice on studying hard and following their dreams, Ventura takes a few shots at the media. "As governor I have to come here and deliver those real serious messages so my friends in the press can go home and say I'm doing my job." Turning the crowd against the media is now a standard gubernatorial practice. "You know, I don't particularly like the press," he says to an enthusiastic cheer. "I never liked them when I wrestled because all they did was criticize wrestling, the most popular thing on TV."

Then he plunges headlong into a defense of his book. "I wrote a book that has become very controversial, as everything I do does with the press. If I sneeze, it becomes controversial. If I stub my toe, it becomes controversial. But I did write a book. I gotta bunch of hypocrites down there [in St. Paul] asking me, should I apologize?"

That brings a chorus of "No! No! No!" from the students.

"Do you want me to tell you what you want to hear or do you want honesty?" he asks the students.

"Truth! Honesty!" they yell back.

"Honesty? Is that what you want?" he asks rhetorically to another huge cheer. "Well, with me that's what you're going to get. Honesty. And I don't apologize for anything. I'm certainly not perfect, but I stand tall and proud for everything I've done in my life, whether it be right, wrong, mistakes or not.... And when they question me, I tell them very clearly I won the young people because I didn't lie to them during the election. I told them the truth."

That brings one more thunderous round of applause as he walks off, promising, "We will catch fish tomorrow!"

Gone Fishin'

It's 4:00 A.M. on May 15, and Ventura and a few old high-school buddies are up getting their gear together for Minnesota's fishing opener. Ventura admits it's been twenty years since he's done any "serious" fishing. Now he's the host of the fifty-first-annual governor's fishing opener, and he knows this is serious business in Minnesota. A million people will be on the state's fifteen thousand lakes today for the traditional opener. The Minnesota Office of Tourism estimates nearly $1.5 billion is spent in the state each year on fishing equipment, along with lodging, food, transportation, and other expenses during fishing trips.

It's drizzling at Ruttger's Sugar Lake Lodge near Grand Rapids as Ventura and company pile into his Lincoln Navigator for the short drive to Pokegama Lake. It's still pitch-dark as they shove off onto the lake in a Crestliner boat with a 220-horsepower Mercury outboard and a smaller trolling motor. Although the official reason he's here is to promote Minnesota's number-one pastime, his primary goal today is to break an embarrassing run of fishing luck for Minnesota's previous governor. During eight years in office, Governor Arne Carlson caught one measly fish. The fish was so tiny that any self-respecting angler wouldn't even consider it a catch.

Ventura is pulling out all the stops to catch the big prize of the day, a walleye, Minnesota's state fish. He's got a top-notch professional fishing guide at his side, along with his buddies from his Roosevelt High School days. He's also stretching his fishing time as long as possible, getting on the lake more than three hours earlier than the 8:00 A.M. start time listed on the official itinerary for the day. As boats full of reporters and photographers head out on the lake in pursuit of the governor, his quiet fishing party eventually swells to a comical flotilla. By noon, the governor's tally includes three northern pike, one perch, and a lake trout. No walleye, but he avoided a shutout.

A couple of hours later Governor Ventura is darting across Sugar Lake, skimming the waves on a personal watercraft, looking like a cross between Aquaman and a character in *Easy Rider*. He's wearing a black custom-made fringed wet suit and a personalized life preserver with "Gov. Jesse" emblazoned on the front. The wet suit and vest are gifts from Polaris, a Minnesota maker of personal watercraft. Ventura and his wife are test-driving new models of personal watercraft that are made to be quieter and reduce emissions by 80 percent. The governor owns five personal watercraft and is opposed to government efforts to regulate them.

"As you can see, the industry will take care of itself," he says, referring to Polaris's efforts to reduce noise and emissions. "We realize there are people that don't like personal watercraft. We need to let the private sector supervise itself." Ventura makes these comments after trudging out of the cold water. "I feel a little bit like the creature from the Black Lagoon," Ventura says, laughing and holding his arms out to let the fringe dangle.

In what I'm certain is the first gubernatorial news conference conducted in a wet suit, Ventura is asked if he feels guilty to be up here fishing and boating while the legislature is hard at work. His response, in a word, "No!" He says they could have been here too if they wouldn't leave all their work to the last minute. "I would encourage the legislature over the next three years that I'm governor to finish their work two weeks ahead of time, and I will happily invite each and every one of them to the governor's fishing opener."

The 1999 session of the Minnesota legislature is meandering to a close on May 17. It's noon on a Monday and the House chamber is nearly empty. With dozens of bills yet to be considered and voted on, most of the work is being done behind the scenes.

With less than twelve hours to go in his first legislative session, Governor Ventura is hunkered down in his office, staying out of the way while lawmakers try to finish up. However, one last-minute piece of business is the first override of a Minnesota governor's veto since 1982. Ventura earlier had vetoed a bill intended to change a so-called seat-belt gag rule. A Minnesota Supreme Court ruling from 1997 doesn't allow automobile-accident victims to sue car manufacturers over defective seat belts. A bill passed by the House and Senate would change that, but Ventura vetoed the legislation, saying that the legislature overstepped its authority by designating what evidence the courts can hear.

Getting the legislature to override Ventura's veto became the personal crusade of Jodi-Michaelle Carlson, who became quadriplegic as the result of a car accident in which she claims defective seat belts failed to protect her. Her vigil in the capitol, sitting outside the House chambers in her wheelchair, helps convince lawmakers to override the governor's veto. Ventura has no comment on the veto, although his spokesperson, John Wodele, says the governor respects the right of the legislature to override a veto.

By early evening both the House and Senate chambers are buzzing with activity as the last-minute flurry of legislation snakes through the system. Governor Ventura leaves the capitol about 8:20 P.M., less than four hours from the constitutional deadline for the session to end. When asked what he'll do if lawmakers don't finish by midnight, he tersely replies, "They better!"

The House and Senate do eventually finish their work. But like college kids completing a term paper that was assigned the first day of the semester, lawmakers use every second up to their midnight deadline. The biggest issue, of course, is tax cuts. During debate over the huge tax-cut bill, some House members worry about the size of the cuts. "I'm worried it may not be sustainable," says Representative David Tomassoni, a Democrat from northern Minnesota. "A downturn in the economy could cause serious problems." Majority Leader Tim Pawlenty states the more optimistic and prevailing argument in the Republican-controlled House. "Taxes have spread out in Minnesota like a bad smell," he says on the House floor. "We are literally being taxed to death. This is a historic tax cut!"

The day after the legislative session ends, Governor Ventura declares himself the winner. "I definitely won," he tells me during an interview in his office. "I think all Minnesotans won is the bottom line. I think that all three of the tripartisan parties can walk out of here winners. I was the engineer of the train, and I suppose you could say that Senator Moe and Speaker Sviggum were shoveling the coal."

Someone's shoveling something, but it's certainly true they all did get onboard the so-called Tax-cut Train. The tax bill that will soon arrive on the governor's desk for his signature reduces income and property taxes by $1.6 billion. That's on top of a sales-tax rebate totaling at least $1.3 billion, meaning taxpayers will receive checks in the mail from $204 to $5,000. However, the governor was unsuccessful in getting any reductions in auto license tabs, one of his key campaign promises. The promise of dramatic property-tax reform also will have to wait for another day.

Ventura is proud of a big increase in education funding that will help lower class sizes. Still, he's no fan of the legislative budget process. "If the private sector were to conduct business the way the public sector does, everyone would be fired," he says.

However, he certainly learned how to play the game in a hurry. After complaining about conference committees and "backroom deals" during his campaign, he says he didn't feel hypocritical taking part in backroom deals near the end of the session.

"You have to make deals to do what's best for the people of Minnesota," he says. "You're naive to think that isn't going to happen." After taking a second or two to think about what he just said, the governor changes his tune a bit. "I don't think 'deal' is the right word. I never made any deals. I simply made compromises where it was needed to get the job done."

With the tumultuous session now over, Ventura takes one more parting shot at his critics in the legislature. "Jealousy's a bad thing, isn't it?" referring to the uproar over his autobiography. "You know, jealousy can be a horrible thing to eat away at people. Why are they so concerned about me? I think people should be more concerned about themselves. Are they doing the right thing? Are they a role model? Are they doing everything they can do in their lives rather than worrying about what Governor Jesse Ventura's doing?"

On May 23 a made-for-TV movie hits the air that the governor hates but can't do anything to stop. It's NBC's hastily produced version of *The Jesse Ventura Story*. Nils Allen Stewart plays the part of Ventura in this movie tracing Ventura's rise from pro wrestler to governor. "It portrays Jesse in a really nice light, and I'd like to believe that's really how he is," Stewart tells the syndicated TV show *Extra* while shooting scenes for the movie in Toronto between matches of a World Championship Wrestling event.

Stewart, by the way, bears only the slightest resemblance to Ventura and doesn't sound anything like him. Nevertheless, producers of the movie say it's an otherwise accurate portrayal of Ventura's life. "We've been scrupulous in trying to be accurate," the movie's executive producer Bruce Saland tells *Extra*.

In reality, the movie is a semiaccurate, over-the-top portrayal of Ventura's road to victory. In one scene he is having a nightmare about his opponents, Coleman and Humphrey, literally beating him up in a wrestling ring. In this cartoonish scene they're kicking Ventura, sticking their fingers in his mouth and kicking him in the ass. One yells, "Jesse, you're a loser, baby!" while the other is biting his foot. The Coleman character taunts him by saying, "I'm the one who brought the NFL back to Minnesota." (Actually, Coleman helped get approval for a hockey arena in St. Paul so the NHL could come back to Minnesota.) Suddenly, Ventura wakes up from his nightmare and looks at his wife, whimpering, "What if we don't win?" The Terry Ventura character just looks at him and says, "You wanna fool around?" She climbs on top of him just as the scene fades to black.

Despite the movie's implication that Ventura's wife provided him with sexual therapy to overcome his anxiety about the election, Saland, the executive producer, says, "We did not try to delve into any intimate parts of his life we don't know about, nor, quite frankly, is it any of our business."

Ventura doesn't think *any* of it is any of their business. "Why do you think I distanced myself from it?" he asks reporters during a photo opportunity at the governor's mansion with former Canadian prime minister Joe Clark. "No, I won't watch it. It had no input from me. It is not accurate from what I've heard in many, many places. Again, my big issue is that a homeless person on the street has more rights than I do, because they could not do a movie like that on a regular citizen and not face legal repercussions. Where I, as a private figure, lose all my rights, and I'm very confused over why we have a situation where you lose your rights. Someone can make a film of you that is not accurate and yet there is nothing you can do. How many in the world will believe this is accurate? Many. And it's not. I think that's highly unfair."

Governor Ventura leaves for California on May 26 to begin what eventually will be a national book tour taking him to Los Angeles, New York, Washington, D.C., and Chicago. Just so the legislature doesn't get too lonely, he leaves behind a going-away present. Ventura exercises his veto pen thirty-seven times, cutting $140 million in spending. "It's called cutting out the pork," he says. To make his point he stamps the veto messages with a picture of a pig.

The vetoes range from $25,000 for a housing program for homeless women and children to $11.1 million in appropriations for campus repairs in the Minnesota State Colleges and Universities system. Ventura also vetoes $150,000 for a state World War II memorial, $4 million for local hockey rinks, and $10 million for bridge repairs. In a written statement about the vetoes, the governor says he's just keeping a campaign promise to reduce reliance on state government.

Whatever the rationale, Ventura manages to tick off the legislature one more time. The problem is, the legislature adjourned eight days ago, so it can't do anything about the vetoes until the next session, scheduled to begin February 1, 2000. Senate Majority Leader Roger Moe vows to put that first on the to-do list. "He has the right to veto and we have the right to override, so we'll see what happens," Moe says. Other Senate Democrats react more harshly, claiming they've been "blindsided" and can no longer trust the governor. House Republicans don't agree with all the vetoes either, but Majority Leader Tim Pawlenty says Ventura kept his promise to hold the line on spending. "It's a gutsy move and probably more than a little overdue."

Leno and Nixon

While lawmakers back in St. Paul wring their hands over Ventura's vetoes, Ventura is in California, trying to make cash registers ring with book sales. In fact, money is the one theme that seems to run through everything about Ventura since taking office. When he boards a plane for Los Angeles, clutching a copy of his book, he's also accompanied by two state troopers who regularly travel with him on state business. A member of his communications staff is also along on the trip. The book publisher will pay Ventura's expenses. Security and staff member expenses will be paid by the state. This, of course, is more buckshot in the barrel for critics of the governor.

Although this is a private trip for Ventura on vacation time, his administration argues it's no different than any other vacation during which the governor would be entitled to his usual security. "The fact that he's not sitting at his desk in the capitol doesn't mean he's not the governor," spokesperson John Wodele says after Ventura leaves for California. "It's important to facilitate communication that a staff member be with him and that he be protected."

Former governor Arne Carlson agrees Ventura should be protected at state expense. "I think it's prudent," Carlson says, noting that he didn't always take security with him on personal trips. "I think it's wise for us to provide security. Suppose the governor were killed in L.A. on a book tour and we, the state of Minnesota, didn't provide security. What would we say then?"

The first stop on the California leg of the book tour is an appearance on the NBC *Tonight Show* with Jay Leno. As my photographer and I pull up to the *Tonight Show* studios on a sunny southern-California afternoon, the sidewalk is lined with palm trees—and hundreds of women in black miniskirts waiting to get into the *Tonight Show*. They don't strike me as Ventura groupies. They're not. So I ask one of them, "Why are you here?"

"Rickeeeee!" is the response.

Mystery solved. Latin music sensation Ricky Martin is getting top billing on tonight's show. The nation's hottest singer and hottest politician will share the same stage.

We work our way through the line of people hoping to get into the show, searching for anyone who is more interested in seeing Ventura. "He's the guy that wants to legalize prostitution, right?" says one guy, apparently telling us the extent of what he knows about the governor.

Finally, we do find a couple of Ventura groupies. "We love Jesse!" says Luke Stedman of Yorba Linda. "He's the hottest political phenomenon today. Forget Ricky Martin. Ricky Martin might be hot in music, but Governor Jesse is soon to be President Jesse."

Ventura appears on the show with Martin and actor Angie Harmon from NBC's *Law and Order.* Despite his penchant for stirring up controversy on late-night talk shows, the governor stays out of trouble this time. He gets big applause when bragging about the tax rebates Minnesotans will be getting, along with a big tax cut. "And they tell you a wrestler can't govern!" he jokes.

The biggest laugh during Ventura's appearance comes when Leno takes a playful shot at him. He tells Leno the only way he'll run for vice president is on a ticket with Colin Powell. "I'll break my promise [not to run]. If he'll run for president, I'll be his running mate," Ventura says, making it clear he's not joking. Leno can't resist. "Yeah, but that's like M. C. Hammer going, 'Bill Gates, you and I, let's put our money together ...'"

Leno and the studio audience howl with laughter. Ventura ignores the obvious slam. "I don't know, Jay, I look at it this way. You've got the Army and the Navy teaming up. Who's going to whip them?"

After the *Tonight Show* appearance, the governor does more book business. His limo heads back to the posh Hotel Nikko in Beverly Hills, where his book publisher wants him to spend an hour pre-signing three hundred to four hundred books for an appearance at the Richard M. Nixon Library and Birthplace in Yorba Linda. He also squeezes in a meeting at the hotel with actor Melissa Gilbert, who talks with him about the possibility of shooting a *Little House on the Prairie* movie in Minnesota. The popular, long-running TV show about a prairie family in Minnesota was never actually shot in the state. If Gilbert makes a movie based on the show, she'd like to bring it to Minnesota with Ventura's help.

"He's quite an interesting man," Gilbert tells me after the meeting. "I was very impressed to actually sit with a politician who is honest and straightforward and candid about his life as opposed to what we're all accustomed to these days. I think it's about time some politician somewhere was honest about their life and their past, and I don't think there should be any recriminations for that."

While I conduct the interview with Gilbert in the hotel lobby, a funny thing happens that illustrates Ventura's appeal to average people. The governor walks in the front door with his two security guards and David Ruth, a member of his communications staff. In their hands are a few bags of the greasiest-looking burgers you can imagine from a Fatburger joint across the street. Here's one of the most famous politicians in the country, a governor no less, staying at one of the finest hotels in Beverly Hills at book-publisher expense, and he's eating greasy food from a hamburger joint.

The California flag blows lazily in the warm breeze above the lush gardens and immaculately manicured grounds of the Nixon Library. The library is adjacent to the small home where President Nixon was born in 1913. The birthplace and library are now surrounded by a patchwork of breathtaking rose gardens. The former home of one of the nation's consummate career politicians is about to play host to the anti-politician.

As Ventura drives up Yorba Linda Boulevard in front of the library, he passes California Reform Party members holding signs that say, "Let's Trade Gov. Davis for Gov. Jesse Ventura" and "California Needs the 'Right' Governor." Ray Mills, state secretary of the California Reform Party, says Ventura is a dream come true for the Reform Party. "The fact that you can have a return to the basic principles of having a representative of the common man come in and run government is why we like Jesse," Mills tells me on the sidewalk out front.

"He's the kind of guy I like," says Joe Schaaf of Yorba Linda, who just shelled out $40 for two copies of the book at a table set up out front. "I'd vote for him in a heartbeat. He's a tough individual. He takes nothing from nobody. That's what I want." A woman writing out a check for a book echoes that sentiment. "I like nonpolitician politicians, if that makes any sense," she says. "I think that he uses common sense, and I think regular politicians don't."

Ventura's appearance is one of the most eagerly anticipated in the history of the Nixon Library. Organizers quickly sold out the six-hundred-seat auditorium for his speech at $15 per ticket. The demand is so great that another one hundred seats have been sold in the lobby, where people can watch the speech on closed-circuit television. They'll all get their money's worth as Ventura delivers what is probably his most entertaining speech yet.

He speaks for more than an hour with no notes. At times he elicits wild laughter, then moments later he's nearly in tears. He starts the speech by introducing a couple of his former Navy SEAL buddies sitting in the audience. He warns the crowd, "Don't yell 'skivvy check!'" This won't be anything like recent speeches at the Nixon Library by the likes of Henry Kissinger and Newt Gingrich.

Ventura engages the crowd by telling the story of how his campaign for governor began. It's the only time I've heard him admit publicly that his campaign actually started as a publicity stunt. "I was doing talk radio. I was criticizing the politicians very strongly and I started to, in a way, at the start for ratings, say maybe I ought to run for governor. And it started to build up and build up. Then something happened in Minnesota that truly angered me."

That's when he launches into the story of how the state kept running up huge budget surpluses and none of it was being returned to taxpayers. "That's what angered me. That's what made me decide I'm going to run."

He says the media and political "experts" shrugged his campaign off as a publicity stunt. Of course, Ventura just admitted it started that way, but he also says he saw a window of opportunity. In 1992, Ross Perot got close to 24 percent of the presidential vote in Minnesota (562,506 votes out of 2,345,448). "That told me 24 percent of the voters out there were willing to step away from the two-party system. It also told me if a Texan can do that in Minnesota, imagine what a Minnesotan can do in Minnesota."

He also uses this speech to launch a spirited defense for writing the book and revealing so much about his past. "Oh, have I been criticized," he says in exasperation. "'You're not a role model! How dare you say these things that children will read. How dare you talk about this sordid childhood you had.'" Ventura says it never occurred to him to sugarcoat his past, especially when so many of his indiscretions happened so long ago. "I don't think there's anyone in this room that, when you were making decisions at eighteen or nineteen, who said, 'You know, I better not do this, because twenty-five years from now I might be a role model.' I don't recall that. That never entered this thick Slovak's head!"

Which brings him to the story in the book about his escapade with a Nevada hooker shortly before being shipped off to Southeast Asia. "I told the story because I thought it was unique and funny. I'm probably one of the only human beings standing on the face of the earth today that's gone to a Nevada ranch and been paid!" The crowd roars with laughter and applause while Nixon probably rolls over in his nearby grave.

It's not every day a politician of any rank, let alone a governor, stands before you and brags about an exploit with a hooker. He points out that prostitution is legal in Nevada and that he was unmarried at the time. Ventura knows that will make the story somewhat palatable for the few prudes that might be in the audience.

"When I got into the ranch, the particular girl looked at me and said, 'I want that belt!'" he says, referring to a belt of spent machine-gun shells he was wearing. "I said, 'Make me an offer.'"

The Nixon Library has never rocked with so much laughter in anticipation of the punch line. "And she said, 'How 'bout a trick and ten dollars?'"

The crowd is now clapping and rollicking while Ventura stands onstage with a big smile on his face, spreads his arms out wide, bends backward, looks to the heavens, shrugs, and yells, "I did it!"

He manages to segue seamlessly from the hooker story into an emotional reflection on what it means to be governor. "I'm very proud to have been given the honor to be the governor of Minnesota. It's a very humbling thing, to hold that office."

He also admits to some frustrations. "Many people criticized me early on. They said, 'He talked reform. He's not making big changes.' Well, they don't know what it's like on the inside. They don't know that this big thing called government is a gigantic wheel and that, if you stand in front of that wheel, it's going to squash you. What you have to do is get onboard and attempt to turn it a little, change it slightly wherever you can."

Ventura says the highlight since his election is the recognition he received from his childhood idol, Muhammad Ali. You'll recall on election night, Ventura borrowed Ali's famous line about "shocking the world."

"A month or so after I won, hand-delivered to me was a letter from the champ." Ventura pauses while he chokes up and holds back tears.

He holds his hand up in front of his face while regaining his composure. A woman in the audience yells, "It shows you're human!" Finally, he resumes. "He's my hero," he says, his voice still cracking. "And he said, 'You shocked the world.' And along with the letter came a pair of boxing gloves, which mean probably more to me than anything else I've ever gotten."

Of course, no Ventura speech would be complete without some good old-fashioned media bashing. "I think all of us will agree the First Amendment is the most cherished one we have, the right to freedom of speech. But with that freedom comes responsibility. With that responsibility comes the fact that the media needs to be honest too."

He gets another big round of applause, but who couldn't get applause bashing the media? "I think that the media needs to be clear and tell the public that, 'Yes, we're out to make money. Yes, we're out to make ratings points, and, yes, that's what our job is now.' Because they are no longer just reporting the news, they are attempting to create it."

Conveniently, the governor is ignoring the fact that a few minutes ago he admitted his candidacy started as a radio-show ratings ploy. Talk about creating news!

After the speech, Ventura sits at a table in the Nixon Library gardens for a two-hour book-signing. The irony here is too rich too ignore. His table is situated not more than twenty-five yards from Richard Nixon's grave and another twenty-five yards from Nixon's birthplace. On page forty-five of the book he is now signing, he tells the story about how his dad always referred to President Nixon as "the Tailless Rat."

Here's more irony: A Republican presidential candidate hasn't won the Minnesota vote since 1972, when Nixon carried the state over George McGovern. Now, twenty-seven years later, Minnesota's Reform Party governor is signing books in Nixon's garden.

There were seven hundred people attending his speech, but his book publicist estimates sales of about twelve hundred books. A couple hundred people are in line for autographs. Most were impressed by the governor's ad-libbed, straight-from-the-heart speech.

"I thought it was great," one gray-haired man of about sixty tells me. "He's very honest, straightforward. A breath of fresh air compared to what we see in Washington." His wife chimes in, "We hope it's contagious!" Another man who looks to be in his mid-forties, balding with a ponytail, two earrings, a leather vest, and gray beard, looks me in the eye and blurts out, "I loved it! He's honest. He speaks from the gut, and he doesn't make it up to see if you like it first!"

After signing books for two hours, Ventura and his Navy SEAL buddies pose for personal pictures. One of them hands Ventura a cell phone to talk with another SEAL buddy who couldn't make it in person.

"Hey, you dirtbag!" Ventura shouts into the phone. His friends laugh as they nudge the governor, reminding him a television camera is still pointed his way. We'd love to hear the rest of that conversation, but his security guards let us know it's time to move along.

CHAPTER 7

"I Don't Have to Do Anything, I'm a Governor"
Ventura's Talk-Radio Comeback

"Jesse, just one important question. How often do you masturbate?"

It's not the sort of question a governor gets asked every day. Let's face it, this might be the first time any governor's been asked that question—at least in public. Anyone who figures Jesse Ventura won't make much news now that his legislative sparring partners have gone home badly underestimates his ability to attract attention.

On June 2, 1999, it looks as if Ventura is in the eye of an electrical storm. Flashbulbs pop furiously as photographers vie for his attention while he signs copies of his book at the Barnes and Noble bookstore in New York's Rockefeller Center. Inane questions pop almost as furiously from one of Howard Stern's radio sidekicks. "Have you ever been attracted to another man?" asks Stuttering John in a follow-up to his masturbation question. The crowd around the governor responds with gasps and groans, wondering how much longer until Ventura piledrives the Stern interloper.

Instead, the governor, after trying unsuccessfully to ignore Stuttering John, is now laughing while he continues signing books. "Where do you stand on abortion, Jesse?" Stuttering John asks as his aimless interrogation continues. Finally, Ventura can't ignore him anymore and looks up.

"I'm here to sign a book, OK?" he says.

"You're a governor, you should be able to answer some of the issues," Stuttering John quickly responds.

Few, however, are as quick as Ventura. "I don't have to do anything, I'm a governor!" he shouts back, drawing a huge laugh and applause from the two hundred people standing in line to get his autograph.

Stern sent Stuttering John to the book-signing in the vain hope of persuading Ventura to appear on his radio show. The governor declined an invitation to appear on the show as part of his book tour because he's still peeved about being bumped off the show when he was running for governor.

"Jesse, just come on the show, man," Stuttering John pleads. "I don't understand. You called us right before you won. But then you don't do the show."

"Yeah, you stiffed me," Ventura says, clearly relishing his chance to even the score after getting "stiffed" shortly before election day. Stern's show attracted a young audience when it aired in the Twin Cities and Ventura was counting on that to get some votes.

"So why don't you do it now?" Stuttering John responds.

"No, you stiffed me!" says the governor. "What goes around comes around."

Someone in the crowds yells, "Way to go, Governor!" Ventura loves to have the last word, especially when taking on someone sent by Stern, the self-proclaimed "King of All Media."

But just seconds after being dismissed by the governor, the intrepid Stuttering John resumes his outrageous line of questioning. "Have you ever cheated on your wife?"

Ventura's Rockefeller Center appearance comes in the midst of a whirlwind, two-day East Coast book tour that will be followed by a quick stop in Chicago. The governor is scheduled to appear on no fewer than eight national television and radio talk shows in New York City and Washington, D.C. Before the encounter with Stuttering John, Ventura faces a more serious interrogation on NBC's *Today Show*. Cohost Matt Lauer sees to it that Ventura's East Coast tour won't be two days of free, feel-good commercials for his autobiography. Lauer begins the nearly ten-minute interview by asking a hypothetical question that kids might ask after reading the book: "Well, Jesse smoked pot, Jesse went to prostitutes, Jesse vandalized a school, and he became governor. So why shouldn't I do it?"

"Maybe that's the point," Ventura responds. "We all do things at a young age that's part of growing up and you grow beyond them."

Lauer is just warming up. "You said this on prostitution and drugs: 'We shouldn't be wasting so much time and so many resources on prosecuting consensual crimes such as prostitution and drug possession.' Do you plan to relax laws on prostitution or drug possession?" he asks.

"No, I don't," Ventura says. "Not at all. I just want to open people's eyes that I think catching murderers and violent criminals is far more important.... Let's get our priorities in order. Lets go after criminals who hurt other people, not people that hurt themselves. You can't legislate stupidity, Matt. People are going to do stupid things."

Next, Lauer zeroes in on the governor's views on gun control. Ventura, growing increasingly agitated by the tone of Lauer's questions, takes a deep breath while listening to the next question. "Katie [Couric, his cohost] just had a segment about the tragedy in Littleton, Colorado. Following that shooting you said this: 'To me it justifies conceal-and-carry more. It should open people's eyes. We have to protect ourselves from attacks such as this. If we can't protect our schools, how can we protect our kids on the streets?' You later, let me say, said you regretted those comments. What did you mean to say?"

Ventura makes it clear the only thing he regrets is stating his views to the news media, but he eventually answers Lauer's question. "I think I want people to listen to a very simple thought. What do we have more value in, our kids or our money? Because we put our money in a bank, don't we? And there's a guard there twenty-four hours a day armed, isn't there?"

Lauer jumps in, "You want armed guards in schools in Minnesota?"

"I'm not saying," Ventura fires back. "But we put our kids in school. What's there to protect them? You have to remember something. This is an act of terrorism. A terrorist is a coward. And a terrorist is going to pick out a place with least-resistance. Schools are prime targets."

Lauer tries to back Ventura into a corner. "So how do you increase the resistance if you're not arming people in the schools?"

The governor heads to a neutral corner. "I don't know. I don't know. I don't have the answer."

"He was known to the wrestling world as Jesse 'The Body' Ventura, one of the great names in wrestling," says Regis Philbin. "Last November all of that changed when he became the governor of the state of Minnesota. And now in his new book he talks about his bumpy and colorful road to success. And, boy, it has been quite a journey. Here he is, Governor Jesse Ventura!" The studio audience delivers rousing applause as Ventura steps onto the set of *Live: Regis and Kathie Lee*.

It's just ninety minutes after the *Today Show* appearance and it's immediately obvious he's on much friendlier turf. "Now I have to treat you with more dignity," Philbin tells him. "We used to fool around in the past, but now you are the governor."

"That's right, I became honorable," Ventura says. "You win an election, you become honorable. It's amazing." If fawning by Philbin isn't enough, this show also features some flirting.

"When you walked in to say hi to me, I got a hot flash," Ventura tells Kathie Lee Gifford before he turns and winks at the crowd.

"You're my favorite governor!" she responds. "Really!" Clearly, no one's going to play hardball during this appearance.

The governor's armed entourage catches the attention of Gifford. "Who are those guys outside?" she asks. "There's lots of traveling guys with you." Gifford is referring to three Minnesota state troopers, two New York state patrol officers, and four New York City cops. The New York officers are provided as a courtesy to a visiting governor.

"It's required by law that you're protected," Ventura says of his Minnesota security contingent. "You have to be protected.... The state of Minnesota must protect me twenty-four hours a day 'cause I'm the governor."

The next day, Ventura has the legal opinion to back up that statement and quiet his critics who claim taxpayers are footing the bill to support his private business interests. The Minnesota attorney general's office in St. Paul issues a formal legal opinion regarding the use of state-paid security on the book tour. The ruling interprets state law as requiring his protection regardless of where or why he's traveling. As long as there's a "public purpose" for the expense, security must be provided by the state.

"While facilitating the governor's promotional book tour is not a public purpose, the *protection* of the governor at all times is a valid purpose," the opinion reads. Many complaints about the governor's use of state security for his book tour have come from legislators. Ironically, laws passed by the legislature are what make the security arrangements possible. "It is significant that the legislature did not limit the requirement of security to the Governor's on-the-job activities, as it easily could have done," says the legal opinion. "Rather, in recognition of the importance of maintaining the Governor's safety, the statute provides for the Governor's security without reference to his whereabouts or the nature of a particular activity of the Governor."

The attorney general's opinion means the state will have to pick up the tab for the three security guards and one staff member who accompanied the governor on the two-day California trip. The state is also on the hook for three security guards and a staff member on the three-day trip to New York, Washington, and Chicago. Ventura takes five vacation days for the trips and has all his personal expenses covered by the book publisher.

Wrestling with Larry King

After his New York stops, Ventura hops on a shuttle to fly down to Washington, D.C. In less than ninety minutes he sells out five hundred copies of his autobiography at Trover's Bookshop on Capitol Hill. Then he heads to a private party at a Georgetown restaurant, where he signs another two hundred books. There's no time to rest after that, because he's got four more national interviews to do in the next seven hours.

There's CNN's *Inside Politics*, the syndicated radio program *The Oliver North Show*, CNBC's *Hardball with Chris Matthews*, and CNN's *Larry King Live*. King gets the governor to talk more in-depth about his wrestling career than at any other time I can recall since his election. During his campaign and in the first few months after his election, Ventura seemed to distance himself from his wrestling past. Not anymore.

King gets the interview off to a rough start by inadvertently referring to Ventura as a "Republican." King catches himself, only to follow up by describing him as the "only independent governor in America." Ventura corrects King by reminding him he's a member of the Reform Party and that the only independent governor is Angus King of Maine.

The one thing King does get right is that Ventura used to be a wrestler. "We have a premise of what the wrestler is," King says. "Is that wrong?" King doesn't explain what the premise is, but we're left to assume he means most people think of wrestlers as big, mindless thugs.

"I think so, because to me they're tremendous performers who give their heart and soul to the business, and they're tremendous athletes." As an example, he tells the story of basketball player Dennis Rodman's one professional wrestling match. Ventura says Rodman told him he could barely get out of bed the next day. "I told Dennis I wrestled sixty-three consecutive nights in a row once, and he said, 'There's no way I could do that.'"

Ventura admits the winners of professional wrestling matches are determined in advance, but says the matches are anything but fake. "It's entertainment. It's ballet with violence.... It's knowing how to wrestle. A lot of people think it's rehearsed. It really isn't. It's ad-lib. It's knowing how to wrestle and it's very much like dancing."

Video clips of him in the wrestling ring are now rolling while King and Ventura talk. King winces when he sees Jesse "the Body" crush someone's hand with his foot. "So, when it looks like you're stepping on his hand ..."

"I'm stepping on it," Ventura says with satisfaction. "But I'm not out to destroy his livelihood. When you take a body slam, you get slammed. And believe me, every wrestler goes through life in pain."

The next clip shows a bare-chested Ventura in red wrestling tights and scraggly blond hair down beyond his shoulders. He's jumping on someone's head. "So, you're hurting that guy now," King says. "You just fell on him!"

"I'm thumping him," Ventura responds. "It's like football.... You get thumped but you still continue to play. But certainly injuries happen."

King asks the governor why he thinks so many people are such big fans of professional wrestling. "Because it's adult soap opera. It's a soap opera of athleticism. And in the older days it was good versus evil. You had the evil wrestler, the good wrestler. Today, it's switched a little bit. Today, you have more personalities and each personality has their following."

Speaking of personalities, King asks him what he thinks about Vince McMahon, Ventura's former boss with the World Wrestling Federation. "Vince is a brilliant businessman," Ventura says of the man he's often battled on a number of issues.

He also brags about the time he sued McMahon in federal court because Ventura thought it was unfair he didn't receive any royalty payments for ninety WWF videos he appeared in. "The jury agreed. The federal judge agreed. The appeals court agreed and the Supreme Court of the United States agreed. So I think I was right." Ventura won a nearly $1 million judgment against McMahon.

The governor also reveals some interesting inside details about how much money wrestlers can earn. "In my court case I found out that at a couple 'WrestleManias,' Hulk Hogan made over a million dollars that night. For one match." Did Ventura make a lot of money wrestling? "I did good. Yeah, I did good. I actually ended up making more as an announcer than I did as a wrestler, but then again, I was the first wrestler who brought in an agent. I got powerful enough to where I made them deal with my agent, Barry Bloom, out in Los Angeles."

Ventura doesn't offer King any details, but court documents filed in his lawsuit against McMahon back up his claims. After he retired from wrestling in 1986, Ventura would often get paid $20,000 to

$25,000 for just a few hours of announcing and promotional work at "WrestleMania" events and other WWF appearances. By June 1990, the WWF prepared to offer Ventura a $1 million, three-year contract for about fifty days of work a year. The deal was never signed, because Ventura had his falling out with McMahon and left the WWF in August of that year. Two years later he signed on as an announcer with World Championship Wrestling, a competitor of the WWF. On March 1, 1992, while serving as mayor of Brooklyn Park, Minnesota, Ventura signed a two-year, $900,000 WCW contract with incentives to make much more based on television ratings.

During his appearance with Larry King, a video clip is shown of Jesse "the Body" Ventura from the mid-1980s in one of his classic wrestling interviews: "I'm so beautiful, sometimes I can't even live with myself. It gets hard to look in the mirror because tears come to my eyes, because I cannot believe that there's anybody on earth that can be as beautiful as me."

Ventura laughs when he sees the clip. He's wearing a leather hat, audaciously big earrings, a long beard, and sunglasses studded with jewels. "Interviewing was my forte, Larry. I could turn it on when the cameras went on."

"Did you enjoy being a bad guy?" King inquires.

"Absolutely," he says. "You can be way more creative. Plus, it's nice because you don't have to be nice to anyone unless you want to."

It's also well established that Ventura and Hulk Hogan had a major falling out years ago. Ventura reveals why. "It was right before 'Wrestle-Mania 2' and it was the perfect opportunity to attempt to unionize because all the publicity had gone out, the match was set. And I had met Gene Upshaw of the NFL Players Association a few weeks earlier and had talked and spoken with him a little bit. And so I came up.... There was only wrestlers in the room, and I said, 'Boys, now's our chance to unionize. If we refuse to do "WrestleMania," we can ask to have a union come in and we can unionize. What can they do?' And I came home a day or so later and Vince McMahon called me and almost fired me for attempting to unionize."

He says it was years later, during a deposition of McMahon in Ventura's lawsuit, that McMahon admitted it was Hogan who told him about the union incident.

"That ended your friendship with Hulk?" King asks.

"Pretty much," Ventura says, "because he had been what I thought a close friend until that point in time."

"You've led an extraordinary life," King says to the governor as they conclude the nearly twenty-minute interview.

"Either that or I can't hold a job too long," Ventura jokes.

Governor Ventura's official schedule of public appearances is more diverse and eclectic than any other politician's in the country. I say this without doing research on the matter because it can't possibly be wrong. Let's take the week of June 7, 1999, as an example. On Monday, Ventura attends a meeting with federal trade officials to discuss ways to open world markets for ailing Minnesota farmers. The day also includes an elegant roast-duck lunch with Crown Prince Haakon of Norway at the governor's residence. The prince is visiting cities in the Midwest with large Norwegian populations, and how could he resist a meeting with the country's most famous governor? On Tuesday, Ventura helps build a Habitat for Humanity home in St. Paul. On Wednesday, the governor meets separately with the mayors of Minneapolis and St. Paul to discuss stadium proposals for the Minnesota Twins. On Thursday, he accepts twelve thousand pieces of underwear on the steps of the State Capitol. That last item needs a little explaining.

It turns out the revelation in the governor's book about his underwear-free lifestyle caught the attention of Fruit of the Loom. The company lends its "support" to the governor by offering him an assortment of Fruit of the Loom underwear. It also offers to donate twelve thousand pieces of underwear to three local charities. The boxers, briefs, and T-shirts will go to organizations that help feed and clothe the poor and homeless.

Ventura graciously agrees to accept the donations at the capitol, but admits to some misgivings about exposing the truth. "Maybe it's sad that I brought it out, because it was kind of an unwritten mystique about the [Navy SEAL] teams, you know, and now it's no longer unwritten. It's right out there in the open being exposed." Fruit of the Loom, of course, just couldn't let this golden marketing opportunity pass without at least a "brief" ceremony on the capitol steps. "When America's most freewheeling politician turns out to be, well, a little bit too freewheeling, we just couldn't sit idly by," says company executive John Wendler.

Ventura says the donations won't change his, shall we say, alfresco lifestyle, but he's glad to see something so positive come out of his book. He says most people never think of donating underwear to charity. "So I think we're fulfilling a tremendous gap. I don't think anyone cares to inherit underwear secondhand."

Back on the Air

Ventura caps off this busy week of June by premiering his new Friday-afternoon *Lunch with the Governor* radio show. He is sitting at his desk, wearing a blue denim shirt with a Minnesota Vikings logo. He's got the daily newspapers spread out in front of him alongside the eagle sculpture Arnold Schwarzenegger gave him as an inauguration gift.

The governor is allowing one pool television camera in his office to shoot the first twenty minutes of the show. He's also allowing reporters to sit in chairs lined up across from his desk to witness this historic event. It turns out there will be plenty to write about. Before his first hour back on talk radio is over, the governor and his callers will discuss everything from underwear and baseball stadiums to sales-tax rebates and oral sex.

At 11:00 A.M. on June 11, Ventura is officially back on the air, not as "the Body" but as "the Governor."

"Now, live from his stately office in St. Paul, unfiltered, unedited, unabashed—this is the Honorable Jesse Ventura, governor of Minnesota." After the female announcer's voice fades away, up comes Ventura's theme music, "Lie to Me," by Jonny Lang.

"Good morning. It's great to be back on the air again," he says, a smile on his face and headphones straddling his bald head. "Imagine that. I'm going to have to control myself, though, and not let my wild and woolly Jesse 'the Body' appear. Ah, we'll let it sneak out every now and then, though. It's got to happen."

The producer of the show, David Ruth, is sitting just a few feet from the governor, monitoring the mike levels and incoming calls. Ruth is a member of the governor's communications staff but used to produce Ventura's radio shows at KSTP and KFAN. The new show will be broadcast on WCCO-AM and a network of twenty-three radio stations throughout Minnesota. Ventura won't be paid for the show, but WCCO will sell advertising and will likely turn a nice profit.

The governor says his show will allow him to communicate directly with citizens of the state without the filter of the media. He also views the program as a platform to make public-service announcements. Less than three minutes into the show, he also leaves no doubt it will be a launchpad for criticism of the media. "This now gives me the opportunity to correct the media," he says, unable to conceal the glee in his voice. "And I want to make sure the public out there understands that the media's not perfect, you know. They make mistakes. And so we're going to be like that little person off sitting in the background now, and when the media makes mistakes, we're going to jump on them with both feet, grind 'em right into the turf, and let 'em know when they make a mistake."

He's laughing now while all the reporters sitting across from him scribble in their notebooks. "No, I'm having a little fun with 'em. Look at 'em all. They're sitting, writing away feverishly now. 'How dare him! How will we fight back!'"

Ventura takes a break from his media-bashing to spend some time explaining how the state's sales-tax rebate will work. He passes along some information provided by the Minnesota Department of Revenue for people who might need to file some tax forms to qualify. "We want to make sure all Minnesotans who qualify for that rebate get it."

After about fifteen minutes of mixing public-service announcements with media-bashing (which are probably synonymous in his mind),

Ventura finally takes some phone calls from citizens. He reminds callers that "we don't have to be totally serious with this."

The attempt to go to the first caller is a bit rough. "Let's go to Linda in Zimmerman, Minnesota. Linda ..."

Dead air. Ventura looks perplexed.

Linda finally pipes up, "Are you there?"

"Yes, I'm there, Linda. Can you hear me?" he says.

"I'll be damned!" she blares into the phone.

"Yeah, heh, heh," Ventura laughs, trying to stop her before any serious expletives pop out. "We got our first FCC violation! We love it!"

Unfortunately, that turns out to be the highlight of the historic first call to *Lunch with the Governor.* Linda rambles on about this, that, and nothing. In fact, she seems uncertain why she even called. Ventura finally asks, "Linda, you're not drinking lunch today, are ya?"

"Just coffee," she says. "I'm like this normally."

"My [computer] monitor says you have an underwear question for me," Ventura tells her.

"Heck no," responds Linda. "I don't give a rip about the underwear."

This riveting phone call manages to drag out for nearly four minutes. Not exactly what Marconi had in mind when he invented radio.

A bit later some technical problems cause a few glitches as Ventura tries to take more callers.

"Nick in Minnetonka." Dead air.

"Cindy in Minneapolis." Dead air.

"Anyone," Ventura says, "tell me who you are. What happened? Did we go off the air, Dave?"

Finally, Cindy in Minneapolis chimes in. "I just want to congratulate you first of all on keeping the people guessing and worrying about what you're going to do or say next," she says while the governor laughs. "I think it's intriguing."

The most intriguing thing now is whether this show will make it through a full hour. Once the technical bugs are worked out, there are calls about stadium financing, education, and legalized gambling. But the highlight of the show comes near the end of the hour from John in St. Paul.

"Would you be interested in repealing the laws that prohibit adults from having oral sex? Because in Minnesota it's illegal for consenting adults to have oral sex."

When the governor stops laughing, he tells John, "We have a lot of laws that need to be repealed. We'll get to it next week. Thanks."

Ventura, still laughing about the oral-sex call, looks over at his communications director, John Wodele. "Wodele's over there nodding up and down, yes, yes, yes!"

You can now hear the laughter from the governor, his staff, and reporters echoing on radios throughout the state. For Ventura, it's just like old times.

Taking on Congress

A week later Governor Ventura walks out of the West Wing of the White House. He's just come out of a meeting with several members of the Clinton administration. It's a warm, sunny day in the nation's capital, and Ventura is holding court with a dozen camera crews and a pack of reporters on the circular driveway just outside the West Wing.

He's here on a two-day mission to lobby anyone and everyone on behalf of Minnesota farmers. As usual, Ventura's schedule is packed from early morning into the evening. His itinerary includes nineteen appearances or meetings on June 23 and 24.

In addition to his White House meeting, Ventura will meet with the secretary of agriculture, Minnesota's congressional delegation, the U.S trade ambassador for agriculture, and the Canadian ambassador. He'll testify before a House agriculture subcommittee, meet with the *Washington Post* editorial board, deliver a speech at the U.S. Chamber of Commerce, and appear on CNBC's *Hardball* show with Chris Matthews.

His primary mission is to lobby the federal government to change the way it supports dairy prices. Dairy price supports are among the most complicated, controversial, and confounding aspects of farm economics.

Ventura jumps into the morass of farm policy by opening his

lobbying effort at the White House with Gene Sperling, the chair of the Council of National Economic Advisers. "I just pointed out to him one of the major things I'm discussing now is a fair and level playing field on the dairy industry within our country," Ventura tells reporters. "They have some very archaic laws that date back fifty or sixty years that set policy here in the United States. I think it's the new millennium, and I think it's time to modernize some of these laws."

The governor didn't come to Washington because he has any magic solutions to the problems facing farmers. He's here because he can bring attention to the issue like no one else. "There's no doubt about it," says Gene Hugoson, Ventura's agriculture commissioner, after watching the impromptu news conference outside the White House. "The governor's ability to attract an audience serves agriculture very well, especially at a time like now."

After leaving the White House, Ventura gets an audience with the *Washington Post* editorial board. Even Katharine Graham, the newspaper's longtime publisher, makes a rare appearance at the meeting with Ventura. Sources also tell me everyone in the room bursts out in laughter at the governor's rendition of his Nevada hooker story. OK, so the whole trip isn't necessarily going to be focused on agriculture!

The governor attends a reception in his honor at the Longworth Office Building on Capitol Hill. Most members of Minnesota's congressional delegation and their staffs attend and marvel at Ventura's ability to draw a crowd.

After sampling hors d'oeuvres, he acknowledges that his greatest strength is playing the part of a carnival barker bringing people into the tent. "That's one of the strong points I bring. If you call it the 'celebrity-status governor,' if that's what it indeed is, but it's also with some substance to it, you know. If you're simply getting attention with no substance, that doesn't do any good.... What I bring out here to Washington is a little dose of commonsense."

Governor Ventura brings his "commonsense" approach to Congress the next day. He's scheduled to testify about the dairy pricing system before the House Subcommittee on Livestock and Horticulture.

There are parts of our federal government where lots of action takes place, where important people perform glamorous duties under a glaring spotlight. This is not one of those parts. For most meetings of the Subcommittee on Livestock and Horticulture, it's probably difficult to get a quorum of committee members together, let alone a crowd of spectators.

That changes on June 24, 1999. Governor Ventura is scheduled to testify before the subcommittee at 10 A.M. By 9:30, a line of people snakes down the hall and around the corner from Room 1300 in the Longworth Office Building. There's so much demand for media coverage, the House TV gallery is forced to set up a television-pool arrangement to reduce the number of cameras in the room.

When Governor Ventura arrives to testify, every seat in the hearing room is filled and a standing-room-only crowd is three deep. Another room is set aside so reporters and an overflow of spectators can listen to an audio feed of the testimony. Suddenly, the House Subcommittee on Livestock and Horticulture is the Capitol Hill hot spot.

Ventura will be one of eighteen people testifying before the committee, but, just as in his wrestling heyday, he's the drawing card. He takes a seat at a table facing the committee members, all of whom, I might add, are present and accounted for. Ventura sits before them with a half-gallon carton of Minnesota-produced 2-percent milk and a glass on the table in front of him.

"It's time to end two-party partisan deadlocks on farm bills and focus on results for the people," Ventura says in his usual blunt style. "Washington needs to stop using the farmer as a political pawn. Every day three dairy farmers go out of business. Nearly one-third of all Minnesota dairy farmers have disappeared since 1993."

A couple of minutes into reading his testimony, the governor pauses and informs the committee his mouth is getting dry. He picks up the carton of milk, pours himself a glass, and guzzles it. When he's done, he lets out a satisfied "Aaahhh." It's the kind of sound kids make to annoy their parents after taking a drink. Ventura is doing it to amuse the committee and make a point. The point is unclear, but the stunt is amusing.

"If there is one reason why I am sitting before you today as the first Reform governor in the United States, it is because the great center of the voting public is weary of politics and business-as-usual. The public is fed up with a farm crisis that never ends. The farmers who I talk with are fed up." Ventura concludes his testimony with the assurance that "I'm here for results, not politics."

When the governor concludes his testimony and leaves the room, the spectators clear out so fast you'd swear a fire alarm went off. It seems there's not much interest in the stimulating testimony about to be delivered by seventeen other witnesses who are actually experts in dairy policy. Most reporters also follow Ventura out of the room.

He walks across the street to conduct a news conference in the shadow of the U.S. Capitol dome. Minnesota representative Collin Peterson, the ranking Democrat on the Subcommittee on Livestock and Horticulture, appears alongside Ventura. "The governor made a big difference today because you folks are here," Peterson says, referring to all the television crews and newspaper reporters. "I'll guarantee you, without Jesse Ventura we would not have this many cameras paying attention to what we've been trying to do over there for the last five or six years in dairy policy. So, Governor, just that alone has been a big help."

Ventura attracts more media coverage an hour later when he appears at the U.S. Chamber of Commerce to deliver a speech about dairy policy. He gleefully shares with the luncheon audience details of a practical joke he played on a member of his staff the night before. It involves a night out with a couple of his old Navy SEAL buddies.

"Naturally, us old frogmen were going out on the town," Ventura says. "That can spell real trouble for the town." He says Wendy Wustenberg, his director of intergovernmental relations, was nervous about him going out before his big day on Capitol Hill. After all, she wrote both the testimony he'll give to Congress and his chamber speech. "Wendy made my friends promise to get the governor in by ten o'clock. After all, 'He's going to testify in front of Congress tomorrow.'" The audience starts chuckling as they sense what's coming.

"I said, we're going to fix her," Ventura continues. "So we concocted a story with my security guys. I told them to come down in the morning and have their sunglasses on and tell Wendy that, 'Oh boy, the governor didn't get in until 4:30. We don't even know if he got out of his suit. He probably slept in it, because they started drinking shooters last night, as frogs sometimes will, and he got in all kinds of trouble.' Lo and behold, it worked! They did a great job."

Ventura says Wustenberg was so frantic she couldn't even finish her breakfast. And he wasn't done yet. "I came down and continued to play the role, and I held my head and I said, 'Is there any way Commissioner Hugoson can talk to Congress today? I don't think I can do it.'" Wustenberg was dumbfounded. "Naturally, Wendy was going to string up my old frogman buddies."

The audience gets a good laugh out of the story, but Ventura says he's also making a point. "That's what I try to bring to government and my staff. I'm going to have fun. We have nothing to lose. After all, they told me I couldn't win. So if I misbehave occasionally, I guess they'll expect it from somebody who couldn't win."

As a matter of fact, just two days later he is "misbehaving" again on his *Lunch with the Governor* radio show. He says his successful trip to Washington, D.C., to promote Minnesota farm interests is an example of the good he does by traveling the country and making national television appearances. Then he gets downright nasty.

"So for all those naysayers out there who say, 'Oh, the governor shouldn't be standing in front of the cameras, the governor shouldn't be bringing attention to himself,' and all that stuff that I get, all the crap from the people that don't like me out there—well, this is in your face now, because you all can shut up!"

He saves special invective for one of his most strident critics, Darrell McKigney, president of the Taxpayers League of Minnesota. Ventura refers to McKigney as "McIdiot." That's just for starters. He also calls him a "fat load" and nicknames him "Lumpy Rutherford," a reference to the overweight kid on *Leave It to Beaver.*

CHAPTER 8

"A Ritual Political Suicide"
Shocking the World Again

It's not long before Jesse Ventura does more to blur the line between politics and the World Wrestling Federation. In fact, the governor all but erases the line by agreeing to take part in a huge pay-per-view wrestling event. If he thought he had critics before, he better hold onto his feather boa and brace for more. On July 12, 1999, his office issues a short release confirming rumors that have circulated for more than a month. "Governor Ventura is scheduled to participate in "Summer-Slam," a pay-per-view wrestling event sponsored by the World Wrestling Federation on Sunday, August 22. The Office of the Governor is not involved in coordinating this event." A news conference will be held the next day to announce more details.

Ventura no longer has "the Body" that initially made him famous. He's put on a considerable amount of weight since his election, so it's unlikely he'll actually wrestle. The speculation is that he'll either reprise his role as a ringside announcer or be a guest referee for a championship match.

What we do know is that the event sold out in just ninety minutes with advance-ticket sales of nearly $500,000. Of course, the big money on this event will come from individual pay-per-view fees at $29.95. Some of that big money will end up in Ventura's pocket. Estimates put the figure in the $1 million range.

Ventura has other money matters on his mind. Not his own

money, but money belonging to taxpayers. He holds a news conference on the State Capitol steps to announce that Minnesota's robust economy has added another $298 million to the state's budget surplus. The $1.25 billion rebate passed by the legislature and signed by the governor in May will now grow to $1.3 billion, the maximum allowed by the legislation. The other $248 million will be carried over to the next year for rebates or tax cuts.

"This will be the largest tax rebate in any state in history," Ventura announces, flanked by his commissioners of finance and revenue. He says the fiscal year ended June 30, the money is in the bank, and now it's time to "settle up" with taxpayers just as he promised during his campaign. The extra money means the average rebate will grow by $24. A married couple earning $50,000 a year will get a check for $1,005. Single filers earning that much will get $805.

It's a significant story, but reporters also want to hear more about the check the governor will soon be getting from the WWF. In a feisty exchange with the capitol press corps, the governor refuses to talk about it. "We're here to talk about rebates, we're at the capitol," Ventura barks when asked about details of his WWF deal. "That has nothing to do with my business as governor."

Ventura's not talking, but his critics have plenty to say. Ron Eibensteiner, chair of the Minnesota Republican Party, calls the wrestling plans an "outrage." He says Ventura's appearance in the wrestling event will "contribute to the cynical opinion that people have of politicians today: that politicians are only looking out for themselves, lining their own pockets and not doing the people's business."

Eibensteiner calls on Ventura to disclose the complete financial arrangements of his deal with the WWF, but not before calling the whole scenario an embarrassment for the state. "Our governor donning tights and performing in a ballet of violence, as he likes to call it, will not bring honor and dignity to the office of governor in our state." Democratic senator John Marty, one of the legislature's leading ethics watchdogs, says Ventura is taking unseemly advantage of the position Minnesotans handed him. "We all know this isn't the sort of thing usually offered to washed-up forty-eight-year-old wrestlers," Marty says.

Senate Majority Leader Roger Moe at least finds some humor in the situation. "Listen, I did tell the governor that I'd wrestle him, but he'd have to come to my weight class," he says with a chuckle.

Although Ventura told reporters earlier in the morning he wouldn't talk about the WWF event until the next day's news conference, the criticism draws him from his corner. He comes out fighting on Minnesota Public Radio's *Midday* program a couple of hours later. He still won't reveal how much he'll be paid or what exactly he'll do at the WWF pay-per-view event, but he steadfastly defends his right to do just about anything he wants.

"There's no rule that says a governor can't have fun," he tells host Gary Eichten. "There's no rule that says a governor on his own time can't be human.... The perception is that people need to be professional politicians and that therefore being a politician is your entire life. Well, it's not Jesse Ventura's entire life, and I think I was elected upon the fact that I came from being a private citizen."

Ventura also points out that he'll take part in the WWF event on his own time on a Sunday and it will benefit Minnesota by putting the state back in the spotlight. Not surprisingly, he seems to have a lot of public support. Several callers to the MPR show tell Ventura to ignore the criticism. "Don't sweat the media quite as much as you're doing," says Harry of International Falls. "When you destroy a Minnesota icon like Skip Humphrey, the media are going to give you hell, even if you were the Virgin Mary!"

After a hearty belly laugh, Ventura tells Harry, "I'll remember that!"

Suck It!

On July 14, the floor of the Target Center in downtown Minneapolis will be the site of the once unthinkable: Vince McMahon and Jesse Ventura sharing the same stage again in a televised news conference beamed via satellite around the world. "SummerSlam" and WWF logos are plastered just about everywhere to fit into any conceivable camera shot for this news conference announcing Ventura's return to the ring. A huge poster hangs above the stage bearing "Stone Cold" Steve Austin's face and a coy, Ventura-related slogan for "SummerSlam": "An out of 'Body' experience."

"There's some media people out there and, I'm sure, some politicians that are scoffing at the fact that Jesse 'the Body' Ventura is going to take part in 'SummerSlam,'" says a scruffy-looking wrestler named X-Pac, wearing sunglasses and black, curly hair down to his shoulders. "Well, you know what? If you ain't down with Jesse 'the Body' Ventura being here at 'SummerSlam,' we got two words for ya!"

X-Pac doesn't have to say the last two words, because a thousand, mostly adolescent wrestling fans on hand to watch the news conference all yell in unison, "Suck it!" I should have known it was coming because X-Pac is wearing a football jersey with the words "Suck it" printed on the front. X-Pac is followed by another class act, the lovely Debra. This walking bundle of breasts steps onstage in a black miniskirt accentuated by a red jacket and black blouse unbuttoned down to her nether regions.

It's difficult to understand exactly what she's uttering into the microphone, but she's mumbling something about taking her "puppies" out for a walk. She starts to unbutton her blouse before she's finally ushered off stage to the disappointment of the adoring adolescents and more than a few mesmerized political reporters in the media seats directly in front of the stage.

Eventually, we get to the main event. Vince McMahon, the WWF chair and Ventura's former archenemy, takes center stage to a healthy round of boos from the partisan crowd.

"It is indeed an honor," McMahon says, ignoring the hostile crowd, "to announce that the guest referee in the World Wrestling Federation championship match to be held at 'SummerSlam' at the Target Center will be Jesse 'the Body' Ventura." The boos turn to cheers for the hometown hero of these rabid wrestling fans.

Ventura appears from behind a curtain to a huge ovation. He's wearing an olive-colored business suit when he walks up onstage as highlights of his wrestling career beam across the arena scoreboard. When he reaches McMahon, Ventura extends his hand as if to offer a handshake, but then pulls it back before McMahon can reach him.

McMahon feigns shock at such mistreatment. The crowd is now chanting, "Jesse, Jesse, Jesse!"

Ventura stands there and soaks it in. "The Body" is home. "I never thought I would ever see the day that my name would be next to the World Wrestling Federation again," he says. "But I'll tell you what. In light of where wrestling is today, it is time to bring back some law and order, and that will be my job at 'SummerSlam' August 22 for the championship match, because I rule here." Another big ovation from the crowd as Ventura turns his attention to McMahon. "I am bigger than you, McMahon. I'm more powerful than you. I am more powerful than the World Wrestling Federation. As long as you're in this state, you hold no power here. It's very simple. 'The Body' rules."

Next Ventura turns his attention to his other favorite foe, the media. "There's been a lot of criticism that I'm not in shape anymore. The two local newspapers have both taken shots at me this week and said a bunch of bull that I'm not in shape anymore. Well, we're going to prove to them August 22 who's in shape. . . . I'm not stepping back in the ring to wrestle, but I'm stepping back in the ring to be a referee—and there will be law and order!"

Then, just like that, he's back to picking on McMahon and baits the crowd into chanting, "Asshole, asshole, asshole!" Clearly, this whole event is orchestrated to make McMahon and Ventura as much money as possible. Somehow, though, the "asshole" chant aimed at McMahon seems refreshingly real.

McMahon steps back up to the microphone in mock disgust as the "asshole" chants continue to reverberate through the arena. "That's Twin Cities hospitality?" he asks. Next up in this carefully scripted psychodrama are wrestlers Triple H and his aptly nicknamed female sidekick, Chyna, "the Ninth Wonder of the World." McMahon steps aside as they make their entrance.

"This is the WWF, so make some noise!" Triple H implores the crowd. Chyna steps up to make a special presentation to Ventura, now seated at a table on the stage. "I certainly remember Jesse 'the Body,' but I thought you might need a little reminder," she says, reaching into a bag. "So, Mr. Ventura, if you would stand up for a moment, I'd like to help everybody remember." She wraps yellow and black feather boas around the governor's neck and hands him a pair of oversized, jewel-studded sunglasses. Ventura happily puts it all on and slips right back into the persona he once vowed to leave behind for politics. "How'd we do it in those old days?" he says before he starts strutting on the stage like the Ventura of old, combining a sort of duckwalk with a head bob.

After introductions and more antics from other WWF luminaries like "Stone Cold" Steve Austin, the Rock, and the Undertaker, the event finally turns into a news conference. First, though, "Stone Cold" presents Ventura with a WWF championship belt Ventura never won while wrestling because, according to Austin, "that crooked-ass promoter [McMahon] never gave the title shot he needed to Jesse 'the Body' Ventura."

During the news conference the governor reveals he'll earn a $100,000 appearance fee and says all that money will go to two charities he's creating. The Jade Foundation, named after his daughter, will get $50,000 to help underprivileged kids. The other $50,000 will go to a scholarship fund in Ventura's name at his alma mater in Minneapolis, Roosevelt High School. However, the big money Ventura will earn will come from videotape royalties and the copyright use of his name. When asked how much that might amount to, the governor will only say, "That's confidential." McMahon can't resist chiming in. "Let me just say, if it's a dollar, it's entirely too much."

Sports-marketing experts peg the estimate of the governor's take at a minimum of $1 million. It's not difficult to figure out why. The WWF claims to be the number-one pay-per-view provider in the world, citing 4.3 million pay-per-view sales grossing $130 million in 1998. One 'WrestleMania' event alone grossed $24 million. The upcoming 'SummerSlam' is expected to draw six hundred thousand to seven hundred thousand pay-per-view customers, putting the gross anywhere from $18 million to $21 million. Imagine what Ventura could command for the "copyright" fee on his name with that kind of money floating around.

As for videotape royalties, the WWF also claims to control 56 percent of the sports video market. If that's not enough, the WWF also generated an estimated $500 million in retail sales of licensed products in 1998. When you consider those figures, it seems like Ventura is getting ripped off if he only gets $1 million. The fact is, Ventura also could command even more because McMahon *needs* Ventura. WWF wrestler Owen Hart died in a wrestling ring in May at a time when the WWF was already under attack for its increasingly violent, raunchy, and sexually explicit content. Criticism doesn't usually seem to bother McMahon too much, unless it costs him money. This time it might cost him money because he's got plans in the coming months to take his company public.

The stock might be a tough sell unless the WWF takes steps to clean up its act. What better way to do that than to feature the one wrestler who made the quantum leap from the wrestling ring to mainstream respectability in the political ring? "Having Jesse back in the World Wrestling Federation is, I think, a considerable influence, a positive influence," McMahon concedes at the news conference.

Other than money, what does Ventura get out of this? That's what I'm trying to find out when I put my life on the line in the midst of the raucous WWF crowd. After I stand to ask a question, someone sticks a microphone in my hand so everyone in the arena can hear. "Some of your critics have been quoted in the newspapers and elsewhere recently saying that your association with the WWF makes a mockery of the office and harms the dignity of the office of governor with the feather boa and the sunglasses. What's your response to that?" I was only about halfway through my interrogatory when the "boo-birds" came out again, this time aiming at me. I could hear one voice louder than the rest yelling, "Sit doowwwn, Tooommm!"

Suddenly, I know what it's like to be Vince McMahon. Ventura tries to answer my question by simply holding his hands up as if to say, "Listen to the crowd—that's all you need to know."

"What's your response to that?" I ask, pressing him and my luck at the same time. "I know their response."

Finally, Ventura responds. "When I was running for this office, the press would never refer to me as 'former mayor.' The press always referred to me as 'former pro wrestler.' So I don't see why anyone would be upset at all if I were a NBA player and I got involved in a NBA basketball game in some manner. I don't think anyone would say anything. I'm not going to stop having fun. My critics didn't vote for me anyway, did they?"

As a follow-up, I ask him why he's getting involved with McMahon after claiming McMahon once cheated him so badly they ended up in court. "That was business seven or eight years ago," Ventura responds. "It's now 1999, and I'm happy to be here and supporting two new charities that I think are going to help a lot of kids in Minnesota." Once again, McMahon can't resist piping in. "And besides, there's nothing that goes on in the World Wrestling Federation that doesn't or hasn't gone on in the White House."

Ventura gets testy when the questions keep turning to how much money he'll make for his one-night stand in the WWF. "It's interesting how the media wants to grill me on what I'm making and all this and all that. Maybe somebody should turn the tables around and say how much money have I brought to the media. Because it's the media that chooses to cover everything I do, whether I stub my toe or anything else."

I don't know about the other reporters, but I get paid the same whether I'm covering Jesse Ventura or a brushfire. As for my television station, I'm guessing we've spent much more money covering the governor than we've made as a result of covering him. Those facts won't get in the way of a good rant by Ventura. "I found it very interesting yesterday that we in Minnesota gave back the largest surplus in history back to the taxpayers, and yet when you looked at your local newspapers today, what was the headline story? Jesse Ventura's participation in wrestling took a bigger headline than $1.3 billion being given back to the taxpayers of Minnesota."

Whether he likes it or not, the governor of a state stepping into the wrestling ring with the WWF is big news. Besides, the rebate story has been reported ad nauseam for six months. The wrestling story raises significant public-policy questions the governor must answer. Patrick Sweeney from the *St. Paul Pioneer Press* tries to get one of those answers when he dares to ask Ventura if it's appropriate for him to have state-paid security guards with him at this wrestling promotion.

"The law says the governor is to be protected twenty-four hours a day," Ventura responds. "If you don't like it, go to the legislature and change the law and say the governor's only to be protected between 8:00 and 4:30 Monday through Friday." Ventura also points out he's taking a vacation day for this appearance and will do so for the WWF event on August 22.

The mood lightens considerably as the news conference/wrestling sideshow nears a conclusion. A local comedian attending the news conference, Fancy Ray McCloney, coaxes Ventura into performing an impressive rendition of one of Muhammad Ali's famous rapid-fire boxing soliloquies. Ventura's face lights up as he slips into Ali's persona. "'I Am the Greatest,' by Cassius Clay, number 73. This is the legend of Cassius Clay, the most beautiful fighter in the world today. Who talks a great deal and brags indeed, with a muscular punch that's incredibly speedy. The fistic world was dull and weary, with a champ like Liston things had to be dreary. Then someone with color, someone with dash, brought fight fans running with cash...."

As the crowd gives him a big ovation, Ventura appears unaware of the irony of how those words fit the occasion.

Naturally, his foray into the WWF receives saturation coverage on Minnesota television and radio stations and in the daily newspapers. But how does it play nationally? At least two television networks, MSNBC and Fox News Channel, carry live coverage of the WWF event. That alone probably makes it worthwhile for McMahon to pay Ventura a million dollars. You can't buy the kind of mainstream news coverage Ventura attracts. He puts the WWF in front of viewers who wouldn't ordinarily give a wrestling pay-per-view event a second thought.

The coverage does raise some eyebrows from media critics wondering if a WWF-produced "news" conference warrants live news coverage. "Jesse Ventura is a political phenomenon," says John Moody, Fox News Channel's vice president for news, in an interview with the Associated Press. "There is no other way to describe him. To come from his background and be elected governor is a political rarity. Therefore, he's newsworthy."

A CNN spokesperson tells the AP that the network passed on airing live coverage because it was concerned about promoting a pay-per-view event. MSNBC not only carries coverage of the wrestling promotion, it interrupts an interview with Arizona senator John McCain about the 2000 presidential race.

Not all the coverage is positive. While watching Ventura prance around the stage in a feather boa and sunglasses, Fox News Channel commentator Dick Morris calls the event "a ritual political suicide.... In the last fifteen minutes, this man has destroyed his political career." A bit of an overstatement, though Morris knows a thing or two about political suicide, after having been caught with a prostitute while working as a key adviser to President Clinton.

Not only has Ventura not committed political suicide, he sees his popularity in Minnesota soar to a record high. In the *Star Tribune/KMSP-TV* Minnesota Poll published July 22, 1999, the governor's job-approval rating hits 73 percent, topping the 72 percent he registered just after his inauguration in January. It's the highest rating ever registered by any of the ten governors measured by the poll since 1947.

The poll surveyed 1,001 Minnesota adults from July 6 through July 14. The last two days of polling were conducted after the governor announced his plans to referee a WWF match. In other words, despite the controversies over his autobiography, his book-tour expenses, and now the wrestling promotion, Minnesotans are taking Ventura on an extended honeymoon cruise. In fact, 57 percent of respondents say Ventura's self-promotion is good for the state.

Reform Party Controversy

Ventura's latest stunning poll numbers come on the eve of the national Reform Party convention in Dearborn, Michigan. It's the party's first national convention since Ventura's election and he's expected to be the star attraction. His victory gave the party a much-needed dose of credibility, and his latest poll numbers confirm he's no fluke. The party won't be nominating a presidential candidate until next year's convention, so the key item on the agenda this year is electing a new national party chair.

Three weeks before this convention, Ventura sent a letter by e-mail to Reform Party delegates, urging them to support Jack Gargan of Cedar Key, Florida, to be the next chair. In the letter, the governor threatens to confine his Reform Party activities to his home state unless new leadership is elected. The current chair of the party is Russell Verney, the only elected chair the party has ever had. Verney is a Ross Perot loyalist and works as a paid political adviser to Perot in Dallas. Ventura is convinced the only way the national party can move forward and build on his victory is with new leadership that isn't beholden to Perot.

"Together, Jack Gargan and I can help make the Minnesota miracle happen in other states," Ventura writes to the delegates. He goes on to say that "if the convention delegates are not willing to elect and support the best person for the job, I'll remain reluctant to fully embrace the national Reform Party. I'll be pleased to keep my party activities within Minnesota's borders."

Verney quickly criticizes Ventura's letter as an "ultimatum" that will harm the party. A week later Verney announces he won't seek reelection as party chair but says his decision has nothing to do with Ventura's support of Gargan. Still, Verney quickly endorses two other candidates to replace him as chair. The stage is now set for a showdown between the Perot faction of the Reform Party and the insurgent Ventura faction.

As Reform Party delegates gather at the Hyatt Regency hotel in Dearborn on July 23, 1999, so do some rather ominous storm clouds. It's been hot and humid in the Detroit area all day, and by late afternoon it looks as if someone flipped off the light switch. The winds begin to swirl beneath the black clouds before lightning and thunder punctuate the start of a heavy downpour.

This is not good news for convention delegates expecting to hear Governor Ventura deliver a speech tonight. Ventura is stuck in a Northwest Airlines plane on the runway at the Minneapolis—St. Paul International Airport. A system of severe weather is crawling through the

Detroit area, and air-traffic controllers won't let Ventura's plane depart from Minneapolis. He sits there for three hours. The excruciating delay is made all the worse by severe back pain from an injury Ventura suffered playing golf a few days earlier. Finally, his flight is cancelled.

Even though Ventura won't make it to the convention in person, he will still cast a major influence on it. The letter he sent to the delegates a few weeks ago is still making waves. "The wording might not have been exactly what he wanted to say in the letter," says Doug Friedline, Ventura's campaign manager, who is at the convention to help Gargan with his campaign for party chair.

Friedline admits some delegates who support Ventura didn't like the heavy-handed tone of the letter, but says the intent wasn't to be divisive. "I think he really wants this to work. He just says if it doesn't look like it's fair and open elections here, if there's some type of shenanigans going on or something, he would pull back and he would just stick with the Minnesota message, and I think that's very important."

Jack Gargan is holding court at his own booth not far from the Minnesota Reform Party booth. The silver-haired retired insurance agent wears a white T-shirt emblazoned front and back with the words "Head Geezer." Obviously, he doesn't take himself too seriously, but he's dead serious about the Reform Party and what it stands for.

"The Reform Party is all about better government," Gargan says before rattling off specific ways the party would create better government. "We're talking term limits. We're talking balanced-budget amendment. We're talking real, honest-to-God campaign-finance reform." That message connected with voters in Gargan's 1998 congressional race, in which he garnered 34 percent of the vote. Of the 154 Reform Party candidates running nationally, Gargan says his vote was second only to Ventura's 37 percent in Minnesota.

"He has talked the talk and walked the walk about what real reform is about," Gargan says. "Governor Ventura has shown the American people that your vote does count. The Republicans and Democrats have been telling us for years, if you have a third-party candidate you've got a wasted vote. They worked it on Perot, they worked it on me and on countless other third-party candidates or independents. Governor Ventura has blown that out."

Gargan says he appreciates Ventura's support but is concerned about the party splitting into Perot and Ventura factions. "Until three weeks ago there wasn't a Ventura faction," Gargan tells me, alluding to the e-mail Ventura sent to convention delegates. "It wasn't even considered. He was doing such a good job in his home state of Minnesota, and the whole eyes of the world were on him doing such a good job." Now that Ventura is taking a more active role nationally by lobbying for Gargan, it's uncertain what impact it will have on the party. "All this has just blossomed out," Gargan says. "And, of course, his letter had some strong wording in there, so it both helped and hurt me. I think overall, though, the help has got to be there, because he's our shining star."

Later that evening Ventura gets a chance to address the convention, but he's forced to do so by telephone hookup from his Maple Grove ranch. Unlike his letter to the delegates a few weeks earlier, Ventura's message is one of unity rather than division. He even extends an olive branch to Perot supporters by publicly thanking Perot. "We owe him a great debt as the founder of our party. We learned from him that a third party can be taken seriously if its leaders use common sense and demonstrate they are in touch with the people."

As always, the governor also uses the opportunity to take a shot at the media. He blames them for all the speculation that he might run for president. "Do not trust the media!" his voice booms through the ballroom speakers. Ventura knows how to unify an audience. On that point, he gets loud applause from both his own supporters and Perot's.

Perot isn't quite as gracious as Ventura when he addresses the convention in person the next day. In fact, Perot doesn't even mention Ventura during his Saturday night speech, although he does seem to refer to the governor when he says the purpose of public service is "to serve, not to cash in." Perot's veiled shot at him notwithstanding, Ventura gets the last laugh at this convention. On Sunday, Gargan is elected to succeed Verney as the national party chair on a 213–135 vote over Pat Benjamin, the current vice chair.

Gargan says he plans to move the Reform Party headquarters from Texas, where Perot is based, to Florida. A vote will be held later to determine the site for the 2000 Reform Party presidential nominating convention. With the Reform Party eligible for $13 million in federal election funds for its presidential candidate, the convention will be very important. Minnesota's delegation is hoping to convince the delegates that Minnesota is the logical site because it's home to the only Reform Party governor in the country.

A week after the convention, the focus is back on Ventura's private moneymaking ventures. The Minnesota legislative auditor releases a report criticizing the governor for using state-paid security for his book-promotion tour in late May and early June. Even though the attorney general already ruled that using the security was legal, several state lawmakers requested a review of the expenses by the legislative auditor, whose office reviews financial activities of all state departments and agencies to check for compliance with state laws and regulations.

The auditor determines the two trips cost the state nearly $16,000. That's the total for the three state troopers and one staff person who accompanied the governor on the trips to Los Angeles, New York, Washington, D.C., and Chicago. The book publisher paid for Governor Ventura's expenses.

The legislative auditor, James Nobles, writes his own five-page opinion regarding the book-tour travel expenses. He begins by acknowledging the attorney general's ruling, but says that doesn't mean this issue shouldn't be explored further. "First, we do not think all discussion should end simply because the Attorney General said it was legal for the state to pay certain book tour expenses," Nobles writes. "There is more to 'good government' than legalities. Moreover, in adding costs to state government by pursuing private business activities, Governor Ventura has raised important policy questions that need more consideration, particularly by the legislature."

Nobles suggests that while the governor may not be violating state law, his use of state security for private business trips borders on unethical. "There is a strong tradition in Minnesota against state employees and officials using public resources for private gain. By law, state employees and officials are strictly forbidden from using state time or other resources to help them obtain private benefits."

Nobles gets a sharply worded written response to the audit report from Ventura's commissioner of public safety, Charlie Weaver. "Our policy has always been, and will continue to be, that we will afford the Governor, his family and elected officials the level of protection necessary to ensure their safety." Weaver says that the obligations of the state troopers who protect the governor don't change depending on the purpose for his public appearances. "The fact is that Governor Ventura is a worldwide celebrity.... I can assure you that anyone intent on doing him harm will be unconcerned with whether an event relates to his public or private business.... If the legislature engages in a public debate and concludes that the Governor is not entitled to state-provided security at certain events, and those types of events are specifically described, it would be like sending an open invitation to any disturbed individual who may intend to harm the governor or his family."

By far the most critical responses to the legislative audit report come from Governor Ventura and his wife, Terry. State representative Carol Molnau, a Republican and frequent critic of Ventura, is among the lawmakers who requested the audit. Molnau saves a voice-mail message left for her by Terry Ventura. "I too am canceling all of my security," she says in her heated voice mail to Molnau. "I am also canceling my children's security. I'm throwing security off of my ranch. We will be here. We will be alone. We will not be protected except by the goodwill of the people who live around us and by our own wits." It turns out Terry Ventura is just blowing off steam because none of the security arrangements are actually changed.

Governor Ventura's response, ironically, comes from San Diego where he's on a six-day vacation to take part in the navy's annual "Fleet Week" celebration. On his weekly radio show, broadcast live from

San Diego (where his security contingent dutifully stands by), Ventura notes that no one questions the security provided to Vice President Al Gore or Texas governor George Bush while they're campaigning for president. "You know what it all comes down to in reality? If you're a Democrat or Republican, it's OK. But if you're a Reform Party person, you shouldn't be doing things like that."

CHAPTER 9

"I'm Proud I'm a Wrestler"
The Body's New Chyna Policy

On August 7, 1999, Jesse Ventura arrives in St. Louis for the third National Governors Conference since his election. He's still the star attraction among the governors gathered at the Adam's Mark Hotel. The summer session of the conference is usually a sleepy affair that doesn't attract much attention. Not this year. Both President Clinton and Colin Powell are scheduled to speak to the governors, heightening the event's profile.

Clinton focuses much of his speech on bad-mouthing a tax-cut bill the Republican-controlled House recently passed in Congress as an attempt to deal with a growing federal budget surplus. The president says it would be disastrous for the nation. "This is not just politics," he tells the governors, "this is arithmetic." He also makes a point Ventura could take to heart because it's the same point the governor makes repeatedly in Minnesota. "A projected surplus is not the same as one in the bank," Clinton says, eliciting a nod of agreement from Ventura.

Naturally, Clinton and Ventura are the two most famous politicians in the room. So guess who dominates news coverage of the president's speech? Well, other than Clinton, it's Ventura, of course. A color photo of the two men graces the top front page of the *New York Times* on August 9. The same photo also appears in the *Los Angeles Times*, the *St. Louis Post—Dispatch*, and many other newspapers throughout the country. The *New York Times* caption with the photo says, "Gov. Jesse

Ventura of Minnesota said that he had listened to President Clinton's speech lambasting the Republican tax cut and promised to keep an open mind in weighing the bill against Mr. Clinton's alternative." More important, the *Times* reports in the story accompanying the photo that Clinton and Ventura also "talked at length about wrestling."

The day Ventura's picture is splashed across the nation's newspapers, looking his gubernatorial best in the company of the president of the United States, the governor jets off to the other end of our cultural spectrum. He's scheduled to appear at the World Wrestling Federation's "Raw Is War" event in Chicago to promote his upcoming referee gig at "SummerSlam." Ventura and his state-trooper bodyguards fly at the WWF's expense from St. Louis to Chicago for the appearance. Allstate Arena is jammed with the usual assortment of crazed wrestling fans here to see wrestling superstars "Stone Cold" Steve Austin, Mankind, and Triple H. They'll get a bonus when the most famous ex-wrestler of all time steps into the ring. So will millions of viewers around the country watching the event televised on the USA Network.

Wrestling announcer Jerry "the King" Lawler goes to the center of the ring to introduce Ventura. "He shocked the world and he will shock 'SummerSlam,'" Lawler yells, straining to be heard over the wildly cheering crowd. "Jesse 'the Body' Ventura!"

The sold-out crowd is up for a standing ovation as Ventura walks down a ramp toward the ring. He stops briefly, preening for the cameras. As he climbs between the ropes, rock music blares through the arena and highlights of Ventura's wrestling antics play on an enormous ringside screen. His fans are ready for Ventura's appearance, holding up signs that say "People's Governor," "The Body Is Back," "Jesse for Prez," and "The Body Is the Law."

Ventura looks more governor than ex-wrestler, wearing a tan double-breasted suit and tie. But when Lawler hands him the microphone, he's all wrestler. Ventura assures this hard-core wrestling audience he'll take care of business in the ring when he referees the upcoming championship match. "We all know who is the power in Minnesota, and we all know why did the World Wrestling Federation come to Jesse 'the

Body' Ventura for a match of this magnitude. A world championship match! Because they know I am the only person who can deliver law and order."

Just then the lights go out in the arena and up comes some incredibly loud music. Triple H and his female sidekick, Chyna, saunter down the ramp. Triple H, one of the wrestlers scheduled for the championship match on August 22, steps into the ring to meet with Ventura face-to-face.

"It's my way or the highway in that ring," Ventura warns Triple H, a menacing-looking man with shoulder-length brown hair who stands six-foot-four and weighs 246 pounds. "Those are the rules. Live with it!" Certainly in this little melodrama, Triple H can't back down from Ventura.

"You must be stuck in the seventies or something," Triple H responds. "I hear you out here talking about former this, former that, 'I was, I used to be.' I'm beginning to think the air up there has gotta be doing something to your brain. It's gotta be throwing you off, making you see and do funny things!"

The crowd starts chanting, "Asshole! Asshole! Asshole!" This obviously is some kind of wrestling ritual not solely reserved for Vince McMahon appearances. Ventura listens to the crowd for a moment, then looks at Triple H and deadpans, "I think they're talking to you!"

Triple H doesn't back down. "Let me make this clear," he tells Ventura, inching closer to the governor. "This is not Minnesota. This is my world. This right here, where your two little feet are standing dead center in the middle of what is 'my' ring!"

Ventura looks over at the announcer, Lawler, and says, "King, you better explain to him that this is *my* country, which is bigger than *your* ring! You better tell him to go look at the *New York Times* today, to go look at the *L.A. Times* today, and see whose picture stood with the president of the United States today." Ventura's face is now just inches from Triple H's.

"You might have been standing face-to-face with the president, but right now you're standing face-to-face, nose-to-nose, eye-to-eye with me," Triple H says, proving to be no slouch with the mouth. "And I don't care who you are and I don't care who you've got with you. If right here in the middle of this ring I feel like kicking your ass, I will."

Just then there's a commotion outside the ring and a big cheer. Shawn Michaels, a former WWF champion and now the WWF commissioner, is on his way down. He steps into the ring to break up what appears to be the makings of a "brawl" between Ventura and Triple H.

Like Clark Kent hopping into a phone booth and emerging as Superman, Ventura the wrestling promoter hops onto a plane that night and heads back to St. Louis and reemerges as governor. The next day he appears on C-Span's *Washington Journal* program. Again, I've not bothered to research this, but I've got to believe Ventura is the first politician in history to appear on the WWF's "Raw Is War" program one day and C-Span the next.

The following week Governor Ventura gets back to his day job of governing Minnesota. On Monday, August 16, he announces he's merging two state departments. The Department of Public Service, which regulates public utilities, will merge with the Department of Commerce, which regulates financial-services industries like banking and real estate. The commissioner of the new Department of Commerce will be Steve Minn, the current commissioner of public service. The governor says he decided to make the move after Commerce Commissioner David Jennings resigned to take another job. "We're going to make the most of today's technology to really improve government's efficiency," Ventura tells reporters. "I've always said we will provide leadership and act upon our beliefs, so we're starting here in our own backyard to cut the size of government."

As usual, this attempt at government reform by Ventura stirs controversy. Lawmakers are upset they weren't consulted before the governor made such a major structural change in state government. In announcing the move, Ventura makes it clear he's determined to reform and reduce government. "It is the prerogative of the governor to organize and manage the affairs of the executive branch," he insists.

Just ninety minutes after that announcement, Ventura makes another appearance outside the Minnesota Department of Revenue, two blocks from the capitol. With great fanfare, he announces the "checks are in the mail." The state sales-tax rebate checks, that is. While spending the weekend at his cabin near Annandale, about fifty miles northwest of the Twin Cities, Ventura says he found out firsthand the checks were already arriving for some taxpayers. "I was riding my WaveRunner and a lady waved me down ... and she called me over and said, 'Governor, thank you, I just got my check today!'"

Ventura can't resist taking a political potshot even on this joyous occasion. He's upset by an ad running in local newspapers in which Republicans take credit for returning the budget surplus. "It says in here the Democrats wanted to spend it and the governor wanted to hold onto it," he says, holding up a copy of the ad. "Well, for a party that expounds on family values, I find it very interesting that telling the truth doesn't seem to be one of the values."

The next day, Governor Ventura makes good on another one of his campaign promises. He sets off on a barnstorming tour of Minnesota cities, trying to sell his idea for a unicameral, or single house, legislature. It's kind of a nerdy issue for a macho former Navy SEAL and professional wrestler to be so wrapped up in, but Ventura is dead serious. He flies around the state, making stump speeches in Rochester, Mankato, Moorhead, and Duluth and on the State Capitol steps in St. Paul. "Unicameral empowers the people, bicameral empowers the legislators," he says in his sales pitch. "Only insiders and those paid to work the system really understand the legislative process. As a result, legislators and lobbyists can easily manipulate it to their advantage."

Ventura would like to merge the Minnesota House of Representatives and Senate into one body and significantly reduce the total number of legislators. There are now 134 representatives and sixty-seven senators. By cutting the two-house system from 201 to one chamber with 135 members, Ventura says the state could save $20 million a year. More important, he says, the legislative process would no longer be a "maze" the average citizen can't navigate. "Under a nonpartisan single house, citizens will not have to track legislation through multiple committee hearings in both bodies and through the conference-committee process," Ventura says to a group of reporters at the last stop of the day on the capitol steps.

The governor does have a point about Minnesota's number of legislators being on the high side. The state has 201 legislators serving a population of five million. California, with thirty-four million residents, has only 120 lawmakers. Texas serves its twenty-one million people with 181 legislators, and Florida's state government has 160 members for its sixteen million people. However, all of those states have bicameral legislatures. In fact, only Nebraska employs a unicameral legislature. Many political scientists say there's good reason for that. Steve Smith, a political-science professor at the University of Minnesota, says the governor's proposal could make government more responsive but less responsible.

"Bicameralism was adopted by most states so that legislating was *not* easy," he says, "so that the hasty actions of one chamber could be checked by the deliberations of the other chamber." But he's not surprised Ventura is pushing so hard for a single house. "Governors are forever frustrated with legislatures," Smith says.

Ventura promises to make a strong push to get the unicameral choice on the ballot when the legislative session begins in February 2000. "We are at a pivotal point in Minnesota politics," he says. "The people are not satisfied with politics-as-usual, and they deserve the opportunity to vote whether to make the change to a nonpartisan, single-house system."

Lawsuits and Complaints

The same day Ventura barnstorms the state, promoting his plan to reduce the size of government, a complaint is filed to restrict the governor's ability to earn outside income. Common Cause Minnesota, the political watchdog group, protests the governor's involvement in the World Wrestling Federation's event to the Minnesota Department of Employee Relations. In its complaint, the group argues that Ventura's contract with the WWF represents a "conflict of interest" and violates state law regarding conduct by a state employee.

In the complaint, Common Cause president David Schultz writes, "there is no question that the governor is an officer within the executive branch and if he is an officer within the executive branch he is thus considered an employee ... and therefore subject to the conflict of interest provisions.... Common Cause contends that the Governor has used his official position to secure benefits for himself which are distinct from benefits available to the general public. Specifically, he has used his office to secure both the compensated referee position and marketing rights to the August 22 event."

Schultz insists this complaint is not a frivolous matter. "There's a law in the state of Minnesota that the governor seems to believe he does not have to follow, but everybody else in state government has to follow," he tells me after filing the paperwork. "He is saying that a law that sets a high standard of conduct for our public officials applies to everybody in the state except him. He can live to a lower standard. That's his argument."

Ventura won't talk about the issue, but his spokesperson, John Wodele, insists the governor isn't violating the law. "It's unconventional, not illegal," he says of the governor's WWF appearance. "Some people just can't accept that."

Schultz, a tall, bespectacled professor of public administration at Hamline University in St. Paul, doesn't buy that argument. He says state law is quite clear that the governor is considered a "state employee" and therefore required by law to avoid conflicts of interest. "The reason why Minnesota and every other state makes the governor full-time, pays him a great salary ... gives him a house is because they don't want him influenced by outside interests." Schultz says, odd as it may seem, Ventura may some day have to rule on a state law that could affect the WWF. "Half the states in the United States regulate professional wrestling; Minnesota doesn't," he says. "Maybe that's an issue that's going to come before him."

Schultz isn't the only one raising a red flag about the governor's

WWF deal. The same day Schultz files his complaint, another familiar foe files suit in Ramsey County District Court in St. Paul. Leslie Davis, president of an environmental group called Earth Protector, asks a judge to issue a temporary restraining order to prohibit Ventura from stepping into the ring. Davis ran an unsuccessful write-in bid for governor against Ventura in 1998. Like Schultz, Davis is a far cry from the opponents Ventura used to face in the wrestling ring. Except, that is, with his mouth.

Davis favors ill-fitting sports jackets to go with his jeans, tennis shoes and salt-and-pepper beard. He's a frequent and obstreperous presence at just about any protest involving the environment or animal rights. Now he's focusing much of his energy on harshly criticizing Ventura on nearly every issue, environmental or otherwise. His organization is marketing $20 T-shirts that say, "Our Governor's I.Q. is lower than your Governor's" and another with a picture of a pointy-headed Ventura with the caption "Legalized Dope."

Call Davis what you want, but you can't question his passion and persistence. His original complaint about Ventura's wrestling appearance filed with the Minnesota attorney general was rejected, so he's now taking the same complaint to court. He too makes the argument that Ventura is a "state employee" violating conflict-of-interest laws. Davis doesn't have to wait long for a decision. On August 20, three days after filing the complaint and two days before the governor's wrestling appearance, a Ramsey County judge dismisses the case.

Judge Kathleen Gearin finds that Davis's case has no merit and he doesn't even have "standing" to bring a "private cause of action" against the governor. "The plaintiff has failed to provide any evidence that irreparable harm will be suffered by him individually or to anyone else as a result of Mr. Ventura's involvement in the World Wrestling Federation event this weekend," Gearin writes in her two-page decision.

Although the judge says Davis has no right to bring action against the governor in this case, she does indicate which way she might have ruled on the merits of the case. In a memorandum attached to her decision, Gearin clearly comes down on the side of the governor. "It goes without saying that the Governor of the State of Minnesota is an elected official and as such, his actions will ultimately be approved or disapproved by the voters of this state in the polling booth. An elected official does not by their election become someone without personal, social, economic, and private interests."

The governor couldn't have asked for a more favorable opinion. And she's not done yet. Gearin goes on to say the "lawsuit has no legal basis," even if Davis had standing to bring it before her. "He has not, in either his arguments or the written materials submitted to the Court, given one concrete bit of evidence as to how the Governor's participation in this event Sunday night comes under this statute." She concludes the memorandum by implying the governor is, in reality, free to do just about whatever he wants to earn outside income "whether it involves refereeing at the World Wrestling Federation or directing a Shakespearean production at the Guthrie Theater."

In his usual outspoken, stream-of-consciousness diatribe, Davis criticizes the ruling and calls the governor's outside activities an embarrassment to Minnesota.

"He's all about money," Davis tells reporters in the lobby of the Ramsey County Courthouse. "He's all about violence with the wrestling people, and he knows that if you put the babes up there with their bras on and their butts sticking out of their panties, people are gonna watch it. So he's gonna make a lot of money doing all of that stuff 'cause what he's about is money, sex, and violence."

Unbeknownst to Davis, Shultz, or even Judge Gearin, a far different opinion of the governor's activities had already been issued weeks earlier but hadn't been made public. On July 30 Sandra Hyllengren, the state ethics officer in the Department of Employee Relations, met with, among others, the governor's chief of staff, Steven Bosacker, and communications director, John Wodele. Wodele says the meeting was intended as an ethics training session for senior staff members. During the meeting, however, they also discussed the ethical ramifications of the governor's WWF appearance. Three weeks before that appearance, Hyllengren wrote an internal memo to the meeting participants to outline her thoughts on the matter.

"We questioned whether the Governor is ... an 'employee,'" she writes. "If you look at the language of [the state statutes] you will find that unclassified employees include those 'chosen by election or appointed to fill an elective office.' I can think of no way he can avoid being characterized as an employee given that inclusive language."

In her written opinion Hyllengren not only questions the propriety of his wrestling appearance, but also his use of state security for his book tour. "Do his activities give rise to a conflict of interest? My *unofficial opinion* is that, were we talking about any other state employee, my answer would be yes, there is a conflict."

Hyllengren says the governor is clearly taking advantage of his position. "We discussed whether his newfound notoriety as Governor directly or indirectly affected book sales or the price he negotiated for the upcoming wrestling event. The statute prohibits use of the employee's official position to secure benefits ... or advantages ... which are different from those available to the general public. It further prohibits the use of 'prestige or influence of state office' for private gain. Again, I find it difficult, if not impossible, to stretch the plain meaning of the statute to the extent that I can justify ignoring an obvious conflict."

The Ventura administration dismisses the memo as an "unsolicited" opinion and chooses instead to abide by Judge Gearin's opinion on the matter.

In the Ring with Mr. Ass

The scene outside Target Center the evening of August 22, 1999, is an odd collection of protesters and wrestling fans. More than one hundred members of the Minnesota Association of Professional Employees are picketing in the slim hope of getting Governor Ventura's attention. The union, representing ten thousand state workers, is having a tough time negotiating a new contract. They've been working without a contract since June and now want Ventura to step in and help them.

"We don't want luxury items, we want basic working conditions that the employees of this state deserve," union spokesperson Deb Shadegg says while leading a picketing line across the street from Target Center's main entrance. She figures on a night when Ventura stands to make more than $1 million for a few minutes' work, they'll try to get him to notice their plight. "The governor is apparently about being fair and impartial in all venues, and he's going to provide that for his paying constituents at this event. We don't want more; we just will not accept less."

It's unlikely Ventura ever sees the state workers protesting. For the most part the wrestling fans ignore the protesters on their way into Target Center. They've paid big money for the hottest tickets in town and couldn't care less about people with an ax to grind with the governor. They want to see Ventura make history when he steps in the ring.

"I've been a wrestling fan ever since the Crusher and the Bruiser," says Ron Hildeen, who's on his way into the arena with his teenage son. He's also a fan of Ventura, both the wrestler and the governor. "I voted for him. He's the best governor we've had so far. I just spent his check," he says, referring to his rebate check. Hildeen is wearing a Ventura T-shirt that says "10,000 Lakes: One Navy SEAL." His son's shirt says "The Governor Is Ready to Rumble." Jeremiah Hildeen is more interested in Jesse "the Body" than he is in politics. "Hopefully, he'll referee a clean match, but he'll probably get hurt in some way. That's what usually happens to referees."

Another wrestling fan on his way into the arena is Dean Barkley, one of the architects of Ventura's improbable election victory. He's now a member of the governor's cabinet as director of the Minnesota Planning Office. As he makes his way into "SummerSlam," he can't help but laugh when thinking about the last time Ventura appeared at a professional wrestling event, during the 1998 campaign. It was at a World Championship Wrestling event at Target Center, the primary rival of the World Wrestling Federation at the time. Ventura attended the event hoping to get some publicity for his gubernatorial campaign. It didn't exactly pan out.

"They did everything they could to make sure that nobody watching knew we were there," Barkley says. "They switched the camera angles around. Every time the crowd started chanting 'Jesse,' they went to a commercial break. They went out of their way to try to ignore us." That won't be a problem tonight.

The wrestling matches leading up to Ventura's appearance feature the sex, violence, and raunchiness that have become the trademarks of the WWF. There's a match between two female wrestlers, Ivory and Tori, where the object seems to be ripping off each other's skimpy wrestling outfits. The match ends with Tori fleeing the ring, breathlessly clutching her unhooked top to her breasts. The predominantly male crowd of more than nineteen thousand is breathlessly disappointed her top doesn't fall off. That titillating match is tame compared to the "Grudge Match" between the Rock and Mr. Ass. This match is the prelude to the championship match that Ventura will referee. It features the usual violence and equal parts of raunchiness and the outright degradation of a woman.

After the Rock is introduced to a big ovation, the bad guy, Mr. Ass, makes his way into the ring. Mr. Ass, also known as "Bad Ass" Billy Gunn, is easy to spot because he's wearing lime green wrestling shorts that say "Mr. Ass" on his ass. He's booed mercilessly. He brings a woman into the ring with him draped in a black sheet. He informs the crowd that the loser of the match will have to kiss the woman's rear end. The crowd howls with laughter as he pulls the sheet off to reveal a homely, overweight woman. She seems to revel in the attention and bends over to reveal a hole in her pantyhose where the vanquished wrestler will have to put his lips.

Mr. Ass assures the crowd the lips won't be his. "The Rock is gonna smell what her ass is cooking," he says, eliciting another roar from the crowd. It doesn't take a genius to figure out where the plot of this match is going. Mr. Ass, in an amazing twist of fate, ends up losing and faces the indignity of having his face rubbed in the woman's hindquarters. She's only too happy to oblige by climbing in the ring, grabbing a turnbuckle, and bending over.

"That was not exactly fair," the ringside announcer says. "Billy Gunn passed out when he had his face jammed into that fat lady's keister. You know what they say—crack kills!" The other announcer can't resist adding, "That's no crack, that's the Grand Canyon."

After eight other matches spanning a couple of hours it's finally time for the main event, the World Wrestling Federation "Triple Threat Championship Match." Reigning champion "Stone Cold" Steve Austin squares off with Triple H and Mankind. The last man standing will be the WWF champion. More head-pounding music blares as the ringside announcer makes the introduction of the guest referee. "Ladies and gentlemen, may I introduce to you the most powerful referee in World Wrestling Federation history, Jesse 'the Body' Ventura!"

Ventura walks out, pumping his fist to fire up the crowd. He's wearing a long-sleeved black-and-white-striped referee shirt as he climbs into the ring to a standing ovation. As he hold his hands above his head while soaking in the cheers, it's obvious he no longer has the sculpted physique that first made him famous. But make no mistake: He still looks capable of mayhem, especially if you're a reporter. He makes that clear when he grabs a microphone at center ring and says a few words to the crowd.

"There's a lot of media saying I'm a disgrace for being here," Ventura says, instantly inciting the crowd to boo reporters covering the event. "But I'll tell you this. I'm proud I'm a wrestler, I'm proud I was a wrestler, and I'm proud to be here tonight!" The crowd cheers and the pay-per-view television announcers chime in with an "Amen to that" and "Jesse for Prez!"

"Scheduled for one fall, it's a Triple Threat match for the World Wrestling Federation championship," the ringside announcer says before introducing the combatants. First, there's the 287-pound Mankind, wearing a white dress shirt, tie, and a mask that looks like it belongs on a rabid dog. The 246-pound Triple H is introduced next with his reliable and Amazon-like sidekick, Chyna, her breasts bursting out of her two-sizes-too-small leather top.

"Jesse's laying the law down to Chyna," the announcer says as Ventura confronts her and Triple H in the ring. "He's telling her she is not in any way, shape, or form going to be a factor in this match."

The other announcer doubts Ventura's ability to keep Chyna at bay. "I don't know if even 'the Body' can control Chyna. No other man's been able to do it!"

Just then the champion "Stone Cold" Steve Austin is introduced, walking confidently toward the ring with the WWF championship belt in his hand. He gets the loudest cheer of the night and doesn't waste any time on formalities. Austin jumps in the ring and immediately starts hammering Triple H in the head. Austin and Mankind team up and both start taking shots at Triple H. They throw him out of the ring, bang his head on the announcer's table, and then, for good measure, repeat the head-banging on the metal steps leading to the ring.

After throwing Triple H back into the ring, Austin and Mankind continue to pound on him. From where she's standing just outside the ring, Chyna starts hitting Mankind, sparking Ventura's first action of the night. He steps in between the two of them to keep Chyna from getting involved. While Ventura's got his back turned dealing with them, Triple H somehow ends up with a metal folding chair (it's always just a matter of time before a metal folding chair enters the picture). He sneaks up on Austin and bangs the chair into his knee.

The announcers (wink, wink) can't believe it! "Jesse can't be everywhere!" one says. "Ventura on the far side of the ring doing his job there, but in the meantime Triple H, being very resourceful, saw how Chyna had 'the Body' positioned, and it was Triple H with a chair shot right on the knee of 'Stone Cold' Steve Austin!"

Ventura hears the roar of the crowd and turns, yelling to the crowd, "Did he hit him with a chair?" While Ventura checks on Austin, Chyna and Triple H start tag-teaming Mankind. Chyna, standing outside the ring, pulls Mankind down from behind, grabs his ankles like a wishbone, and pulls him until his crotch repeatedly pounds against the corner post. This time, Ventura sees what happens and finally lays down the law.

"Hey, get her ass out of here!" he yells at Triple H, as the crowd begins to chant, "Jesse, Jesse!"

The announcers can hardly contain themselves. "Did the referee see it? 'The Body' saw it and 'the Body' is ejecting Chyna at ringside!" one yells. "Jesse rules! I don't recall off the top of my head anybody who's ever ejected Chyna!"

Meanwhile, Triple H is wrapping Austin's knee around a ring post like a pretzel while Mankind also bangs away on Austin. Ventura is just wandering around the ring now, not doing much in the way of refereeing.

"It looks like a war zone out here," screams an announcer. "Ventura is letting these men do what the fans want, beating each other to a pulp until we have a winner."

Austin manages to get away from the double team and knocks Mankind to the mat. He jumps on top of Mankind and Ventura begins the three-count for the pin. But just before he hits three, that pesky Triple H returns with the metal folding chair and slams Austin in the back, knocking him off Mankind.

"What's this bullshit?" Ventura yells at Triple H. "I told you about that! I told you about that! No way! I ain't countin' nothing you do with that chair. You got that?" Apparently not, because seconds later Triple H picks up the chair again and hits Mankind in the head.

Triple H jumps on Mankind, expecting Ventura to count him down for the pin. But Ventura just stands in the corner of the ring, shaking his head. "Look at Jesse," the hyped announcer says. "He's saying hell no, you're not going to win it that way. Jesse rules here. 'The Body' rules here at 'SummerSlam'!" The crowd joins in with another chant of "Jesse, Jesse, Jesse!"

Triple H hops up and threatens Ventura. They square off in the ring with fists up. "Here we go," screams the announcer. "I been waiting for this!"

Just in the nick of time Shane McMahon (Vince McMahon's son) jumps in the ring to intervene. "Who do you think you are?" he yells at Ventura, wanting to know why he wouldn't let Triple H pin Mankind. "That's your job!"

Ventura stands his ground. "He hit him with a chair," Ventura says.

"I don't care!" McMahon yells back. "That's your job!"

Ventura's heard enough. "Don't you come out here and tell me shit!" he says to McMahon.

Austin finally manages to get back up, grabs McMahon from behind, and spins him around. He flips McMahon the finger with both hands before slamming him to the mat. Ventura then picks McMahon up, grabs him by the back of the neck, runs him across the ring and throws him over the top rope. With a television camera in his face, Ventura leans over the rope looking at a supposedly unconscious McMahon and yells, "That's for your old man, you little bastard!"

Three minutes later, after somehow knocking out both Triple H and "Stone Cold" Steve Austin, Mankind pins them both. Ventura, with sweat pouring down his face and neck, holds Mankind's hand over his head, declaring him the new WWF champion. In an appearance that lasts all of twenty-two minutes, thirty seconds, Ventura just made his easiest million yet.

The 1999 "SummerSlam" is another financial bonanza for the World Wrestling Federation. Nationally, the pay-per-view is expected to generate more than $20 million. Among the Twin Cities customers was Minnesota representative Tim Pawlenty, the Republican House majority leader.

Pawlenty is among those who think Ventura made a mistake by taking part in the wrestling event. "I used to watch wrestling all the time, but this is very different than [former pro wrestlers] Verne Gagne and Nick Bockwinkel bringing a foreign object into the ring once in a while. This is a whole new level of raunchiness that I don't think is appropriate for the governor to be involved with."

Pawlenty says he's not concerned about the money Ventura is making or whether he's abusing his office or has a conflict of interest.

He's concerned about the image the governor projects to the rest of the country. "I think this crosses a line," Pawlenty says. "The governor's a leader. The governor's a role model. We want him to project an image, particularly for young people. Common sense should tell a governor, 'I shouldn't be here. I shouldn't be doing this.'"

But Pawlenty stops short of advocating new laws to restrict the governor's outside activities. He says it's up to voters to determine what's right and wrong. "People could call in, write letters, send e-mails, or they could speak at the next election if he runs again."

Ventura's critics might not be happy, but at least two people must be thrilled: Ventura's accountant and WWF chair Vince McMahon. After his WWF payday, Ventura has earned a conservatively estimated $2 million in outside income since his election just nine months earlier. This includes as much as $1.5 million from the wrestling appearance and the reported $500,000 advance, plus royalties, for his autobiography.

It should also be pointed out he's raising a lot of money for charity. There's the $100,000 "appearance fee" from the WWF he's using to start two new foundations, plus another $100,000 from the sale of licensed merchandise through Ventura for Minnesota.

Some observers, however, find Ventura's association with McMahon and the WWF more than a little hypocritical, considering Ventura's recent criticisms of professional wrestling.

Wade Keller, publisher of a weekly wrestling newsletter, *Pro Wrestling Torch*, says Ventura's drumbeat of criticism of Vince McMahon and working conditions for wrestlers seemed to disappear the moment he was offered big money to referee a match. "I think there is a little bit of concern with the hypocrisy of him speaking out against the WWF and then basically getting a check from them and saying, 'No, they're all right.'"

Keller has a theory on why Ventura is willing to set aside his past differences with McMahon and the WWF. "When you think about Jesse Ventura, he associates with and compares himself and judges himself based on rich and famous people. Hulk Hogan is a big rival of his. Hogan has earned seven figures every year for the past fifteen years, or at least the last ten years. Jesse Ventura hangs out with Arnold Schwarzenegger, who's a multi-multimillionaire. Jesse Ventura last year was working for a radio station doing a talk show. He wasn't making seven figures. And so here comes an opportunity to capitalize on the notoriety he has as governor and make seven figures. He's going to take that opportunity and set principle aside."

Vince McMahon is only too happy to pay him. Ventura's involvement in the WWF is a two-for-one deal for McMahon. Ventura brings mostly positive mainstream press coverage of the WWF, which, in turn, could attract many new paying customers after Ventura's come and gone. "Jesse's worth to the World Wrestling Federation? Seven figures, easily," Keller says. "Just from the intangibles of having a sitting governor basically endorse a controversial product by being part of it.... In a way, it lets wrestling fans who are given a hard time for being wrestling fans go, 'Hey, our governor's part of it. Why can't I watch it?'"

"Pioneer Porn"

Five days after the wrestling appearance, Ventura makes what should be a triumphant return to the Minnesota State Fair, where his campaign for governor caught fire in 1998. This year, instead of handing out campaign stickers and signs, the Ventura booth looks like a mini-retail outlet selling licensed products like T-shirts, hats, mugs, even bookmarks with his bald head sticking out the top. The bookmark includes the caption "Governor Ventura says 'Train Your Brain ... Stay in School.'" The funniest item on sale is a T-shirt with the governor's face on the front bearing the caption "Got Underwear?"

Ventura is here to broadcast his *Lunch with the Governor* radio show. It quickly becomes obvious he's going back to war with the media, particularly the *St. Paul Pioneer Press* newspaper. He's broadcasting live from the WCCO Radio State Fair broadcast center. Ventura is sitting in the glass-enclosed booth with his producer, David Ruth, newspapers spread in front of them. Hundreds of people are standing behind a railing outside the booth on a warm, sunny day.

Ventura, wearing a white golf shirt and reading glasses, begins the show innocently enough by reading a quote from a once-embattled Abraham Lincoln: "If I were to try to read, much less answer, all the attacks made on me, this shop might as well be closed for any other business. I do the very best I know how, the very best I can, and I mean to keep doing so until the end. If the end brings me out all right, what's said against me won't amount to anything. If the end brings me out wrong, ten angels swearing I was right would make no difference."

Ventura says he can relate to Lincoln's plight. He uses the quote to set up what's about to become an hour-long slam of the *Pioneer Press*. "There will be no guests, because I have such a hot topic," he tells the crowd and radio listeners across the state. "This is a hot topic! Triple hot!"

The governor is about to get even for the harsh criticism he took for his wrestling appearance, and he's especially incensed by what he read in the *Pioneer Press*. "How many people out there know what a hypocrite is?" Many in the crowd raise their hands. "The *St. Paul Pioneer Press* are a bunch of hypocrites, from top to bottom."

Ventura is outraged by several news stories and editorials published by the *Pioneer Press* about his WWF gig. He grabs a copy of one editorial and reads it to his listeners. "'Don't you wonder about the intelligence of parents who would take young children to a live World Wrestling Federation event such as Sunday's SummerSlam at the Target Center? Judging from news reports there was enough raunch there to fill at least a PG-13 movie and maybe even one rated R. Raw language, violence, sex, SummerSlam had it all. Take your pick.... Have they tuned out to the warnings about behavior and messages that degrade women? Hello, is anybody home?'"

Ventura puts the newspaper down. "That's out of the *Pioneer Press*, right? That's their editorial, which they're certainly entitled to have. But remember hypocrisy!" Be patient, he's building to a big finish.

Ventura goes on to complain about other *Pioneer Press* columnists who took shots at him, including sports columnist Tom Powers, who wrote about the old days of wrestling when there were "good guys" like Verne Gagne. Ventura concedes that's true, but points out there were also plenty of bad guys whose personas often bordered on racism. "Every Japanese wrestler was sneaky and threw salt," Ventura says. "Every German wrestler was a Nazi. Every Russian wrestler was a Communist. Every Arab wrestler was a sheik with a harem of women. That's what old wrestling was."

It's not the Powers column that upsets him as much as the others about sex and degradation of women at the WWF event. He brings up the Powers column primarily because of its placement in the sports section just above several ads for pornography. "Five ads!" the governor exclaims. "Here we got 'em." He holds the ads up to the booth window to show the audience at the fair.

"'Sophia Staks is at Dream Girls,'" Ventura says, reading an ad for a strip joint. "And they list all the times she's appearing there. Along with it, 'Triple X Videos, thousands to choose from. Better, safer, and faster than Viagra.'" The crowd is getting a big laugh, hearing the governor read newspaper ads for X-rated businesses.

"So, are they not in the pornography industry?" he asks about the *Pioneer Press*. "In essence, think about it. They are lining their pockets with pornography because they get paid salaries. And the paper makes their money by the advertising they choose to sell. So they are working together with the X-rated industry right here in their paper, and I'm showing it to the crowd so they're very clear." He holds up the newspaper again.

Ventura then backtracks to the editorial he read earlier about him and the WWF. "At the end of their editorial it says, 'Have they tuned out to the warnings about behavior and messages that degrade women?' Well, I always have heard that pornography degrades women. Let me hear by applause, is that hypocrisy or what?" The crowd responds with enthusiastic applause.

Ventura says the newspaper will argue it's a First Amendment issue because these businesses have a right to advertise. He's ready with a comeback. "They can turn down an ad. This newspaper has the ability to say no, we're not going to accept those kinds of ads. But instead their greed, their lust for money allows them to say we don't care."

Ventura tells his audience that even former Minnesota Twin Kirby Puckett brought his kids to "SummerSlam." Puckett is one of Minnesota's most beloved sports figures of all time. "[The *Pioneer Press*] would maybe rather have Kirby take his kids to one of these video stores or maybe down to see Sophia Staks."

The governor is now zeroing in for the kill. "So I'm going to move forward with some very radical decisions here. First of all, I'm no longer going to refer to the *Pioneer Press* any more as the *Pioneer Press*. I'm going to refer to it as the *Pioneer Porn*." The crowd outside the broadcast booth responds with a big laugh and some groans. "There's nothing that goes better, according to the *Pioneer Press*, than what? Sports and sex. They go hand in hand. It has a good ring to it, *Pioneer Porn*."

He also says he plans to cancel the *Pioneer Press* subscriptions in the governor's office and possibly cancel all interviews with the newspaper's reporters. "I don't want people thinking that we at the capitol in some way support a newspaper that supports pornography.... I think I will not be a hypocrite. I will not participate with the *St. Paul Pioneer Porn* any more."

In downtown St. Paul, meanwhile, *Pioneer Press* executives are trying to figure out how to respond to Ventura. As with many of his outbursts, there's at least a kernel of truth in what he says. He's got the newspaper backed into a corner, but *Pioneer Press* editor Walker Lundy doesn't shy from a good fight. Lundy defended the newspaper after the governor criticized its coverage of the University of Minnesota basketball scandal. And he proves to be a worthy adversary again.

"The main point is that the governor's angry because some of our columnists and an editorial criticized him," Lundy tells KSTP-TV in a live interview six hours after the governor's radio show. "He compared himself to Abe Lincoln today. I'd remind him of another president, Harry S. Truman, who liked to say, if you can't stand the heat, stay out of the kitchen."

It's easy to criticize the governor's thin skin. The difficult part is justifying the ads for pornography and strip clubs prominently displayed in the sports section. The *Star Tribune* recently moved such ads from the sports section to the classified ads. Lundy says his newspaper's advertising department is separate from the news department and he knows of no such plans to make a similar move. "I happen to agree with their policy, which is that they accept advertising from any legal business. I think that's in the spirit of the First Amendment."

Ironically, Ventura could make the same argument. He accepted a job with a legal business, the WWF, and a court ruling told him there was no legal reason why the governor couldn't take part in the event.

Ultimately, Ventura doesn't cancel his *Pioneer Press* subscriptions or stop doing interviews with the newspaper's reporters. But Lundy couldn't let the opportunity pass for one more shot at the governor. He says the governor's criticism is actually "great publicity" for the newspaper and issues a challenge to Ventura. He says Minnesotans should read the *Pioneer Press* and the governor's autobiography and decide which is more pornographic.

"Let's have a citizens jury," Lundy says. "In fact, I challenge him to that. Isn't that what they do in wrestling? I challenge him. I don't think the governor's got the guts to do that."

CHAPTER 10

"Organized Religion Is a Sham"

Playboy!

In early September 1999, national Reform Party leaders pick California as the site of the party's 2000 national convention where the presidential nominee will be chosen. The choice of Long Beach over four potential sites in Minnesota is viewed as a slap in the face to Jesse Ventura. After all, he's the highest-ranking elected Reform Party member in the country and its standard-bearer. What better place to rally around a new presidential candidate than in the only state to elect a Reform Party candidate in a statewide election? It seems like a no-brainer.

So why the snub? The Ross Perot faction of the Reform Party pulls off one of its last, desperate power plays. The outgoing chair of the party, Russell Verney, engineers a vote of the party executive committee in favor of Long Beach. Verney is a Perot loyalist who will be replaced as chair in January 2000 by Jack Gargan, who was endorsed for the job by Ventura. Verney defends the executive committee's decision by saying a convention in Ventura's home state would hurt the party's presidential nominee.

"Whoever the nominee is, you wouldn't want him overshadowed by the celebrity in the party," Verney says. "We've also got some people who think that Ventura's celebrity status would bring more attention in other states rather than in Minnesota."

Ventura and Minnesota Reform Party officials are seething over the loss of a convention that could draw more than four thousand people and the national spotlight to Minnesota. The governor won't comment on the convention decision directly, but his spokesperson, John Wodele, makes it clear where the governor stands. "Maybe what it shows is that the Reform Party, just like the Democratic Party and the Republican Party, is capable of petty politics," Wodele says. "Governor Jesse Ventura is the embodiment of the Reform Party movement, and to say that would overshadow whatever they're trying to accomplish . . . I would then question what they're trying to accomplish."

Doug Friedline, Ventura's campaign manager and a Reform Party activist, is equally incredulous. "We plan to run between fifty and one hundred candidates next year for state races," Friedline says. "What better place to showcase the Reform Party than here in Minnesota?" Minnesota Reform Party chair Rick McCluhan vows to conduct a vote of party delegates from every state to overturn the executive committee decision.

Brothel Battle

In his autobiography Governor Ventura takes delight in recounting his exploits at a Nevada brothel the day before he was shipped to Vietnam with the Navy SEALs. You know, the one about trading a military souvenir to a hooker for a "trick and ten dollars," thus becoming one of the few customers ever to be paid for sex by a prostitute. It's one of the governor's favorite and funniest stories. He doesn't find it so funny when the brothel tries to cash in on this famous connection.

The Moonlite Bunny Ranch publishes ads in newspapers in some western states, using Ventura's name in what appears to be an endorsement of the brothel. Following lines in the ad like "Minutes from Reno" and "Not just sex, an adventure" is a supposed quote from Ventura that says, "I had sex at the Moonlite!" He's quoted along with Larry Flynt, publisher of *Hustler* magazine, and Al Goldstein of *Screw* magazine. Ventura isn't exactly thrilled to be keeping such company.

His attorney fires off a letter to the owner of the Moonlite Bunny Ranch, Dennis Hof. "It has recently come to our attention that you or your organization have been advertising 'The Moonlite Bunny Ranch' with print advertisements that incorporate the name or image of Jesse Ventura. This is to let you know that, unless you first obtained express written permission from Jesse Ventura or Ventura for Minnesota, Inc., you may be violating the law.... While we appreciate your support of Governor Ventura, we must nonetheless ask that you immediately cease any advertising that states or implies his endorsement."

In an interview a few days later, the governor's attorney, David Bradley Olsen, tells me this isn't an issue of Ventura wanting to be paid (obviously times have changed since the governor's visit to the brothel thirty years ago!). "We're not asking for any damages or any money, we're just looking to protect the governor's name and image," Olsen says. "Obviously we don't want people around the country thinking the governor endorses the Moonlite Bunny Ranch."

If Olsen thinks a stern letter from an attorney is going to dissuade Hof from using the governor's name, he's underestimating his foe. "He doesn't understand what this means," Hof tells me by phone when I call for his reaction to the letter. "I'll have his ass!" Hof isn't going to roll over and play dead. He tells me this is a promoter's dream—in this case, a promoter of prostitution. The day after the KSTP-TV story about the brothel battle, the story ends up on the Associated Press wire and gets picked up all over the country.

"He's the one who brags about being the first guy to get paid here," Hof says of Ventura. "If he can use the Bunny Ranch to promote his book, I sure as hell can use him to promote the Bunny Ranch! He doesn't know who he's dealing with. I have connections. I'll have *Extra* [the syndicated television show] on my doorstep tomorrow!" It seems like the guy's just full of bluster, but two nights later there he is, featured on *Extra* as he takes on the governor of Minnesota.

The unseemly national news coverage notwithstanding, Ventura's attorney says he has little choice but to protect the governor's rights to his own name. "If we at some point cease trying to enforce the governor's rights to the commercial use of his name and likeness, we will eventually lose those rights," Olsen says.

Hof admits he made up the governor's quote, "I had sex at the

Moonlite!" He says he just condensed what Ventura wrote in his auto-biography. As a small concession, Hof says he might change the quote to more accurately reflect exactly what the governor says in his book. Beyond that he seems more interested in going to war with Ventura. He's already working on a room at the brothel he'll dedicate to the governor, changing the name of a bedroom from "Monica's Oral Office" to the "Jesse 'the Body' Ventura Suite."

Trump for President

The presidential election is still more than thirteen months away and Ventura repeatedly says he doesn't want to talk about it until after January 1. He also repeatedly denies having any interest in running for president. But in September he shakes up the presidential race anyway. At what seems to be a routine appearance at a Rotary luncheon in the Minneapolis suburb of St. Louis Park on September 13, the governor announces a surprise possible choice for the Reform Party nomination.

"I'm leaning not totally, but very strongly, in support of Donald Trump for president," Ventura says in response to a question from the audience. He also says he doesn't think Pat Buchanan would be a good fit in the Reform Party, although he wouldn't challenge his right to join the party.

"If Mr. Buchanan wants to join the Reform Party, that's fine, I have no problem with him doing so. But if he is simply doing it to get $13.5 million to run for president, I personally would prefer the Reform Party to field its own fresh candidate and not a candidate that couldn't succeed in another party."

A few hours later, after delivering a speech at Carleton College in Northfield, Minnesota, the governor tells students that candidate might be Trump. "I've had three conversations with Donald Trump, and he's starting to pique my interest a lot," says Ventura, draped in a black academic robe as he meets informally with students gathered around him on the steps of Carleton's Skinner Memorial Chapel. "He came out with a new book in which he quotes me a lot, and he thinks a lot like me."

His remarks may seem off-the-cuff and somewhat inconsequential, but once again Ventura makes national headlines. *USA Today*, several other national newspapers, and the television networks pick up the story. Within a week, *Time* publishes a three-page story headlined "Take My Party, Please ... Jesse Ventura may not run for President in 2000—but he wouldn't mind if Donald Trump joined the fray." The story highlights the possible scenario of Ventura and Trump forming a tag-team of sorts to deny Buchanan the Reform Party nomination. The governor single-handedly gives a Trump candidacy some legitimacy.

Playboy!

As if going to battle with a pimp and Pat Buchanan isn't enough to handle, Ventura is about to go to war on every front imaginable. It begins on Wednesday, September 29, 1999, a day when he faces a fairly routine schedule, by his standards. It's packed from morning to night. There's a 9:30 A.M. news conference at the State Capitol to announce formation of a new crime-fighting initiative. The conference is followed by a noon luncheon and speech at the Saint Paul Hotel; a 5:00 P.M. live appearance on the *Jason Lewis Show* on KSTP-AM radio; and a 7:00 P.M. live appearance via satellite from the governor's residence on CNN's *Late Edition with Wolf Blitzer.*

While Ventura is on the run, his communications office releases a media advisory that day about the governor's plan to host a series of events in October to unveil "The Big Plan: Strategic Directions of the Ventura Administration." A news release quotes the governor as saying, "I'm excited that we've developed a plan that very clearly expresses my vision for the future of the state, and I'm eager to share it with the citizens of Minnesota."

Unfortunately, his vision for the state will be clouded by his eagerness to share with the world some unorthodox and inflammatory views on everything from religion to women's undergarments. The *Playboy* interview is about to hit the newsstands and shake the core of the Ventura administration.

At about 8:15 P.M. on the evening of September 29, I get a call at home from our 10:00 P.M. producer, alerting me that details of the *Playboy* interview are on the Associated Press wire. My jaw about hits the ground as he reads just a few of the quotes to me.

The governor says, "Organized religion is a sham and a crutch for weak-minded people."

He calls the Navy's Tailhook sexual-harassment scandal "much ado about nothing."

Ventura tells *Playboy* his thoughts on fat people: "Every fat person says it's not their fault, that they have gland trouble. You know which gland? The saliva gland. They can't push away from the table."

When asked what he'd like to be if he could ever be reincarnated? "I would like to come back as a 38 double-D bra."

The producer asks me if I think I should come in to report this story live on the ten o'clock news. By the time he asks, the phone is dangling off my kitchen counter because I'm already racing to the station.

It was common knowledge that a *Playboy* writer spent time with the governor over the summer of 1999. And in early September, when the October issue of the magazine hit the newsstands, *Playboy* promoted the upcoming Ventura interview for the November issue by saying, "The Body reveals his response to daily death threats, defends his remarks about Columbine and tells how a wrestler could become president." In journalism that's called burying the lead. There is no mention of the governor's most explosive remarks.

On September 9 I asked Ventura about the upcoming interview during a news conference with a group of Japanese travel executives. He admits he doesn't remember everything he said, because the interview was a couple of months ago. He says *Playboy* wanted to do the interview shortly after his election, but he put the magazine off. He was clearly flattered by the request. "Through the years that interview is done by a lot of provocative, interesting people, so it's kind of an honor to be asked to do it." President Jimmy Carter once admitted to "lusting" in his heart in *Playboy*. The Ventura interview is Carter times one hundred.

It's hard to imagine that in one interview Governor Ventura could find a way to offend billions of people around the globe who belong to organized religion, millions of "fat" people, and millions of people who find sexual harassment to be serious business. The interview comes off as a smorgasbord of insults blanketing nearly everyone in America in some fashion or another. And we haven't even gotten to his controversial political views.

He says protesters have a right to burn the American flag ("If you buy the flag, it's yours to burn"). Prostitutes and drug offenders shouldn't be sent to prison ("The government has much more important things to do"). He's staunchly opposed to almost all gun control ("You want to know my definition of gun control? Being able to stand there at twenty-five meters and put two rounds in the same hole. That's gun control").

The *Playboy* interview starts off innocently enough. Ventura jokes about what he likes best about being governor: "It's good to be the king. The best thing is that there's no one in this state who can tell me what to do." He reveals a humorously candid moment that happened shortly after his shocking election victory: "The day after we won the election we all met in my kitchen and looked at each other and said, 'What the hell do we do now?'"

Ventura offers a funny assessment of his job description as governor: "My job is somewhat of an oxymoron. I do everything and yet I do nothing." And he describes a hypothetical scenario in which he could win the 2000 presidential race: "I would let Gore and Bush hang each other with all the rope they have, to the point where the public can't stand either of them. Their disapproval ratings would skyrocket. Then you enter the race three months before the election and take the whole thing." Little does he know that, because of this interview, his own "disapproval ratings" are about to skyrocket.

The trouble starts with his response to a question about legalizing prostitution. He's long been on the record as favoring some sort of legalized prostitution, but that's not what gets him in trouble. It's his bizarre defense of that view that sets off a land mine:

VENTURA: Prohibiting something doesn't make it go away. Prostitution is criminal, and bad things happen because it's run illegally by dirtbags who are criminals. If it's legal, then the girls could have health checks, unions, benefits, anything any other worker gets, and it would be far better.

PLAYBOY: This isn't a very popular position in America, is it?

VENTURA: No, and it's because of religion. Organized religion is a sham and a crutch for weak-minded people who need strength in numbers. It tells people to go out and stick their noses in other people's business. I live by the golden rule: Treat others as you'd want them to treat you. The religious right wants to tell people how to live.

The irony is that the *Playboy* interviewer, Lawrence Grobel, never asks about religion. Ventura just serves it up as a defense of his views about prostitution. It turns out his critics find his absurd defense of legalizing prostitution more offensive than his desire to legalize it.

Ventura then lobs another hand grenade in response to a question that couldn't have been more innocent. It's a question about the governor's reading habits:

PLAYBOY: Ever read any Hemingway?

VENTURA: No, Hemingway lost his credibility with me when he killed himself. I've seen too many people fight for their lives. I have no respect for anyone who would kill himself.

PLAYBOY: That's a pretty harsh thing to say without knowing the circumstances.

VENTURA: No it is not! It's an easy thing to say. If you're to the point of killing yourself, and you're that depressed, life can only get better. If you're a feeble, weak-minded person to begin with, I don't have time for you.

If Ventura's goal is to be provocative, mission accomplished. But there's more: this time it's a response to a question about a scandal in the U.S. Navy:

PLAYBOY: What do you think of the sexual harassment charges that are brought against the Navy, as in Tailhook?

VENTURA: I don't condone what happened, but I understand it. These are people who live on the razor's edge and defy death and do things where people die. They're not going to consider grabbing a woman's breast or buttock a major situation. That's much ado about nothing.

In the midst of this interview is another exchange that in some ways foreshadows the controversy that will rage when the interview is published. It's a question about why he seems to "thrive on attacking" the media. Once again, it results in a completely unrelated attack on another significant segment of the population:

VENTURA: And when I criticize them everyone gets upset with me. I love how people can dish it out but can't take it.

PLAYBOY: Which is just what Barbara Carlson, the former governor's ex-wife, told *Mirabella* about you: "He can dish it out but can't take it, and that's going to be his downfall."

VENTURA: Consider the source. This is a woman who struck the former governor with a frying pan, who had a name for his private parts. So you have to take it with a grain of salt. She's also a woman who's had her stomach cut out so she don't eat so much. What happened to willpower? I love fat people. Every fat person says it's not their fault, that they have gland trouble. You know which gland? The saliva gland. They can't push away from the table.

By the time Ventura concludes the interview by saying he wants to be reincarnated as a 38 double-D bra, it's difficult to even muster a gasp. The interview is so full of vitriolic statements that the bra comment is much-needed comic relief. When this thing hits the newsstands, it's no laughing matter for the governor or his administration.

Spin Control

John Wodele's pager starts to beep about eight o'clock on September 29, the night the *Playboy* Interview is released. The beeping won't stop for two weeks. Wodele is officially the governor's director of communications. Unofficially, he's the administration's fire chief. He's called on to put out so many public-relations fires, he should have a dalmatian roaming his office.

When I call Wodele that night for a response to include in my 10:00 P.M. report, he tells me the governor's office received a copy of the interview at about 4:30 P.M. He knew immediately it would be a long night. "The governor is provocative and always will be," Wodele tells me in a quote for my story. "He's freewheeling in interviews, and because he does that, he's going to be controversial." Wodele also knows Ventura's comments about religion will require the most flame retardant.

"The governor is talking about extremists of the religious right, who are often intolerant," he says. "This governor cannot stand intolerance." Wodele expands on that by saying the governor's family belongs to a church in Maple Grove. These explanations on the 10 P.M. news do little if anything to blunt the nationwide uproar the Ventura administration is about to face the next day.

"Good afternoon, Governor Ventura's office, could you hold a moment? Thank you. Good afternoon, Governor Ventura's office, could you hold, please? Good afternoon, could you hold, please?" The governor's receptionist, Sonna Olson, finds herself on the front line of an honest-to-God public-relations firestorm.

"Please hold. Thank you. Governor Ventura's office. OK, let me put you through to our citizen comment line." Hundreds of phone calls flood Ventura's office the morning after the release of the *Playboy* interview. E-mails jam the computer system. Letters come across fax machines, not just from Minnesotans but from people all over the country.

Wodele's cell phone rings incessantly. At times he's talking on his office phone and cell phone at the same time while glancing at his pager. Propped on his desk is an invitation sent out earlier in the week to various citizens and state leaders, inviting them to the kickoff of the governor's "Big Plan" for Minnesota. Promoting that event will now take a backseat to the "Big Pain" from the *Playboy* interview.

"I'm not surprised in the reaction to anything that Governor Ventura does," Wodele tells me as I take my turn in a conga line of reporters waiting to interview him in his office one floor below the governor's office. He admits it's the first time he's lost sleep over a controversy involving Ventura.

It's now 11:00 A.M. on September 30, just over twelve hours since the interview made national news. So far, Wodele is doing all the talking because Ventura won't. Publicly it appears the governor is trying to blunt criticism by ignoring it, possibly hoping that by not responding to his critics they'll go away. However, Wodele admits Ventura is surprised by the vehemence of the criticism. The two men had a long conversation about some of the governor's more controversial remarks.

So how does one go about explaining what Ventura told *Playboy?* First, Wodele tries to explain Ventura. "He always has been and always will be a provocateur. He says what's on his mind. He lays it out there for discussion. Some of it's going to be more popular. Some of it will not be. He will always be a controversial governor."

Wodele tells me he sat in on only parts of Ventura's sessions with the *Playboy* interviewer. He apparently missed the good parts. He didn't hear any of the comments about religion, Tailhook, or suicide. Wodele makes it clear, however, that the governor doesn't deny saying any of the things *Playboy* published. "Governor Ventura is a very unconventional politician, and we see examples of it every day," Wodele says. "He believes that people would rather in the long run have him be brutally honest than to avoid, keep secret, manipulate."

"Is there any line which the governor feels he should not cross?" I ask Wodele. "I'm not aware that there is," he responds. "But I think that's probably a good question to ask the governor."

So far, though, the governor isn't talking.

Everyone else *is* talking. The Reform Party's national chair, Russell Verney, finds the story hard to believe. "We have been building the Reform Party based on principles, integrity, and values, and this story is just so humiliating," Verney tells reporters. "It is contrary to everything we have been building in the Reform Party."

The chair of the Minnesota Republican Party weighs in with a call for the governor's resignation. "Jesse Ventura's attacks show he has a fundamental lack of understanding of the world he lives in," Ron Eibensteiner says in a written statement issued to the media. "It is incomprehensible that our governor could have such obvious contempt for people—whether they are Jewish, Muslim, Christian or others— who have deeply held religious beliefs.... As governor, Jesse Ventura cannot continue to make these outrageous attacks. Jesse Ventura should know it is wrong to grope women. He should know it is wrong to attack and be intolerant of people of faith. If Jesse doesn't know his comments are wrong—maybe he should consider stepping down as governor."

For most of the day Senate Majority Leader Roger Moe keeps his criticism in check. He initially hears about some of the governor's comments on the radio and chalks them up to just another Ventura rant. Moe declines several requests for interviews until he hears more details about the governor's comments. He finally alerts the capitol press corps he'll be available in the afternoon for a response to the Ventura interview.

With television, radio, and newspaper reporters crammed into his office just off the Senate chamber, Moe reads one of the governor's quotes out loud. "'I don't want people to think I'm some kind of erratic nut running the State of Minnesota,'" Moe says, quoting the governor responding to a question in *Playboy* about why he believes the U.S. government was part of a conspiracy to assassinate President Kennedy. "Well, Governor," Moe adds, his voice cracking with anger as he puts his notes down, "if you want to ensure that this is not the impression you are leaving here in Minnesota and around the nation, then I would suggest that you apologize for your recent comments. Minnesotans do not embrace your views on religion, on women, on prostitution, on drugs, or on conspiracy theories."

Moe says Minnesotans also don't embrace another view expressed by Ventura in *Playboy:* "'It's good to be the king. The best thing is that there's no one in this state who can tell me what to do.'"

"Governor," Moe responds defiantly, "every citizen in this state has a right to tell you what to do, and, Governor, you have a responsibility to listen to them. That's what being a public official and public service is all about."

Ventura is scheduled to make appearances the following week on both the *Late Show with David Letterman* and on *20/20* with Barbara Walters. Moe says Ventura should use both forums to apologize for "tarnishing our national image." He says it's a unique opportunity for Ventura. "The governor has to understand nobody compares with that position for commanding the bully pulpit. And no governor is getting the publicity our governor is getting. Use that opportunity, Governor, to get good publicity for the state. Talk about the positives. Talk about how good we are. Talk about the great things Minnesotans have done. Don't talk about the things you're talking about, because they do not reflect Minnesota's values."

Moe, you'll recall, lost to Ventura as Skip Humphrey's running mate in November. I couldn't resist asking the senator to reflect on that in light of the *Playboy* controversy. "Senator, if Ventura had said these things prior to November 3, is there any way in your estimation he would have been elected governor?"

Moe's terse response: "There's no way he would have been elected governor!"

Criticism is also pouring in from religious organizations throughout Minnesota and the nation. The Catholic League, a Roman Catholic organization based in New York, calls the governor "Jesse 'the Bigot' Ventura." The Archdiocese of St. Paul and Minneapolis is more restrained, releasing a statement, saying, "We realize that Governor Ventura is undergoing a learning process during his first term in office.... [Our hope is] he will choose to educate himself fully on the importance of church and religion in our society."

A group of churches and family organizations says it plans to publish newspaper ads condemning the governor's comments and demanding an apology. They plan to remind Ventura he is one of only three governors who refused to sign a "National Day of Prayer" proclamation earlier in the year, yet he saw fit to declare a "Rolling Stones Day" in Minnesota. The conservative Minnesota Family Council releases its own statement slamming Ventura. It says, in part, "The governor has once again brought shame on the office of governor and further contributed to the moral deficit plaguing our society."

Another frequent critic of the governor chimes in. Darrell McKigney, president of the Taxpayers League of Minnesota, says Ventura's comments are just the latest in a long line of embarrassments. "The trouble is not that the governor is making an idiot and an ass of himself; he makes an idiot and an ass of all the people of Minnesota," McKigney says. "We are becoming a laughingstock all around the country."

A target of Ventura's comments in *Playboy* chimes in with her own sharply worded attack on the governor. Radio talk-show host Barbara Carlson, the victim of Ventura's criticism of "fat" people, launches a tirade on her KSTP-AM radio show.

"Listen, Jesse Ventura," Carlson says in a shrill counterattack, "you have finally gone too far. First of all, you insult me and every large person in the world. You are not a thing of beauty yourself. And another thing, when you say Tailhook is understandable ... how can you say touching a woman's breast and buttocks is acceptable behavior? You have gone too far, Jesse Ventura!"

Most of the callers to the show agree. One woman calls him an "embarrassment to the state." Another female caller simply says, "This guy is an idiot!" A few callers defend the governor's candor and honesty, if not his specific views. "He tells it like he sees it," says one male caller, "so lay off, would ya!"

Keep in mind that all the reactions to the *Playboy* comments you've just read poured in less than twenty-four hours after the release of the interview. It shows no signs of letting up, and by late in the afternoon of September 30 Governor Ventura still hasn't made any public statements about the flap. Finally, at 3:58 P.M., he faxes to the media a copy of a letter he just sent to religious leaders in the state. The conciliatory letter aims to soften the harsh edge of the criticism he's receiving about his controversial view of religion.

"I want to be clear about one thing," the Ventura letter says. "I respect the role that religious organizations play in our communities and more importantly, that faith plays in people's lives.... My recent quotes about organized religion only reflect a portion of my thoughts on the matter. While organized religion has not been a major influence in my adult life, I respect the beliefs and choices of others, including my close family members. Tolerance is at the core of my own personal beliefs. I have always been an advocate for freedom of religious expression."

So why the sweeping condemnation of organized religion in *Playboy?* Ventura tries to explain. "My views about organized religion were dramatically shaped by my military experience in the Vietnam era and make me skeptical," he says in the letter. "I witnessed many instances of so-called religious leaders zealously marketing their beliefs to people too uneducated to comprehend what they were talking about and too poor to afford the money they were being asked to hand over. Yet there they were, handing over their last dollar for a baptism that they were promised was essential. And there were the religious marketers accepting that last dollar. I would think the spirit of religion would put the needs of people and families first and profit last. Further, I have always been offended by the imposition of extreme beliefs on another. I've witnessed in recent years an intolerance by some right wing leaders that disturbs me."

The letter is a step in the direction of cushioning the blows the governor's taking, but it's clearly not enough. He covers so much ground in the *Playboy* interview, and says so many outrageously damning things, that he really has no choice. He must come out and publicly explain why he said the things he said in *Playboy*. After consulting with his staff, the governor abruptly announces just after 4:30 P.M. that he'll meet with the media in the governor's reception room at 5:00 P.M. It will be one of the most extraordinary news conferences in Minnesota political history.

Ventura Finally Responds

At precisely 5:00 P.M. Governor Ventura emerges from his office and steps into the adjacent governor's reception room. He takes a sip from a Diet Coke and puts the can on the podium. The room is packed with reporters and television cameras. KSTP-TV is carrying the news conference live because we happened to be set up to do a live interview with John Wodele about the *Playboy* interview. After a short, awkward silence between the governor and the reporters, Ventura begins by saying he's had a productive day with his commissioners doing "the state's business." He says they attended an all-day retreat to prepare for the unveiling of his "Big Plan" for the state. Obviously, reporters are more interested in how he plans to explain what he said in *Playboy*.

Someone asks him about the letter he just sent to religious leaders, explaining his views stated in *Playboy*. "The letter speaks for itself," Ventura responds. "My comments were made on my own behalf and my own beliefs and my position in life that I don't particularly need organized religion. But I don't condemn anyone that does. Obviously they play an important role, and I certainly don't want to offend or alienate them, because I certainly need them in our 'Big Plan.'"

Questions about the religion issue dominate the news conference. "Governor, are you surprised by how your words carry this much weight, especially dealing with religion?" a reporter asks. "This is a line a lot of [politicians] don't cross."

Ventura doesn't hesitate to put a positive spin on what would seem to be an impossibly negative situation. "I separate church and state, and I will always be honest, and I think that's my problem. The career politician won't be honest. When the career politician gets asked a question, they'll give the answer they're supposed to. They'll give the answer that's politically correct. They'll give the answer that you need to give to get reelected. That's not me."

"Governor, do you regret anything you said in this *Playboy* interview?" a reporter asks, as the focus of the news conference switches to other issues raised in the magazine.

"No," Ventura answers, "because in light of that it's *Playboy* you're doing it for, you're supposed to be provocative. I know now I'll never do an interview for a wrestling magazine, because if I get in my wrestling mode, there's no telling what you all will do to me."

Is he concerned that his controversial views might hurt the Reform

Party's national image? Or that party chair Russell Verney calls the interview "humiliating" for the Reform Party?

"No, I'm not, because they told me when I made the comments during the election, when I talked about prostitution and drugs … leaders of the Reform Party said I'll never win the election, and I proved 'em wrong, because, again, it was a case of honesty. And I'm gonna be honest."

The governor is also asked to explain his views on the Navy's Tailhook scandal. "It was bad behavior, there's no doubt about it. But as I said, I don't condone it, I simply understand how it can happen. When you put ten, fifteen, twenty, thirty of these people in a room and start serving alcohol, bad situations can arise from it. These people are put and trained to do a specific thing that many others can't [he's referring to how they are trained to kill the enemy]. That's why they're very special in what they do. It goes back, if you want to a little bit, to 'You want me on that wall, you need me on that wall, yet you question the very freedom which I provide for you.'"

He's quoting Jack Nicholson's character in the movie *A Few Good Men*. Everyone in the room starts chuckling, but Ventura is serious.

As this remarkable twenty-minute session with reporters draws to a close, John Wodele reminds the governor to address the quote in *Playboy* when he says, 'It's good to be the king.'"

The governor is both amused and irritated that he has to explain. "Well, for those of you who don't know, that's a line from Mel Brooks's *History of the World, Part One*. It's a comedy film that, on certain portions of the film Mel turns to the camera and says, 'It's good to be the king.' Well, that's kind of an interoffice joke we have around here and it stems from …" Ventura pauses for a moment with a disgusted snicker. "And I'm sitting here having to defend this. It's silly. The problem was I didn't sit and say that's a joke, that's a joke, that's a joke. Which is my policy that I have to do now—is say, 'It's a joke,' because no one gets it."

This is probably one of the more amazing news conferences conducted by any governor in history. Not a word about tax policy or education or transportation issues. There's plenty of talk about *Playboy*, religion, sexual misconduct by Navy officers, and lines from Hollywood movies. In the end, Ventura says none of this has anything to do with how he performs as governor. Although he leaves open the possibility he was wrong for some of what he said in *Playboy*, he refuses to apologize.

Perhaps the most amused witness to this uproar is the man who conducted the *Playboy* interview, Lawrence Grobel, one of the magazine's contributing editors. Grobel is surprised by the reaction and says it seems Ventura's critics are just louder than his supporters. In an interview with KSTP-TV, Grobel says he thinks there are more people who agree with what the governor said than there are people who are "morally outraged."

Grobel leaves little doubt about his opinion of Ventura after spending nearly a week with him doing the interview. "I loved him. I've talked to a lot of people, including Nobel Prize winners, and what I like about Governor Ventura is he is an honest, direct, no-nonsense man."

Grobel says he wouldn't be surprised if Ventura becomes a serious presidential candidate. In his view, the governor's straightforward approach is refreshing even if it is controversial. He illustrates the point with a story he tells about doing the interview with Ventura.

"I think he was a little wary of me when I first walked in. He called me a 'liberal weenie.' He would point his finger and say, 'I know who you are, I know what kind of liberal type you are. You don't think we should have guns in our houses.'

"And I said, 'I don't understand hunting. I don't understand handguns.' And he told me I should put up a sign outside my door that says, 'This house has no guns.' I told him I thought that would make me a target. And he said, 'That's exactly my point. At least people who don't know if you have a gun in your house may not try to get into your house because they think you might.'

"That's *your* governor!"

CHAPTER 11

"You Have Brought Shame . . ."
No Apologies

On Friday, October 1, 1999, Jesse Ventura is back on the air for his weekly *Lunch with the Governor* radio show. His critics have been having *him* for lunch for two days now, and it's finally his chance to respond without the "filter" of the media. "I've learned that you will have an extremely difficult time if you get elected to high office and you're honest," Ventura tells his statewide listening audience. He's broadcasting from his office with a larger-than-usual contingent of reporters listening and recording the audio feed of the show in the adjacent reception room.

To his credit, Ventura takes calls from several listeners, including harsh critics and some supporters. "Keep up the good work, Jesse," says a caller named Bob from Minneapolis. "I back you 100 percent, and just keep in mind that since the first day you were elected, people had a microscope at you. And when they look that closely, they can find something wrong." Bob says he didn't vote for Ventura in 1998, but he will vote for him if he runs again.

During the hour the governor takes twelve calls, including six positive calls, three negative calls, and three about other topics. The negative callers don't seem as concerned by what Ventura said in the *Playboy* interview as they are by how he's responding to all the criticism. "I don't think you're being honest with Minnesotans many times, and you are backtracking like many politicians have in the past on quotes that you've given that get you in trouble," says a female caller named Terry, who says she's upset by the governor's comments about the Tailhook scandal.

Critics calling his radio show are the least of his problems. Later in the afternoon the chair of the national Reform Party sends a letter to Ventura demanding his resignation from the party. Russell Verney faxes the letter to the governor and simultaneously posts the letter on the Reform Party's Web site.

The letter is short and scathing. "Your comments in the November 1999 Playboy article about religion, sexual assault, overweight people, drugs, prostitution, women's undergarments and many other subjects do not represent the values, principles or ethics upon which this party was built. Members of the Reform Party from coast to coast are outraged about your comments. In just one interview you have managed to severely damage the credibility and integrity of thousands of Reform Party members. You have brought shame to yourself and disgrace to the members of the Reform Party. You can stop the cascading damage to the reputation of the members of the Reform Party by accepting personal responsibility for your actions and the attendant consequences. For the good of the members, you should resign now from the Reform Party of the United States of America."

The golden boy of the upstart Reform Party is asked to resign in disgrace.

Rick McCluhan, Minnesota's Reform Party chair, won't have any part of it and e-mails the governor to tell him he's still a member in good standing of Minnesota's Reform Party. McCluhan says it's just another attempt by Verney to discredit Ventura with the state and national party. "I think there's still a very demonstrable level of support for him out there. Here's a governor who has had the highest approval rating in the history of Minnesota. I really don't feel that this is going to have a significant impact on the core approval rating that he's had."

Several prominent national politicians join the cascade of criticism. Christian Coalition founder Pat Robertson says Ventura is "off his rocker." Regarding Ventura's comments on religion, Republican Senate

Majority Leader Trent Lott of Mississippi asks, rhetorically, "Can you believe a governor of a state in America would say such an insensitive, bigoted thing?" Republican presidential candidate Gary Bauer, another Christian conservative, takes it a step further. "I'd like to suggest to the governor that maybe a better name for him might be Jesse 'the Bigot' Ventura."

The governor's remarks about suicide also are reverberating through the State Capitol and the U.S. Capitol. Two state lawmakers whose close family members committed suicide denounce Ventura's insensitive statements. U.S. senator Paul Wellstone of Minnesota harshly criticizes him on the Senate floor while preparing to offer an amendment to a mental-health care bill. "I am so outraged by these remarks," Wellstone tells his fellow senators. "I want Governor Ventura to understand that all these families have gone through so much pain. They need support. They do not need ridicule.... We need to understand that this is not a moral failing. This is an illness. Suicide is the result of an illness, and, with treatment, we can prevent these deaths."

In Minnesota criticism pours in from every imaginable corner. "The governor's interview with *Playboy* magazine is a continuation of a line that cannot be characterized as free speech; rather it is abuse of free speech," writes Amin Kader, president of the Islamic Institute of Minnesota, in a letter released to news organizations. "His remarks regarding religion as 'a sham and a crutch for the weak minded' is indeed an insult to all of us who believe in God. If Mr. Ventura does not believe in a God that is his privilege but he has no right to insult people who do."

Editorials in both of Minnesota's major daily newspapers offer their assessments of Ventura's *Playboy* fiasco. The *Star Tribune's* editorial is surprisingly tame. The headline, "Jesse and Playboy—Refusing to be shocked," suggests the newspaper is numbed by the governor's frequent controversies. "As we've said, he's a hybrid—part entertainer, part politician, and you never quite know which Jesse you'll get," the editorial says. "Actually, the entire *Playboy* interview is a jolly good read. Taken in context, the governor comes off as a quick, almost thoughtful, straight-shooter. . . . Obviously we don't agree with everything he says. But the Playboy interview makes clear that Ventura possesses a kind of plain-speak directness that citizens (and editorialists) can admire."

The *St. Paul Pioneer Press*, the governor's frequent sparring partner, also isn't shocked by Ventura's *Playboy* interview. "By now, the jaw drops less often in response to outrageous statements by the governor," the newspaper's editorial reads. "One comes to expect shocking comments when he opens his mouth around the media, much as Pavlov taught the world about the conditioned reflexes of dogs. . . . Jesse Ventura knows that his box-office appeal—his value as a political and cultural phenomenon—goes up each time he says something scandalous, especially something best left in the boys' locker room."

Ironically, the one thing the *Pioneer Press* finds most offensive is Ventura's quote from Mel Brooks's movie *History of the World: Part One*. It's the line when Brooks looks into the camera and says, "It's good to be the king." *The Pioneer Press* editorialist doesn't get the joke. "For all the shocking comments in the Playboy interview, the most deeply unsettling is the governor's reference to himself as 'king' and belief that 'there is no one in this state who can tell me what to do.' Governor, 4.7 million residents of this state are your bosses and have the right to tell you what to do. You disregard or dismiss them at your own peril. You ought to familiarize yourself with the concepts of servant leadership."

Recall Effort

Before the end of the day on October 1 one of Ventura's frequent critics announces plans to attempt to recall the governor from office. Leslie Davis, the man who sued Ventura to try to keep him from participating in "SummerSlam," plans to invoke a relatively new Minnesota law. In 1996 Minnesota voters approved a constitutional amendment providing for recall of constitutional officers, legislators, and judges. The 1998 legislature enacted the law establishing the process by which a recall election could be initiated. Davis plans to be the first to use the new recall process.

All he needs to do to begin the process is get twenty-five signatures from eligible voters on a petition and pay a $100 filing fee with the Minnesota secretary of state. The next steps aren't so easy. The chief justice of the Minnesota Supreme Court will have ten days to rule on whether the facts presented in the recall petition, if proven, actually constitute grounds for recall. If the chief justice agrees there are sufficient grounds, a "special master" (who must be an active or retired judge) is appointed to conduct a public hearing within twenty-one days to determine if there is sufficient evidence to warrant issuing a recall petition.

If the special master issues a report finding that the recall standards have been met, the report is forwarded to the entire Minnesota Supreme Court. The court has twenty days to determine if it agrees with the special master's report. If it does, the people bringing the original recall complaint have ninety days to circulate another petition to actually call a recall election. This time they would need a lot more than twenty-five signatures. The recall law requires the number of signatures to equal 25 percent of the votes cast in the last gubernatorial election. In this case, that means Davis would need the signatures of 522,748 Minnesotans to force a vote on whether Ventura should be thrown out of office.

After the governor's controversies involving state-paid security for book tours and his involvement in "SummerSlam," the *Playboy* interview makes Davis more confident than ever he can finally take Ventura down. "In addition to the conflict-of-interest matters, all of these statements he has made attacking religion and accepting Tailhook, I think he has fried himself now," Davis says boldly. "He is finished as governor."

You know you've captured national attention when the cast of *Saturday Night Live* lampoons you in their opening skit. On Saturday, October 2, that's exactly what happens to Governor Ventura. The show begins with impersonators of Pat Buchanan, Ross Perot, and Donald Trump sitting in a room, discussing who should be the Reform Party's presidential nominee.

All of a sudden a maniacal-looking bald man bursts through the wall, sending debris flying through the room. "It's Jesse! Run for your lives!" yells Perot in a high-pitched Texas twang. "Ventura," played by Will Ferrell, grabs Perot and starts swinging him over his head while Perot screams, "I want to be your vice president!" Ventura tosses Perot aside while Trump and several showgirls escape out a side door. "What are you looking at, America?" Ventura bellows, staring into the television camera. "You think I'm a joke? Well, you won't when I'm your president! Oh yeah, live from New York, it's *Saturday Night!*"

The real Ventura decides to address the growing national criticism on a Sunday-morning television show on which he's grown comfortable, *Meet the Press.* The governor actually taped the interview on Friday, the day after his *Playboy* interview became public.

Ventura laughs when host Tim Russert begins by holding up a copy of the *Playboy* issue featuring Ventura's interview and a cover photo of a female boxer covering her breasts with boxing gloves. The governor is appearing via satellite from St. Paul, dressed in a blue crew-neck Navy SEAL instructor sweatshirt. Russert puts Ventura's "organized religion" quote up on the television screen and reads it back to him in all its "weak-minded" glory.

"Do you believe in God?" Russert pointedly asks Ventura.

"Absolutely!" Ventura quickly replies.

"Do you consider yourself Christian?"

"Yes, but I don't believe necessarily that I need a church to go to," Ventura says. "My religious beliefs can be by a lake. They can be by a hill. They can be in the solitude of my own office."

Russert gets the governor to admit some of the things he said to the *Playboy* interviewer were nothing more than a publicity stunt. He asks Ventura if the interview was done for "shock value," much like the things a professional wrestler says to stir things up. Ventura's response is telling. "You do an interview for *Playboy*, *Playboy* wants a provocative interview. They want something that's going to sell issues. It doesn't mean I carry this *Playboy* interview in with me and do policy with it. That's ridiculous! It's one interview in many, many that I do."

His explanations on a Sunday-morning national talk show do

nothing to quell the uproar in Minnesota's religious community. He spends part of Sunday morning outside the governor's mansion, greeting runners along the Twin Cities Marathon course on Summit Avenue. He is not with his wife and daughter when they attend the church service at St. John's Evangelical Lutheran Church in Maple Grove, where the family worships.

After that service Terry Ventura is approached by a reporter from the *Star Tribune* and asked about her reaction to the governor's *Playboy* interview. "I am not ashamed of my husband—ever," she says in a vigorous defense of her besieged spouse. "He believes the state of Minnesota is a wonderful place and his job as governor is to make it better. He's been working steadily toward that goal." The newspaper reports she wipes away tears while standing with the couple's daughter, Jade. "What he says in an interview is his business," Terry Ventura says. "All I know is that I love him and the congregation loves him."

A minister at the church reads a statement to the congregation. It says, in part, that the governor "has apologized to each of his pastors for any problems or embarrassment his public comments have caused our congregation and assured us that he did not intend to include congregations such as our own in his comments. Any further concerns we have with his statements are matters of pastoral concern between us and him."

Former archbishop John Roach of the St. Paul and Minneapolis archdiocese writes an opinion piece that appears that Sunday morning in the *Star Tribune*. "I look back over a quarter of a century playing my role in organized religion, and I treasure my relationship with governors holding office during that time," writes the former archbishop. "Gov. Jesse Ventura's statement on organized religion in *Playboy* magazine is a serious departure from that relationship. I know that the governor has now qualified his statement to narrow it to what he describes as 'extreme' organized religion.... It may be gratuitous, but I would encourage the governor to find greater precision of language in his public statements."

Roach reminds Ventura about the role of religion in public debates that shape legislation. There is a separation of church and state in this country, but Roach argues that doesn't mean the church has no influence on public policy. "Governor, you need to look more deeply into the public role of organized religion. Not for the world would I presume to give you advice, but with your public image, do try to couple a reflective image. Try to spend a little time in quiet reflection. Be alone with your God. He has things to whisper in your ear."

By Monday, October 4, the national uproar over Ventura's *Playboy* interview has taken its toll. A new Minnesota Poll published by the *Star Tribune* shows the governor's approval rating in a serious nosedive. After reaching a pinnacle of 73 percent in July, the new poll gives him an approval rating of just 54 percent. The *Playboy* interview takes the shine off his administration. The poll of 624 Minnesotans was conducted October 1–3, the first three days after the *Playboy* release and also after the governor's various explanations and defenses of his opinions.

Ventura dismisses approval polls as "fickle" and says they "blow with the wind." He also reminds everyone again that opinion polls once showed he had no chance to be elected governor.

Bad poll numbers aren't the only feedback he's getting. In the two business days after the release of the *Playboy* interview, the governor's office received 971 unfavorable phone calls about his comments. Another 343 callers support the governor. These are just the callers who could get through the jammed phone lines. During the week of October 4 the numbers even out a bit, with 292 unfavorable calls and 269 favorable calls logged by the governor's Citizen Outreach office. Among the callers, nineteen ask Ventura to resign while twelve others say he should run for president. Remarkably, the calls came in from at least thirty-eight states.

Ventura's national profile will grow as the week goes on. Barbara Walters announces plans to interview him in New York for an upcoming *20/20* segment and also for her annual *Ten Most Fascinating People* special, both on ABC. Ventura is also a hot topic of discussion on Walters's ABC morning show, *The View*. One of the show's cohosts, Meredith Vieira, poses the question, "Can you cross the line into a buffoon? He is the governor of a state."

Walters jumps in with a spirited defense of Ventura. "I don't want to be the only one in the whole world defending him, because he does say very outrageous things," she says. "It's one of the reasons he got elected, because everybody says, 'Right or wrong, he's honest.' Now, he says a lot of very, very upsetting and very, very shocking things. But from day one he has always said everything that's on his mind, good, bad, or indifferent. In a way, and I'm certainly not going to condone what he said—I mean, I don't want to be a bra and you know I don't think religion is for the weak-minded and so forth—but I do give him credit for saying, no-holds-barred, 'I'm going to be honest.'"

Ironically, Minnesotans have been reading *about* Ventura's *Playboy* interview for five days, but haven't been able to actually read the interview, because the new issue hasn't hit Twin Cities newsstands yet. The demand is expected to be tremendous. It turns out *Playboy* will be sharing space with another national magazine featuring a major story about Minnesota's governor. *Newsweek* puts a big picture of Ventura on its cover with inset photos of Warren Beatty and Donald Trump, two other celebrities considering a run for president. The cover headline reads, "The Wild Bunch: Ventura, Beatty and Trump Stir Up Campaign 2000."

Long before the *Playboy* flap threatened to swamp Ventura's ship of state, the first week in October was pegged as the time to unveil the governor's "Big Plan" for Minnesota. It's the blueprint for how he will lead the state into the next century, with emphasis on reforming government and making people more "self-sufficient" so they need less government. It incorporates many things he talked about during the campaign, like creating a simpler tax system, reducing government regulation, seeking a single-house legislature, and improving transportation. The "Big Plan" doesn't strike most observers as particularly inventive. In some ways it seems almost ripped out of a utopian civics textbook. But it does at least serve as a scorecard by which to judge Ventura's term in office.

The governor travels to Mankato, about one hundred miles south of the Twin Cities, to unveil part one of the "Big Plan." Unfortunately for him, few of the reporters gathered here are interested in many more details about the "Big Plan." *Playboy* still rules the airwaves and newspapers.

A reporter asks Ventura if he thinks his *Playboy* remarks will hinder the cooperation he needs from the legislature to implement aspects of his plan. "I don't answer questions dealing with media feeding frenzies," he blurts out. "We're here to do business." After answering a few questions about the plan, a reporter takes a stab at another *Playboy* question, asking how it will affect his governing. "Judge me by my policies," Ventura responds, lightly banging his fist on the podium to emphasize his point.

Finally, an exasperated reporter asks him whether he even realizes his views stated in *Playboy* might affect how the public receives the "Big Plan." "If I went on public opinion, I wouldn't even be here as governor, would I?" Ventura fires back. "Because public opinion said I couldn't win." Once again, it's difficult to argue with his tortured logic.

House Republicans in the Minnesota legislature manage to stir up an argument. They dismiss the "Big Plan" as "long on rhetoric but short on details and implementation." But mostly they chide Ventura for releasing the plan details after the *Playboy* interview and just before jetting off to New York for interviews with Barbara Walters and David Letterman.

"Last week organized religion was a 'big sham' and this week he comes with the 'Big Plan,'" says House Majority Leader Tim Pawlenty. "We hope the governor becomes serious about governing and less concerned about various entertainment ventures." House Speaker Steve Sviggum puts it more succinctly. "Trying to govern between controversial and confrontational interviews does not serve the state of Minnesota or its people well."

Harvard Man

On October 6, Ventura boards Northwest Flight 148 headed for Boston, where he's been invited to Harvard University's John F. Kennedy School of Government. The high-school-educated, had-a-cup-of-coffee-in-junior-college, biker-turned-wrestler-turned-governor is about to become a "Haaavaaad" man. Harvard University in Cambridge, Massachusetts, is America's oldest university, opening its doors in 1636. Harvard has produced six U.S. presidents, thirty Nobel prize winners, and, now, one invitation to a body-slammin' governor from Minnesota.

They must be *really* smart at Harvard because the invitation was extended weeks before publication of the *Playboy* interview. Students in the Institute of Politics invited Ventura to take part in a monthly "Pizza and Politics" session with nearly one hundred undergraduates. The topic of discussion is supposed to be "Youth Involvement in Government and Politics." But post-*Playboy*, the number-one topic on everyone's mind is still, "What the hell were you thinking?"

What began as a one-hour session scheduled with students grows into an additional meeting scheduled with Harvard faculty members, a one-on-one interview with ABC's Sam Donaldson, a *New York Times* interview, and a guest appearance on a special edition of CNBC's *Hardball* show broadcast live from the university.

When Ventura arrives at Harvard it's immediately obvious he's tired of talking about *Playboy*, at least with Minnesota reporters. Several of us have followed the governor to Harvard. After checking into the Charles Hotel adjacent to the campus, he walks across a courtyard to another wing of the hotel for his interview with Donaldson. Ventura, surrounded by his usual entourage of staff and security, refuses to answer any of our questions. He doesn't even look at us to acknowledge our presence as he brusquely walks into a hotel conference room where Donaldson is waiting.

Donaldson will interview Ventura live on the ABC News Web site. They've turned the conference room into a makeshift television studio. Ventura asks for some makeup to knock down the shine on his bald head from the dozen or so television lights flooding the room. Like every other journalist in the world, Donaldson wants to talk about *Playboy*. "How are you holding up since the *Playboy* interview?" Donaldson asks.

"I'm doing just fine," Ventura replies. "I conduct business and do my job as governor, and I don't get tangled up in the press's problems."

He dismisses the criticism as an example of the press taking his quote about organized religion being a "sham and a crutch for weak-minded people" out of context. He says everyone neglects to mention that his quote ends with a reference to the "religious right." Donaldson pulls out a copy of the interview. "Now, at the very end of the last sentence in there, it does say 'religious right,'" he acknowledges. "But the antecedent was 'organized religion is a sham.' Shouldn't you use the words 'religious right' [at the beginning]?"

"I probably should've, Sam," Ventura admits. "And I'm not making excuses, but I do three to five interviews a day. If you multiply that out five days a week, that's twenty-five a week, which for the year means I'll do well over a thousand."

Despite the steady drumbeat of criticism for more than a week now, the governor says he still doesn't owe anyone an apology. "I have freedom of speech," he reminds Donaldson. "Getting elected I don't think takes away your First Amendment right. I think you're still allowed your own thoughts and your own freedom of speech. If people were offended by it, I didn't mean to offend people. I just speak my mind and what I believe in."

Ventura also tells Donaldson he thinks it's unfair for people to judge his ability to govern based on this controversy. "Judge me by how I govern, not by how I do an interview or say something to *Playboy* magazine."

When he leaves the interview with Donaldson, Ventura again gives the Minnesota media the silent treatment. Even Donaldson, who made a living out of badgering presidents and other public officials, is amazed by the governor's open disdain for the local media. But he understands why Ventura gets so much coverage by the local and national press.

"First of all, Jesse Ventura is a very fascinating character," Donaldson tells me after his interview with the governor. "And I use the word 'character' in the best sense of the word. Second, here's the governor of an important state who says all of these things and they're, to him, honesty, but to a lot of people ... they're offensive. So that makes him hot copy."

Although Ventura is taking tremendous heat for his controversial views, Donaldson doesn't believe the governor's viability for reelection in Minnesota or election to a national office is irreparably harmed. Not yet, anyway. "I don't think he's dead, if that's what you're asking me—politically, nationally—because of this one *Playboy* interview. But if he keeps saying things that offend large groups of people, he's not going to be elected. That's just obvious."

Donaldson isn't surprised that the governor's comments about religion and Tailhook dominate the coverage of the *Playboy* interview. "The rest of it isn't what's newsworthy. It's interesting, I think, but it's like Jimmy Carter. He did a long *Playboy* interview, and as the interviewer was leaving, Carter stopped him at the kitchen door and says, 'I want you to know one more thing—I've known lust in my heart.' Well, who remembers anything else he said in the interview!"

CNBC's Chris Matthews agrees with Donaldson that Ventura isn't dead in the water yet. Matthews stops to talk with reporters on his way from the Charles Hotel to the Harvard campus, where he's preparing for tonight's live broadcast of *Hardball*. Ventura has already been on *Hardball* a few times, and Minnesota's governor clearly intrigues Matthews. "There's a record number of Americans now looking for an alternative to the two parties, and he is probably the most dramatic prospect to fill that void," Matthews says. "They used to say the first thing you have to do is get the donkey's attention. He's gotten attention, and the question now is, what does he do with it?"

Matthews says Ventura is tapping into a part of the electorate that he practically has all to himself for now. "The very fact that he's in *Playboy* probably is the statement that he is of interest to younger voters and people less connected to politics. The kind of person that would read *Playboy* is certainly not the kind of person that would read the *Weekly Standard* or the *National Review* or *New Republic*."

But *Playboy* can be a double-edged sword as Matthews knows all too well. He used to work for former President Carter. "*Playboy* is a very treacherous terrain to do an interview because, I think, inevitably whenever you sit down to talk to those reporters or editors, you end up talking their lingo. You end up talking the '*Playboy* philosophy.' I mean, even Carter, my old boss, talked about having lust in his heart. You try to reach common ground. It's not like you're addressing the National Council of Churches. And that's probably what people do, they retail. And I'll bet that's the worst thing I could say about Jesse Ventura. He was retailing that magazine. He was playing to that audience of guys out there, some of whom read that magazine with one hand."

At a news conference after the meeting with students, Governor Ventura faces a pack of reporters, television cameras, and newspaper photographers. Again, everyone wants to talk about *Playboy*. Ventura pulls out a photocopy of the interview to blast what he views as distorted news coverage of his comments. "I guess I'm not used to dealing with the fact that Jesse Ventura today can say words that will cause a thunder throughout the world. You know this whole interview here and everything that you're grilling me on? This is old news! I said it all on talk radio! It's just that nobody cared then. When I said it on talk radio it didn't shake up the world! Now I say it and the world is shook!"

Of course, there is a world of difference between being a talk-radio show host and the governor of a state. So a reporter asks Ventura if his blunt talk now hurts his credibility and his effectiveness as governor. "I don't have time to worry about that. I can only be me. I will continue to be me. I was elected being me. I like being in the position I'm in because I can speak freely and not worry about getting reelected or not. This isn't my career."

A few minutes after that news conference Ventura is introduced on *Hardball*. He bounds up onto a stage in the middle of an auditorium surrounded by eight hundred cheering students at Harvard's John F. Kennedy School of Government. "Sounds to me like I got a hometown crowd here," Ventura boasts. Once again *Playboy* is the prime-time topic.

"I was asked recently if I would do a *Playboy* interview," Matthews tells Ventura. "Do you recommend that I do that?"

"I'd say do that before the foldout," Ventura deadpans, drawing a big laugh from the crowd.

Matthews catches Ventura a bit off-guard when he asks a simple question: "What kind of country does Jesse Ventura want to live in?" After pondering the question for several seconds, the governor rattles off an answer that doesn't seem particularly well thought out. Or, at best, it's geared to justify his *Playboy* interview more than to articulate his vision for America. "I want to live in a country that supports all the amendments of our Constitution. I think they're very, very important ... that we never lose sight of the fact that freedom of speech is so very important."

One Harvard graduate student in the audience refuses to believe Ventura could actually mean what he said about religion. "I'm a Hindu, and while I agree with you I don't need to be in temple to be practicing my religion, I don't think people who do believe they have to do that are weak-minded," the student says, looking Ventura straight in the eye. "I don't think you necessarily believe that either."

Ventura doesn't back down. "Read the question [in the *Playboy* interview] and then read the whole answer. Not just things pulled out.... There's not necessarily a bad connotation on being weak-minded." Chuckles ripple through the audience. "No, there is not. If faith and religion fulfill that void for you, then you obviously do need it."

Matthews probes the religion question too. The question has been asked of Ventura so many times, he's desperate for a new approach. "When you walk by a church, Governor," Matthews says as the audience begins to chuckle again, "and you have that moment where you look up at the place and you keep walking, what goes through your head?" The crowd is laughing now, but Ventura gives a serious answer. "I have nothing at all against religion, people's beliefs, and the freedom that we're allowed to practice them here in the United States of America. What goes through my heart and thoughts are that it's a sanctuary, that if people desire or need it, it is there for them."

Ventura and Matthews cover a lot of ground in their one-hour interview. An inordinate amount of time is devoted to a discussion of Ventura's views on the Kennedy assassination. In *Playboy* he said he thinks the U.S. government was involved in Kennedy's death. "I believe

Kennedy was going to withdraw us from Vietnam and there were factions that didn't want that," Ventura told *Playboy*.

Matthews wants to know what makes the governor believe that. "You said that we killed Kennedy," Matthews says.

"I cannot buy the fact personally that Oswald acted alone," Ventura replies.

Matthews goes to great lengths trying to dismiss Ventura's theory, saying it would require us to believe everyone from the Secret Service to the Dallas Police Department were in on the conspiracy. It leads to the funniest exchange of the night. "How far will you go with this?" Matthews asks after Ventura explains his conspiracy theory. The governor tries to ask Matthews questions about the Kennedy case.

"Let me fire another one at you," Ventura says.

"No, I'm asking you the questions," Matthews interrupts.

"No, no," Ventura fires back, "I'm a talk-show host, too!" The crowd is laughing and applauding as the two mix it up.

When the show ends, Matthews and Ventura stand up and shake hands. But as the credits for the show roll, Matthews can't resist grabbing Ventura from behind, trying to put him in a wrestling hold while grunting like a wrestler. This is not politics-as-usual.

The governor hangs around for about fifteen minutes after the show, talking with students and signing autographs. He signs copies of his autobiography, someone's hat, and even a few copies of the now infamous *Playboy*. The Harvard students seem to enjoy Ventura's appearance, but they also offer insightful critiques of what they heard.

"I guess I was a little bit disappointed," Harvard student Jonathan Laurence tells me afterward. "I thought there was a little bit more developed ideology behind his frankness. I was impressed by his honesty. I guess that's what a lot of the media attention can be ascribed to, that he speaks in a straight manner whereas a lot of people do not. But on the other hand, I didn't think he had that much to say. He was repeating a lot of clichés from what we learned in civics class."

If Ventura wants to avoid interview land mines, New York is probably the last place he should be, but that's where he's headed after leaving Harvard. He's mixing some state business with his entertainment ventures in New York. He's got his commissioners of the finance and revenue departments along on the trip for a meeting at Standard & Poors bonding house to discuss Minnesota's credit rating. Even in New York, Ventura draws a crowd of media and onlookers outside an office building in the shadows of the World Trade Center, just off Wall Street. His car is waiting for him in the loading dock of the building. When he drives away after offering a few brief comments to reporters, several New Yorkers cheer him on.

"Jesse 'the Body!' Oooh, Jesse!" two guys yell to Ventura as they strike wrestling poses. "Jesse, we love you in New York! Be our governor!" He rolls down his window and gives them a wave as he drives off.

Some thought the *Playboy* interview would turn Ventura into a pariah. Instead, it's raised his celebrity to stratospheric heights. He heads to the Ed Sullivan Theater for a taping of *Late Night with David Letterman*. It's a bit of a trick for the governor's two-car motorcade to get near the stage entrance. That's because the street is blocked for a much larger motorcade expected to pass by soon. President Clinton is at a fund-raiser a couple of blocks away and plans to drive by the Ed Sullivan Theater when he departs. So Ventura gets out of his car on Broadway and walks to the stage entrance, puffing on a cigar and surrounded by security.

Ventura is the featured guest along with ZZ Top. "Of all the wrestlers turned governors, the first guest is my favorite," Letterman says to a big laugh. "Please welcome from the great state of Minnesota, Governor Jesse Ventura!" As Ventura walks onstage and the applause signs light up, Letterman is ready to stir up some trouble with the governor.

"You know, last time you were here, we were kidding around with you and we said, 'Which do you like better, St. Paul or Minneapolis?' And there was some trouble there, wasn't there?" Ventura doesn't take the bait, instead choosing to poke fun at himself about *Playboy* before Letterman can get to it: "I've learned that I can get in trouble now without you."

Letterman laughs and the audience applauds as they all realize he's referring to *Playboy*. As Ventura sits there with a smirk on his face, soaking up the applause, he's plotting more trouble for himself. "By the way, that's not the president's motorcade outside, that's mine," he tells Letterman, who earlier broadcast live pictures of the motorcade driving by the theater. "The president's still back in the hotel with the interns."

Now the audience is groaning over the governor's audacity. Letterman just shakes his head in wonder. "Do you think I'm in trouble again?" Ventura asks Letterman.

Letterman tells Ventura he's amazed by his willingness to say just about anything that's on his mind. "Hardly anybody says anything anymore that they really are called to task for. There's very little accountability because nobody will say anything wrong. Everybody knows exactly what to say because they know what people want to hear. So they tell them exactly what people want to hear. You're a little bit different. So why is it all hell breaks loose whenever you say something?"

"I don't know," Ventura says. "Two years ago no one cared. And in reality, Dave, all the things I say I've said before. They're not new. But now all of a sudden when I say them, apparently they're going to have a major effect on world policy."

Letterman points out to the governor what should be obvious. "The difference is now when you speak, you're no longer just speaking for yourself. You're speaking as a representative of the people who voted for you and you're speaking as a representative of the state of Minnesota."

"That's true. But you know what? They voted for me, and they knew I was outspoken when they elected me."

About ninety minutes after the Letterman taping, a black limousine pulls up outside the Trump International Hotel and Tower. Ventura is having dinner with Donald Trump and actor Woody Harrelson and it's the worst-kept secret in New York, which explains the swarm of reporters and camera crews standing at curbside. "Nice and easy, fellas," a bodyguard says to the photographers jostling for position. Then out steps Harrelson, followed by Ventura and Trump.

They all ignore questions being shouted about whether Trump plans to run for president and if Ventura plans to help him. Earlier in the day, however, Trump made it clear in a television interview he's considering a bid.

"We're probably going to be making a decision in January or February," Trump says. "The polls have come out. They've been unbelievably strong. They say I'd win. But we're going to look at—we're going to look at it very seriously." It must be an internal poll he paid for because every legitimate national poll so far shows him to be a long-shot candidate, at best.

Playboy Explanation Tour

God knows he's trying to dig himself out of a hole, but someone needs to tell the governor to put the shovel down and back away slowly. His "*Playboy* Explanation Tour" takes him next to an interview with Barbara Walters for ABC's *20/20*. Again, he raises a few eyebrows. Ventura manages to compare people hooked on cocaine or heroin to people "addicted to Hostess Twinkies." He comes to the conclusion that "I don't think you need to treat them criminally, because they suffer from an addiction." He reiterates his position that prostitution should be decriminalized and says banning assault weapons would be a "fraud." Ventura says they're "no more dangerous than a deer rifle."

But once again he really steps in it when the discussion turns to religion. Walters brings up the "organized religion is a sham and a crutch for weak-minded people" quote.

"So you made a little mistake," she says. "You went a little too far."

"I'm human," Ventura tells her. "And when I get asked a question, I may not clarify as clearly as I want to say it.... It just came out and then I was left to defend it. And I'm not backing up. I believe what I believe and I will not apologize."

"But your wife goes to church. That's organized religion."

"So?" Ventura replies.

"So you don't say she's weak-minded. Or do you?"

"Yeah."

"You do?" a surprised Walters responds.

"Because weak-minded doesn't necessarily have to be bad," Ventura explains." "It means you have a weakness and if it's—if going to church will strengthen that mind, then for that person, fine. I'm just speaking on my behalf. I don't have to do it."

"So have you said to your wife, 'Darling, you're weak-minded'? I want to hear that!"

"Well, come on over."

Walters concludes her interview by asking Ventura about running for president. He says he doesn't want the job, but Walters wants to know if he did run, does he think he could win. "Yes, I believe I could," Ventura says. "And I'm not saying that bragging. I've traveled around the country and I see the same thing nationally as I saw in Minnesota when I ran for governor. The people are tired of the in-the-box career politician, created politician. And they're looking, I think, for something that's true and real."

Walters can only marvel at his confidence. "Governor, as they say, you are a piece of work," she tells him with a smile.

"So are you, Barbara," he replies.

On Sunday, October 10, Ventura is on national television again, this time on *This Week* with Sam Donaldson, Cokie Roberts, and George Will. The three hosts flew to St. Paul to tape the interview with the governor at the State Capitol on Friday. It starts innocently enough with softball questions about Donald Trump and whether Ventura would support him as a Reform Party candidate for president. After a couple of questions about Pat Buchanan's potential shift to the Reform Party, Will tries to ask a question about *Playboy*.

Ventura interrupts him, points at Donaldson (who set up this interview), and says, "You told me we weren't going to get to *Playboy!*" Donaldson just laughs, saying of Will, "I can't control him any more than anyone else can, Governor." A source in the governor's communications office tells me Donaldson arranged the interview with the vague promise that they didn't plan to dwell much on the *Playboy* interview. The governor is tiring of talking about it. By my calculations, approximately twelve minutes of the sixteen-minute *This Week* segment with Ventura end up devoted to discussion of the *Playboy* interview.

In fact, it's soon obvious that Donaldson planned to grill the governor about *Playboy* all along. Why else would they all fly to St. Paul for the interview?

The interview on *This Week* finally hits on the larger questions surrounding the governor in the wake of the *Playboy* fiasco.

In a roundabout way, Donaldson, Roberts, and Will essentially ask Ventura: "Are you nuts?"

Cokie Roberts gets the ball rolling. "There are polls in the newspapers saying that the majority of people are now saying instead of your attitude being refreshing, that it's embarrassing. There's a recall petition out for you."

"Oh, come on! That guy! That's a joke. Don't even bring up the recall. This guy [Leslie Davis] has brought up four or five lawsuits against me that have been tossed out. He's meaningless."

"What about the general public?" she asks.

"The general public? Remember, I like to quote my friend Jack Nicholson sometimes: 'You can't handle the truth.' And there's points where if you do tell the truth and it makes people personally uncomfortable they get irritated not being able to face the truth and have it put in front of them. A lot of people don't like that."

In Ventura's mind his "opinions" are the "truth," and it seems no amount of arguing to the contrary will convince him otherwise.

The interview on *This Week* ends with George Will practically picking a fight with Ventura. It's obvious Will can't stand the notion of Ventura as a political folk hero.

"Do you think that when you became governor—voluntarily, no one made you do this—that you took on a certain obligation to worry about the country's sense of dignity?"

"The state's sense of dignity ..." Ventura tries to correct him.

"You're a national figure too," Will reminds him.

"So what! I'm the governor of the 'state' of Minnesota.... How have I been undignified?"

"Well, you want to be reincarnated as what?" (A 38 double-D bra, according to *Playboy*.)

"Oh, come on! Come on! Have we gotten to the point, George, I have to get elected and lose my sense of humor?... I also was a wrestler. They tell me that's not dignified. Yet the majority of the people of Minnesota elected a wrestler, an undignified wrestler." (Actually, a plurality of 37 percent of the people elected him, not a majority.)

At this point Will uses Ventura's belief in a possible conspiracy theory implicating the U.S. government in Kennedy's assassination as an example of why people question whether the governor and the Reform Party can be taken seriously.

"I don't have the answer of who did [the assassination]," Ventura tells Will. "But don't sit and tell me I have to accept the Warren Commission. Don't sit and tell me in the light of O. J. Simpson being innocent that I now have to accept the Warren Commission being a fact."

"Let's stipulate that people can disagree," Will says, "but there's a political problem here, and that is that since Ross Perot said the CIA may have disrupted his daughter's wedding, there has been a cloud of nuttiness perhaps associated with the [Reform Party] franchise."

"I don't think so," Ventura fires back, although he mostly ignores the Reform Party "nuttiness" crack because he's focused on the Kennedy assassination. "Let me ask you this, George. If he did it, Oswald, this little disgruntled Marine, why did we have to put all the evidence in the archives until the year 2029 because of national security? How, in what way, could this little Marine private affect our national security as a nation, if that's true?"

"Beats me," an exasperated Will responds as the interview comes to an inglorious end.

The exchange with Will exemplifies why Ventura has such broad appeal. He can take an intellectual heavyweight like George Will and reduce him to a simple, "Beats me" as a counterargument to Ventura's seemingly far-fetched Kennedy-assassination theories.

The same day Ventura is sparring with Cokie, George, and Sam on ABC, the incoming and outgoing chairs of the national Reform Party spar *about* Ventura on NBC. Outgoing party chair Russell Verney, who earlier asked Ventura to resign from the party, tells NBC's Tim Russert on *Meet the Press* that Ventura's collection of off-the-wall remarks in *Playboy* were "an affront to the values of the members of the Reform Party." Incoming party chair Jack Gargan admits to some uneasiness about the *Playboy* interview. But he says Ventura is still the star of the party and should remain a member. "It was unfortunate, and that's putting it mildly. But he never said he was speaking on behalf of the Reform Party. He was speaking personally. And my e-mail I've received is overwhelmingly in favor of the governor."

Gargan's e-mail might support the governor, but a new CNN/ *USA Today*/Gallup Poll shows Ventura's national popularity falling rapidly. The impact of a nonstop, two-week barrage of reports and interviews about the *Playboy* interview shows up in another poll. A survey of 973 adults across the nation indicates that 37 percent have a favorable opinion of Ventura. That's down from 51 percent in a similar national poll just a month earlier. The poll published on October 14 also shows his unfavorable rating jumps from 25 percent in September to 45 percent in the new poll.

While those numbers are certainly not positive, they could be a lot worse. When you consider that 90 percent of the coverage of Ventura's *Playboy* remarks has been negative, a drop of just 14 percent in a national popularity poll is rather remarkable. *Saturday Night Live* has lampooned him, hosts of Sunday morning political shows have blindsided him, and Minnesota newspaper columnists have skewered him. Yet 37 percent of the nation has a favorable impression of Governor Ventura. More amazing still is the fact that national publications are even doing polls about his popularity. Name one other governor in the nation who gets that kind of attention.

The negative coverage won't let up just yet. A few days after the *This Week* appearance, George Will makes a comeback from his lame "Beats me" response to lash Ventura in his *Washington Post* column. Will unleashes some of the funniest one-liners yet written about Ventura since his election.

"Jesse Ventura ... has Minnesota so well in hand he has time to give interviews promiscuously—25 a week, he says. Nowadays these include interviews to tidy up after interviews." Talk about biting the hand that feeds you! Just days after flying to St. Paul to interview him for *This Week*, Will is ridiculing Ventura for having the audacity to agree to the interview.

"Ventura's mind is quick and his temperament constantly pops the clutch that connects his mind to his mouth," Will writes. "He knows next to nothing about the Constitution. Asked by Playboy about his statement that government should not create jobs, he indicates no awareness of rather a lot of history surrounding the clause that says Congress shall 'provide for ... the general welfare.'"

Will calls Ventura's frequent "I'm only telling the truth" excuses "arrogance in drag. There is no vanity quite like that of a populist man-of-the-people who is too darn humble to concern himself with anything as highfalutin' as manners. And it is plain bad manners to insult and embarrass constituents."

Near the end of the Will column is the biggest gem of all. It's the epitome of a backhanded compliment. "Ventura seems to be a meanness-free zone in today's politics. He is a genuinely friendly man, curious about the world, and without pretense, other than the delusion that it is a public service for him to give public tours of the mansion of his mind, regardless how sparsely some rooms in it are furnished."

In the midst of the withering local and national criticism, Ventura wins another key court battle. He fends off the effort to recall him from office when Minnesota Supreme Court chief justice Kathleen Blatz dismisses the recall petition. The decision is so overwhelmingly favorable to the governor it would seem to open the door to just about any outrageous endeavor he could dream up.

In his recall petition Leslie Davis makes several allegations about Ventura's use of state-paid security for a book tour and conflicts of in-terest for accepting compensation from a book publisher and wrestling promoters. Blatz picks apart the Davis petition point by point.

"Assuming the factual allegations in the proposed petition can be proven, most of the conduct challenged is in the realm of the governor's personal and private life, not the performance of his official duties," Blatz writes in her decision. "But the general standard for recall stated in both the constitutional and statutory provisions applies expressly to acts 'in the performance of the duties of the office.'"

As for using state-paid security for a book tour, Blatz writes, "Continuous protection of the governor by state personnel has long been the practice, whether the governor is performing official duties or engaged in private activities. This protection is a practical necessity of the office."

In regard to whether Ventura used his position as governor to increase the money earned for his book and wrestling deals, Blatz says, "The fact that a public official enjoys greater personal opportunities as a result of holding office" is not sufficient grounds for recall. She rules that receiving outside compensation also doesn't meet the recall standard, because Ventura didn't accept money in the "performance of official duties." Finally, Blatz dismisses an allegation that the governor's "outrageous" conduct is designed to increase his opportunities for personal gain.

Ventura isn't commenting on the court decision, preferring not to give Leslie Davis's allegations any credibility. His spokesperson, John Wodele, says the governor and his staff spent little time worrying about the outcome of the case. "The ruling is something we expected. We felt from the beginning that it was unworthy of the recall process. It was a frivolous attempt by an individual who seems bent on going after the governor for whatever reasons he can conjure up."

Across the street in the State Office Building, Davis conducts a news conference and responds in his usual vitriolic way.

"When people like Justice Blatz ignore the law, the outlaws will rule," Davis says, referring to Ventura. "Based on the calls and letters I've received, I'm convinced that if the voters were given a second chance, they would vote Ventura out of office. If Governor Ventura has any brains at all, he'll start to govern Minnesota in ways that we need Minnesota governed and not as his own little piggy bank."

With so much controversy swirling, Ventura does his best to put the focus back on governing. Each week in October he's unveiling another part of his "Big Plan" for Minnesota. On October 19 he's headed north to Brainerd to outline a plan to improve government services.

But even during his appearance at Mississippi Horizons Middle School in Brainerd, Ventura can't escape the *Playboy* topic. Students submitted questions in writing for the governor. The little slips of paper are pulled out of a plastic pumpkin one by one and read to him.

"What's the most embarrassing thing that's happened to you while you were in office so far this year?" a student reads to him. Ventura laughs because it's an easy question to answer. "I guess my most recent interview that got so much publicity." Everyone laughs along with the governor, but it's a revealing moment for Ventura because, for the first time, he acknowledges he's embarrassed by some of the things he said in *Playboy*.

CHAPTER 12

"Blatant Political Garbage"
The Reform Party Implodes
While the Governor Stands Alone

Governor Jesse Ventura gets a chance to shake off the *Playboy* fiasco by trying his hand as an international statesman. On November 3, 1999, he wakes up halfway around the world at the Hotel Okura in Tokyo. He's leading a Minnesota trade delegation in Japan and will spend the first anniversary of his improbable election victory visiting his roots. His wrestling roots, anyway.

With a busload of Minnesota reporters and a handful of Japanese television and newspaper reporters in tow, Ventura visits a "sumo shrine" that, from the seventeenth to nineteenth centuries, was the site of major sumo tournaments in Tokyo. Near the shrine is a hundred-year-old monument honoring Japan's sumo grand champions, all of whom stood six-foot-seven or taller (three inches taller than Ventura). Ventura's hand is dwarfed when he checks out handprints each of them made in concrete. "They remind me of Andre the Giant from my days in pro wrestling," he marvels.

Ventura is accompanied by one of his former tag-team partners, Japanese wrestler Masa Saito (wrestling fans will remember him as "Mr. Torture"). Their visit to the shrine includes a purification ritual, in which they wash their hands before donning white ceremonial vests.

Bong! Bong! Bong! The somber sound of a drum reverberates through the shrine while Ventura and Saito approach the altar, bow, and clap their hands after making a wish.

A few minutes after the ceremony, a Japanese reporter informs Ventura that Japanese politicians often come here for "luck, prosperity, and purification." The governor can't resist a wisecrack. "Politicians would probably need that," he jokes.

Halfway through his trip to Japan the governor sells out a noon luncheon at the Foreign Correspondents Club in Tokyo. Of course, in Japan many of the foreign correspondents are Americans. No matter where Ventura comes in contact with reporters, there's potential for a sparring match. This event is no exception.

"Governor, usually when a governor of a state such as Minnesota comes to Japan, he gets to meet with fairly high-ranking Japanese officials, if not the prime minister," a Tokyo-based Associated Press reporter says after Ventura offers to take some questions after his speech. "There's definitely an appearance that you've been snubbed by high-ranking Japanese government people. Do you feel that they don't respect you as a governor or are they afraid of you?" The last line draws laughter from everyone but Ventura.

"Sure, it would be nice," he responds in a measured tone. "But I'm here to do business, and I'm meeting with the people here in Japan that I think can expand business opportunities for the state of Minnesota. No, I don't feel at all snubbed. I could care [he wants to say "less," but resists the temptation] . . . I mean, if I do, I do. If I don't, I don't. It's not going to make or break this trip for me."

It's true Ventura isn't scheduled to meet with any high-ranking Japanese trade or government officials. But just before the correspondents luncheon, the governor did meet with U.S. ambassador Tom Foley at the American embassy in Tokyo. He's also meeting with several key Japanese business leaders who actually make decisions about doing business with Minnesota companies. Still, the American reporters in Japan remain skeptical. "I'm always a bit skeptical about these sort of schmoozing trips when politicians turn into salesmen," a *Forbes* magazine reporter says to Ventura in a somewhat condescending tone. "Have you actually gotten any sort of harvest? Is there anything concrete to report from your trip? Has some new business emerged?"

Ventura is doing a slow burn as he listens to the question. "The trip's not over," the governor says, turning on the deep, menacing voice he so often employed in his wrestling days. "I'm always a little skeptical too when they make me talk to the press the whole trip. I could be meeting with businesses right now, but instead I'm entertaining you!"

The reporters all laugh, appreciating the refreshing bluntness of Ventura's response. He could have done what most politicians would do and point to a pork-export agreement he planned to sign during the trip and mention some tourism initiatives that are in the works. Instead, he goes for the media's solar plexus.

Ventura might be thousands of miles from Minnesota, but that doesn't mean his critics back home can't still get under his skin. The day after that press luncheon, the Taxpayers League of Minnesota issues a news release criticizing the governor's trip to Japan. The conservative taxpayer-advocacy organization is a frequent critic of Ventura. This time it fires its most vicious shot yet all the way across the Pacific.

"The governor is spending $10,000 a day on a 10-day vacation to Japan," the one-page news release says, "where he is meeting no high government officials, and meeting with far fewer Japanese than Americans. The trip appears to be nothing more than an expensive vacation for Jesse and his buddies to sightsee and go to the season-opening games of the Minnesota Timberwolves." The Timberwolves are in Tokyo to play two NBA games against the Sacramento Kings. "It is scandalous that $100,000 of taxpayers' money is being spent to accomplish nothing real for Minnesota's citizens or businesses. The 'trade deal' the governor announced with Minnesota pork producers and a Japanese company was completed before the governor even arrived. Minnesota taxpayers shouldn't be on the hook for $100,000 so the governor and his buddies can have a good time visiting Japanese shrines and watching basketball.... Perhaps after this trip is over, Governor Ventura can write a book entitled, 'How to Visit Japan on $10,000 a Day.'"

Ventura is just minutes from starting his weekly *Lunch with the Governor* radio show at the CBS News Bureau in Tokyo when a reporter hands him a copy of the Taxpayers League news release. Needless to say, he blows his top. "You read this article and tell me if this is a factual description of what we've accomplished over here," Ventura rants to the Minnesota reporters on hand to cover his radio show. "This ought to tell you right here and destroy the credibility of this particular group, because this is just blatant political garbage. And you all as reporters have been here every step of the way, and I certainly hope you'll report on this."

A rather remarkable request, considering his constant insistence that we're unable to accurately report anything.

Ventura's communications director, John Wodele, motions the reporters and television photographers to back off so the governor can get into the radio booth. There are still several minutes until airtime, but Wodele appears to fear the governor is about to say something he'll regret. Ventura keeps blowing off steam anyway. "That just shows me the Taxpayers League of Minnesota has no credibility at all. Don't even ask me to respond to this phony group anymore."

Remarkably, the governor shows enough restraint to not even mention the news release during his radio show. It's remarkable because the governor has a legitimate beef. While you can debate the value of these trade missions, Ventura isn't doing anything differently than other governors. The previous governor, Republican Arne Carlson, went on more than a dozen international trade missions in his eight years in office without so much as a peep from the Taxpayers League or anyone else. As for traveling to Japan while the Timberwolves are in Tokyo, Ventura would be a fool not to coordinate the two events. What better way to maximize the amount of exposure Minnesota can get in Japan than to pair the state's NBA team with a visit by the most famous governor in America?

One funny thing does come about as a result of the Taxpayers League news release. While Ventura doesn't respond to the criticism on the air, he spends the final commercial break of his show complaining about it to television photographers shooting video in the radio booth.

"I really think it'll hurt 'em," Ventura says about the Taxpayers League. "What shred of credibility they had." He has his headphones hanging around his neck while he's talking. He's so focused on the Tax-payers League, he forgets to put the headphones back over his ears and can't hear the pleadings of his producer David Ruth back in Minnesota as the commercial break is coming to an end.

"Governor Ventura! Governor! Governor! Governor Ventura! Are you there? Governor, we gotta wrap it up! Allllll right! We'll just wrap it up from here."

A few seconds later Wodele and Ventura put their headphones back on and can't figure out why there's dead air.

"We must be done," Ventura says.

After his trade mission to Japan, the governor picks up where he left off back in Minnesota. In other words, he's right back in the national spotlight. Thanks to the provocative *Playboy* interview, ABC's Barbara Walters features Ventura as one of her *Ten Most Fascinating People of 1999* in a special broadcast to air at the end of November (sharing the spotlight with singer Ricky Martin, New York Yankees manager Joe Torre, former White House intern Monica Lewinsky, Tour de France winner Lance Armstrong, circus ringmaster Jonathan Lee Iverson, soap star Susan Lucci, King Abdullah of Jordan, communications titan Sumner Redstone, and John F. Kennedy's daughter, Caroline Kennedy Schlossberg).

More important, the Ventura administration announces that Minnesota has run up yet another huge budget surplus. It is, according to the state's finance commissioner, a "boatload of money." Just in time for the holidays, Ventura and the legislature find themselves with a $1.6 billion projected budget surplus through the end of the 2001 fiscal year.

The Minnesota Department of Finance says revenue is booming from collection of individual income taxes, sales taxes, corporate taxes, and motor-vehicle sales-tax receipts. It's especially remarkable coming on the heels of the big tax cuts enacted during the last legislative session. "It's a lot of fun being governor when the times are good," Ventura says at a news conference announcing the surplus. "Santa Claus is coming to town," chimes in Republican House Majority Leader Tim

Pawlenty at another news conference a short time later. "Unbelievable numbers," says DFL Senate Majority Leader Roger Moe. It's a rare instance when all three branches of Minnesota's tripartisan government agree on something. It doesn't last, of course.

The three sides immediately renew the debate over how to deal with the surplus. Governor Ventura wants another sales-tax rebate and a significant lowering of automobile license-tab fees. House Republicans want income-tax cuts and a rebate. Senate Democrats say they want some tax relief, but also view this as an opportunity to spend more money on things like education and transportation. Keep this early debate in mind. A few months from now, it will set the framework for a remarkable compromise at the end of the 2000 legislative session a few months from now.

The governor is passionate about giving surplus money back. He's even more passionate about Minnesota Timberwolves basketball. People around the nation know Ventura often shares political opinions on talk shows. Basketball fans also know he likes to share an opinion or two with NBA referees at the Target Center in Minneapolis. Ventura is a season-ticket holder and rarely misses a game. He doesn't always sit courtside, but he's usually close enough to get the attention of referees. At a game in early December 1999, an outburst aimed at referee Ron Elesiak gets the attention of just about everyone in the arena and in a local television audience.

"He got this crowd going," a Timberwolves television announcer says during a telecast. "One entire end of Target Center on their feet chanting, 'Jesse, Jesse!'"

Ventura is yelling because the referee is trying to have another fan thrown out of the arena. The governor is coming to the fan's defense, much to the delight of the crowd. He's pointing at the referee and giving him that familiar scowl from his wrestling days.

A couple of days later Ventura is explaining the outburst to reporters during a photo opportunity with the governor of a Chinese province and his delegation. He says the incident began when the referee blew a kiss to a woman at courtside after she made comments to the referee. "The referee made a gesture to the woman sitting courtside, and the husband jumped up to defend his wife, and then the referee wanted the husband thrown from the game," Ventura explains in front of a thoroughly perplexed Chinese delegation. "I realize they do take a lot of abuse down there, but they have no business making any type of gesture toward a fan."

After the referee asked security to throw the fan out, the governor admits he yelled at security to arrest the referee. "Jokingly," Ventura says, "because the fan was not at fault. It was initiated by the referee. I had fun. That's Timberwolf basketball!"

Say what you will about the governor, but he gets results. Ultimately, the referees allowed the fan to stay in his seat.

Reform Party Rumble

While Ventura battles NBA referees, the Minnesota Reform Party continues to battle the national Reform Party. On December 6 the state party claims it successfully wrested the right to hold the party's national convention in August from Long Beach, California. After a vote of seventy-five national committee members, state-party chair Rick McCluhan says forty-five members voted to overturn the executive committee and move the presidential nominating convention from California to Minnesota. It culminates a two-month effort to reverse the selection of Long Beach, but the battle isn't over. Outgoing national party chair Russell Verney calls the mail-in vote a "farce."

The dissident Minnesota group fights on, suing in federal court to temporarily stop the national party from entering into convention contracts in Long Beach. But the whole issue is thrown into limbo by the end of December when a federal judge denies the request for an injunction, calling it an internal matter that needs to be sorted out by the party. The dispute sows the seeds of a political-party implosion unprecedented in recent history. As 2000 begins it becomes clear the Reform Party is going to have one major Y2K problem. It will nearly take a fistfight to determine the future direction of the party.

Meanwhile, Donald Trump continues his flirtation with a presidential campaign by traveling to Minnesota to attend a Ventura fundraiser and test the waters for a possible bid for the Reform Party endorsement. In reality, his appearance at the Northland Inn in Brooklyn Park on January 7, 2000, has all the markings of a book-tour stop. Trump denies that his potential candidacy is a publicity stunt, but tables outside the ballroom where he'll speak to about six hundred businesspeople are stacked with copies of his new book, modestly titled *Trump: The America We Deserve.*

Trump delivers a fifteen-minute speech peppered with sales pitches for his book and ideas for how he'd run the country as president. As for his potential candidacy, Trump says "we've done some internal polling that's been amazing," but says he won't run unless he's convinced he can win. As for Pat Buchanan, Trump says it would be a "disaster" if Buchanan were to win the party's nomination.

Speaking of looming disasters, at a joint news conference with Trump after the speech Ventura denies that his rift with the Reform Party over the national convention and party leadership will cause him to leave the party. "I'm not a quitter," he tells reporters. "Never have been. And again, I don't cross bridges until I get to them, and at this point in time I'm still an active member of the Reform Party. I'm still the only elected Reform Party official at a high level anywhere in the United States of America. And when I was being asked to leave the Reform Party a few months ago, I had far more people calling me begging me not to."

Ventura's problems with the Reform Party will have to wait because another battlefront is opening at the State Capitol. The wildly popular Governor Ventura of 1999 got nearly everything he wanted from a legislature that often feared to stand in his way. The Governor Ventura of 2000 is still popular, but an emboldened legislature has noticed chinks in his armor.

His approval ratings have bounced back up, and, on a bus tour of several small Minnesota towns in mid-January, Ventura is still greeted and mobbed like a conquering hero. The latest Minnesota Poll in the

Star Tribune shows Ventura with a 68 percent approval rating, up from 54 percent after the *Playboy* interview and just a tad below his all-time high of 73 percent.

However, the *Playboy* interview is still fresh in the minds of his political opponents. So is the constant barrage of insults he hurls at lawmakers. Although it doesn't seem to be reflected in the polls, they sense that a segment of the public is beginning to tire of Ventura's combative style and might actually be looking forward to legislators standing up to him. There will be no shortage of opportunities.

On January 14, 2000, Ventura unveils his capital bonding budget for 2000. State agencies and local governments requested bonding for more than $1.5 billion worth of building projects. These funding requests are often accompanied by assurances from individual lawmakers that they will fight for funds that will come to their districts. But after Ventura reviewed all those requests, he proposes a lean bonding budget of $462 million.

"There is not a lot of pork in this plan and there shouldn't be," Ventura says during the formal budget presentation at St. Paul's World Trade Center. There aren't even any thin slices of bacon for lawmakers to take back to their districts. There's no money for new ball fields or a water park in Minneapolis. No money for a cold-weather testing facility in International Falls on the Minnesota-Canada border. Lawmakers might not like it, but they'll have a tough time going after the governor on this one. A new law passed by the legislature in 1999 says to qualify for bonding money, projects must have some kind of "statewide or regional significance." The idea is to put an end to pork-barrel politics, and Governor Ventura plans to stick to the letter of the law.

After the gavel falls to begin the 2000 legislative session on February 1, Ventura faces resistance on a wide range of issues. Although he wants to focus on the bonding bill this session, House Republicans immediately call for another round of income-tax cuts. "We have had fifteen projected or actual surpluses in a row in the state of Minnesota," says House Majority Leader Tim Pawlenty. "We are not going to be duped for a sixteenth time."

House Republicans also announce plans to repeal the millions of dollars earmarked for light-rail transit during the last session after a strong push from Ventura. The governor faces opposition on other issues in the Senate, including a bruising confirmation process for one of the governor's cabinet appointees. And Senate Majority Leader Roger Moe makes it clear he's no fan of allowing a vote on changing to a unicameral legislature, one of Ventura's pet issues.

Ventura is not about to back down. On the second day of the session he takes a rare step for a governor by testifying before a legislative committee. At 10:00 A.M. on February 2, 2000, he arrives in Room 112 at the State Capitol and takes a seat before the Senate Transportation Committee. "I know this is not the way things are usually done," Ventura jokes as he sits down. He says his reason for being here is simple: He wants to look them in the eye to make sure there's no underestimating his commitment to light-rail transit. "I am absolutely committed to breaking the twenty-year-old LRT logjam that has produced millions of dollars in studies but not one foot of progress."

With House Republicans threatening to rescind the light-rail-transit funding approved last year, the Senate is much friendlier territory. "We won't waste this committee's precious time on undoing light-rail transit," Democratic committee chair Carol Flynn assures Ventura. But the support isn't unanimous. The state originally was supposed to be on the hook for only $100 million, with the federal government kicking in the balance of the $446 million project. But the estimated cost of the eleven-and-a-half-mile line is already climbing over $500 million and still rising. The state's portion is still supposed to remain at $100 million, but there are plenty of lawmakers with doubts about the final cost and the ongoing operating expense.

"In the nine years that I've been in the Senate, the light-rail proposal is the worst damn proposal in nine years," Republican Senate Minority Leader Dick Day tells the governor and his fellow committee members. "I call it the train to nowhere."

Governor Ventura must have enjoyed mixing it up directly with lawmakers because less than a week later he's testifying before another committee. This time he's promoting a unicameral-legislature bill that would give Minnesotans a chance to vote on a proposal to combine the House and Senate into one body of 135 members by 2003. "My support for a single-house legislature is grounded in the belief that government should be accountable, responsive, and limited," he tells the lawmakers in a packed, standing-room-only hearing room. "The legislative process doesn't need to be complicated to be effective."

Although it's an uphill fight, Ventura has some key allies in the legislature. Also testifying at this joint House-Senate committee are two unlikely allies, Democratic Senate president Allan Spear and Republican House Speaker Steve Sviggum. "If you're looking at reform of the legislative process, the accountability, the addressing of the concentration of power, this is the bill," Sviggum tells the committee.

Opponents of the unicameral idea, like former secretary of state Joan Growe, testify there's no proof a one-house legislature would achieve all that Ventura and others say it will. "It certainly would be dramatic," Growe says. "It would be drastic. But the question is, would it be better?"

It's a fairly rational discussion until Governor Ventura gets baited into a tussle with Representative Phyllis Kahn, a Minneapolis Democrat and one of the legislature's more outspoken members. She wonders out loud at the hearing whether the only reason Ventura wants a unicameral legislature is so he can be "king," as he mentioned in *Playboy*.

An angry Ventura leans into his microphone, glares at her, and delivers a brief lecture. "First of all, Representative Kahn, obviously you don't watch comedy," he says. "And obviously you don't understand when a person makes a comedic answer. 'It's good to be the king' is out of Mel Brooks's *History of the World, Part Two* [actually, it's *History of the World, Part One*, but what the hell, he's on a roll]. And if anyone in their right mind can possibly take a Mel Brooks movie as being serious, then I believe they have serious problems. And that's all that was, a comedic answer. It was no seriousness meant to it at all, and I think you better bone up on Mel Brooks a little more."

He leans back in his chair, disgustedly shaking his head, and mutters, "Unbelievable!"

When the committee chair restores order a few seconds later the focus turns to a discussion of what James Madison said in the *Federalist Papers* about a bicameral legislature. That officially makes this the first time anywhere that the works of Mel Brooks and James Madison were each cited to make an argument about the best form of democratic government.

Although the governor is getting more actively engaged in the process, the legislature will continue to flex its political muscle. A Senate committee takes the rare step of refusing to confirm one of Ventura's cabinet appointments. A few months before the session began, the governor announced plans to merge the Department of Public Service into the Department of Commerce. He named Public Service Commissioner Steve Minn to be commissioner of the newly merged departments. The deck is stacked against Minn from the start.

First, the former Minneapolis City Council member has a rocky relationship with several lawmakers after butting heads with them on a number of issues. Second, legislators aren't thrilled the governor unilaterally decided to abolish a state department without consulting them. A Senate committee votes eighteen to one against Minn for the commerce job and seventeen to two against him for the public-service job. In so doing, committee chair Senator Steve Novak sends a clear message to the governor. "We have a law in this state that says governors cannot abolish state agencies when the legislature is not in session," Novak tells Minn.

Ventura tersely responds to Novak at a news conference a few hours later. "My response to him is that if he wants to be governor, he ought to run for it." The governor vows to fight on and get Minn confirmed by the full Senate later in the month.

Before he'll get a chance to do that, Ventura has another fight on his hands. He's about to make a decision that will make headlines across the country. It's a decision that will serve as a major setback to the third-party movement. And it all starts innocently enough while the governor is on a whirlwind bus tour of several Minnesota cities.

A motor coach with a sign on the front that reads "Governor Jesse Ventura: Tour 2000" is reminiscent of his "Drive to Victory" tour during the campaign. Cruising along Highway 10 north of the Twin Cities, the bus makes a stop at Dixie's Diner in Royalton. Ventura steps off the bus and is mobbed by about two hundred people. He stands outside in the chill February wind, dressed only in a sport coat and turtleneck. Surrounded by state troopers on the sidewalk, he's answering impromptu questions from the crowd.

"Who's your favorite wrestler?" someone shouts.

"My favorite wrestler?" Ventura responds. "Chyna."

"Are you going to go back in the ring?" someone else yells about another pressing state issue.

"I hadn't planned on it, but if the decimal point's in the right spot.... You never say never!"

After a quick lunch at Dixie's, the governor stops in at a bar next door for a beer. No, this isn't part of his normal routine. He's just forcing the owner to make good on a bet. The owner of Mel's on 10 said he'd donate $5,000 to the local fire department if Ventura stopped in for a beer.

The caravan then makes its way to several more towns, including an overnight stay in Alexandria, where the governor spends time shooting an ice-fishing segment with Lisa Ling, one of the cohosts of ABC's *The View*. In the midst of this traveling Ventura love fest, you'd never guess he's about to pick a nasty fight that will leave the national Reform Party bruised and bloodied.

One of the last stops on this bus tour is St. Augusta Township, located an hour northwest of the Twin Cities. It's a fairly nondescript town thrust into the spotlight by getting so caught up in Ventura mania it's considering officially renaming itself Ventura, Minnesota.

Just after he walks out of a town meeting on this cold February afternoon, Ventura mania again spins out of control. Reporters covering the bus trip are hearing rumors that Governor Ventura will soon announce he's quitting the Reform Party. He's peppered with questions about it when he steps outside. He brusquely refuses to answer questions about his future in the Reform Party until a news conference scheduled for the next day. We keep asking the questions anyway. "You all seem intelligent to me," Ventura says sarcastically as he stops on a sidewalk lined by deep snowbanks. "And when I give you an answer, why doesn't it sink in the first time?"

The questions continue. So do the refusals to answer. "The reason the press conference was called for tomorrow was exactly the reason that's happening here right now," says a clearly frustrated Ventura. "Because you're going to take that and make it a lead story instead of the story that should be the lead of me going out and relating to Minnesotans and talking to them."

That sounds reasonable. Unfortunately for the governor, a key member of his administration is leaking the information about his pending announcement. The story can't be ignored. "Oh, don't give me that!" Ventura barks when informed where the information is coming from.

"Nobody from this administration is leaking anything!" communications director John Wodele insists as he tries to push the governor away from reporters.

Ventura keeps firing back anyway. "Nobody's leaking anything! Nobody from my administration knows a thing about it.... That is fully untrue!"

An angry Wodele finally gets the governor aiming for the bus. "We're done! We're done!" Wodele says, glaring back at reporters who dared to question the administration's handling of the situation. "I resent that!"

Just one month after telling reporters he wasn't contemplating leaving the Reform Party, vowing he's "not a quitter," Ventura quits the Reform Party and essentially lights a fuse triggering the party's implosion. One day after refusing to confirm his plans, the governor calls a 1:00 P.M. news conference on the steps of his official residence on St. Paul's Summit Avenue. Outdoor political news conferences in mid-February are rare in Minnesota, and this particular day is a good example why.

It's a crisp, sunny day that is actually tolerable if you're standing in the sun. Unfortunately, at this time of day the front steps of the governor's mansion are in the shade. Television satellite news trucks line Summit Avenue to beam the news conference throughout Minnesota and across the nation on cable-news networks. Ventura's stunning announcement makes the frostbite worthwhile.

At one o'clock sharp he walks out the front door, wearing a Rolling Stones leather jacket prominently featuring a tongue hanging out of a mouth. Ventura then proceeds to stick *his* tongue out at the national Reform Party. Figuratively, anyway. "I am disaffiliating myself from the national Reform Party completely as of this day," he announces, standing alongside state Reform Party leaders and Lieutenant Governor Mae Schunk. "And I'm going to encourage the state party of Minnesota, which was the Independence Party prior to the Reform Party, to disaffiliate also and to go back to what we were before.... I believe that the national party is going in directions that are not conducive to what we believe here in Minnesota of what we want the party to be. And I believe that the national-party problems are being destructive to us here in Minnesota."

He points to the controversy over the party's 2000 national convention and efforts to oust Jack Gargan as the national party chair. "You have a small group of power brokers in this party that won't allow it to grow nationally, and that's not conducive to what we want to do in Minnesota," Ventura tells the two dozen reporters and seventeen camera crews assembled in the snow piled on his front yard. He then refers to former party chair Russell Verney, whom he blames for many of the problems, as Russ "Varmint" and Russ "Vermin." Ventura also says he can't be part of any party that would consider having Pat Buchanan as its presidential nominee. Instead, Ventura says, he wants to focus on strengthening the third-party movement in Minnesota "without the distractions of this dysfunctional national party."

While the governor is holding court on his front steps, a few Minnesota Reform Party supporters are protesting on the sidewalk just beyond the mansion's black wrought-iron gates. One St. Paul man who will give only his first name of Andrew is wearing a cardboard sandwich board that reads, "I voted for Jesse the Grump." It's his way of protesting the governor's decision. "I wanted Jesse to know that I was disappointed with him. You know, I voted for him and voted for him as a Reform Party candidate, and I thought he was going to be a leader in that party. He's only been a year on the job and he's gone."

Another protester, Paul Larsen of Fridley, is wearing a big fur hat and holding a sign with a picture of Ventura in an Uncle Sam–type pose that reads, "I want you to quit the Reform Party." Larsen is also disappointed by the governor. "It just kills the third-party movement on a national level," Larsen says. "You're just back to big money and big business as usual." He doesn't see the sense in leaving a growing third party and starting another party out of that. "I don't know how much happier he can be being a splinter of a splinter."

Ventura's decision sets off a chain of events over the next twenty-four hours that is nothing short of spectacularly amusing. Ventura attends a state Reform Party meeting the next morning at which he successfully lobbies party leaders to take a preliminary vote in favor of splitting from the national party. There is verbal sparring between the governor and some state committee members, but it's nothing compared with the a full-fledged fiasco going on in Nashville, Tennessee. That's where the national Reform Party is conducting a special meeting to consider voting Jack Gargan out of office as party chair. It gets so out of control you'd swear the World Wrestling Federation had rights to a pay-per-view telecast of the event.

It begins with Gargan refusing to call the meeting to order at the Nashville Marriott because he and his supporters claim it was called improperly. "Would you call this meeting to order and ask the secretary to call the roll?" bellows Russell Verney, the former party chair. "Mr. Secretary, would you call the roll!"

With Gargan continuing to withhold the gavel and refusing to call the meeting to order, all hell breaks loose. "If you can't run this meeting, resign!" a woman yells at the silver-haired Gargan, who by now is looking a bit overwhelmed.

"We want a voice!" screams another wild-eyed Gargan opponent. "It's our party!"

Two men, one a Gargan supporter and the other an opponent, nearly come to blows right in front of the podium where Gargan is holding on for his political life. "Do you want to get physical?" the Gargan supporter asks.

"Yes, I do want to get physical," comes the response. "You better get out of here!"

Someone steps in to break them up while people are screaming and pointing fingers in every direction.

A party official eventually steps to the podium with a warning. "Ladies and gentlemen, on the advice of the hotel security staff, they have told us if we refuse to act like adults, this meeting will be terminated for safety reasons," he says amid a flurry of catcalls. "So we need to sit down and calmly go through what we came here to do, whatever it is."

With Verney clearly pulling strings behind the scenes, the Gargan supporters are outraged. "Russ Verney is the cancer of this party," a woman shrieks to her fellow delegates. "Russ Verney is the cancer of this party!" The Verney forces eventually prevail and, through some parliamentary maneuvering, manage to get the meeting called to order.

While the party secretary is calling out the roll call of state delegates, Gargan sits just a few feet away from the podium on the edge of the stage, conducting a television interview. "This is the same group of people—since the day I got elected, they've been doing this," Gargan says in a whisper. "This is nothing new. Unfortunately, it makes me look like a dictator or something. I just won't roll over and play dead for them. I'm for the people. I'm the grassroots candidate, and somebody has to speak for the grassroots. This is mob rule here."

Although Ventura's defection from the Reform Party clearly precipitated the melee in Nashville, Verney is convinced his departure will have minimal impact on the party's future. "Last summer Governor Ventura threatened the delegates at the national convention to elect his choice as chairman [Gargan] or he would leave the party," Verney says.

"Then the Minnesota party threatened we had to have the convention in Minnesota or they would leave the party. Then the governor threatened that if we nominated Pat Buchanan, if the members chose Pat Buchanan, he would leave the party. I think he had the opportunity to be a leader or a leaver. He could have come to this meeting to help solve the problem he created or he could leave. He chose leaving."

Verney clearly has blinders on if he thinks damage to the party can be minimized. Videotape of that meltdown in Nashville is shown over and over on national news programs and talk shows. The pictures do nothing to dispel the notion among some critics that the party is made up of crackpots and half-wits. Ventura is invited the next day to appear on ABC's *This Week* with Sam Donaldson and Cokie Roberts and rips the national Reform Party again. Dean Barkley, one of the architects of Ventura's election and a cofounder of Minnesota's Reform Party, completely supports Ventura's decision. "I think being attached to the national Reform Party in its current state is sort of like a stagecoach hooked up to a team of raving lunatic horses ready to go over a cliff," Barkley says. Two days after the Nashville implosion, Donald Trump announces he won't seek the Reform Party nomination, because the party is "self-destructing."

Governor Ventura is gone from the Reform Party, but he's clearly not forgotten. A week after his surprising announcement, he is in Denver checking out that city's light-rail transit system and giving a speech to the Colorado Press Association. On the same day, Pat Buchanan is in Minnesota, seeking support for the Reform Party presidential nomination. With Ventura out of town, he doesn't hesitate to take some potshots during a news conference at Bloomington's DoubleTree Inn. "I believe [Ventura] has run away from a fight, which would have been a good fight for the folks of Minnesota," Buchanan tells reporters. "I think it would have been a great contest. I think we could have brought the whole national press corps up here for that battle. And I think it would have put a focus on the issues and the struggle for the soul of the Reform Party."

When Ventura is told of Buchanan's remarks shortly before his speech to the Colorado Press Association, his response is classic Ventura. "Notice he came to town when I left," he barks just outside a hotel ballroom. "What does that tell you? Did he ever serve in the military? No. I think I'll rest it at that."

Of course, he doesn't leave it at that. Instead, he quotes again from *A Few Good Men*, one of his favorite movies. "When he's served his country and put his life on the line, or in the words of Jack Nicholson, I'd say, 'Pat Buchanan, have you ever stood a post? Put your life in the hands of another man? Have him put his life in your hands? When you've done that, Pat Buchanan, come and talk to me!'"

Ventura's battles with Buchanan and the Reform Party mark the beginning of a spate of bizarre confrontations during the 2000 legislative session. It starts when the Minnesota Senate votes, as expected, to reject the governor's appointment of Steve Minn as commissioner of the new Department of Commerce and Public Service. After the vote on February 24, Minn is diplomatic. "I think it's just appropriate for me to say public service is an honor and a privilege, and I just regret the way the senators treated me," he tells a pack of reporters waiting outside the Senate chambers.

As Minn makes his way down a flight of stairs to the governor's office, pursued by a thundering herd of television photographers, he jokes, "It's not every day you get to attend your own funeral!"

Ventura doesn't find anything funny about the Senate vote. He steps out of his office after meeting with Minn and instructs the photographers to roll their videotape because he's about to tell us exactly why Minn was rejected. "Because the Senate has shown me very clearly that qualifications don't matter, butt-kissing does."

The man knows how to get our attention. He also takes dead aim at Senate Majority Leader Roger Moe, who Ventura suspects of railroading Minn out of the job. It's the first time a gubernatorial appointee has been rejected for a commissioner's post in about thirty years. Just as he often did in his wrestling career, Ventura delivers a low blow. "That says 'Jesse Ventura, Governor,'" he says, looking back at the nameplate outside his office door. "It doesn't say 'Roger Moe, Governor.' If I recall, he finished third!"

By late February 2000 Ventura is rebounding from the Minn defeat and the Reform Party debacle. He surprises many people by announcing he won't deliver a State of the State address this year, but there's little doubt about the state's economic health. A new budget forecast shows Minnesota has an additional $229 million in surplus revenue projected through 2001. That means the state's "boatload of money" is beginning to look more like a cruise liner. When the 2000 legislative session began, the projected surplus was $1.6 billion. Now it climbs to more than $1.8 billion. It's a pleasant problem for the governor and legislature.

The governor also remains in demand on the national political scene. Vice President Al Gore even makes time during a campaign stop in the Twin Cities to have breakfast with Ventura. Gore is running neck and neck with George W. Bush and courting the governor, whose independent block of voters is suddenly becoming important to presidential hopefuls. Gore even shows up dressed like Ventura, in blue jeans and cowboy boots.

Bizarre Behavior

You'd think Ventura would simply ride the wave of the state's good fortune and his growing national stature. Instead, he lets a couple of minor setbacks set him on a binge of bizarre antics. I first get a taste of it when I air a story on March 3 in our 10:00 P.M. newscast that analyzes how Ventura played a key role in sparking the Reform Party fiasco. It seemed to be a balanced story. The governor doesn't see it that way. In fact, he's enraged. He calls the KSTP-TV newsroom, demanding to speak to me. An assignment-desk editor tells him I've gone home and she's not allowed to give out home telephone numbers. He demands to talk with someone else. When she finally convinces him there's no one available that late on a Friday night, he hangs up as one very unsatisfied viewer. She immediately calls me at home to tell me the governor is angry about my story. She says she's still shaking from the conversation.

The next day, I get a call from my assistant news director, Mark Ginther, who says he's gotten a call from John Wodele. Wodele tells Ginther that the governor wants to see me in his office on Monday to discuss complaints he has about the story. There's no reason I have to go, but I wouldn't miss this for the world. When I walk in for what's supposed to be a fifteen-minute appointment, a calm and relaxed Ventura tells me he's "upset" and "disappointed" about my story. He claims he never threatened to leave the national Reform Party if Jack Gargan didn't get elected chair, as I reported in my story. He also claims Gargan wasn't his "handpicked" candidate for chair, as I also reported.

I inform him that delegates at the national party convention in Michigan received an e-mail from Ventura that said, in part, he would "remain reluctant to fully embrace the national Reform Party" if Gargan isn't elected, adding, "I'll be pleased to keep my party activities within Minnesota's borders."

For good measure, I slide a copy of the e-mail across his desk. He puts on his reading glasses, looks at it for a minute or two, then throws it down, and says, "I didn't write that e-mail." He tells me he couldn't have written it, because he doesn't use a computer and doesn't send e-mail. I explain to him it was sent to all the delegates, and details of it were first reported months ago in the *Dallas Morning News*, a respected daily newspaper. Ventura looks at me and says, "It's not respected. There's no such thing as a respected newspaper."

I later find out the e-mail was actually written and sent out under the governor's name by a Minnesota Reform Party official with the governor's authorization. Anyway, my fifteen-minute appointment stretches to nearly an hour as he rants about a wide range of media sins, some real and some ridiculous. Finally, as I get up to leave, the governor says, "Tom, I think you do a good job. You're as good as they come. But Tom, I gotta tell ya, the bar isn't set very high." I look back at him and respond, "Well, Governor, I guess journalists and politicians will just have to wallow in the muck together."

My episode with Ventura is nothing compared with what's still to come. A week later a House committee deadlocks in a five-to-five vote on Ventura's unicameral-legislature bill. Unless someone changes a vote, the governor's favorite piece of legislation is essentially dead for the session. Ventura isn't about to give up. He embarks on a previously scheduled twelve-city tour of southeastern Minnesota and plans to take time on each stop to urge people to call their legislators and stir up support for a single-house legislature. During a stop in Rochester he calls lawmakers "gutless cowards" for not advancing the unicameral bill. When asked by a reporter if he really thinks they're gutless cowards, Ventura says, "I just speak the truth as I see it. If they won't put unicameral on the ballot and allow people to decide, yes, sure they are."

That's typical bravado from the former Navy SEAL and pro wrestler. Which makes what happens the next day all the more remarkable. He's giving a luncheon speech to a business group at Slippery's restaurant in Wabasha, a scenic Mississippi River town where the *Grumpy Old Men* movies were shot. During the speech the governor does a 180-degree turn from the previous day. He's making his usual sales pitch for lower automobile license-tab fees, property-tax reform, and a unicameral legislature. Then comes the about-face. "I believe we have tremendous legislators," Ventura tells the group amid a great deal of laughter. Everyone's aware of the "gutless coward" label he tattooed on lawmakers the day before. "Write that down! And I do! I believe we have tremendous people that are elected and serve over there as legislators, but the problem is the system."

He tells them that, in addition to the bicameral system, he doesn't like the two-year election cycle for House members. "The first year they're getting acclimated. They don't know nothing about what's going on. I didn't hardly know anything and I was the governor! Did pretty good, though, for not knowing much." Everyone's laughing now, even a couple of legislators at the luncheon. It's clear the governor is doing some fence-mending after his caustic remarks the day before.

What comes next is totally unexpected. He concludes by urging the audience to call legislators about license tabs, property-tax reform, and the unicameral proposal. "And I want to finish with this to you," Ventura says as he softens his voice. "Because while the legislature has caucuses for the Democrats, they have caucuses for the Republicans, I don't have a caucus. I stand alone, but I have you." The governor is now choking back tears and his voice is cracking as he struggles to continue on. "Don't let me down, because you're all I got. I got elected alone and I stand alone and I need you, because if I don't have you, I can't be successful. Thank you very much." The audience delivers rousing applause and a standing ovation.

Some would view this as a heartfelt attempt to make up for his legislative insults the day before. Some might view it as the result of the cumulative stress of the previous few months when he's defended the *Playboy* interview, ditched the Reform Party, and battled with the legislature. Still others might see it as nothing more than a ploy to sell books. It turns out the title of a new book he's got coming out is *Do I Stand Alone? Going to the Mat against Political Pawns and Media Jackals.*

It's probably a bit of all three. After all, he has recently turned up his war with lawmakers for no readily apparent reason. It certainly hasn't helped advance his cause in the legislature. Senate Majority Leader Roger Moe isn't buying the emotional, repentant governor routine. Moe says he hasn't forgotten the governor has essentially boiled legislators down to "butt-kissing gutless cowards."

The governor's mercurial behavior becomes fodder for a grandstanding move on the Senate floor by a senator tired of taking the verbal abuse. Gary Laidig of Stillwater tries to amend a bill to add a provision that would prohibit Ventura from carrying a concealed handgun on the State Capitol grounds.

"While I may be a 'gutless coward,' I don't think I have to bring a .357 Magnum to work each morning," Laidig says. Ventura doesn't actually carry a gun to the capitol, but he does have a permit to do so. Laidig says the governor's recent behavior indicates he shouldn't have such a permit. "In my own personal judgment, we have a governor with his own gyroscope," he says on the Senate floor. "I mean, he's all over the place. One day he whines, the next day he weeps. He's poured more gasoline on more legislators and lit 'em on fire than any other governor in the history of the state of Minnesota. And then he laments that he doesn't

have anybody to turn to but the public: 'Nobody loves me in the legislature.' One moment he's for light rail, the next moment he's just railing."

Senate president Allan Spear finally steps in and cuts off Laidig's
amusing rant. "We generally do not allow personal attacks on the governor or other state officials," Spear informs him. Having made his
point, Laidig withdraws his amendment and sits down with a satisfied
grin on his face.

The next bizarre episode transpires on a statewide public-television
broadcast on March 22, 2000, exactly a week after the "gutless coward"
remark. Governor Ventura appears on a special broadcast to discuss controversial transportation issues under consideration in the legislature.
Appearing alongside the governor is Republican representative Carol
Molnau, the House Transportation Finance Committee chair, Republican Senate minority leader Dick Day, and Ventura's transportation
commissioner, Elwyn Tinklenberg. The debate is heated at times as
Ventura and Tinklenberg essentially face off against Molnau and Day.
The two Republican lawmakers are staunch opponents of the light-rail
transit system favored by the Ventura administration. This broadcast,
however, won't be remembered for any transportation issues. Instead,
it will long be remembered, with apologies to M. C. Hammer, as the
"Can't Touch This" debate.

Molnau is wearing a button pinned to her lapel that says, "Gutless
Coward." Many lawmakers are wearing them now as a badge of honor.
The discussion becomes rather animated between Molnau and Ventura,
who happen to be seated next to each other on a couch. Molnau tends
to be rather demonstrative when she talks, using her hands to gesture
and occasionally touching the person during a conversation to make
sure she's got their attention. After the fourth time she touches the
governor's arm on the broadcast, he's had enough.

"Please, please, I'm not touching you!" Ventura says, backing
away and holding his hand up to keep her away. "I'm sorry for touching
you," Molnau responds. "I didn't want to hurt you. I know you're frag-
ile." Members of the studio audience snicker and roll their eyes while
witnessing this exchange.

Needless to say, this incident "touches" off a talk-radio bonanza. Naturally, the governor starts it all on his *Lunch with the Governor* radio show. On Friday, March 24, two days after the public-television broadcast, he's seething about a column written by Joe Soucheray in the *St. Paul Pioneer Press*. "First of all, he doesn't respect my office," Ventura complains of Soucheray. "He doesn't respect me, because he refers to me as Governor Turnbuckle." Most of the column focuses on criticism of Ventura's support for light-rail transit. Only two of sixteen paragraphs in the column deal with the "touching" incident. Ventura seizes on that and won't let it go until he explains his version of what happened.

"She put her hand on my thigh," he says. "She grasped my arm. She put her hand on my shoulder and then she patted me on the back." For the record, a careful review of the unedited videotape shows she touched him four times and each time on his right arm. "If I were sitting next to the president of the United States, I wouldn't be touching him," Ventura continues. "I would not touch the president even though I'm a governor. I wouldn't put my hand on the president's thigh. I wouldn't grasp his arm. I wouldn't pat him on the shoulder."

The governor also mentions that a new button is already being circulated at the capitol that says, "Don't touch me!" He complains legislators are making fun of his "sensitivity" and wonders out loud what would happen if he did any of the things he claims Molnau did.

"Would that be grounds for a sexual harassment [suit]?" Ventura asks John Wodele.

"There would be hell to pay, Governor, I guarantee you," Wodele responds.

An hour later, Molnau gets a chance to tell her side of this now ridiculous story. She appears on *Facts and Snacks*, a program WCCO Radio airs to give lawmakers a chance for a rebuttal to Ventura's *Lunch with the Governor*. Molnau is a broad-shouldered farmer who, legend has it, once beat Ventura in a celebrity beer-keg-tossing competition years ago. In other words, the governor doesn't intimidate her. However, she says she meant no disrespect to him on the public-television show.

"As you do on occasion to get someone's attention, you place your hand on their shoulder or your hand on their arm, and that's actually what I did," Molnau says. "And the governor somehow felt I was invading his space." Her colleague, Senator Dean Johnson of Willmar, appears on the radio show with her and comes to her defense. "Carol, I watched the show that evening, and as you know we have sensitivity training in the House and Senate. I've been in the military for twenty-nine years. I'm a chaplain in the military. I'm a Lutheran minister. I know what sexual harassment is. Governor, it was not sexual harassment."

Ventura can't possibly let them have the last word in this inane argument. So he agrees to appear on another talk-radio show later that afternoon. And guess what? It's Joe Soucheray's show on KSTP-AM. Yes, the same Soucheray who wrote the newspaper column that started all this. "If I were out in Washington and I were sitting with the president, I would not be touching the president," Ventura says to Soucheray, referring to President Clinton.

"No, but there's a fighting chance he'd be touching Molnau," Soucheray jokes, irritating Ventura even more.

The governor stays focused on his claims that Molnau touched him on the thigh. "OK, I'll give you thigh," Soucheray says, "but the only one I saw was, I think, shoulder."

It goes on and on like this until finally an exasperated Ventura asks Soucheray, "Would it be OK for me to feel someone's breast?"

In Governor Ventura's world, it's easy to move seamlessly from a low-brow debate about breasts and thighs one week to highbrow testimony before a congressional committee the next. On March 30, 2000, he appears before the powerful House Ways and Means Committee in the Longworth Office Building on Capitol Hill to testify in favor of allowing China to join the World Trade Organization. Is Ventura an expert in world trade issues, you ask? Between body slams and pile drives years ago, was he secretly boning up on the General Agreement on Tariffs and Trade? No. He does, however, have an appeal to people who might not otherwise pay attention to this issue. President Clinton recognizes this and personally invited the governor to get involved in helping him to promote China's admission to the World Trade Organization. As a result, Ventura is invited to testify before Congress about how China's entry in the WTO would help states like Minnesota.

Minnesota exported $315 million worth of farm products and manufactured goods to China in 1998. If China is allowed to join the WTO, trade with the United States could triple by 2020, according to the U.S. Chamber of Commerce. Ventura tells the House Ways and Means Committee before a standing-room-only audience that he's not a trade expert, but he knows a good deal when he sees one.

"What I do bring to you today is a dose of common sense. China's participation in the WTO and a permanent normal trade relation between China and the United States is the number one market opportunity of the twenty-first century, and it's being handed to us on a silver platter." As an example, Ventura holds up a cell phone. A Minnesota company makes some of the little plastic panels attached to the phones and the company is doing a growing business with China. "Now every time you make a call, you can think of Minnesota," he tells committee members. "I'm here to tell you who cares about this China issue in Minnesota. Farmers care. Business both big and small care, and, finally, a lot of ordinary people with commonsense care." The governor closes his remarks in classic Ventura style. "Please help me by saying yes to China. Please don't blow it."

After his testimony, he stops by the offices of Representative Henry Hyde to lobby in favor of a Hmong citizenship bill on behalf of Minnesota representative Bruce Vento, who is ailing with cancer. During the meeting Hyde jokingly engages Ventura in an arm-wrestling match. The governor laughs and poses for pictures with their arms interlocked. Ventura's rule about "touching" appears to be different for members of Congress.

Abortion Land Mine

As the 2000 legislative session nears a close, Governor Ventura finds himself backed into a corner on the one issue most politicians prefer to avoid: abortion. There's no way to win, because voters are split so passionately on this topic. The focus of the 2000 legislative session is clearly on tax cuts and the capital bonding bill. However, the abortion issue has been lurking in the background all session.

The Republican-controlled House passes a bill on April 5 known by its supporters as the "Woman's Right to Know" bill. The primary provision in the bill requires abortion providers to make available to patients information about alternatives to abortion at least twenty-four hours before their appointment. Opponents of the legislation refer to it as the "Women Are Stupid" bill and say it's just the first step toward further restrictions on abortion services.

Into this morass steps a reluctant Governor Ventura. He describes himself as socially liberal, but his stance on abortion is confusing at best. He makes the mistake of trying to walk a tightrope on the abortion issue and please both sides. No other politician has successfully done this and neither will he.

On August 11, 1998, Ventura filled out a questionnaire for the Minnesota Family Council when he was running for governor. On the form he unequivocally states he's opposed to a ban on partial-birth abortions, but he walks the tightrope on two other key questions. One questions asks, "Do you support a constitutional amendment ending judicially mandated taxpayer funding of abortions in Minnesota?" Ventura doesn't check the "yes" or "no" box. Instead, he writes on the form, "I support a checkoff system on the state tax forms that would allow individuals to designate whether or not their tax dollars would be used for abortion-related services. I do not believe that a constitutional amendment is necessary."

He's also asked, "Do you support a 'woman's right to know' legislation requiring a twenty-four-hour waiting period before an abortion can be performed?" Again, he doesn't check "yes" or "no" on the candidate questionnaire. He writes, "I would not promote the legislation, but I would sign it if it were passed by the legislature." Those words will come back to haunt him in 2000.

Two days after the House passes the abortion bill Ventura is reluctant to discuss it, even though House Republicans claim key members of his administration helped draft language in the bill they thought the governor would accept. On his weekly radio show Ventura goes out of his way to avoid the topic. In fact, he spends the first thirty-seven minutes of his show that day discussing rock music, the new XFL football league, and *The Man Show*, which airs on Comedy Central. He says he's particularly amused by the fact that each episode of that show ends with big-breasted women jumping on a trampoline.

It's about thirty-nine minutes into the show when Duncan from St. Paul calls with a question about Minnesota Timberwolves basketball. It's obvious he asked that question because it was the only way he could get on the show. He follows up the basketball question by asking Ventura if he plans to veto the abortion bill.

"First of all, it's like this," the governor responds, clearly peeved that this call got through. "We have a current bicameral system that I oppose. You know I like unicameral. So the House can pass anything they want. The Senate still has to pass something and then it has to go to conference committee. So really, the whole thing is much ado about nothing. It's just a media hoorah. Until a bill arrives on my desk, I really don't have to deal with it."

Just when it appears he's going to deftly dodge the question, Ventura finally hints at which way he's leaning. "But I will tell you this. I am not going to infringe on a woman's right to choose. That is a court decision that was made by the courts. If people want to challenge that they should do it in the courtroom." Once he dispenses with Duncan, it's on to a call about wrestling. (I learn later "Duncan" was actually the fictitious name of a Democratic legislative staff member trying to get Ventura to reveal his intentions regarding the abortion bill.)

Although Democrats control the Senate, an increasing number of them are "pro-life" Democrats. The Senate passes the twenty-four-hour notification abortion bill just a few days after the House. Now Ventura must deal with it because he has to sign it, veto it, or let it become law without his signature in three days. However, he won't discuss any aspect of the bill with the capitol press corps or any local reporters, even though his office is being swamped with thousands of phone calls on both sides.

Instead, Ventura leaves for Washington, D.C., where he's been invited for dinner at Vice President Gore's home. While in the nation's capital he does answer questions about abortion on National Public Radio. He drops another hint, this time saying a mandated twenty-four-hour waiting period for an abortion is unnecessary. "It's not like driving into a McDonald's and pulling up and saying, 'I want a number-four cheeseburger.' You have to make an appointment."

He also talks about the issue on ABC's *Good Morning America*. He tells Charlie Gibson he hasn't made up his mind which way he'll go, but it's becoming obvious. "It's a very difficult decision to make, because, really, what I think the question comes down to is, how involved in our personal, private lives do we want to interject government?"

When the governor arrives home at the airport after his trip to Washington, he once again gives the local media the brush-off. "I just got off an airplane and it's not the proper time or place to do it," he says when asked to comment on the abortion bill. It appears no time is a good time to communicate directly to Minnesotans where he stands on this important issue. No issue is too important to stand in the way of his private war with the local media.

On Friday, April 14, the governor finally has to announce his decision. We're told he'll make his announcement at 4:45 P.M. in the governor's reception room. Only his staff and reporters with special credentials will be allowed in. That means no lobbyists, no lawmakers, and no members of the public. He'll simply read a statement and no questions will be answered. Security will be tight because of the heated passion this issue stirs up on both sides. The bill is known by various names, but to Ventura it's simply referred to as Senate File 3387, a bill he ultimately vetoes.

"I have decided it is wrong for government to assume a role in something I have always believed was between a woman, her family, her doctor, and, if she chooses, her clergy." Ventura discovered belatedly what most other politicians already knew. "We learned that there is no middle ground here, so now we move on."

He won't move on without some major political damage, however.

House Republicans are furious he vetoed the bill after they were told by some of his top aides the language in the bill would get Ventura's approval. House Speaker Steve Sviggum is so livid about the veto he raises his voice at a news conference afterward. "This was a centrist bill!" Sviggum tells reporters. "This was a moderate bill! To not be able to vote for this bill, to not be able to sign this bill, Governor Ventura, you have to almost be the extremist! The radical!"

The conflict over the abortion bill won't make it easy to wrap up the other important work of the legislative session. The legislature and governor are once again locking horns on many issues and time is becoming a factor. House and Senate leaders originally promised to have the session wrapped up by Easter. With so much time and energy expended on the abortion legislation, that deadline is out the window.

Essentially, the stalemate boils down to this: The state has about $549 million in projected surplus that can be used for spending or tax cuts, but the House, Senate, and governor can't agree how to divvy it up. The House Republicans want income-tax cuts, Senate Democrats want to spend more money on education, and Ventura wants his long-sought-after automobile license-tab reduction.

Legislators accuse the governor of not being engaged enough to help reach a compromise. He does, however, make time to meet with Arizona senator John McCain, who is in Minnesota to campaign for a Republican congressional candidate and to sign copies of his new book at the Mall of America. After a meeting in Ventura's office, McCain quashes any talk that he might run for president as an independent and that Ventura could be his running mate.

As one maverick politician to another, McCain says he admires what the governor accomplished in getting elected. He points out that Ventura was the first to make extensive use of the Internet during his campaign, one of many things McCain says he learned from Ventura for his own campaign for president.

"I also believe that Governor Ventura, by straight talk, by telling people not only what he thought they wanted to hear but what they should hear, was also a model for our campaign." Naturally, McCain couldn't resist joking that he could beat Ventura in a "two falls out of three" wrestling match. "I've been working on my atomic backbreaker drop."

Take Me Out to the Ballgame

Ventura might be tempted to use such a move to get the legislature to break its stalemate. Instead, he invites legislators to breakfast at the governor's residence. It's a productive meeting, if only because it eases some of the leftover tension from the abortion battle. "The governor's proud of the fact he's kind of a common person, and we were glad to see he eats breakfast in his boxer shorts like most other Minnesotans," cracks House Majority Leader Tim Pawlenty, one of the sharper wits in the legislature. Back at the capitol, it's not so funny. Pawlenty and other Republicans claim the Senate Democrats are "pirates" trying to make off with the state's "boatload of money." Senate Majority Leader Roger Moe says Republicans are using "phony numbers to prop up a phony tax cut."

Ultimately, Moe comes up with a proposal Ventura quickly endorses. It's now known in Minnesota political lore as the "Third, Third, Third" deal. Moe says that since the three sides can't agree on what to do with the available money, why not split it three ways and let each side do with its third whatever it wants? Under Moe's proposal each side would get $175 million. He calls it a truly tripartisan compromise.

"It's intriguing," Ventura says. "You know, I think it shows initiative on their part to try to reach something of a favorable compromise before the session ends." House Speaker Sviggum isn't so quick to agree. "I think, again, they're just coming at it from the wrong premise, the premise being that it's the politicians' money to spend."

The three sides do eventually agree to the "Third, Third, Third" deal. When the crucial deal is reached on May 3, Ventura isn't around to celebrate or even personally take part in the deal-making. He's in Chicago singing "Take Me Out to the Ballgame" at Wrigley Field. It's part of an effort to promote Minnesota tourism that had been scheduled long before the governor knew the legislative session would drag on so long. Earlier in the day he broadcast his radio show from the ESPN Zone restaurant in downtown Chicago. He also walked the streets with Minnesota tourism officials, handing out *Explore Minnesota* newspapers.

His entourage is surrounded by a huge pack of television crews and newspaper reporters from Minnesota and Chicago. With his well-known dislike of the local media, Ventura says he puts up with us here because media exposure for Minnesota is what he's after. We're sort of a necessary evil, he says. "It's like the famous quote from Jerry Garcia," he tells me while walking along Michigan Avenue. "If you're picking the lesser of two evils, it means you're still picking evil!"

When he later gets in the press box to sing "Take Me Out to the Ballgame" during the seventh-inning stretch, there's a huge cheer from the sun-splashed and beer-drenched crowd. The crowd quickly turns surly when Ventura introduces the song by saying, " I want to hear this all the way back to the great state of Minnesota!" That brings a lusty chorus of "Boo!"

They cheer him again, however, when he finishes the song and holds a Cubs jersey out the window that says "Ventura" with the number "98" on the back. As he's leaving the press box he's informed that the "Third, Third, Third" deal has finally been agreed to back in St. Paul. "I guess it's nice to hear," he says as he stops in a stairwell. "We got the job done, if it's true. I guess for a second time in a row, we've showed that tripartisan works."

The three sides do exactly as promised. House Republicans use $175 million to cut income taxes. Ventura will use $175 million to reduce license-tab fees, with a goal of a maximum fee of $99 for a car more than one year old. That would be a savings of hundreds of dollars for many Minnesotans. Senate Democrats plan to use $175 million primarily to boost education funding, with some also earmarked for human services and natural resources. Another $640 million of surplus money that's already in the bank (as opposed to the projected surplus they divvied up) will be sent back to taxpayers in another round of sales-tax rebates. While everything seems to be going smoothly on the surface, don't think for a second there's not some resentment toward Ventura being harbored by lawmakers.

On May 9 the legislature plans to wrap up its work in a marathon session, pass the major pending legislation, and then recess for a week. Why? They remember what Ventura did to them last year. After they adjourned and went home he vetoed several bills and they had no way to override any of them until the next session. This time they'll wait to see what he vetoes, then come back and attempt to override vetoes before final adjournment.

But when May 9 rolls around Ventura once again is out of town. He's been invited to the White House for a gathering of dignitaries who support President Clinton's plan to allow China to join the World Trade Organization. Rather than doing the dirty work with Sviggum and Moe at the State Capitol, Ventura is in the East Room of the White House with President Clinton, Vice President Gore, and former Presidents Ford and Carter. Not to mention Secretary of State Madeleine Albright and former Secretaries of State Henry Kissinger and James Baker.

"It is just profoundly humbling for me to look across this sea of faces," President Clinton says as he begins his speech promoting the China trade legislation. Governor Ventura has a front-row seat and will get the recognition that comes with it. "It's by far the most important national security vote that will be cast this year. It's an American vote. You know, it unites Henry Kissinger ... and Jesse Ventura. And not at a wrestling match! I thank you for being here, sir. You didn't have to come today, and I really appreciate it."

While Ventura basks in the international limelight, legislators facing a long day and night of work are seething. When a last-ditch effort comes up to pass Ventura's unicameral bill, there's little enthusiasm. "We gotta governor that cares about this issue so much that the last day of the session, when it's crunch time, he's out in Washington promoting himself again," says feisty Representative Tom Rukavina, a Democrat from Minnesota's Iron Range. "I think it's about time we kill it because the guy pushing it doesn't give a damn about it. Why should we?" House Speaker Steve Sviggum also says "the governor ought to be here," pointing out that Ventura only met with him and Senate Majority Leader Moe once the whole session.

On the White House lawn after the ceremony with President Clinton, Ventura is asked how he defends himself from the criticism he's getting back home. "Defend what?" he responds. "I have a staff. You have one of those things in your hand that's called a cell phone. I can be reached any moment of the day. I can be briefed. I can give a decision. In the modern technology era that we live in today, traveling to Washington for one day in a session is not going to make or break a session. We have very capable people back there on my staff that are handling it."

He saves his sharpest response for Sviggum. "Maybe if the speaker was ever personally invited by the president, he might have somewhere to talk from. When the president calls you on a national policy, you go. Then again, when you're only involved in local politics, maybe you don't know anymore than that."

That's a rather stunning statement for a man who not so long ago ran for office as a "man of the people." Now he can't be bothered with "local politics."

The final day of the session lasts until 7:00 A.M. the next day, going nearly twenty-one hours straight. It wasn't really the "last" day of the session. As expected, Ventura vetoed fourteen pieces of legislation. Most of them were line-item vetoes of money for capital bonding projects. The legislature comes back a few days later and overrides four of the vetoes, which preserved $6.5 million for various projects, including a new Guthrie Theater in Minneapolis. Legislators failed to get enough votes to override ten other vetoes.

Until now, veto overrides were rare in Minnesota, with only three on record for the past twelve governors. In just one day Ventura has overridden more than all other Minnesota governors combined since 1939.

"They're all sitting here thinking I'm upset," he tells me afterward. "I wear it as a badge of honor."

CHAPTER 13

"10,000 Lakes and One Goofy Governor"
From *The Young and the Restless* to the Lincoln Bedroom

Despite the veto overrides and the nearly constant rancor, it would be difficult to describe Governor Jesse Ventura's second legislative session as anything but successful. For the second year in a row, income taxes have been cut. He helped hold the line on spending in the capital-bonding projects bill, which totaled $539 million, or about half the size of the previous bonding bill two years ago. Another sales-tax rebate check is on its way to Minnesotans. He fended off legislators who wanted to eliminate funding for light-rail transit. And he made good on one of his main campaign promises by dramatically reducing license-tab fees for car owners. To top it off, he somehow managed to become a major player in Washington, D.C., with both President Clinton and Vice President Gore courting him for their own needs, Clinton for China trade and Gore for his presidential campaign.

Of course, there were plenty of failures. The governor and legislature didn't do anything to address long-term transportation needs of the state. And, of course, Ventura's unicameral legislature never really had a chance despite mustering all his political clout behind it. During my interview with the governor in his office the day after the 2000 session ends, he declares war on the legislature for defeating his unicameral bill.

"The war has just begun," he says, staring me down with a gleam in his eye as he relishes the idea of political combat. "They think what they did, they started the war. Now I'm going for term limits too. That's next." He seems to be forgetting a term-limits bill, like unicameral legislation, would require passage by the very legislators he's declaring war on.

Ventura's not going to let that stand in the way of a battle plan he's formulating for the 2000 campaign. He won't be up for reelection until 2002, but he vows to campaign against lawmakers who voted against the unicameral bill. "First of all, what I'll say is, vote them all out. Vote out all Republicans and Democrats and vote out all incumbents. That's going to be my campaign message. Let's clean house over here. Then I'm going to focus on bringing unicameral again so people can vote on it in 2002. I'm going to focus on bringing term limits in. I want the people to be able to vote for term limits so we can have a constant turnover of fresh people in our government, which is what we need to have a good, responsive government."

Another remarkable thing about Ventura's 2000 legislative session was his ability to overcome the dark days after the *Playboy* interview. Many people were tempted to give him up as politically dead. Ventura tells me there was no coordinated effort to overcome the damage. "I've never operated with spin doctors. You saw that during the campaign. My two opponents had spin doctors all around them, and the reason I won is because I don't have them."

It becomes obvious he doesn't have spin doctors a few seconds later when he goes on to blame the *Playboy* fiasco on the media and compares his situation to a man who has become a social pariah. "Look at John Rocker. He seems to be doing OK. I mean, they wrote him off. They said, 'His career's over, this guy destroyed himself.' He's signing more autographs now than he ever has. Sure, he's getting booed occasionally, but I think Rocker, even though I don't support what he said, I think he ultimately got sympathy because of the feeding frenzy the media did to him. It created people saying, 'I feel sorry for this guy.'"

This is all news to me, because I don't know anyone who feels sorry for John Rocker, the Atlanta Braves baseball player who made inflammatory remarks about gays, minorities, and others in a *Sports*

Illustrated interview. "I think people saw the media go after Rocker the way they saw the media go after me. And I think in the end you end up being a hero in your own way because you fought off these media sharks, you know, who will do anything to rip you about, tear you down, and carve you up."

He also takes aim at legislators who unsuccessfully fought during the last session to keep Ventura from earning outside income on his book tours and his World Wrestling Federation appearance. "If I choose to work on vacation, that's my business, isn't it?" Ventura asks me without waiting for an answer. "Tom, if you go on vacation and you decide to help a friend roof houses, is KSTP going to fire you because you went on vacation and worked and made other income? No! No! Well, why am I any different? Have I lost my rights because I've been elected? I don't think so."

The Young and the Restless

Less than a month later Governor Ventura again tests the limits of what he can do with his "vacation" time. In June he embarks on a trip to California that will include the fulfillment of a Hollywood dream. He's going to play a part on his favorite soap opera, *The Young and the Restless*. Not just any part, but one opposite his favorite character on the show, Victor Newman. It may be a dream for the governor, but his frequent travels continue to raise eyebrows. This will be his twenty-third trip outside the state since taking office, including business trips, book tours, and vacations. State travel records show that Ventura has spent part or all of seventy days outside Minnesota. That's two-plus months he's been away out of eighteen months in office. The travel for the governor, his staff, and security has cost the state $304,000 so far (that figure doesn't include some travel costs paid for by his book publisher, the WWF, and some network television shows).

Spokesperson John Wodele defends the governor's travels. "Could we save money by not traveling?" he asks rhetorically. "Yes, but there is value in traveling. There is value in talking about public policy in various environments around the country. There is value in traveling to sell the state of Minnesota." Again, there's also plenty of expense. In addition to the travel expenses, overtime for his around-the-clock security force is also adding up. In the first eighteen months of the Ventura administration, overtime for troopers protecting the governor totals nearly $1.1 million. By comparison, during the last eighteen months of the previous administration, security overtime totaled $361,000.

Ventura's total will climb on this trip because he's got three state troopers traveling with him and he plans to keep them busy. In addition to making his *Young and the Restless* appearance in Los Angeles, he will also speak at a political forum in Monterey hosted by former White House chief of staff Leon Panetta, he'll play golf with Clint Eastwood at Pebble Beach, and he'll make another appearance on *The Tonight Show* with Jay Leno.

Minnesota Public Safety Commissioner Charlie Weaver says the overtime cost to protect Ventura can't be avoided because he's the highest-profile governor in the nation. "If Governor [George W.] Bush and Governor Ventura were walking down some main street in the Midwest, I'd guess more people would recognize Governor Ventura," Weaver tells me. "He does start early. He goes late. Unfortunately, overtime is just a budget reality for us. When we elect someone, we grab their life for twenty-four hours a day for those next four years."

On June 14, 2000, Ventura and his security guards arrive at CBS Studios in Los Angeles for his long-awaited appearance on his favorite soap opera. The set for *The Young and the Restless* is just around the corner from where *The Price Is Right* game show is taped, but this isn't a big moneymaking venture for the governor. He'll be paid the union scale of about $700, which he plans to donate to charity. When Ventura's entourage arrives on the set just after 10:00 A.M. the place fills up quickly. His security guards, wife, and a staff member all jockey for position with camera operators, sound and lighting technicians, and floor directors. To cash in on all the free publicity, the soap-opera producers allow all the television news crews and newspaper reporters to go into the studio to cover Ventura's cameo appearance.

"Quiet, please!" the director calls out from the control booth. "Roll tape. This is a fade-in." Ventura's appearance begins with him knocking on Victor Newman's office door and Newman's surprise at this visit from Minnesota's governor. They sit down at Newman's desk for a few forgettable, yet amusing minutes of television.

"You haven't really answered my question, Jesse. What brings you by Genoa City?" Newman asks.

"It's not another campaign contribution, if that's what you're worried about, Victor," Ventura responds.

"Cut!" calls the director. "We were off-mike on a shot."

Remarkably, that's the only foul-up along the way. While Ventura isn't bucking for an Emmy nomination, he doesn't screw up any lines and certainly knows his way around a television studio.

After the tape rolls again, the two get to the point of Ventura's fictional visit. "Why did you decide not to run for president?" Newman asks. "I mean, come November it would have been far more interesting." In real life, Ventura claims to dislike all the presidential talk about him. In make-believe soap-opera land, he stirs it up himself. "Well, there's always 2004. That is ..."

He stands up for dramatic effect and leans over Newman's desk. "Why don't you run with me?" Ventura asks in his deep, raspy wrestling voice. "We'd be a dream ticket." The director apparently agrees, as she blurts out in the control room, "I love this guy!"

As for Newman, he's not so sure. "That's an interesting possibility, except ..."

"What's that?" Ventura asks.

"Who would take the top spot?" Newman wonders.

"That would be a problem," Ventura agrees. "If our two egos were to clash, I don't think the country could survive it!" Some things are just as true on soap operas as they are in real life.

At a news conference after the taping, Ventura admits he had some butterflies before the show, but says he quickly calmed down once taping started. He says he used to wrestle in front of nineteen thousand screaming fans, so acting in a crowded television studio doesn't bother him. A reporter asks the governor how he would assess his performance if he were a reviewer. "I would assess it very good, because as a reviewer I wouldn't want to meet me later," he jokes, "because I read what the press writes!"

Eric Braeden (aka Victor Newman) says Ventura did a "damn good job," but he's also impressed by the governor's political abilities. "Jesse Ventura represents what is symbolic and what is good in America, that someone from that background can rise to these heights and be taken very seriously. I have enormous admiration for him. He's a man's man. He says what he thinks. So do I, and I have respect for that. And, to be quite frank with you, the fact that he's not taking PAC money, for example, to run his campaigns, I find that enormously admirable."

The show is scheduled to air a few weeks from now, on July 10, and Ventura jokes he might "declare it a holiday in Minnesota." In an interview after the news conference, he tells me he's not concerned about the criticism of his travel for television appearances and book tours. "The only people who give me heat are political opponents. And you know what? They'd probably give me heat if I didn't leave the state. They'd probably say I'm not engaged, out there fighting for Minnesota. So I can't control what they do or what they say, and, frankly, I don't care."

Still, there is room for criticism. The governor's six-day trip to California will cost Minnesota taxpayers about $10,000, even though only three or so hours on one day of the trip approach anything that could be considered state business. Those three hours were spent at two tourism-related meetings in Los Angeles. Most of Ventura's expenses are paid for privately by the hosts of his speaking engagements and by *The Tonight Show.* The state is on the hook for the expenses of two staff members and three state troopers traveling with the governor.

Although Ventura brushes off the criticism he clearly has it on his mind when he appears on *The Tonight Show* the day after the soap-opera taping. During his appearance with Jay Leno, the governor brings up the fact that a major taconite mine in northern Minnesota is closing, putting fourteen hundred employees out of work. In an effort to show he's still on the job, Ventura makes a sales pitch to any company that might want to take over the plant. "There's a railroad, a power plant up there," he says, looking into the camera. "If you want to move to Hoyt Lakes, Minnesota, and have fourteen hundred great workers, give me a call at the capitol in St. Paul." You can't blame him for trying. In fact, he actually got a few calls.

During the rest of the summer and fall of 2000 Ventura keeps a fairly low profile as the presidential race and Minnesota's U.S. Senate campaign take some of the political spotlight off him. He still manages to get his share of national attention, however. It's hard to avoid when Vice President Al Gore and his wife, Tipper, accept an invitation to visit the Venturas at their Maple Grove ranch. In late June the two couples attend a horse show where the Venturas' teenage daughter is performing and later spend the night at the ranch. It's the third time Gore and the governor have visited each other in the past three months, twice in Minnesota and once in Washington, D.C. Gore is obviously courting Ventura and his block of independent voters, but Ventura stops short of endorsing him.

A few days after the visit in late June, Ventura also tells ABC's Sam Donaldson on *This Week* that he doesn't think Gore would ask him to be his vice-presidential running mate. "I don't like that lifestyle," he says on the Sunday-morning talk show. "You have to live in a bubble. I had the Secret Service scared to death. You should've seen them. I wanted to take the vice president out in my Porsche and drive around … they were panicked!"

Governor Ventura also has what he considers an unwelcome moment in the spotlight in the Republican presidential race. Minnesota's Republican Party chair, Ron Eibensteiner, appears at the National Republican Convention in Philadelphia to help officially cast Minnesota's delegate votes for George W. Bush. It's traditional for each delegation to come up with a flowery way to describe something unique or memorable about their state. Eibensteiner begins his introduction by saying, "From the great state of Minnesota, the land of ten thousand lakes and one goofy governor …"

Ventura is incensed. He seethes about it for three days until he gets a chance to fire back on his weekly radio show. He refers to Eibensteiner as "Ebenezer" and chastises him for name-calling. "It's very disrespectful," Ventura says. "He, as a leader of a party, should get over the fact that they lost. Get over it! What we should be doing is promoting Minnesota and not standing out on a national forum and embarrassing our state simply because you're angry because you couldn't win an election."

Lest we forget, Ventura is the same man who used his radio show once to refer to another political opponent as a "fat load" and "McIdiot."

The criticism of Ventura's frequent travels does nothing to stop his rapid accumulation of frequent-flier miles. In September he embarks on a nine-city tour spanning sixteen days to promote his second book, *Do I Stand Alone? Going to the Mat against Political Pawns and Media Jackals.* He goes coast to coast, bashing career politicians and reporters.

In early October Governor Ventura is invited to testify before Congress again on the issue of international trade. But he also receives a surprise invitation that will become the highlight of his trip. President Clinton calls and invites him to spend the night in the White House. After a stay in the Lincoln Bedroom, Ventura broadcasts his weekly radio show from Washington the next day and regales his audience with tales about the evening.

"Just had great conversation with the president," Ventura tells his listeners. "We were up until four o'clock in the morning. He's a night owl, the president." He tells communications director John Wodele on the air that Clinton even gave him a twenty-year old cigar. Wodele asks if he smoked it. "You can't smoke in the White House, no," Ventura responds. "But you can go out on the balcony and drink beer and smoke." Wodele asks him if they went out on the balcony.

"Yeah," Ventura says.

"What kind of beer?" Wodele inquires.

"Anything you want!" Ventura tells him, hinting that he and the president consumed several beers.

Naturally, that story gets retold in many television and print news stories across Minnesota. There's just one minor problem: much of the story isn't true. The story about staying at the White House in the Lincoln Bedroom and spending some time with the president *is* true. The story about the cigar smoking and beer drinking was made up by the governor to entertain his listeners and probably to fool reporters. Wodele fields many calls from irate reporters wondering why the governor would make up a story like that, knowing it would be reported as fact. "The fact is, the governor never in the entire course of the radio show actually says that he drank beer or smoked a cigar," he says. "He never states it as fact."

Wodele admits the governor probably left the strong impression with listeners that he was up smoking and drinking with the president all night. "It is very possible that listeners could go away taking what the governor said as fact," he tells me. "But the important thing is that there is a big difference between a listener and a reporter who has a responsibility to ferret out the facts."

It's also apparently now our job to double-check every single thing Ventura says because there's at least a fifty-fifty chance he's making it up just for the hell of it. And don't forget, the governor said one reason that he wanted his own radio show is so he could communicate directly to citizens without the filter of the news media. Perhaps he needs the filter to protect him from himself.

XFL

By the time the presidential election ends in a dead heat on November 7, Ventura becomes all but invisible on the national level because "the Great Recount of 2000" dominates the airwaves and newspapers. If your name isn't Bush or Gore, you're going to have a hard time getting yourself on television news. However, I've learned never to underestimate the ability of Governor Ventura to break through the media clutter and commandeer the spotlight.

First, a Broadway producer is working on a musical based on Ventura's life. Ventura sold the rights to his story several months earlier, but now Pierre Cossette announces he's completed the first act that will include the Ventura character singing with his Navy SEAL buddies back when he was known by his real name, Jim Janos. It also includes a scene in which Jesse "the Body" Ventura learns the ropes in the professional wrestling ring. The second act will likely include a musical candidate debate loosely based on the 1998 gubernatorial campaign and another number based on his inauguration.

Later in November, Ventura drops another entertainment bombshell. He reveals he'll soon begin moonlighting as an announcer for the new XFL football league. He makes the announcement at a news conference at the KARE-TV studios in Golden Valley, an affiliate of NBC, which will own part of the league and broadcast its games. Ventura will be reunited with two men from his wrestling past, Vince McMahon of the World Wrestling Federation and Dick Ebersol, chair of NBC Sports.

"Some fifteen years ago in another life in a far, far away galaxy, the three of us were united in another venture," Ebersol says to begin the news conference, flanked by black football helmets with "XFL" emblazoned in red. "It turned out for four or five years not only to be wildly successful, but also one of the most fun things in my life." Ebersol is referring to the WWF's popular *Saturday Night Main Event* broadcasts on NBC in the mid-1980s. Ebersol and McMahon say the XFL could become another big hit on Saturday nights, kind of a WWF with cleats and helmets.

They envision the league as more "honest" than the NFL because nothing will be hidden from the fans or viewers and announcers won't be afraid to criticize. "Who better to communicate that honest approach," McMahon says, than Jesse Ventura because of his "communication skills with the common man, with middle-class America.... In the NFL, everyone's nice to each other, at least seemingly so on the air. Whereas here, if Jesse Ventura disagrees with a play called by a head coach or anyone like that, he's going to say so. 'What a stupid call that was!' I don't think you've ever heard that in the NFL."

Naturally, a roomful of middle-class reporters wants to know how much the governor will be paid for his new weekend job. Ventura fumes when asked if the public has a right to know. "Do they have a right to see my tax returns? No. You're a public reporter, do we have a right to know your salary?" he asks Jim Ragsdale from the *St. Paul Pioneer Press*. Ragsdale offers to show him, but Ventura scoffs at the idea. When Ragsdale continues to press him on the issue of the public not knowing how much the governor has made off any of his private deals, Ebersol jumps in to defend Ventura. "It seems like the people in your state are pretty happy with him. I saw the poll in one of your papers, it's about 71 percent. They're pretty happy."

The governor is also asked about rumors the XFL will include raunchy, sexual overtones and nearly naked cheerleaders. "I see that every Sunday, scantily clad cheerleaders," Ventura says, dismissing questions about whether he'll make a good role model. "Whenever the NFL goes to a break, they usually focus in on cleavage before they go. I'm not buying into that. I'm here to do football." He also guarantees the XFL job won't interfere with his day job. "State offices are closed on Saturdays and Sundays anyway," he says. "I don't traditionally work then. But let's be very clear: in my contract with the XFL it's clearly in the contract that, if at any time my governor duties are such that I can't make it [to a game], that's fully accepted by the league and NBC. Being governor naturally always comes first."

The XFL's eight teams will play a ten-week regular season with a two-week play-off. Ventura has some previous NFL announcing experience with the Minnesota Vikings and Tampa Bay Buccaneers, but it's clear he's been tapped for this role because of his fame and ability to get press coverage.

"We think this is going to be tremendously successful based upon the interest from the media and the controversy that this league has already created," McMahon says. "That's good for business. We're very long-range oriented and, with the business model we've set up here in the XFL ... in my view this can't fail."

Ventura's latest moonlighting gig brings more howls of protest from state legislators. Among the first to jump into the ring is Senator

Ellen Anderson, a Democrat from St. Paul. She announces she will introduce a bill during the 2001 legislative session that will make the office of governor a "part-time position." She proposes a salary of about $30,000, about a fourth of what the job pays on a full-time basis. "I am confident Governor Ventura will want to join me in creating a truly part-time citizen government so there will be no issue of 'professional politicians' profiting from public service," Anderson says in a news release. "Rather, a part-time governor would be expected to pursue additional employment, just like part-time legislators."

While other legislators promise to author bills to prohibit the governor from earning outside income, criticism comes from other quarters as well. David Schultz, a professor of public administration at Hamline University in St. Paul and a former Common Cause president who battled Ventura about his WWF referee job, says the governor continues to damage the image of his office. "How would we feel if we knew that all the people who work in government use their position to line their pockets?" Schultz wonders. "We'd call that bribery. We'd call that corruption."

The governor also takes it on the chin from some callers to his radio show a couple of days after the XFL announcement. "You belong to the people 100 percent, twenty-four hours a day, seven days a week," one caller tells Ventura.

"I do?" Ventura responds. "So, in other words, I shouldn't be coaching high-school football either?"

"No, that's a different story," the caller says. "Because you're doing that for kids. That's good. That's good for the dignity of the governorship."

The dignity of the governorship had already taken a hit a couple of weeks earlier for reasons that have nothing to do with Ventura or the XFL. The governor's chief of staff, Steven Bosacker, was cited for indecent conduct in a steam room at a local health club. According to the complaint against him, Bosacker was caught making sexually suggestive gestures to a male undercover Minneapolis police officer. The story leads our 10:00 P.M. newscast and is reported in detail in local newspapers.

Ventura has some faults, but a lack of loyalty isn't one of them. He immediately says he won't fire Bosacker. His loyalty, however, leads to a bizarre defense of his chief of staff on the *Chad and Barreiro* talk show on KFAN sports radio. On November 21 Ventura agrees to an interview on the station about the XFL. The show hosts also can't resist asking Ventura about Bosacker.

"Propositioning people in public places happens all the time. Go to a pickup bar," Ventura says, calling in to the show by phone.

"Yeah, but not in the way Steve Bosacker was doing it," says Chad Hartman.

"I'm not condoning what he did," Ventura continues. "Steven is seeking help. He's getting it. But I judge him by the job he does as an administrator in my office, and there is none finer. My view is simply this: The man made a mistake. He's paying for it dearly. I am not going to add to that mistake without giving a person a chance to redeem themselves from it."

Ventura would be fine if he stopped there. He doesn't stop. Dan Barreiro prompts him by saying, "Where Bosacker's lost me is he has encouraged the notion that he is the victim here, that in some way this is about his sexuality. And I'll tell you, Jesse, in a steam room nobody should have to be subjected—hetero, homo, whatever—to the possibility of that sort of activity or alleged sort of activity going on."

The governor's response is vintage Ventura. "As an alpha male, I know in my alpha-male world, 'cuz I consider myself an alpha male, and I know in my alpha-male world I've been in situations like that. I don't call the police. And this is just me personally … I would laugh it off."

Again, not a bad place for him to stop, right? Forget it. He's on another talk-radio roll. "Let me put it to you this way. Let's change it a little bit, OK? Let's say it's a coed steam room and that same male cop would have gone in there and saw a female take her top off, touch herself. Would he have done the same thing [cite her for indecent conduct]?"

"I would hope so," Barreiro responds.

Ventura thinks otherwise. "I think you'd have twenty of his buddies get called up saying, 'Hey, get down here!'" Not exactly a ringing endorsement of law enforcement. Oh, and he's not done yet. "[For heterosexuals], it's acceptable to go out, have sex in public places. We can do it and people just shake their fingers at us and say we're 'spirited.' My point is this: is there any of us talking here that hasn't gone out and had sex in a place we're not supposed to?"

Add that to the growing list of things you never thought you'd hear a governor say in public.

Bosacker quietly takes a leave of absence from his job and that controversy quickly fades away. The XFL controversy will prove to have considerably more staying power. On November 20, 2000, Senate Majority Leader Roger Moe sends a letter to the state attorney general asking him to rule on whether the governor is subject to the state's code of ethics for employees in the executive branch. The code of ethics prevents state employees from using their official position to get benefits that wouldn't be available to other citizens. It also restricts state employees from accepting outside employment that might "affect the employee's independence of judgment in the exercise of official duties." You'll recall much of this ground was already plowed back in the summer of 1999, when Ventura took his WWF referee job. Ventura survived a court challenge then, but the judge didn't rule on the merits of the complaint.

The attorney general takes a different position in a ruling issued November 28, 2000. "It is the opinion of this office that the governor, like all other employees of the executive branch, including all the other state constitutional officers, is subject to the state code of ethics," writes Alan Gilbert, the chief deputy and solicitor general in the attorney general's office. Gilbert dismisses Ventura's argument that the legislature doesn't have the power to impose restrictions on his conduct beyond what is called for by the Minnesota Constitution. "The governor's attorney states that 'short of committing acts constituting corrupt conduct in office or other impeachable offenses, the governor is answerable only to the voters of this state.' We believe this argument lacks merit. If it had validity, then no state law would affect the conduct of the governor."

While the attorney general's position is that the governor is an "employee" subject to the ethics code, the ruling stops short of saying Ventura's XFL job violates the code. Gilbert says a ruling on that requires findings of fact, rather than a legal opinion, and is outside the jurisdiction of the attorney general's office.

Moe invites reporters to his office to discuss the ruling. He says he's glad the attorney general agrees that the governor is subject to the ethics code and isn't surprised he didn't rule the XFL contract specifically violates the code. "That, I think, is really a question that's going to have to be determined in the court of public opinion," Moe says. "Did he get this position based upon being governor or did he get this position based on being a former professional wrestler and movie actor?" Moe doesn't plan to take the action any further, but several other lawmakers are already lining up to author bills to specifically prohibit the governor from taking outside employment.

Ventura quickly launches a defense of his XFL job in his favorite forum, talk radio. On Minnesota Public Radio he insists he has a right to earn money just like anyone else. "You know, I was taken to court on this, and the court's clearly stated that I do not lose my rights because I become elected," Ventura tells *Midday* show host Gary Eichten. "You know, I was elected because I was going to be different. I was elected because I was reform-minded. I wanted to change the way we viewed government and the way it operated, and yet, when I try to do that, I get criticized for it—the very essence of why I was elected. Now I guess they want me to be a status quo politician. Get elected on a reform agenda, but once you get elected, become the status quo. Just become like any other politician."

While I give the governor credit for a passionate defense, I'll have to mark him down for at least one inaccuracy. No court ruled on what rights he does or doesn't have to earn outside income. The case in Ramsey County District Court from 1999, as I pointed out earlier, was dismissed without an official ruling. As for his comments about being elected as a "reform-minded" governor, I think most Minnesotans who voted for him had "government reform" in mind, not reform of how professional football is broadcast on television.

The day after that radio appearance Ventura travels to Tampa, Florida, to deliver a speech in a forum that is all too rich in irony. He's been invited to speak to the national Council on Governmental Ethics Laws, which was founded during a 1974 conference at the Watergate Hotel in Washington. I'm not making this up. He was invited to speak long before the XFL issue came up, primarily because of his interest in campaign-finance reform. He sticks to that topic during most of his speech. But many of the questions afterward are about his XFL deal. He sends up another spirited defense.

"I mean, here's people talking about me leaving on Saturday night and doing football. Well, how long has it been since Governor Bush governed Texas? Two years? And this is not criticism on him. Don't think I'm criticizing him [for running for president]. I'm talking about the system here. It's considered OK to go out and campaign for two years for a higher job. Isn't that using the position you're in to get another one? Sure it is. Yet I get criticized if I go do a football game."

Ventura also tells the group, in response to a question, that there should be no limit to what he can earn outside his office. "No, because you ultimately answer to who put you in office. That's the voters. The voters are the ones who hire and fire you. Not the pundits. Not the political adversaries. It's the voters who do that." Then someone tosses him a softball question, asking if he thinks the Minnesota media spends too much time focusing on his celebrity and not on his governing. "The press is dishonest. The press doesn't tell the people why they're here. They're here to make money. The same as everyone else, they're here for ratings points. I'm ratings points! I sell. So therefore it's more easy to focus in on the things that have nothing to do with me governing, but they know people will tune in and people will read."

While I don't agree with his portrayal of the press as dishonest, I have to agree with some of what the governor says. For the most part the Minnesota media does a fair, balanced, and thorough job of covering Ventura's job performance. However, it is true newspapers and television stations at times spend a disproportionate amount of ink and airtime on things that have nothing to do with his ability to govern. It's true many of his extracurricular activities are so unusual or outrageous they demand coverage, but not at the expense of coverage of things that actually have an impact on many Minnesotans.

Two examples come to mind. When Ventura went to Washington, D.C., in 1999 to testify about dairy issues, KSTP-TV was the only Minnesota television station to send a reporter (the two major local newspapers assigned reporters from their Washington bureaus). When I asked one of my colleagues from another Twin Cities station if they planned to send anyone, she said no, "that's just ag stuff." The last time I checked, the agriculture industry was fairly important to Minnesota. Another example is when one of the local television stations led its 10:00 P.M. newscast with the breathtaking story of a new, officially licensed Jesse Ventura Air Freshener. That couldn't possibly have been the most important thing going on in state government that day.

It's also true the governor's new job with the XFL isn't the most important thing going on in state government. But it's still getting most of the attention of lawmakers and the media. The controversy turns up a notch when the commissioner of the Minnesota Department of Employee Relations rules that Ventura's "outside employment" with the XFL "does not" constitute a conflict of interest under Minnesota law. Commissioner Julien Carter, a Ventura appointee, says his department has authority to make such rulings regarding executive-branch employees. Carter says he believes the law is "ambiguous" and that the language of the law doesn't support the attorney general's ruling that Ventura is a "state employee."

He concludes that, even if the governor is considered an employee subject to the ethics code, "his actions would not be deemed to be a conflict of interest at this time." In making that decision, he says that there's no evidence Ventura used his "official position" to get the job and that there's no official business between the XFL and the state that would cloud his "independence of judgment in the exercise of his official duties."

The conflicting rulings over the governor's possible conflicts spur a rare House committee meeting just six days before Christmas, even though the 2001 legislative session begins in two weeks. "I felt it was important to deal with this issue while it is certainly in the public's mind and the public's eye," Representative Phil Krinkie explains to members of the House State Government Finance Committee, which he chairs.

A bill that would have clarified that executive officers, including the governor, are "state employees" and covered by the ethics code was considered during the 2000 session but didn't make it out of committee. "I think most of us assumed that, upon not passing the bill, that things seemed to settle down and we were in a bit of a stage where there was not a lot of public acrimony about whether the governor would be covered by state ethics laws," Krinkie tells the committee. He says that all changed in November with the XFL deal.

The first to testify before the committee is Sandra Hyllengren, the former state ethics officer who issued an opinion in 1999 critical of the governor's involvement in the WWF "SummerSlam" event. She later resigned, she says, because of stress related to criticism directed at her from some members of the Ventura administration. She stands by her assessment that state law identifies the governor as an employee.

"It defines for purposes of payroll state employees as those who are hired, appointed, or elected," Hyllengren testifies. "I don't know how he can avoid being characterized as a state employee. You can't be a state employee for some purposes and not for others." She also says it seems clear to her that Ventura got the WWF contract by using his position as governor of Minnesota.

Alan Gilbert, who wrote the attorney general's opinion, agrees with Hyllengren's assessment of the governor as a state employee. "It's incongruous to suggest that the code of ethics for employees in the executive branch applies to all employees except the governor," he tells the legislators. "It's the governor that can exert the most influence over the transaction of state business." Gilbert describes Commissioner

Carter's ruling that the governor isn't an employee as an "absurd interpretation of the law."

Carter also testifies and stands by his ruling, saying the law is too vague. He also testifies that Governor Ventura did not try to influence his ruling. "In no way, shape, or form was I put under any pressure about this matter," Carter says.

The legislators are split on their level of concern about this issue. Representative Jim Rhodes, a Republican, says, "The court of public opinion has not really been very vocal or adamant against this [XFL job]." "I believe the governor has a fairly high approval rating and popularity," he tells his fellow committee members. "There's no question about the popularity issue. Why isn't the public outraged?"

The public might not be outraged, but outrage is expressed by one of his fellow Republican House members on the committee. "If the governor of this state is off doing color commentary in Arizona or California when a natural disaster were to hit or some crazy blows up a building in downtown Minneapolis, and he's not here to handle the situation, because he's off making millions of dollars doing color commentary on wrestling or football, I think there's going to be war," warns Representative Doug Reuter. "Maybe not in the literal sense, but there will be political war!"

The war starts less than an hour later when Governor Ventura blasts lawmakers for even considering legislation to block his XFL deal. "I think they ought to worry about their lives a little bit more and worry about the state of Minnesota a little bit more than worrying about me," he says when we track him down for comment outside his office door. "This is a personal attack obviously being done, and who cares? Even if I am a state employee, which that's fine if I am, no one has come out and said I've broken any ethics, have they?"

He's told by reporters some legislators say he has violated ethics rules by taking a job that wouldn't necessarily be available to a member of the general public. "But they are available to the general public!" Ventura fires back. "Anyone could have been hired for the XFL. Any other governor could have been hired. You could have been hired. Each and every one of us, anyone could have been hired for that job. Please explain to me how I've used my position to get the job."

He doesn't wait for anyone to offer an explanation. He's tired of reporters and the legislature. "They want to come after me, bring it on! Bring it on! If that's all they've got to do, then let 'em do it. I'm conducting state business. You're wasting my time here with all of this stuff." With that XFL rehearsal out of the way, he turns his back to us and walks into his office.

CHAPTER 14

"This Governor Is Out of Bounds"
Moonlighting with the XFL

On January 3, 2001, Governor Jesse Ventura finally does get a chance to get back to state business. It's the start of a new legislative session, the third with Ventura at the helm, and, for the first time, he has a true ally in the legislature. Bob Lessard, a longtime Democratic state senator from International Falls, defects to Ventura's Independence Party. He becomes the only member of the governor's party among the 201 state legislators. Ventura campaigned for several Independence Party candidates during 2000, but his coattails have proven to be shorter than the wrestling shorts he used to wear. In fact, no member of his party that the governor has supported at the state or federal level has been elected to office. But he'll take legislative allies any way he can get them.

"Who knows? When you get one defection, there could be more," Ventura says at a news conference introducing Lessard in the governor's reception room. Senate Majority Leader Roger Moe, who loses Lessard from his party, isn't impressed by the move. "As a new member of the Independence Party, if he's waiting for the governor to call him and get advice from the governor, I think he's going to end up being lonelier than the Maytag repair man," Moe tells reporters outside the Senate chambers.

The next day Ventura gets his chance to set the tone for the new legislative session with his State of the State address in the House chambers. This will be just the governor's second such address because he declined to deliver one at the start of the 2000 session. He makes up for it on this one because it goes on for one hour and fifteen minutes. It's a long speech for good reason. He makes perhaps the boldest, most far-reaching proposals for changing the state's tax system in Minnesota history—proposals that would simultaneously change how the state funds public education, lower property taxes, deliver another sales-tax rebate, expand the application of the sales tax, reduce income taxes, and cut automobile license fees even further. He would do all this while holding the line on spending and the growth of government.

"We are poised to provide Minnesota citizens with a reformed tax system that not only lightens their load but also makes the tax system more fair, simple, and accountable to taxpayers," Ventura says to a joint session of the House and Senate. The governor says he knows some of his proposals will be controversial, but he believes they will prepare Minnesota for the rapidly changing new economy. His prime target for an overhaul is the property-tax system. "The property tax needs to be reformed so it is smaller, simpler, fairer, and more truly a local tax—and we can do it this year!"

Ventura's plan calls for the state to begin paying the full cost of K–12 public education out of the state's general fund rather than through local property taxes. The plan would eliminate a state-mandated general education property-tax levy by local school districts that now shows up on every homeowner's property-tax statement. The net effect, according to Ventura, would be property-tax relief of about $800 million per year for Minnesota taxpayers. He promises double-digit property-tax reductions for homes, businesses, apartments, farms, and cabins.

To help pay for that property-tax shift and the state's new responsibility for 100 percent of school costs from the general fund, Ventura makes his most controversial proposal: he wants to lower the sales tax from 6.5 percent to 6 percent, yet broaden it to include many services not currently subject to the sales tax. Ventura points out that 40 percent of the purchases Minnesotans make are for goods like books, tools, tires, and furniture. But he claims 60 percent of what we buy are for services, including haircuts, piano tuning, boat docking, car washes, and dating services. Those things, he says, are mostly untaxed. Ventura says that sixty-forty split is almost the exact opposite from when the current sales-tax law was written. He wants to alter the sales-tax system to reflect the new economy.

Ventura is aware some people will view his sales-tax plan as a tax increase, a notion he quickly tries to dispel. "It's about making a tax system fairer. Overall, it's about cutting taxes. And, in the end, it is about the ability for all Minnesotans to have more money in their pockets and for the state of Minnesota to have less in theirs."

Aside from these proposals for major tax reform, the governor can't pass up an opportunity to tweak the noses of his captive legislative audience. He reminds them he's disappointed they killed his unicameral bill last session. So now he outlines a series of reforms in the legislative process, essentially telling lawmakers how they should do their jobs. Ventura challenges them to start each session by reviewing and repealing "obsolete" laws before considering any new laws. He asks them to set "real spending targets" early in the session so they don't leave all the important decisions until the final days of the session. He also asks that every legislator be guaranteed the opportunity to introduce a "priority bill" that will get heard in committee and a floor vote (no doubt he has his new ally, Bob Lessard, in mind). He even tries to help them with scheduling, asking that no committees meet after 10:00 P.M. so that average citizens are able to attend.

"Implementing these changes will help ensure a more open, accountable, and responsive government," Ventura says. "Of course, I still believe that a single-house legislature would be the best way to fix the problems inherent in our two-house system. Rest assured, if the legislature fails to reform itself in this session, to paraphrase my good friend Arnold Schwarzenegger: Unicameral will be back!"

It's taken three years, but Ventura is finally setting the table for the bold reform in government he promised voters during his 1998 campaign. In addition to the tax and legislative reform, he also calls for changes in campaign-finance laws. He wants to limit "soft money" and give voters better access to information about where candidates are getting their money. "I promised the people that I would have the courage to challenge the status quo and shake up the system. I believe that this agenda fulfills that promise, and I believe it does it in a very responsible manner."

As he concludes his lengthy speech, Ventura makes just one subtle reference to the controversy over his XFL job and other moneymaking ventures outside the governor's office. He warns the House and Senate to choose carefully when deciding which legislation is most important. "As the business of this body begins, we can choose to debate these bold reforms that are so important to the people of this state or we can choose to focus on the personal, the political, and the petty."

With such a heavy emphasis on tax cutting and tax reform, it's no surprise most Republicans in the legislature are delighted by the speech. House Speaker Steve Sviggum practically gushes over what he heard from Ventura. "I think right now I can shake the governor's hand and say we will be able to meet him on his agenda," Sviggum tells reporters in the House gallery a few minutes after the governor's address. "You know, we'll tweak a few things here and there, but, Governor Ventura, House Republicans will be there for you and with you for the citizens of the state."

Republican Senate Minority Leader Dick Day isn't so impressed. He doesn't care for Ventura telling legislators how to do their jobs, especially with questions about the governor's own work ethic. "I really resent him playing us against the public all the time," Day says. "He'll take off now and we'll see him again in about three months."

Democrats don't like Ventura's message for other reasons. "If you drive an expensive vehicle and have a second home on a lake, his message was a good message," says Senate Majority Leader Roger Moe. "But if you're a senior citizen that's fighting for prescription drugs, he doesn't say anything." Representative Wes Skoglund, a Democrat from Minneapolis, had other complaints that will be loudly echoed through the rest of the session. "I think Democrats were disappointed he didn't talk about education in terms of funding it," Skoglund says. "If you're going to have good schools, you gotta pay for 'em, and there was not a word about putting more money into education."

All the lofty talk about tax reform and education funding will have to wait because there's still that pesky XFL matter to resolve. Despite Ventura's plea to not focus on the "petty," in mid-January a House committee hears testimony regarding a bill that would prohibit the governor and other statewide elected officials from taking second jobs. The author of the so-called "moonlighting" bill, Republican Representative Phil Krinkie, is obviously outraged by more than just the governor's amazing ability to earn money while in public office. Although the XFL's first games are still two weeks away, Krinkie is convinced the league will be so tawdry and degrading toward women that Ventura's involvement will be a major embarrassment to the state.

"This state, like our nation, has a long tradition of decency, civility, and accountability, which Jesse Ventura's predecessors have understood," Krinkie somberly explains to members of the House Governmental Operations and Veterans Affairs Policy Committee. "This governor is out of bounds in many ways, the 'color commentary' being only the latest and perhaps the most flagrant example. Governor Ventura does not understand the tradition of civility. It's time to take action."

As it turns out, committee members are about to see plenty of action. Krinkie brought along some clips of XFL cheerleader television commercials to prove his point about the indecency of the governor's new job. The first ad begins with soft music and close-up shots of a beautiful woman's face, followed by the deep intonation of an announcer: "The eyes. They tell us who she is. They tell us she is intelligence. She is strength. She is dignity. She is kindness." All of a sudden, the soft music abruptly ends and you hear what sounds like a phonograph needle screeching across an album before hard rock music blares. "She is wearing the shortiest, shorty shorts I have ever seen! The XFL cheerleaders. Coming February to NBC."

Suddenly, the usually staid House Governmental Operations and Veterans Affairs Policy Committee is one swingin' group. I've never seen so many grown men and women try their damnedest to suppress laughter. Most succeed. After all, they don't want to besmirch the committee's reputation for dullness. They face another challenge when the next commercial comes up, this one featuring a number of nearly naked, busty cheerleaders gyrating to music and narrated by the same deep-throated announcer: "She is strength. She is dignity. She is making me feel like I did when I was a little boy and my mom and dad took me to the circus.... There were clowns and monkeys and ... Daddy wants some popcorn!"

Krinkie, the master of the straight face, asks the committee members to "judge yourself whether this is the type of activity that the highest-ranking official in the state of Minnesota should be promoting and involved with." The committee takes no action on the bill at this hearing, but promises to conduct another one in the coming weeks to finish up testimony and take a vote. That should give Krinkie enough time to round up more videotape. If word leaks out about this hearing, they might have to sell tickets next time.

Ventura is more than happy to sell the use of his name and likeness to promote the XFL, but he's still a stickler about anyone else trying to make money off his name without him getting a cut. As the 2001 session gets under way, the *St. Paul Pioneer Press* announces plans for a new "VenturaLand" comic strip that will run on its editorial page each week. The governor stews about the planned comic strip for a few days without comment until he's delivering a speech about his tax-reform proposal at the Humphrey Institute of Public Affairs at the University of Minnesota. He's literally in midsentence when he spots a *Pioneer Press* editorial-page writer, Steve Dornfeld, sitting in the audience. Dornfeld is one of Ventura's harshest critics, and the two often spar at news conferences.

"The sales tax when it was put into effect—oh, by the way, Dornfeld, nice to see you! I'm glad your newspaper is going to make money off me now with your cartoon," Ventura says in midspeech. "Maybe you'll write an editorial dealing with that. You know, of your newspaper exploiting me to gain money with a cartoon. Interesting."

The cartoonist who will draw the strip, Kevin Lenagh, says it won't focus only on Ventura, but also many of his political opponents. "If he looks at the strip long enough he's going to see that I'm an equal opportunity cartoonist and that some of the people in the legislature that have been sniping at him are going to get theirs too," Lenagh says.

That doesn't satisfy Ventura, and he threatens legal action because he views the comic strip not just as editorial comment but commercial use of his name. "They're using my name and likeness without any approval from me at all," he tells reporters after his speech at the Humphrey Institute. "I would like some input in it. If they're going to use my likeness and they're going to make money off of me, I think I deserve the right to have input into it as I would with anything that's marketed with my likeness on it. "

There's little the governor can do to stop publication of the cartoon. He can't overcome minor inconveniences like the First Amendment and his standing as a public official. Naturally, the first "VenturaLand" cartoon pokes fun at Ventura's new job with the XFL. The governor isn't amused, but he's powerless to stop it.

Ventura tries to ignore the continued uproar over his XFL job and stays focused on getting out his budget proposal. His first budget back in 1999 was due so quickly after his election that it didn't call for the major reform he promised in his campaign. The two-year budget he proposes in 2001 attempts to make up for lost time. As promised during his State of the State address, Ventura calls for sweeping tax reform and reductions along with barely inflationary increases in spending for the 2002–2003 budget period. His budget plan calls for across-the-board income tax cuts, a sales-tax rebate averaging $440, another reduction in the motor-vehicle registration fee, double-digit property-tax relief as the state moves to take education funding off the property-tax rolls and a reduction in the state sales tax while broadening it to include many services. It's one of the most ambitious and far-reaching tax-reform proposals in state history.

Just as in 1999, Ventura says there was no input from lobbyists in the shaping of his budget plan. "Elected officials who dismiss this proposal out of hand are listening more to lobbyists paid to represent special interests than they are to the taxpayers," he tells lawmakers and members of his administration in a budget address at the Science Museum of Minnesota in downtown St. Paul. Why the Science Museum? "I've often observed that putting together a budget is very much like physics," Ventura explains. "For every action there is an equal and opposite reaction. When you spend one more dollar, you have to create one more dollar. And, of course, if you know anything at all about biology, you know that one more dollar does not grow on a tree."

After his science lesson, the governor quickly learns something about human nature: People are resistant to change. The businesses that provide services now proposed to be included in the sales tax quickly cry foul. Business associations representing everyone from barbers to advertising agencies say the new tax plan would hurt Minnesota. The ad agencies say a lot of their work would now go to competitors in other states where the work isn't taxed. Ventura says it's a matter of preparing the state's economy for the future. "We should not squander the opportunity to adjust the tax code to improve our competitive position in this global economy," he says in defense of his sales- and property-tax reforms.

The loudest complaints about the budget come from educators, both at the K–12 level and in the colleges and university system. At the University of Minnesota, the governor proposes a $56 million budget increase over two years. The university requested $221 million. Less than ninety minutes after Ventura proposes his budget, university president Mark Yudof appears in the capitol press-corps offices to begin making his case to the public for more money. He says the governor's $56 million proposal isn't even enough to cover the university's expected $58 million increase in employee health-care costs.

"We'll have to cannibalize positions," Yudof tells reporters, warning of possible job cuts and double-digit tuition increases if the governor's budget proposal passes. Two days later he paints a doomsday scenario in testimony before the House Higher Education Finance Committee. "The scenarios are quite bleak," he says, stressing that his initial budget request wasn't padded with extras and that he's trying not to overreact. "And I always feel badly saying that. Every year you hear from agencies that 'the sky is falling, the sky is falling.' Eventually you know how to discount that. But the sky *is* falling!"

The committee chair, Representative Peggy Leppik, agrees with Yudof's assessment of Ventura's proposal. "It's left a lot of people with their jaws hanging," she tells him.

The same can be said for the governor's $123 million proposal for K–12 education funding. His budget calls for a 1.4 percent increase, or about $65 million over two years, in the per-pupil funding formula. That's the portion that goes directly to fund students in the classroom. Ventura reminds educators that in 1999, K–12 education funding increased 17.9 percent, or $1.3 billion over two years. "That $1.3 billion increase in funding doesn't magically go away when this budget cycle ends," he says. "It will be there in the next budget cycle." Funding for public schools is by far the single biggest budget item in the state, and Ventura isn't afraid to play hardball with the powerful education lobby.

Opening Night

Playing hardball with the legislature and lobbyists will have to wait, however. Governor Ventura's ready for some football. On February 3, just over a week after unveiling the historic budget plan in St. Paul, he arrives in Las Vegas for opening night in the not-so-historic XFL. It's a few hours before game time at Sam Boyd Stadium, where the University of Las Vegas–Nevada plays its home games. It's now also the home of the Las Vegas Outlaws, one of eight XFL teams.

Governor Ventura transforms himself again into Jesse "the Body" Ventura for opening night in the XFL. He's sitting in a special booth built into the stands so the announcers can sit among the fans while calling the action. Ventura, dressed in a black XFL golf shirt and matching black hat, is chomping on a cigar a few hours before game time, going through a rehearsal with play-by-play announcer Matt Vasgersian.

It's a warm, crystal-clear day with the nearby foothills of Las Vegas framed by a bright blue sky. "Looking for a ticket! Anybody got a ticket?" Outside the stadium, ticket scalper Richard Peterson is happy to have professional football in Las Vegas. The game is sold out, with thirty-one thousand fans expected at the game. Peterson says most tickets sold for $18 to $25, but he thinks he can get twice that by scalping. Sporting a flattop haircut, the gray-haired Peterson is holding a Coors Light and a sign that says "I need a ticket." He says Jesse Ventura's involvement in the XFL just adds to the excitement over the new league. "He's going to be great. I don't know what he knows about football. What did he know about governorship?"

Nearby, dozens of tailgate parties are under way in the parking lot. Preston Goodman of Las Vegas is cooking bratwurst, hamburgers, and potatoes wrapped in tin foil, stuffed with onions and green peppers. "I think he's the perfect choice," he says about Ventura's job with the XFL. "He's got the personality. He's a man's man. He's a macho guy. We want to see some real football and some real commentary." Goodman doesn't understand all the fuss back in Minnesota about the moonlighting governor. "I think the guy's life is his own. As long as he's taking care of his responsibilities back home, he should be able to enjoy the XFL just like the rest of the country."

Just how much the rest of the country will enjoy the XFL remains to be seen. XFL founder Vince McMahon stands at the fifty-yard line just before game time and turns on his growling wrestling-announcer voice. "To our worldwide television audience, to fans all over North America, to fans here in Las Vegas, this … is … the … XFL!" Fireworks explode, the fans scream, and the cheerleaders—well, they're practically naked. Before the game, the much-ballyhooed XFL cheerleaders got their own pregame introductions in the stadium. Their shorts are, um, short, and there's cleavage aplenty, but not much more than we've come to expect on the sidelines of most NFL games.

From a television standpoint, the game is like most other football games. There are some innovations, like dozens of microphones on players and coaches. A daredevil camera operator wearing a helmet occasionally runs on the field and follows the play up close. Another camera operated by remote control hangs over the field and captures the action from above. Players are allowed to put any name they want on the back of their jerseys and one player for Las Vegas, Rod Smart, chooses "He Hate Me." Combine all that with Ventura in the booth and what do you get? A snoozer. The Las Vegas Outlaws win 19–0 and even Jesse "the Announcer" Ventura can't save this one. The game is so dull NBC pulls the plug on the Las Vegas game at the end of the third quarter and switches most of the nation's viewers to a game between the Chicago Enforcers and Orlando Rage.

Ventura wasn't a great color commentator in his previous stints with the Buccaneers and Vikings in the NFL, and he's more than a bit rusty in his XFL debut. At a postgame news conference, Vince McMahon didn't exactly pile on the praise for his star announcer. "I thought he did a good job.... I think he can do a little better," McMahon tells an eclectic group of reporters covering the game. Unlike NFL games that are covered by sports reporters, most of the reporters in Las Vegas are from wrestling publications, television entertainment shows, and, of course, Minnesota's capitol press corps.

"I thought there was the right complement of sexuality and a right complement of confrontation ... the right complement of really hard-hitting football," McMahon says. "I think the viewer really experienced the game. One of the things Jesse did really well was not talk. And I don't mean that disparagingly." No offense taken, at least by the political reporters.

The governor didn't make any outlandish or controversial statements during the game. He admits he wanted to. "I only wish that you all wouldn't criticize me, I'd turn it loose even more," says Ventura, while smoking a cigar and sitting between McMahon and NBC's Dick Ebersol. "I know what would happen if I did that. I mean, if I really let it go. I, in fact, said to Vince, 'You know, if I'm not in office three years from now and we're still doing this, you watch and see what happens then.' Let's face it, I had to be careful tonight. Don't you all agree? Because if I wasn't a bit careful, I know my local media in Minnesota would have hung me up by my thumbs."

Ebersol said the network projected the XFL Saturday-night game would average a 4 or 5 percent rating over the twelve-week season. The rating is the percentage of all television homes in the country tuned into a program. If it performs as projected, Ebersol would consider it a rare Saturday-night success. "I mean, Saturday night is the one night of the week none of the networks can get arrested," he jokes. "There hasn't been a hit there since *Golden Girls*, and most of the people who watched that are deceased."

When the overnight ratings come out, it's clear many live bodies were propped up in front of their television sets. The overnight rating in the nation's forty-nine biggest markets is a 10.3. The Minneapolis–St. Paul market has the second-highest rating in those markets with a 14.9. Only the Las Vegas market, with a 17.7, registered a higher rating.

Unfortunately for Ventura and the XFL, television critics were among the viewers. A review in *USA Today* gave the governor a grade of C-minus, calling him "loud" and "unprepared." The headline in the *Star Tribune*'s review says it all: "It's worse than imagined.... Bad conduct, bad announcing, bad football equal bad TV." As for legislators who have criticized Ventura for taking the job, most are relieved the governor didn't get involved in any tawdry comments about the cheerleaders. Most also didn't think much of his football broadcasting ability, including Republican House majority leader Tim Pawlenty, who offered his own succinct review: "I don't think John Madden needs to worry about his job security."

The following week, the XFL ratings fall off dramatically for the nationally televised Saturday-night game, even though it featured teams from two of the XFL's biggest markets, Chicago and Los Angeles. It draws a 5.1 rating, a steep drop from the 10.3 the week before. But Ventura has more important things to deal with than declining XFL ratings. He's taking serious heat over his funding proposals for K–12 education and higher education. As usual, he doesn't back down. Instead, he wonders out loud where all the money is going, calling the education funding system a "dark hole" and an "endless pit." It's against that backdrop that he ventures to St. Peter, Minnesota, about an hour south of the Twin Cities, and steps into the ring with a five-foot-tall opponent of his education proposal.

Dawn Sandborg, a twenty-eight-year-old mother of a seven-year-old daughter, is waiting for Ventura when he arrives in St. Peter. The governor is on the road trying to drum up support for his budget, including his education proposal and his sales-tax plan. He plans to go door-to-door in downtown St. Peter, talking to business owners and customers. When he walks into the Nutter Clothing store, Sandborg is waiting between the tie racks and the winter jackets. She tells the governor his budget proposal will force her daughter's school to lay off teachers and increase class sizes.

"Let me say this to you," Ventura says, towering over Sandborg and her daughter as he politely but pointedly responds. "Do you know how much K–12 education has gone up in the past decade? Can you give me a quote?" She can't. But guess what? He's got the figure memorized. "In the last decade K–12 complete spending has gone up 100.7 percent—100.7 percent! There are no more kids in school today than there were in 1990. So you better get both sides of the story. I'm a public-education advocate!"

"I'm not attacking you," Sandborg replies, sensing the governor's a bit on the defensive.

"I know, and I'm saying to you in the last budget we raised it $1.3 billion," Ventura says. "That rolls over to this budget too. That's not onetime money. That's continuous money."

Sandborg suggests that instead of rebating all the surplus budget money, some of it could be used to pay for education. "And so you're willing to give up tax cuts altogether?" he asks. "You're willing to give up property-tax, double-digit relief in property taxes to do that?"

She stands her ground. "I am willing to give up whatever it takes so my daughter gets a good education and is taken care of because the teachers are providing so much."

Ventura insists schools are not being held accountable for how they're spending their money. "Something's wrong," he says, pointing a finger to make his point as he heads out of the store. "I'm just trying to find out what it is. Something's wrong out there, and I have the guts to ask it, what's wrong."

After the governor leaves, reporters ask Sandborg what she thought of Ventura's explanation. "I think it's kind of a runaround," she replies matter-of-factly.

The governor heads down the street in search of another forum to promote his budget plan. He finds one in George Lesnar's barbershop. Ventura plops down in a barber chair and shoots the breeze with Lesnar while he's finishing up a haircut. Reporters crowd into the small, basement-level barbershop with the "Gone Fishing" sign hanging above the sink, and someone asks the governor if his plan to expand the sales tax to services like haircuts will be a tough sell. "I don't think it's a tough sell if all the facts are put out, but they're not," Ventura shoots back. "All people like to say is, 'Oh, expansion of the sales tax,' and they don't say anything more. If you tell them we're lowering property taxes and lowering income taxes, then I think most people sit back and say, 'That's not a bad idea.' All the polls show, and I agree, that the sales tax is the most fair tax out there because you choose to pay it. It's not a tax you're required to pay. You choose to pay it by what you purchase."

Although Lesnar has cut a lot of hair in fifty years on the job, he's a man of few words. He does wonder, though, why the state would require him to charge his customers an extra 6 percent.

"Why bother when you have a surplus already?" Lesnar asks.

"Yeah, but we're going to lower the property taxes and income taxes, George," Ventura says, leaning forward in his chair. "We're just shifting it. We're going to make it so you pay less income tax and property taxes."

As hard as he tries to keep his focus on state business, legislators are determined to keep public attention on Ventura's private dealings with the XFL. On February 19, the "moonlighting" bill is back before the House Governmental Operations and Veterans Affairs Policy Committee. There are no sexy videotapes this time. Instead, Arne Carlson will appear before the committee in a rare instance of a former governor testifying against a sitting governor. Needless to say, the bland and cerebral Governor Carlson isn't thrilled by Ventura's gubernatorial high jinks.

"I can just imagine a future governor appearing on television on an ad, saying, 'After having a tough day with the legislature, I like to open a can of suds. It makes me relax,'" Carlson jokes. "When President Reagan became president of the United States, he didn't drag his Hollywood career with him and continue to do Hollywood service on the side."

Carlson says when he served as governor, he presumed ethics rules prevented him from taking outside employment, just as he'd expect the same rules would prevent the attorney general from opening a private legal practice on the side.

The bill passes the committee, but with one major change so that it doesn't appear to be aimed solely at Ventura. The new law wouldn't ban constitutional officers from outside employment until January 2003, meaning it would affect the governor only if he is elected to a second term. Ventura doesn't have any comment, although I'm told he's privately seething about a former governor testifying against him. The only response from his administration is from his spokesperson, John Wodele, who calls Carlson's testimony an "extremist view" and says it's up to voters to decide if Ventura's behavior is unacceptable. "The governor is spending a lot of time talking about his budget, trying to sell his budget, meeting with legislators, traveling the state. That's what we're focused on. And for anyone to suggest that his outside activities or private interests are interfering with that is just plain wrong."

Jackal Badges

It turns out the governor is also busy dreaming up new ways to tweak the media. A couple of days after the House Governmental Operations and Veterans Affairs Policy Committee hearing, a surprise is waiting for members of the capitol press corps. The governor's staff delivers new media credential badges accompanied by a memo from Wodele that says the new badges are needed for "security" and "accountability of who attends official Governor's Office events." One look at the badges and you know there's more to it than that. The laminated credentials are bigger than normal, four inches wide and six inches high. They're red and white and feature a picture of a smiling Governor Ventura, dressed in black and pointing his finger at the camera. In big, black type it says "Media 2001." Underneath the name of each reporter is the title "Official Jackal." On the back, it says the "Governor's Office reserves the right to revoke the credential for any reason."

While some of us find them to be amusing, others view it as an affront to our profession, even an assault on the First Amendment. The reporters at the *St. Paul Pioneer Press* give it the old "we don't need no stinkin' badges" routine. They all return their badges to Wodele. The Associated Press orders its reporters not to wear the badges and even puts a story about them on the news wire. Suddenly, the jackal badges become national news and the governor's office is getting requests for them from all over the country.

Wodele says the "Official Jackal" title on the badges is just a little humor in response to "Media Jackal" T-shirts the capitol press corps had printed after Ventura began referring to reporters as jackals. He says news coverage of the governor won't be any more restrictive and he doesn't understand the uproar. "We obviously didn't just come down with yesterday's rain," he tells me in his office while fidgeting with a stack of jackal badges on his desk. "We've heard of the First Amendment." Governor Ventura gets more to the point a couple of days later when he appears at his first news conference since issuing the badges. "By the way, I noticed that only a few people are wearing their credentials today. Congratulations for having a sense of humor, for those that do. And for those that don't, go stick your head in the mud!"

The use of the media credentials never is enforced and the governor drops the whole idea less than two weeks later. Of course, not until he's gotten two weeks of free publicity for his second book, which, you'll recall, includes the subtitle *Going to the Mat against Political Pawns and Media Jackals.*

On February 28, 2001, a new budget forecast is released that, for the first time in many years, shows some cracks in Minnesota's tight financial ship. In November, the projected surplus through 2003 totaled just over $3 billion. A revised forecast now projects about a $2.4 billion surplus, a decrease of $618 million, or about 20 percent. Although it's the first downward trend in a budget forecast since 1992, Governor Ventura says it will require only minor adjustments to his budget plan because he had left some surplus money unallocated anyway. He's not overly concerned about the state's economy. "It's like professional wrestling— it always goes up and down a little bit. It's like riding a ship in the navy: the seas aren't always flat."

House Republicans prefer to look at the bright side of the budget forecast. There's still a $2.4 billion surplus and House Speaker Steve Sviggum says, "The tax cut is still real. It is still possible." Ventura agrees. "If our national [budget] forecasters are right, this is a very temporary slowdown and not the beginning of a long-term downturn."

Democratic House Minority Leader Tom Pugh tries to temper their enthusiasm. "We're going to have to be a bit more cautious than we were under the November forecast, and we're going to ask the governor and House Republicans to do the same." A few days later Ventura makes his adjustments by calling for a slightly smaller income-tax cut and postponing a further decrease in automobile license-tab fees, a reduction of about $571 million in his proposed tax cuts.

The state's budget surplus isn't dropping as precipitously as the XFL television ratings, however. The March 19 game between the Birmingham Bolts and the Las Vegas Outlaws registers just a 2.1 overnight rating, making it one of the lowest-rated prime-time sports programs in history. The ratings have steadily dropped since opening night and Ventura has been paired with a variety of announcers to juice things up, including WWF announcer Jim Ross and former NFL players Mike Adamle and Dick Butkus. They've resorted to cameras in the cheerleaders' locker room and even a public feud between Ventura and Rusty Tillman, head coach of the New York/New Jersey Hitmen.

Ventura started the feud by calling Tillman "gutless" for kicking a field goal in a game rather than going for a touchdown on fourth-and-goal from the one. The next week Ventura announces Tillman's game again and tries to goad him into a postgame interview on the sidelines just after the game. The governor is wearing a blue rain poncho and XFL cap as he tries to keep up with Tillman, who's doing his best to ignore him. "Rusty, why won't you talk to me?" Ventura asks, as the rain falls and the Chicago fans cheer as they listen over the stadium public-address system. The scene is somewhat reminiscent of the many times the jackals try to get a word in with the governor.

The whole thing is obviously a publicity stunt dreamed up by Vince McMahon and Tillman isn't buying in to it. "I told them when I signed on to coach this team, I'm not going to do this WWF garbage," he tells the *Washington Post.* "First of all, that whole 'gutless' business on and after the game was manufactured by them to get me going. I'm a football coach. I'm not going to embarrass myself on national televi-sion. I'm not going to embarrass my friends and family. I'd like to whip [Ventura's] butt, but that's not going to get me anywhere. I don't like this WWF stuff. I think their TV announcers are awful. Jesse is terrible."

Even McMahon seems to agree with Tillman. Two weeks later in an interview with the *Los Angeles Times,* McMahon says Ventura is on "thin ice" and might lose his job. "We've made some mistakes," McMahon says in an article published March 15, just six weeks into the XFL's inaugural season, "and I think our biggest one was our selection of announcers. We need football announcers, not WWF announcers."

In an interview a few days later, Ventura tells me he's convinced it's all just another publicity stunt. "It's Vince's business. He's the one that orchestrated the whole thing.... He probably got what he wanted. He got plenty of press." Even if it isn't a publicity stunt, he says his contract calls for him to get paid no matter what. "Oh, he will continue to pay me!"

Just one night after feuding with Rusty Tillman on national tele-vision, Ventura seamlessly transitions to a formal White House dinner as part of the latest National Governors Conference. As Ventura and his wife approach President Bush and First Lady Laura Bush in a receiving line, the president reaches out his hand first to Terry Ventura and jokes, "I can't wait to meet the most patient woman in America!"

Patience for Ventura's budget proposal is in short supply at the State Capitol. He continues to draw fire from critics of his education funding.

This time even a ninety-two-year-old former Republican governor joins the chorus. Elmer L. Andersen served as governor from 1961 to 1963 and is one of the state's revered elder statesmen. Andersen uses a wheel-chair and doesn't get out in public much anymore, but he accepts an invitation to address the state Senate on March 19 to talk about the importance of higher-education funding. Andersen is sometimes diffi-cult to understand at his age, but he's in good voice on this issue. He criticizes Ventura for shortchanging the University of Minnesota and says it shows he's "lacking in experience." He warns legislators not to get too caught up in demands for tax cuts and rebates and to focus on investing for the future.

Andersen can't resist deadpanning one wisecrack about Governor Ventura's extracurricular activities. "I got a call the other day from the XFL, saying they were thinking of making some changes in their per-sonnel. They asked if I would be interested." It's been a long time since there was so much laughter in the usually formal and stodgy Senate chambers.

Andersen isn't the only former governor protesting Ventura's bud-get proposal for the University of Minnesota. Former governor Arne Carlson is back for another round of criticism for his successor. "What we're trying to do is to alert the public and the legislature to the fact that we want them to really assess this budget very, very, very seriously," he testifies before a Senate committee. During Carlson's two terms he was one of the state's most visible boosters of the university, often show-ing up at basketball and football games in his "M" sweater. Joining him in criticizing Ventura is yet another former governor, Wendell Anderson, a former hockey player at the U of M and later a member of the U.S. Olympic hockey team as well as a member of the university's Board of Regents. He says in the twenty-five years since he served as governor, it's the first time he's publicly criticized a sitting governor. "I thought I had to step forward and differ with the incumbent governor on his bud-get proposal for the university," Anderson says. "It is grossly inadequate."

University students also rally at the capitol. "One, two, three, four, Jesse don't shut the door!" is the rallying cry at one protest. "Five, six, seven, eight, we're the future of the state!" Ironically, that same day Ventura appears at a 150th birthday party for the University of Minnesota in the capitol rotunda. "If you believed everything you read in the newspapers these days, you'd think I don't care about the University of Minnesota and you'd be wrong," he says in brief remarks alongside university president Mark Yudof. "I do care!"

Yudof and Ventura are cordial to each other despite their differences on the budget. "I think he does care about the university," Yudof tells reporters afterward, "but I think he has a fiscal vision for the state, which, in my judgment, does not fit the needs of the university."

Ventura is less cordial with public-school officials who continue to organize student protests of his budget plan for K–12 education. Hardly a week goes by without grade-school, middle-school, and high-school students filling the rotunda. They display signs like "My school is not a black hole" and chant protest slogans like "S-c-h-o-o-l ... we need teachers, not the X-F-L!"

Ventura delivers a blistering attack on these tactics by school administrators on March 14 at a Minnesota Chamber of Commerce luncheon in downtown St. Paul. "The TV cameras love to capture the sad faces of the kids who, according to the teachers and administrators, will suffer because of the Ventura budget," he says. "Why doesn't someone point the finger back at the administrators and ask them why they spent more money on labor contracts than they had in their budgets?" He says he's tired of being portrayed as the "evil governor" and tired of kids being used to make him look that way. "Enough is enough. It's time for honesty and accountability. And for sure, it's time for adults to stand up and debate these issues without using innocent kids as pawns in a game of deception."

As the 2001 legislative session grinds to a scheduled adjournment in mid-May, it becomes increasingly obvious the House, Senate, and Governor Ventura are more polarized than ever on many issues. Political time bombs are ticking everywhere. One of the most explosive is the abortion issue. After failing to pass the "twenty-four-hour notification" bill on its own merits in 2000, this time House Republicans are threatening to attach it to a huge Health and Human Services bill. Ventura threatens to veto the whole $6.7 billion spending bill if it includes the abortion provisions. A veto would shut down welfare programs, nursing homes, and health-care programs for low-income Minnesotans. There is also no agreement on any of the major spending bills, including the contentious K–12 and higher-education bills.

"Hunting Man"

Among the few issues not getting much attention are those dealing with the environment and natural resources. Governor Ventura changes that in one fell swoop of his mouth. It happens when he summons *Star Tribune* outdoors writer Dennis Anderson to his office to discuss a critical column Anderson wrote about the governor and his Department of Natural Resources commissioner, Al Garber. Anderson criticized the two for what he considers inadequate support for conservation. According to transcripts of the April 3 meeting the *Star Tribune* posted on its Web site, Ventura tells Anderson he's insulted by his insinuation that "Commissioner Garber and I somehow aren't reputable people" and that "somehow I don't know about wildlife, hunting and fishing."

Ventura then chides Anderson about never serving in the military. "Well, Commissioner Garber and I have. He has two tours to Vietnam and I have one as a Navy SEAL and then 17 months in Southeast Asia and I'll just tell you this: Until you've hunted man, you haven't hunted yet. Because you need to hunt something that can shoot back at you to really classify yourself as a hunter. You need to understand the feeling of what it's like to go into the field and know your opposition can take you out. Not just go out there and shoot Bambi."

The transcript goes on like that for twenty-five pages with thirteen references to "hunting man." Due to my long-standing policy of never making fun of anyone who "hunts man," I have nothing further to add on this matter.

By mid-April the legislative gridlock and a continuous series of controversies begin to take a toll on Governor Ventura's job-approval rating.

The *Star Tribune*'s latest Minnesota Poll indicates 57 percent of Minnesotans approve of his job performance, a significant drop from the 71 percent approval rating in the same poll when the 2001 session began. On his weekly radio show broadcast from the Blue Moose Bar in East Grand Forks, Minnesota, Ventura begins a serious campaign of shifting the blame for the gridlock on tax and spending plans. He's upset by comments he's hearing from lawmakers that they might not be able to finish the session by the constitutional deadline of May 21. "How can they not finish their work on time, that they need a special session?" he asks his radio listeners. "Well, I can tell you right now I'm not calling it. And I'm the only one that can. And if they don't finish that work on time, then look for a government shutdown come June 30."

Despite that warning, the 2001 legislative session will be a mad scramble to the finish. The usual partisan debate and discord at the capitol is replaced, if only briefly, on May 9 when the Dalai Lama arrives to address a joint session of the legislature and meet with Governor Ventura. The exiled spiritual leader of Tibet, in his halting English, delivers a message about cooperation that should be taken to heart by the lawmakers. "If we carry this basic human spirit, or human good qualities, then many problems suddenly, I think, can reduce. In some cases, I think we can eliminate."

After his appearance in the House chambers the Dalai Lama, dressed in his flowing robe, walks to Governor Ventura's office for a private meeting. If you ever wondered what Ventura would say to one of the world's most revered religious figures, well, the moment of truth has arrived and Ventura doesn't disappoint.

"I asked him the most important question, I think, that you could ask him—if he'd ever seen *Caddyshack*," Ventura reveals in a radio interview on WCCO. He's referring to a scene from the 1980 film starring, among others, Bill Murray, who brags about once caddying for the Dalai Lama. The real Dalai Lama tells the governor he doesn't know anything about the movie. The governor, however, can't resist a little embellishment when recounting the story on the radio. "Before he left, he looked at me and said, 'Gunga, gunga, la gunga,'" Ventura says, reciting a line from the movie. "Which means, of course, that when I die, I'll have total consciousness, and so I got that going for me, which is nice."

And that's good, because a day later he no longer has the XFL announcing job going for him. On May 10, just nineteen days after the last forgettable game of the season, NBC and the WWF put the league out of its misery. The news first appears on the Associated Press news wire at about 5:00 P.M. "Hey, we just heard that the XFL folded," one of our KSTP-TV photographers says to Ventura as he walks out of a speech at the Minneapolis Convention Center. "I don't care," he responds without stopping. "I don't work for 'em anymore."

It didn't appear the governor was even aware of the XFL's demise. That suspicion is confirmed about an hour later when spokesperson John Wodele happens to be in my office in the basement of the capitol when he takes a call on his cell phone. It's a WWF spokesperson, and he's talking so loud even I can hear what he's saying. "John, I wanted to let you know that the WWF is disbanding the XFL. We wanted to make sure the governor knew before anyone asks him about it. Do you know if he knew about it?"

Wodele just shakes his head in amusement as he tells him some reporters already asked him about it an hour ago. Wodele suggests to the now-embarrassed WWF guy that "it might be a good idea" for Vince McMahon or someone to call the governor directly and tell him what's going on. He gives the guy a couple of phone numbers where Ventura can be reached, then snaps the cell phone shut, laughs, and says, "That guy would go crazy if he knew I was in a reporter's office!"

It often gets lost in the shuffle, but don't forget there's still plenty of legislative business to finish up in the next eleven days. The first order of business is to avoid a shutdown of the state's key social services. As promised, on May 10 House Republicans pass the 680-page Health and Human Services bill with the four pages of controversial abortion language. Also as promised, Governor Ventura says he'll veto the bill. "This twenty-four-hour waiting period has every right to be part of this session and to be passed into law," Wodele says. "But it should be done on its own merits and not in a way that holds the sick, the poor, and the elderly hostage."

On Friday, May 11, the Senate passes the same bill and it's expected to be on the governor's desk the following week. I'm scheduled to interview the governor live on our five o'clock newscast that night from Pequot Lakes, Minnesota, where he's hosting the annual governor's fishing opener. When he shows up for the interview, Ventura informs me he will talk to me about fishing and nothing else. I tell him there's no way I can conduct an interview with him entirely about fishing with so much important pending legislation waiting for him back at the capitol. "Well, you do what you gotta do and I'll do what I gotta do," he tells me as the clock ticks closer to 5:00.

"If you ask me about something other than fishing, I might just walk away," he warns me. I'm down to about three minutes before airtime, so I get on my cell phone and call my news director, Scott Libin, to quickly outline the problem. Libin tells me to go ahead with the interview as planned and "roll with the punches." I'm not thrilled with his choice of words.

The interview comes off with no bloodshed as I ask Ventura an obligatory question or two about fishing and tourism and then hit him with an abortion question. He starts inching away from me but can't resist the opportunity to criticize the legislature for playing political games. "Why couldn't they let it stand alone?" he says of the twenty-four-hour notification provision. "Why did they have to duck and hide and attach it to the Health and Human Services bill?"

On May 15 the Health and Human Services bill finally gets to the governor's desk. He quickly vetoes it and sends it back to the legislature, asking for a bill without the controversial abortion provisions. The problem now is that there are only six days left in the session and the tax bill and every major spending bill still need to be passed. On May 16 Governor Ventura comes back to the capitol for a late-night meeting in his office with House and Senate leaders for one last-ditch effort to broker a deal. The two sides remain far apart on a tax bill. The House wants $2.3 billion's worth of tax cuts and rebates. The Senate proposal calls for $1.7 billion. The House wants more of the property-tax relief targeted toward businesses. The Senate wants more for homeowners. Until they agree on a tax bill, the final spending targets for such things as transportation, health and human services, K–12 education, and higher education also can't be set.

The meeting in the governor's office is acrimonious. It breaks up after forty minutes with the three sides saying chances for an agreement in time to beat the May 21 deadline are all but dead. There's serious talk of a so-called "lights on" strategy of simply passing enough funding to keep government running and deferring decisions on tax cuts and spending until the 2002 session.

When Monday, May 21, 2001, rolls around, it's obvious this won't be the usual mad dash to the finish of a legislative session. The House and Senate chambers are empty most of the day. Meeting rooms are locked up because conference committees don't have any bills to debate. Most of the action is taking place in a capitol hallway where Minnesota Public Radio is broadcasting live with some of the key participants in this mess. Governor Ventura finally admits he'll probably be forced to call a special session of the legislature. "If and when there is one, I don't think [legislators] should be paid nor should they get per diem for it," he says in an interview. "They should come in on their own dollar because this is overtime for them that was caused strictly by them."

That brings a stinging response from Senate Majority Leader Roger Moe. "What we should do then is we should ask the governor to give up his pay that he made doing second jobs and then maybe he can help reimburse members," Moe says just a few feet from where the governor is being interviewed. "With all due respect," adds House Majority Leader Tim Pawlenty, "his job is more than just giving a State of the State address and then disappearing for three months. He needs to be in here working as well."

Governor Ventura refutes Pawlenty's assertion and points out that he's taken part in fifty-five meetings with either individual legislators or groups of legislators during the session. Ultimately, Ventura comes back to his familiar scapegoat for this legislative gridlock. "Be assured that if there's a government shutdown July 1, it's not the fault of the administration. The bicameral system is a broken-down system that leads to problems just like this, where the unicameral system would not allow that generally to happen."

Moe is tired of hearing that one. "That's a perfect illustration of why the governor doesn't know what he's talking about." In wrestling parlance, you could say Moe has taken out the brass knuckles.

The 2001 regular session of the legislature comes to an inglorious end with every piece of major tax and spending legislation left unfinished. Ventura is resigned to the fact he'll have to call a special session to avoid a government shutdown when the state would run out of money at the end of the fiscal year on June 30. Actually, there's nothing all that "special" about special sessions. According to the Minnesota Legislative Reference Library, there have been forty "special" sessions since 1857. Seven were called during the 1990s, including one dedicated to the failed effort to build the Minnesota Twins a new baseball stadium. Ventura isn't a fan of going to overtime. "How is a special session going to change any of the differences you have right now or any of the players at the table?" he asks.

Four days after the regular session ends, Ventura thinks he's finally broken the budget "logjam." He makes a proposal that gives something to all sides. House Republicans get a little more property-tax relief for some higher-valued homes. Senate Democrats get a little more funding for K–12 education and higher education. The governor gets to maintain his goal of holding spending growth to about 7 percent over two years. Initially, each side tentatively agrees to the deal.

Within hours, however, the deal starts to fall apart. Senate Democrats are convinced the plan is still too heavy on tax cuts without enough new spending for education. When June 1 rolls around and there's still no agreement, Ventura uses his radio show to warn the legislature the government will shut down in thirty days. "It's a reality to us because the clock is ticking, time is running," he says, pointing out that by law layoff notices will have to be sent to many of the state's fifty-three thousand workers by June 18.

The first few days of June come and go with no agreement. One of several candidates expected to take on Ventura if he runs for reelection in 2002 is using the stalemate to get an early start on his campaign. Republican Brian Sullivan, a wealthy Twin Cities businessman, begins running a thirty-second television commercial that places the blame for the special session squarely on Ventura's leadership style. "I'm running for governor because I believe Minnesota's government should be run by people who listen—not just people who shout," says one line in the ad.

At a news conference to unveil the first ad of the 2002 campaign, the thirty-nine-year-old Sullivan says Ventura focused too much on "irrelevant reforms," like the unicameral proposal. "I think you need to be traveling the state," Sullivan adds, pushing for issues that are more meaningful to people. "I think you need to be working with the legislature. Shouting and bullying isn't leadership."

On June 7, with an agreement between the House and Senate still out of reach, Ventura provides some leadership. He decides to call a special session without a prior deal, hoping pressure will build once they're in session on the public dime. He orders them to begin a special session on June 11. "If the legislature does not act next week, the state will soon have to begin to expend tax dollars to prepare for a government shutdown on July 1. I don't think that the legislature should be playing this game of chicken."

House and Senate leaders don't think much of the idea, but have no choice but to go along. The governor only has the power to call a special session; it's up to the legislature to decide how long they stay. Moe says he thinks the governor just gave up all his leverage. "If he's going to go ahead and call a special session I think he's all but given up his ability to negotiate whatever it is he wants."

Ventura uses his radio show again to stir up the public about the dangers of a possible government shutdown. "As far as public safety goes ... there would be no state troopers out on the roads," he warns. "There would be no prison guards. So, as we get closer, we've come up with an idea that's called 'Host a Convict.' We're going to look for legislators and people that would like to volunteer to take a few convicts into your home" during a government shutdown. He admits he's joking about the "Host a Convict" idea, but he says he's serious about troopers and prison guards being forced off their jobs.

On June 11 both the House and Senate do go into session as ordered, but it's little more than window dressing. The Senate meets for all of thirty-two minutes, introducing thirteen bills and immediately laying them all on the table. The House meets just a few minutes longer. After a brief flurry of activity in the morning, it's back to the frustrating calm of a budget stalemate.

Of course, they didn't have much pressure on them. Governor Ventura is at a country club playing in a charity golf tournament when the session begins and isn't the least bit concerned that House Speaker Steve Sviggum criticizes him for that. "That's certainly the House Speaker's opinion," Ventura responds, "but in my job description it didn't tell me to run the legislature."

On and on and on it goes. The rhetoric gets so repetitive that at one point I put a story on the air using clips from the movie *Groundhog Day*, when Bill Murray's character keeps living the same day over and over. There are some lively moments, like the night Sviggum pleaded with the Tax Conference Committee to reach an agreement. "It's time to go home! I'm tired of being here!" he said, just before angrily storming out of the meeting.

Ventura tops that by stomping away from a television reporter during an on-camera interview in the backyard of the governor's residence. That's what happened when KARE-TV reporter Kerri Miller accuses him of fear-mongering by telling listeners of his radio show that state troopers and prison guards would walk off their jobs. Miller claims Ventura knew that those are considered "essential" state workers who wouldn't leave their jobs even during a government shutdown. The governor doesn't like the line of questioning, so he gets up and storms away.

The Ventura administration continues to play its part in the political brinkmanship. The governor orders preparations to lay off all but essential state workers, like prison guards and state troopers. State parks are taking steps to close for the busy Fourth of July weekend, and state highway-construction projects are starting to be mothballed. If there's a government shutdown, about twenty-four thousand workers would be sent home and unemployment and welfare services would be greatly reduced.

Finally, on June 22 there's agreement on the framework of a deal. This time the House gets a guarantee of a 10 percent cut in business property taxes. The Senate gets more money for education, and Governor Ventura gets everyone to agree to earmark $250 million for the budget-reserve account to cushion the state in case of an economic downturn. It still takes eight days to hammer out all the details and pass all the spending bills and the tax bill.

The session ends the way it began, with complaints about funding for K–12 education and higher education. The University of Minnesota eventually gets $110 million in new funding, about half what it requested but nearly double what Ventura originally proposed. The governor takes some abuse during the Senate debate over the final bill. "I have never seen a governor pay such little attention to higher education and be so dismissive of higher education as what we have seen this year," says Senator Richard Cohen, a Democrat from St. Paul. "And we have not had a single bit, not a single minute, of public discussion from the governor relative to his vision for higher education and in particular the University of Minnesota. Instead, he's dealt with sound bites, cheap rhetoric, and demagoguery." The university has already announced double-digit tuition increases. Senator John Hottinger, a Democrat from Mankato, says he'll refer to them as "Jesse taxes" on students.

The K–12 education funding that finally passed also far exceeded what Governor Ventura proposed, with a $381 million increase approved over a two-year period. He had proposed a $123 million increase. Teachers unions and many Democrats say the new education spending level of $8.7 billion still isn't enough. Republican Senate Minority Leader Dick Day defends the governor's efforts to hold the line on education spending. "Eight-point-seven billion dollars is not enough? When is enough?"

After six months of rancor and acrimony, the session finally ends at 3:30 A.M. on June 30. Ironically, a late-night snag developed when Governor Ventura threatened to veto the state-government finance bill, the last bill in limbo, if legislators didn't remove the provision designating him a "state employee." The last-minute move angers Representative Phil Krinkie, the bill's author. "In my opinion, the reason we're in special session is because the governor didn't show up for work on time," he says, referring to Ventura's XFL moonlighting. "He wasn't here during the regular session." The provision is dropped and the final bill falls into place.

For Governor Ventura, the session represents another major victory. He manages to pass what some consider the most historic property-tax reform and relief in state history. Education funding is taken off local property tax rolls and will instead come from the state's general fund. The result will be double-digit property-tax cuts for homeowners, businesses, cabin owners, and farmers, one of the primary goals of his 1998 campaign for governor. The broadening of the sales tax didn't pass, but Ventura isn't giving up hope. "You can rest assured, I am not done yet," he says during a tax-bill signing ceremony at the Department of Revenue just a few hours after the legislature adjourned.

The governor thanks his staff and even manages to be gracious to legislators as he puts his signature on their work. "Thanks for keeping the dream alive. Thanks for the debates. Thanks for the insight and thanks for never giving up."

CHAPTER 15

September 11, 2001
Minnesota's Commander-in-Chief
Wages War on the Media

AP—PLANE CRASH—WORLD TRADE CENTER—URGENT—*There's word of a plane crashing into the World Trade Center in New York.*

Those chilling words cross the Associated Press news wire at 7:49 A.M. CDT on Tuesday, September 11, 2001. Life will never be the same in Minnesota, the United States, or the world. Four minutes earlier, terrorists struck the first blow in what will become a holy war, or jihad, against America. It will be the defining test of leadership for politicians and government leaders throughout the nation as President George W. Bush boldly declares a "war on terrorism." It also opens a bizarre new chapter in Governor Jesse Ventura's jihad against the media.

Within an hour of the World Trade Center attack and the subsequent attack on the Pentagon, Governor Ventura orders the opening of Minnesota's Emergency Operations Center in downtown St. Paul. It's a telecommunications command center that can be quickly staffed by FBI agents, state troopers, hazardous-materials experts, emergency medical personnel, the National Guard, the American Red Cross, and others who may be needed in times of crisis. It has been used as a command center for natural disasters like floods or widespread severe weather, but now will serve as a sort of lookout post for evidence of terrorist threats in Minnesota. With the cataclysmic events unfolding in New York and

Washington, D.C., and near Pittsburgh, no one's willing to dismiss the possibility terrorists could strike anywhere at anytime.

By 10:30 A.M. Governor Ventura and his commissioner of public safety, Charlie Weaver, call a media briefing in front of the State Capitol. "The tragic events of this day are staggering to the sense of security, peace, and calm that we in Minnesota and the United States are used to in our daily lives," Ventura says on a warm, clear day that belies the horror nearly every American has now witnessed on television. "This is a time of great shock, great sorrow, and great concern, but this is a time we must be confident that we can meet the very difficult challenges put forth by these senseless and tragic acts."

He says he's put the National Guard on alert and some public buildings in the Twin Cities have been secured. "Further, I am advising schools to keep students in school, but to take measures to make their buildings as secure as possible.... This is truly a time of extraordinary apprehension, but I would ask that the people remain calm. Calm, but alert."

Weaver steps up to the microphones and says the World Trade Center in downtown St. Paul, the IDS Center in Minneapolis, and the Mall of America in Bloomington all have been evacuated and closed. However, he says those measures are purely precautionary. "There is absolutely no hint of any target in Minnesota," he tells reporters. "I can't emphasize that enough. What terrorists want is for Minnesotans to panic. The reason we're on the front steps of the capitol today is to show that we aren't panicking."

Ventura compares the attacks to Pearl Harbor, calling the terrorism an "extremely vicious, cowardly attack." It happens to be primary election day in Minnesota and he insists the voting will go on as planned. "We are not calling off the elections," he says defiantly. "I think now, more than ever, is the time to show the power of democracy."

Within hours of the attacks Governor Ventura orders his staff to begin organizing a memorial service on the front lawn of the State Capitol. He invites the mayors of Minneapolis and St. Paul to take part in organizing an event he hopes will attract Minnesotans from every corner of the state. It's to be called "Minnesota Remembers: A Memorial from the Heartland."

The turnout on Sunday, September 16, exceeds the expectations of organizers. Despite overcast skies and drizzle, an estimated thirty-five thousand people show up. It's a testament to how deeply Minnesotans have been touched by witnessing the loss of so many innocent lives.

The ceremony features patriotic and religious music, prayer and honor guards representing the military, police officers, and firefighters. The crowd cheers when two fighter jets perform a stirring flyby. The excitement spurs chants of "USA! USA!" There are speeches by several Minnesota dignitaries, including former vice president Walter Mondale. He's later followed by Twin Citian Erik Aamoth, who delivers a moving and courageous speech in honor of his brother Gordon Aamoth, who is missing and presumed dead at the World Trade Center, where he worked. Minnesotans from all walks of life listen in rapt attention, united by patriotism, compassion and fear.

Governor Ventura is the last to speak at the nearly two-hour-long ceremony. As he looks out over the podium he sees hundreds of flags waving in the breeze, people embracing each other for warmth and comfort, and Minnesotans looking for confidence and leadership in a time of crisis. "I wanna say I'm proud to be your governor today, but I'm even more proud to be the commander-in-chief of the National Guard of the state of Minnesota!" he says to a tremendous ovation. "We stand ready to protect Minnesota, and we stand ready to assist President Bush and the United States of America in anything they might ask of us!" He's wearing his leather National Guard bomber jacket and looking every bit the part of the commander-in-chief. He also does an effective job of playing the part of grief counselor. "I stand here today humbled but comforted by your presence. That's what family is for, to share with each other the hurt, the sorrow, and the sadness."

The governor exudes the right blend of comfort and courage. It's just the type of message most people are seeking. "We will overcome this tragic moment. We must and we will move forward. We will move forward in fairness. We will live together with tolerance. We will extend our hands to the people of the world in solidarity and unity. We will pit honor against dishonor. We will promote good against evil. And finally, we will together restore our sense of freedom by conquering this enemy! We will do all of this and we will not fail! Hooyah!"

Ground Zero

The now familiar U.S. Navy SEAL battle cry punctuates an impressive response by Ventura in the five days since the devastating terrorist attacks. Along with Public Safety Commissioner Charlie Weaver, the governor has shown strong leadership in assuring Minnesotans everything possible is being done to keep them safe. If Ventura can harness just some of the goodwill and spirit of cooperation sweeping the state and nation, he could use it to accomplish great things as he approaches the end of his first term as governor.

But, for reasons not entirely clear, he chooses to pick a nasty fight with the Minnesota media at the worst possible time and place: during a trip to Ground Zero in New York City.

On September 27 Governor Ventura mentions during a speech in Rochester, Minnesota, that he plans to visit Ground Zero with New York governor George Pataki the following week. The news hits the Associated Press wire later in the afternoon, so I call spokesperson John Wodele to get details. He tells me Ventura will be delivering thousands of condolence cards handwritten by Minnesotans at the capitol memorial service. He'll visit Ground Zero and appear on ABC's *Good Morning America* to deliver the cards to Pataki on behalf of Minnesotans. I ask Wodele what kind of access the media will have to any of this, and he admits he doesn't know yet. But, he adds, "Tom, you don't want to miss this one." In other words, it seems at a minimum some kind of "pool" camera situation can be arranged at Ground Zero if the number of cameras and reporters is restricted.

The timing of the trip is problematic for the governor. On Monday, October 1, after protracted and failed contract talks with the Ventura administration, more than twenty-two thousand state employees, nearly half the state's workforce, go on strike after failing to reach agreement on wages and health-care benefits. It's the first strike by state workers in Minnesota since 1981. The strike date originally was set for two weeks earlier, but the two unions representing the workers agreed to postpone the strike as a gesture of goodwill after the September 11 attacks. When they do strike, Minnesota National Guard troops are assigned to fill in for workers at more than one hundred state hospitals, nursing homes, and veterans homes. Some road-construction projects and other state services simply grind to a halt. Ventura is scheduled to leave for New York on October 2.

The governor is taking heat from union members for not doing enough to solve the labor dispute even before he leaves for New York. At a rally on the State Capitol steps on the first day of the strike, hundreds of striking workers chant, "Where is Jesse? Where is Jesse?" Ventura is scheduled to make a couple of public appearances that day, including one at the Mall of America to show people it's safe to go to the popular tourist attraction and to get people shopping again. However, he cancels his appearances due to a bad back, further frustrating union members who want to hear what he's doing to resolve the contract impasse. They're not going to be hearing from him anytime soon, because his bad back isn't going to keep him from leaving the next day for New York City.

The governor's trip has one component of official "state business." His first appointment when he arrives in New York on October 2 is a meeting with representatives of two bond-rating agencies. Ventura and his finance commissioner are discussing Minnesota's credit rating and issues related to the state's ability to borrow money for capital bonding projects in the 2002 legislative session. While the governor conducts that meeting at his hotel, I'm on the phone with Wodele, trying to determine if we'll have access to the visit to Ground Zero later in the day. Wodele assures me he's doing everything possible to get us access, even if it's just one pool television camera and one newspaper photographer. He indicates to me it would be a great opportunity for people in Minnesota to see the governor handing out the cards from Minnesotans to the recovery workers.

There is one problem. Wodele says Governor Pataki's office made an arrangement with ABC's *Good Morning America* to have exclusive access to the visit. In other words, no other cameras or reporters allowed. I ask Wodele if Governor Ventura could persuade Pataki or ABC to allow a pool camera for the Minnesota media. Wodele indicates that Ventura could probably make it happen, but says the governor is unwilling to intervene.

"His view is that we're the guests and he's the host," Wodele says, explaining why Ventura won't do anything to help. He also tells me the governor views this as the media's problem, not his. Wodele sounds frustrated. He says he'll keep working on it, but doesn't sound optimistic. We all get a taste of the governor's mood a couple of hours later when he leaves his hotel headed for Pataki's Manhattan office. Ventura brushes by all the waiting reporters without so much as looking at us, let alone answering questions about the bond meeting or the state-workers strike. It's the first skirmish in what will soon be an all-out war with the Minnesota media.

At the time, I'm a bit reluctant to make too big of a deal out of this situation. It strikes me as kind of unseemly to get involved in a dispute about who gets to visit a site that is a graveyard for thousands of people. I've also got the advantage of working for an ABC affiliate. There's at least some hope I'll get videotape of the visit from *Good Morning America*, although so far the show hasn't agreed to give us anything. In the end, the Minnesota television crews and newspaper and radio reporters get zero access to Ground Zero during Ventura's visit. Fortunately, I do end up getting videotape of the visit from ABC for my 6:00 P.M. and 10:00 P.M. reports.

On the ABC tape you can see that smoke continues to billow from the World Trade Center wreckage even though it's been three weeks since the towers collapsed. Governor Pataki and Governor Ventura are wearing blue windbreakers with "State Police" emblazoned across the back as they make their way to the site. "You'll see steel I-beams three or four blocks away, and that's mostly from when the planes actually hit," Pataki says as he escorts Ventura, his wife, Terry, and a few other members of Ventura's party. "The first few days, everything from the Hudson River to the East River was covered with two or three inches of dust. Everything. All of the ground, all of the plants, all of the trees and the buildings, and it was like you were walking on the moonscape."

"My God, Terry, look at this!" Ventura exclaims as he and his wife get their first glimpse of the devastation. Terry, dressed in a Salvation Army jacket, is overcome by emotion. Her husband walks over and puts an arm around her. Their visit comes on a particularly poignant day. The bodies of several firefighters are found in the debris. Each time a body is found all work stops and everyone on the site stands in silence as firefighters somberly carry the body out on a stretcher draped by an American flag. The New York firefighters refer to the grim process as "bringing a brother home."

A recovery worker tells Ventura and ABC's Charlie Gibson he's seen that repeated too many times. "When you're working and you come across something like that, it hits home. You go down the block and you see the memorial of all the families and see the people coming here and crying. It's a terrible thing."

Ventura and his wife do what they can to lift spirits, handing out some of the condolence cards from Minnesotans, shaking hands and giving hugs when needed. The governor even climbs into one of the huge construction cranes to greet workers. While shooting his segment for *Good Morning America*, Gibson reads one of the handwritten messages Ventura is delivering from Minnesotans: "'The country and the world are here for your support. May God bless you and keep you in the palm of his hand.'"

It's an emotionally wrenching experience for the Venturas, so much so that at a news conference back at Pataki's office an hour later, Terry Ventura still has tears in her eyes. Governor Ventura said it had a profound impact on him. "It's made me question even more, why? Why would someone do this? Why?"

Unfortunately, the news conference also turns a bit ugly. It starts when a reporter asks Ventura to respond to complaints from striking workers that he should be home trying to settle the strike rather than in New York. It might be the angriest I've ever seen him.

"They're going home to dinner tonight, they're going home to their children tonight," Ventura says of anyone complaining about his trip. "These people here in New York have orphan children today, and I take offense to anyone who would question why I'm out here. I take great offense to that! To anyone who would question the fact of why I came out here.... I lead the state of Minnesota, and I came out here representing the state of Minnesota. How dare them! How dare them!"

He's not much happier when asked if it was unusual to visit the site representing the state and not allow any Minnesota media along. "So!" he responds with a glare. Governor Pataki steps to the microphone to defend Ventura. "This is still a very busy site," Pataki says of the World Trade Center area, "and it's a very dangerous site, and we have been very, very prudent in controlling access to the site.... You have heavy equipment. You have people risking their lives. You have welders on the pile. You still have fires there, and I think it's even more admirable that the governor, out of the sight of the cameras, was hugging the people and turning those tears into smiles. It's always easy to do it in front of a camera, but the most important thing was to be there, to lift the spirits of the people, to let them all know that Minnesota was with them without disrupting or creating additional risk at an enormously dangerous site."

That's an admirable defense, but there are a couple of factual holes in the story. First, Governor Ventura did not make the visit "out of the sight of the cameras." By my count from a careful review of the unedited *Good Morning America* videotape, at least three television cameras followed him every step of the way, along with a sound technician holding a boom microphone over his head. Second, neither Pataki nor Ventura would own up to the fact there was an exclusive arrangement with ABC to cover the visit, even though ABC freely admits there was such an agreement. ABC also reveals it paid for Ventura's airfare to New York and his hotel.

The next morning, when Ventura appears with Pataki on *Good*

Morning America, there's obvious tension between Ventura and the Minnesota media allowed into the studio to watch the show. As soon as Ventura steps off the set when the interview is over, a reporter for the *Star Tribune,* Kevin Diaz, asks him if ABC paid for exclusive access to his visit to Ground Zero by footing the bill for his trip.

"You tell me where I was compensated," the governor angrily responds. "Show me the check. Show me how I got paid." Wodele steps in and is equally angry about the accusation. "We did not do that!" he says, raising his voice to Diaz. "We did not do that!"

This argument is taking place only about twenty-five feet from where Diane Sawyer is about to begin the next segment of the show and you can hear the floor director giving her the last few seconds of a countdown to a live camera. As the show resumes, a member of the *Good Morning America* public-relations staff gently begins nudging Ventura, Wodele, and Diaz toward the door.

Once they get out in the hallway, the argument really gets ugly. Ventura's security guards try to keep other reporters away while the argument with Diaz continues. Ventura eventually storms away, vowing to not do any interviews with the Minnesota media ever again. Wodele stays and continues the battle and, unbeknownst to Wodele, a Minnesota Public Radio reporter records the whole argument.

"I spent an hour-and-a-half on the phone, while my wife sat by herself, trying to work with *Good Morning America* and the New York governor's office to get you access to everything the governor does, and for you to come to me today and say, 'We had an arrangement,' I'm offended and I'm done talking to you!" Wodele says to Diaz, practically shouting he's so mad.

"Who made the decision, John?" Diaz asks.

"I am done talking to you!" Wodele responds again.

"John, calm down. We're not—" Diaz doesn't get to finish.

"You're the one that got me going again! You accused me of doing something unethical!" Diaz denies making that accusation.

"Yes, you did!" Wodele retorts. "Yes, you did! You are—you have questioned my integrity. You have questioned my fairness, and you have questioned my responsibility to work hard to give the Minnesota media access to what the governor does, and I'm offended by that, Kevin!"

To say relations between the Minnesota media and Ventura's office are a bit chilly at this point would be akin to understating how cold a Minnesota winter can get. When the governor arrives at Minneapolis–St. Paul International Airport later that afternoon, he doesn't say a word to the media assembled there waiting for him. He just stands out front, waiting for his car to be brought around, staring straight ahead, arm around his wife, ignoring all questions. So far he's making good on his promise to not talk to the local media anymore.

That pledge, like other vows of silence he's taken while in office, lasts roughly twenty-four hours. The next day, he agrees to appear on Joe Soucheray's afternoon talk-radio show on KSTP-AM. Ventura tells Soucheray he doesn't consider "talk radio" to be part of the local media. It seems his beef is mostly with the capitol press corps. He tells Soucheray the controversy over the New York trip stems from nothing but jealousy on the part of some reporters. "I think it's a case of sour grapes because many in the media feel they're entitled to go anywhere they want to, regardless of the situation. They feel they have a right to be there. I don't believe they do in certain situations."

While on the show Ventura also makes his first public comments about the state-workers strike which is now in its fourth day. He tells Soucheray the state's current offers to the two unions are final: "There's no hidden money that I know of." When he leaves the studio parking lot in his black Lincoln Navigator, Ventura zips by dozens of striking workers picketing outside. He rolls down his window a bit and gives them a wave but doesn't stop to talk.

The appearance on Soucheray's show is just the beginning of a talk-radio blitz by the governor. Just days after he takes his vow of silence, you can't spin the radio dial without hearing his growling voice. When he needs to communicate with the public, he says, he'll use his own weekly radio show or other shows. He explains his rationale on October 10 when he appears on KFAN, the sports-talk station where he used to work. "I enjoy the talk-radio format because it gives me a chance to not deal in sound bites and allow people to pick and choose what they want to say that I said," he says. "It gives me the ability to explain my positions to where people can understand them clearly."

To a certain extent I can understand that reasoning. However, the very next thing to come out of Ventura's mouth is an argument for why he should consider doing less talk radio. "The other reason [I like talk radio] is because of the war. We are changing. We are not putting out my schedule anymore, because certain people and certain things are going to be natural targets for terrorists, and if we put out a schedule on the Internet, you can damn well be sure the terrorists know the schedule if they want to know it."

In other words, he's convinced himself he's a potential target of terrorists. Never mind that President Bush continues to distribute his daily schedule to journalists. Never mind that, after I make calls to all forty-nine other governor's offices, no other governor admits to withholding or even *considering* withholding a daily schedule. That list includes other high-profile governors like Jeb Bush of Florida, Gray Davis of California, and even George Pataki of New York.

Two sources in the governor's office tell me that withholding the schedule is Ventura's idea, partly to anger the Minnesota media and partly because he *does* think he could be a target. When I ask Wodele about it after the KFAN Radio appearance, he won't confirm it's the governor's idea, but he also won't deny it. "While security has always been a concern for Governor Ventura, a very high-profile governor, there is heightened concern right now. And the fact that someone could track his whereabouts is a concern to those who are responsible for his security."

So, is it Ventura's idea? "I wouldn't comment on how the policy was developed." Wodele also won't comment on the irony of the governor telling Minnesotans to go about their normal daily lives while he seems to be growing increasingly concerned about his own safety.

There are suspicions that another reason Ventura doesn't want his schedule published is that he doesn't want striking state workers to know where they can picket him. They manage to find out anyway. On

October 12 he's in Willow River in east-central Minnesota, to broad-cast his weekly radio show from a correctional facility. His touring bus is greeted by more than one hundred striking workers, some carrying signs that read "Jesse 'the Scab' Ventura." When his bus leaves the facility later in the afternoon, the governor isn't on it. He had a state helicopter fly him out.

Two days later the striking workers reach a settlement with the Ventura administration and agree to go back to work on October 15. The two unions got slightly bigger pay raises and less-expensive health benefits than the state originally offered. The settlement will cost the state about $6 million more than budgeted, so it came attached with a warning from Ventura about possible layoffs to make up the difference. "Now that the strike is over, it is important to note that there is even more difficulty ahead," he says in a written statement. "Because our country is at war and our economy is in recession, it was especially important to get this strike settled." Besides, he has a war to resume with the media.

Anthrax

Before warring again with the media, Ventura first has a new terrorist threat to deal with. Anthrax has been turning up in tainted mail in network news offices in New York and on Capitol Hill in Washington, D.C. More than thirty people in Senate Majority Leader Tom Daschle's office were exposed to anthrax spores from just one tainted letter. On October 17, it's revealed that anthrax spores have been discovered in Governor Pataki's Manhattan offices, the same offices where Ventura had his combative news conference two weeks earlier. This, of course, gets the wheels spinning in Ventura's office.

A late-afternoon news conference is called in Governor Ventura's reception room to discuss the growing nationwide fear of anthrax and how the state is prepared to deal with it. It's the type of event where you would assume the governor himself would appear to assure Min-nesotans everything is under control. Instead, he leaves it up to Public Safety Commissioner Charlie Weaver, state epidemiologist Harry Hull, and two National Guard representatives. Ventura's absence is left unexplained, but it's obvious he's not going to let the war on terrorism interfere with his war on the media.

Weaver reveals at the news conference that, because of the "potential threat to our elected officials and innocent citizens," a special National Guard biohazard response team will test for anthrax at the governor's official residence in St. Paul, at his Maple Grove ranch, and in various parts of the capitol complex. Among the areas to be tested are the offices of the governor, the attorney general, the secretary of state, mailrooms, even the capitol press-corps offices. That prompts jokes about whether they would be testing for anthrax in the press-corps offices or planting it.

At least one legislator says he's not amused. Representative Mark Gleason of Richfield sends out a news release calling the anthrax testing a "publicity stunt," adding, "The governor is doing exactly what average citizens are being told not to do, which is panic and divert scarce resources. He should be exhibiting courage and calm, reasoned leadership."

Despite the ominous sight of Minnesota National Guardsmen in biohazard suits testing for anthrax, Weaver admits it's all just a precaution and they don't expect to find anything. "There remains no evidence of a specific threat here in Minnesota of chemical, biological, or any other kind of attack by terrorists."

Ventura's obsession with the possibility he might be a target of terrorism is too easy a target for humorist Garrison Keillor to pass up. In an op-ed piece published in the *New York Times* on October 19, the governor's fellow Minnesotan skewers Ventura, referring to him in the piece as "Larry, so as to throw terrorists off the trail." Keillor also refers to Ventura as the "stealth governor" and writes, "Perhaps Larry even now is hunkered deep in a Minuteman silo in North Dakota, sitting at a control console in front of an electronic map of all 87 counties in Minnesota, running state government via a secure telephone, secret couriers disguised as seed salesmen bringing him state papers concealed in burlap bags."

Governor Ventura eventually allows his daily schedule to be released to the media again. However, it will no longer be posted on the Internet. A few days later one of the items on his schedule is another talk-radio appearance. This time he's not just appearing on Joe Soucheray's KSTP Radio show, he's going to host it because Soucheray is on vacation. With so much frightening stuff going on in the world, you'd think this would be a good chance for the governor to listen to the people who call in, gauge how they're coping, and maybe offer constructive leadership.

Instead, Ventura turns the show into an almost uninterrupted two-hour diatribe about the media. Among other accusations he says reporters "blatantly lie" and "distort the truth" to destroy people.

Obviously, three weeks is not enough time to temper his anger over the New York trip. Ventura says for the second time since he was elected he's quit reading newspapers and watching television newscasts. He then urges all Minnesotans to do the same. "I did it before but I got sucked right back into it again, reading the paper and watching the evening news. Now I do not do either, and life is grand. I highly recommend it, people. People that are out there, if you truly want to live life with freedom, live life with not being poisoned, not be determined for yourself what's going on around you, and concentrate on doing the right thing yourself, don't read either newspaper and don't watch the evening news. Because then you will not be infiltrated with the half-truths, the *National Enquirer* journalism that's practiced today, because it is."

Instead of reading newspapers and watching television news in these times of crisis, "listen to talk radio," the governor advises. "I'll tell you, it's more accurate on there. I'll tell you that."

The next day he's back on talk radio, this time on a Minnesota Public Radio talk show. Even though he's resumed releasing his daily schedule to reporters, he's still defending his previous decision to stop releasing it and his rationale is getting more bizarre.

"You gotta remember something," Ventura says. "If the media knows [my schedule], so does the terrorist and bin Laden. If the media know it, so do they, because you think they don't watch television? You think they're not walking among us? You think they're not here? They're here in some way, shape or ... they're out there. Clearly, they are or they couldn't have attacked as successfully as they did on September 11. So the thing is, see, that's the fine line you have to draw. When you're at a time of war, you lose some of those freedoms. And the media must understand they're going to lose some of the freedoms they had. We're not going to be as open with the media. We're not going to tell the media everything we're doing, even though the media might whine and complain about it. They're going to have to learn to live with it."

The governor who launched his campaign on talk radio is right back where he started. For better or worse, Ventura is now governing through news releases and by ping-ponging up and down the radio dial. It's unconventional, but you have to give him credit for resiliency. No matter how much off-the-wall behavior he exhibits, his popularity so far remains unmistakable. A *Star Tribune* Minnesota Poll in mid-October 2001 shows the governor's approval rating at about 58 percent, the same as six months ago. It's down from the heady days of 73 percent approval ratings, but it's remarkable nonetheless. He's maintained an acceptable approval rating despite a bruising 2001 legislative session, the first state-workers strike in twenty years, and a feud with the media that seems so out of place in a world at war against terrorists guilty of unspeakable horror.

In fact, the governor's approval ratings have withstood nearly constant battles with the media, public educators, and legislators, not to mention his outrageous moneymaking ventures outside his office. But the real test of his leadership is still ahead. For the first time in ten years the state is about to show a projected budget *deficit*. With the nation simultaneously at war and in a recession, Ventura will have to make some unpopular decisions without benefit of the reservoir of goodwill he had in 1998.

Something remarkable happened in October 2001 that illustrates the point. At a Minnesota Wild hockey game at the Xcel Energy Center in St. Paul one night, a hockey fight broke out and one of the players was bleeding. The scoreboard plays a clip from *Predator*, in which Ventura utters his famous line, "I ain't got time to bleed." From the crowd comes a chorus of booing and hissing. A week later at another Wild game, one of the arena cameras finds St. Paul mayor Norm Coleman sitting in the stands and his picture is flashed on the scoreboard. The man Ventura beat in the 1998 governor's race gets a standing ovation. Of course, hockey fans are partial to Coleman because he was a driving force in getting this new hockey arena built and bringing the Minnesota Wild to town, but it's still amazing the difference a few years can make.

As Ventura enters the final year of his first term as governor, he's learning that the old saying "Live by the sword, die by the sword" is more than a cliché. Just two weeks after urging Minnesotans to rely on talk radio for all their "accurate information," he finds out talk radio isn't always such a comfortable place. On November 6, he appears on Minnesota Public Radio again, this time in the midst of controversy over a plan by Major League Baseball owners to eliminate the Minnesota Twins franchise through contraction because the team can't get public help to build a stadium.

A caller named Bill gets under the governor's skin. "I remember the day and the time and the place when the Washington Senators announced they were coming to Minnesota," Bill says. "And now, because of the lack of leadership in this state and especially by the legislature and the governor—" Bill doesn't get to finish.

"That is not true!" Ventura retorts. "Give me a break!"

Bill is primed for battle. "Don't interrupt me!" he yells back.

"No, I'll interrupt you," Ventura barks. "I'll interrupt you because I find that atrocious!"

"Don't interrupt me!" Bill yells again.

"Governor," says *Midday* show host Gary Eichten, "let him get his question on here."

"At least let me finish my thought," Bill says. Ventura is steaming. He leans into the microphone and tells Eichten and the caller, "I'll just take my headset off." He pulls the headphones off and all Bill can do is exclaim, "What a leader you are! My gosh!" The clip of that exchange is played repeatedly on Twin Cities television newscasts.

Three days later, talk radio bites Ventura again, this time on his *Lunch with the Governor* show. He's broadcasting live from the Mall of America to promote tourism in Minnesota. Unbeknownst to him, a man who wants to take his job in the 2002 gubernatorial election bought sixty seconds of airtime immediately preceding the show. Ventura is sitting in the mall rotunda surrounded by people watching the show, wearing his headphones and waiting for his theme music to begin. Several television cameras are pointed at his face when a "radio commentary" by Republican gubernatorial candidate Brian Sullivan begins to play:

> What does Minnesota need more, entertainment or leadership? This is Brian Sullivan. Consider for a moment the difference between our governor, Jesse Ventura, and leaders like President Bush and Mayor Giuliani. President Bush is bringing people together and solving problems. But Jesse Ventura knows only how to divide us. Mayor Giuliani walks the streets of New York and provides serious leadership. But Jesse Ventura? He hides. Retreats to his radio studio. Fights with the press. Refuses to publish his schedule.
>
> And when South Dakota convinces Minnesota companies to create new jobs in their state instead of ours? Our governor responds with jokes instead of producing a real economic plan. In an economic downturn we need real leadership to promote job creation and make our state a better place to do business.
>
> We deserve a governor who demands results for us instead of demanding attention for himself. I'm Brian Sullivan, and I think Minnesotans should expect more from our governor than entertainment. Thanks for listening.

Governor Ventura does his best to stay cool in front of the cameras while the ad is playing, but you can tell he's irritated. He begins his program as if nothing happened, but he seems distracted when trying to talk about tourism. He's still months away from deciding whether he'll seek a second term, but just a few minutes into the show he can't help launching what might be one of the first counterattacks of the 2002 campaign.

"I heard that ad before I came on the air, and I guess maybe Minnesota will follow just like all these other states, where we'll get a candidate that'll spend millions of their own dollars to get elected to the job," Ventura says of Sullivan, a wealthy Twin Cities businessman. "That's what Brian Sullivan's going to do, right? He's going to spend, like, millions of his own money to get elected. That's the latest trend, you know, in politics. Rich guys spending their own money to get elected. And I'll go back to my father. My father always said, 'Why does one spend a million dollars for a job that pays a hundred grand a year?' That might be a good question for Brian Sullivan. What's in it for him? Spending millions of his own dollars for a job he's only going to make a hundred thousand a year on. But we'll fight that battle later. I look forward to it!"

As 2001 draws to a close, Ventura faces multiple challenges. After an initial reluctance to get involved in the fight to save the Minnesota Twins from contraction, he suddenly becomes quite active in the effort. Bowing to pressure from constituents calling and writing his office, and opinion polls showing the Twins' importance to Minnesotans, Ventura becomes the de facto spokesperson for frustrated baseball fans everywhere. He even testifies before Congress on December 6, 2001, about baseball's antitrust status and gets high marks for a head-to-head battle with baseball commissioner Bud Selig.

In one exchange with Selig before the House Judiciary Committee, Ventura says the economic losses claimed by baseball owners aren't as bad as they say because they get huge tax write-offs. "But I guess, Governor," Selig responds, "I'd have to say to you, if you want to have a tax loss and lose fifty or sixty million dollars, I think there are better ways to create a tax benefit than to have a sixty-million-dollar loss." Ventura, sitting next to Selig, stares him in the face and says, "That's why I have a hard time believing it, Mr. Selig, that they're losing that kind of money and still paying the salaries they're paying. It's asinine. These people did not get the wealth they have being stupid."

It's exactly what nearly every baseball fan would love to say to Selig. Ventura still won't support public funding for a new Twins stadium, but he will draw as much attention as he can to baseball's mind-boggling and self-inflicted economic problems.

Unfortunately, the governor suddenly has Minnesota's own mind-boggling economic problems to deal with. The state Department of Finance issues its updated budget forecast through the end of 2003. For ten straight years these forecasts have offered almost unlimited good news about budget surpluses. Not this time. A recession and the September 11 attacks combine to push Minnesota to the brink of a $2 billion budget deficit. That means since Ventura took office, the state has gone from a $4 billion surplus to a projected $1.95 billion deficit.

The governor says he'll first look to spending cuts to balance the budget, but says he won't rule out anything, including tax increases. It's a remarkable turn of events because in his first news release announcing his candidacy on January 26, 1998, Ventura said, "As governor, I will veto any new taxes and any increase in existing taxes. And I keep my word." In his first campaign brochure he repeated that pledge, adding, "If the tax is truly necessary, or that popular, the legislature only has to override the veto to implement it." At the 1998 Minnesota State Fair he told anyone who would listen, "I will veto any new tax that comes on my desk. There's not an excuse they can give me for it!"

Ventura is going to need all the help he can get from veteran legislators and others to turn things around. Senate Majority Leader Roger Moe says he'll work with the governor and the House of Representatives to find solutions, but he can't resist spotlighting the irony. "Who does the chief administrator of this state, the governor, need now to help solve this problem? He needs the people he has villainized for three years—the press, the legislature, and local elected officials."

On January 3, 2002, Governor Ventura delivers what could be his final State of the State address. He chooses a venue that breaks more new ground in Minnesota politics: the living room of the governor's mansion in St. Paul rather than in the traditional setting of the House chambers at the State Capitol. It will just be Ventura and a camera. No legislators, no Minnesota Supreme Court, no dignitaries or audience of any kind. He wants to deliver a serious message on television and radio about the state's economic problems without the constant interruptions of partisan applause whenever Democrats or Republicans sense he's leaning one way or the other. It's just as well. With all the bad news to deliver, there wasn't going to be much applause anyway. He's also probably avoiding the embarrassment of a few boos.

"This past year the longest-lasting economic expansion in United States history came to an end," a somber Ventura says to begin his speech. "For years we had been warned that what goes up must come down—and indeed it did. Last March the country quietly slipped into a recession. However, while there was little notice at the time, it all came crashing home on September 11, 2001." It's a stark contrast to his first State of the State address in 1999, when his proclamation that the "State of the State is great" was met by thunderous applause.

Now each phrase is met with deafening silence. Ventura is dressed in a turtleneck sweater and sport coat. He's trying to look relaxed, but the presentation comes across as somewhat flat and awkward on the three Twin Cities television stations that chose to carry the speech live. In Ross Perot–like fashion he goes through several charts and graphs on an easel as he explains in simple terms where the state's revenue comes from and where it's all going. Fitting, considering Ventura got his start in Perot's Reform Party. He vows his first priority in balancing the budget will be in spending cuts and emphasizes that everything is on the table. "In this process there should be no sacred cows," he says firmly.

That includes tax increases. Ventura is about to learn what many career politicians have learned before him: campaign promises can create their own political minefield. After his 1998 "no new taxes" pledge, the 2002 version of Jesse Ventura says, "I have said that every legitimate option should be on the table, and, therefore we should talk about taxes that could be raised." He goes on to suggest possible increases in gasoline taxes and cigarette taxes, and extending the sales tax to clothing and services that are currently tax-exempt.

Although more than forty states face budget deficits, some Democratic lawmakers are already blaming the governor for Minnesota's, calling it the "Ventura Deficit." He is undaunted despite the flip-flop on his campaign promise about taxes. During his first legislative session in 1999, the state had a projected $4.1 billion budget surplus through 2001. Now he faces a projected $2 billion deficit through 2003.

"After I was elected, I pledged that I would leave the budget in as good a shape as it was when I took over," he says with determination. "Whether I leave this job this year or five years from now, I will not go back on that promise."

One week later, on January 10, 2002, Governor Ventura moves a bold step closer to violating his "I will veto any new tax" pledge by proposing several tax increases. In the middle of a seven-page speech unveiling his budget-balancing plan, he takes a couple of gulps of water before describing his tax-increase plans. "My throat has to be lubricated to get to this next part," he jokes. He then rattles off proposals to raise taxes on gasoline, cigarette and tobacco products, and newspapers, magazines, and shoppers guides. Ventura also proposes extending the state's 6.5 percent sales tax to auto repairs and legal services. Combined with several other changes in the tax code, his proposal would increase taxes by nearly $400 million through 2003 and by another $1.35 billion through 2005, a total of $1.75 billion. He proposes spending cuts in areas like K–12 education, higher education, and aid to local governments totaling just over $2 billion through the same period.

Naturally, the tax increases get the most attention from Ventura's political opponents in the legislature. In fact, two members of the legislature with their eyes on the 2002 governor's race go out of their way to remind Minnesotans of Ventura's 1998 campaign promise about taxes. At a news conference less than an hour after the governor released his budget proposals, Democratic Senate Majority Leader Roger Moe refers a half-dozen times to the "Ventura tax increases." He makes it so transparent that once, when he simply refers to them as "tax increases," he pauses and says, "I mean, the 'Ventura tax increases.'" Republican House Majority Leader Tim Pawlenty is blatant right from the get-go.

"You'll remember we had the 'Jesse Checks,'" Pawlenty says of the rebate checks Ventura often took credit for. "Well, I think we should refer to this bundle of tax increases as the 'Jesse Taxes.'"

By the time he releases his new budget plan, which he refers to as "the Big Fix," Ventura seems reinvigorated and refocused on governing. He seems to enjoy the challenge of balancing the budget in the midst of a war and recession and says he's "inclined to run again." His tax-increase proposals will be a major factor in the 2002 race if he does run. He spent his entire 1998 campaign criticizing "career politicians" who say one thing to get elected and then do something else once in office.

When this is pointed out to him at his budget news conference, Ventura doesn't flinch. "We used to always say in the navy you don't gotta like it, you just gotta do it," he says in response to his campaign promise flip-flop. "I have the great freedom of not worrying too much about the political repercussions because I look at it this way: if I get beat for telling the truth, then I don't want the job anymore."

Just before the governor concludes, a reporter asks him if his proposed tax on newspapers and magazines has anything to do with his long-running feud with the media. His response is classic Ventura. "I don't sit down and think, 'Who am I going to get?' You know, I don't have time to do that. I love all of you!"

Another Ventura news conference ends with uproarious laughter.

Hide-and-Seek

On Monday, January 28, the day before the 2002 legislative session begins, Governor Ventura is sending off 109 members of Minnesota's Air National Guard to help wage the war in Afghanistan. He shows up at a military hangar at Minneapolis-St. Paul International Airport with cigar in hand, wearing blue jeans, tennis shoes, and a Champlin Park High School sweatshirt. "You don't bring suits when you deploy, you bring cigars," Ventura says, explaining his ungubernatorial attire. By now he seems to prefer the ceremonial duties of governor, like his job as commander-in-chief, to the day-to-day grind of dealing with the legislature.

He makes that clear during his remarks to the troops and their commander, Major General Eugene Andreotti. As Ventura sends the members of the 133rd Airlift Wing away from their families and into war, he makes it sound like he'd rather be in their shoes. "General, I thought about going with this time," he says. "After all, I have to face the legislature on Tuesday or Wednesday, whatever the hell day that is." For the record, it was the next day, Tuesday. That caustic remark sets the tone for what will end up being the governor's most remarkable legislative session yet.

When Ventura announced his budget plan earlier in the month, he demanded that legislators take action on erasing the deficit early in the legislative session. If they don't act fast, he threatens, he'll use powers granted to him by the state constitution to begin slashing state spending on his own to balance the budget. Shortly after convening on January 29, House Republicans pass a resolution calling for a hiring freeze on state workers as a first step in cutting the budget. Ventura isn't convinced such a move would save much money and resists the idea, preferring instead that lawmakers focus on a comprehensive budget-balancing plan.

While waiting for the legislature to act on his own budget plan or come up with another one, the governor unveils a package of anti-terrorism measures that would cost about $17 million. He's convinced another major terrorism attack is a strong possibility, possibly in the Midwest. "When, where, and how they will strike again we don't know, but rest assured, there still looms a great possibility it could happen," he tells reporters at a news conference. The package includes money to help local law enforcement prepare for possible terrorism and for more security at the State Capitol. The plan also calls for expanded wiretapping authority on cell phones and gives the health commissioner new powers to quarantine Minnesotans and share health information in cases of bioterrorism. The state attorney general and others raise questions about possible violations of civil rights under these proposals. Ventura is undeterred. "[Terrorists] want to kill civilians, and, in light of that, the rules are going to change a little bit," he says.

The governor's continued preoccupation with the war on terrorism will play a vital role in a budget debate with the legislature that quickly turns ugly. Both the House and Senate come up with plans to erase the budget deficit that starkly differ from Ventura's proposal in one key area: Neither body proposes raising taxes. The House proposes to cut spending by $654 million, pull $811 million from various budget-reserve accounts, and shift $554 million from a tobacco-settlement account. The Senate proposes more than $200 million in spending cuts, $653 million from reserves, and $900 million in accounting shifts. Both plans feature a controversial proposal to eliminate automatic inflation adjustments in state spending that increase the size of the state budget each year.

The key thing is the Republicans who lead the House and the Democrats who control the Senate manage to isolate Ventura as the state's only major political figure proposing a tax increase to balance the $1.95 billion deficit through 2003. It's a 180-degree turn from the 1998 campaign, when Ventura derided "career politicians" for their free-spending ways and tax policies that made Minnesota one of the most highly taxed states in the country.

After getting a look at the legislative-budget plans, Ventura calls a news conference on February 8 in the governor's reception room. Only Minnesota's governor would quote *Mad* magazine in his response to the plans. "This is the classic Alfred E. Neuman 'What me worry?' scenario," he says. "This problem is real and cannot be solved by wishing it away." He calls the elimination of automatic inflation adjustments a "gamble" and says both plans would jeopardize the state's triple-A bond rating. He also criticizes them again for not raising taxes. "It's really quite ironic that they don't want to raise cigarette taxes this year, but mark my word, if they don't, next year they will have to consider raising taxes like sales, income, and taxes on business."

Ventura says his plan, with a mix of tax increases and spending cuts that will balance the budget through 2005, is much more responsible than the House and Senate plans. "They remind me of the homeowner who makes house repairs with cheap materials that last just long enough for them to sell it to someone else," he says. "Then the new owner comes along and gets stuck with all the bills when the place falls apart. I don't want our citizens to get suckered into this cheap trick."

The same day Ventura makes those remarks blasting the legislature, a former governor takes aim and blames him for the state's fiscal mess. Arne Carlson, a Republican and Ventura's immediate predecessor, says Minnesota is paying the price for Ventura's three years of inattention to public policy. "We saw a governor come into office and, frankly, use that office for personal gain and personal enrichment more so than [at] any time in American history," Carlson tells a breakfast meeting of the Twin West Chamber of Commerce in a Minneapolis suburb. "And so now we are three years later paying that price of having an administration with one foot in Hollywood and one foot in St. Paul, and it does not work. Governing is a full-time responsibility, seven days a week, twenty-four hours a day."

A former governor isn't alone in pointing the finger of blame at Ventura. So is a would-be governor, Judi Dutcher, Minnesota's state auditor. In announcing that she will seek the Democratic endorsement for governor, Dutcher says she decided to run as she watched Ventura deliver his 2001 State of the State speech and propose a small increase in funding for education. She says he didn't appear to have a vision for Minnesota. "Instead, we got a governor who said, 'Here is an inadequate amount of money. Legislature, you deal with that. Media, don't ask me any questions, and maybe, *maybe*, I'll be back before the end of the session to let you know what I think.' That is not governing, that is not leadership, and that is why I'm running for governor of the state of Minnesota."

Ventura's support from the people of Minnesota is also suddenly in a nosedive. The bruising budget battle and, perhaps, his proposal to raise taxes seem to be damaging his popularity. A *Star Tribune* Minnesota Poll conducted in February shows his job-approval rating at 49 percent, the first time he's fallen below 50 percent. That's still not a fatal blow, considering he was elected with just 37 percent of the vote in 1998. What is troublesome for the governor is that only 29 percent of those surveyed say he deserves to be reelected. Sixty-three percent say someone new deserves a chance. "I've never been concerned with polls and never will be," Ventura says, continuing a pattern of touting good polls and ignoring bad polls.

The House and Senate come up with a tactic that could put Ventura down for the count. In a surprise move, a tag team of House Republicans and Senate Democrats secretly negotiates a compromise budget solution without the governor's input. The past three sessions he aligned himself with one side or the other to get what he wanted, often playing one side against the other. This time House and Senate leaders make no secret that they believe input from his administration is often counterproductive in efforts to reach compromise.

On February 19 House and Senate leaders schedule a news conference to announce the bipartisan budget deal, which calls for using $1.46 billion in various surplus accounts in state government and borrowing money from a tobacco-settlement endowment. There's also $505 million in spending cuts. The agreement eliminates the automatic inflation adjustment in state spending to reduce future projected deficits. Again, the key element is what the deal doesn't call for: tax increases. "It's tough to make everybody happy, but I think we have a real balance that represents the true interests and the true principles of Minnesotans," House Speaker Steve Sviggum tells reporters. "I would say the governor's budget does not do that."

The budget agreement certainly serves the political interests of two participants in the deal. House Majority Leader Tim Pawlenty and Senate Majority Leader Roger Moe are both now officially running for Ventura's job. The Republican Pawlenty needs to avoid tax increases to satisfy his supporters, and Democrat Moe needs to avoid deep spending cuts to satisfy his constituency. This political gamesmanship is not lost on Ventura.

"I can honestly sit up here and tell you that every decision I made hasn't been made on getting reelected," he says in a speech to a group of energy-company executives in downtown St. Paul the day after legislators announce their budget deal. "I believe when you start making decisions on what's best for reelection, well, then you're not in public service anymore, you're in self-service.... It's a solution for politicians. It's a solution to protect your elected status. It is not a solution that is going to solve Minnesota's problems."

One day after Ventura makes those remarks, legislators pass their budget bill off the House and Senate floors with amazing speed. There's reason for that: In just a few days the state finance department will announce the latest economic forecast and it's expected to show an even bigger projected budget deficit. Lawmakers want this bill on the governor's desk ASAP so it will become law before the new numbers come out. The last thing they want is for Ventura to have more ammunition to aim at their budget plan.

It's Thursday, February 21, and if the bill gets to the governor today, by law he'll have to sign it or veto it by Monday, two days before the new economic forecast comes out. If he vetoes the bill, they would still have a day to override him before the new forecast is announced. If they're going to get the bill to his desk, however, they'll have to find him first.

Just before 5:00 P.M. on February 21, Michele Timmons, the state's revisor of statutes, heads to Governor Ventura's office to deliver the budget bill. It's usually a mundane task, but not this time. At about 11:00 A.M. Timmons notified members of the governor's staff that the bill would arrive before 5:00, but when she calls back about 4:00 to arrange to drop off the bill, no one will take her calls or return her messages. Sensing something unusual is happening, she walks from her seventh-floor office in the State Office Building across the street to the governor's first-floor office at the State Capitol.

"We knocked on the door several times and no one answered," Timmons says, noting she's never had this kind of trouble from the governor before. So she goes up one floor to Senator Roger Moe's office and informs him the bill hasn't been delivered. Moe marches down to Ventura's office while his staff rounds up members of the media from the capitol press offices. When a few cameras are in place, he knocks on the door, showing that no one is answering. "The governor is not discharging his duties the way he should be as required by the constitution," Moe says, accusing Ventura of purposefully avoiding acceptance of the budget bill by closing his office early. "Why would you be afraid of making a decision on this bill? Accept the bill. Look at it. Read it. You got three days to make a decision.... When it's time to do the job he was elected to do, where's the governor?"

Moe then instructs Timmons to deliver the bill to Ventura at the nearby governor's mansion, but when she arrives she's told he's not there. His spokesperson, John Wodele, tells reporters by phone that he won't reveal the whereabouts of the governor or his staff, but he does admit Ventura isn't going out of his way to accommodate acceptance of the bill.

Moe consults with his legal counsel about what to do next. Even House Majority Leader Tim Pawlenty shows up to help plot strategy. Talk about strange political bedfellows: two men who want Ventura's job are now engaged in a game of hide-and-seek with him. Timmons is sent to the governor's ranch in Maple Grove, more than thirty miles from the capitol; with several reporters and camera crews in tow, she arrives at about 10:00 P.M. With television lights glaring him in the face, a Minnesota state trooper guarding the ranch refuses to say whether Ventura is there. All of this plays out on the ten o'clock local-television newscasts. One station even superimposes a photo of the "missing" governor on a milk carton.

Friday morning that gag is taken a step further by legislative staffers distributing "missing" posters with the governor's photo that say, "Have you seen me? Last seen 2/21/02 before 4:30." Ventura is not amused, chiding legislators for playing political games and accusing the media of making it into a big deal to boost ratings. He said he had a "normal night," eating dinner at the mansion and then watching the Timberwolves game at his ranch. Moments later, though, he tells reporters he wasn't going out of his way to be found, because he wanted an extra day to review the budget bill: "This is such an important bill. Why wouldn't I?" Some lawmakers point out he could have been reviewing the bill Thursday night rather than watching basketball.

Ventura can forget about having an extra day. "We contend that the clock started yesterday because of our numerous attempts at presentment on Thursday," says Michele Timmons, who's finally managed to deliver the bill Friday morning to the governor's office. That means he has until Monday to sign the bill, veto it, or let it become law without his signature.

Ventura isn't tipping his hand on what he'll do, but he quickly begins trying to build a coalition with House Democrats. If he vetoes the bill, House Republicans will need votes from the Democrats to get the required two-thirds majority to override. The Democrats aren't happy about cuts to education in the budget-balancing bill and are threatening to sustain a veto. The governor recognizes this, and, after a meeting with House and Senate leaders on Friday afternoon, walks out with his arm around Democratic Minority Leader Tom Pugh's shoulders. "I just want to say that Tom is my favorite legislator," proclaims a broadly smiling Ventura. Pugh looks a bit sheepish in front of the television cameras.

Ventura calls another meeting with lawmakers Saturday morning as he continues a desperate attempt to make some mark on the budget-balancing deal. He's hoping to make sure a veto is sustained or, failing that, to give input on a second phase of budget balancing that will be required if the new economic forecast shows a bigger projected deficit. With his back against the ropes, he pulls out the war card.

"I've been accused of breaking a campaign promise that I would never raise taxes," says Ventura, standing outside his office with several legislative leaders. "Well, I want to tell you at a time of war and in the defense of my country, I will break any campaign promise to get the job done." For good measure the governor is wearing a Navy SEAL cap and he's about to pull a wad of cash from his pocket and wave it in front of the television cameras. "I'll break 'em all if it means fighting this war. I'll break 'em all because when I made that promise, there was no war. So if that means I have to reach in my pocket and pull out some money and say, OK, here, take this from me now and go fight and win the war—here it is. That's my contribution, and if the rest of Minnesota does not want to make the contribution to fight this war, well, then, maybe I don't want to be governor of this state."

He looks and sounds sincere, but several of the lawmakers standing behind him look away and roll their eyes. In an editorial a couple of weeks later, even the *Wall Street Journal* pokes fun at Ventura for acting as if "Minnesota's state budget is financing the Pentagon." The newspaper also says his tax-raising efforts and other antics could turn him into a "one-term wonder."

Ventura won't back down. On Monday, February 25, he calls a news conference at 4:00 P.M. to announce his decision on the budget bill. Earlier in the day he had the finance department move up its announcement of the new economic forecast. As expected, it shows the state's deficit through 2003 grew by another $336 million and now stands at nearly $2.3 billion. That means the budget bill passed by the legislature will still leave a gap of about $400 million. The governor vetoes the bill and proceeds to rip into legislators.

"These politicians did not fix this budget deficit," Ventura says to the media and several legislators crowded into the governor's reception room. "They made things worse by putting a contaminated Band-Aid on a wounded economy." He blames the Al-Qaida terrorists for "devastating" the American economy and Minnesota's along with it. "Our citizens were there for New York in the immediate aftermath of September 11, and I believe they will be willing to sacrifice now to counter the long-term effects of the war on the Minnesota state economy.... Unfortunately, our legislators do not seem to understand that taxes and personal sacrifice are the price we pay for freedom." He urges the legislature to put politics aside and go back to work on a new solution "with the courage of a patriot and the honesty of a public servant."

After the speech, a reporter asks Ventura if he's questioning the patriotism of legislators. "You're darn right I'm saying that," he responds, adding that he's asking legislators and all Minnesotans to "step up to the plate and be patriots instead of carpetbaggers."

Legislators are incensed by his comments. "Let me first say his decision [to veto] is wrong, it's unwise, and it's quite personal," House

Speaker Steve Sviggum says with a tinge of anger. "I think what Governor Ventura wants to do is make himself unilateral dictator of the state of Minnesota." The most fiery response comes a half-hour later in a Senate Tax Committee hearing. Senator Steve Murphy, a former Marine, can hardly control his anger. "That's a big slap in the face," he says of Ventura's patriotism comments. "You can tell the governor that, as far as I'm concerned, that crossed the line, and I don't know if he can come back and repair those wounds. But that is just, well, to use some of the governor's frankness, it's bullshit!"

The next day, the House attempts to override Ventura's veto but falls three votes short of a two-thirds majority needed to do so. Many Democrats vote against the override to protest cuts to education in the budget deal, not because they're taking the governor's side. It's only a temporary victory for Ventura. One day later, after some backroom negotiating, the veto is reconsidered on the House floor and is overridden on a ninety-nine to thirty-three vote, nine votes more than necessary. The Senate follows suit and votes sixty to seven to override the veto, officially putting the legislature's budget-balancing plan into law.

Later that week Ventura broadcasts his radio show from an elementary school in Roseville, a suburb of St. Paul. First, he puts on a red-striped Dr. Seuss hat and reads *The Cat in the Hat* to a group of first-graders. He later admits to them that his favorite book isn't a Dr. Seuss book. No, he tells the impressionable seven-year-olds that his favorite book is *Helter Skelter*, the story of Charles Manson's murder spree in the late 1960s.

Later in the program, the governor jabs the legislature for overriding his veto and putting what he calls an "inadequate" budget bill into law. After the broadcast, he tells reporters that he's particularly irked because the bill cuts the budget for his personal security detail by $175,000. He hints that he might save the money by closing the governor's mansion so state troopers no longer have to guard it. "When dignitaries would come, we could have them up to the capitol and we could order Chinese and Domino's [pizza]," Ventura says, only half-joking. He also seems to be only half-joking when asked if he'd start carrying a concealed handgun for protection. "They might make me," he says, after opening his coat and showing reporters he's not packing heat today.

Ventura can't resist a final dramatic ploy to draw attention to his displeasure. On March 7, a week after the budget bill went into law, he shows up unannounced at the office of state senator Dean Johnson. "This large body stood in my door," says Johnson, a Lutheran minister who chairs the Transportation and Public Safety Budget Committee that recommended and passed the cuts in Ventura's security budget. "He said, 'I'm not taking security away from my wife, from my children, from the lieutenant governor, and you're not taking it away from me.'"

Ventura tells Johnson he'll carry through on his threat to close the governor's mansion on April 30 and move permanently to his Maple Grove ranch to save money on security costs. Ventura rarely spends time at the mansion anyway, other than for ceremonial events and meetings. Clearly, the governor takes the cuts to his security very personally. In fact, at a meeting with House and Senate leaders two weeks earlier, after first learning of the possible cuts, he asked them, "Why do you hate me and my family?" Johnson is still trying to convince him that has nothing to do with this decision. "And I told the governor, 'We don't hate you,'" Johnson says. "That's not the point of this. This is not personal. This is not about Jesse Ventura. This is about trying to balance a budget."

Ventura can't be convinced it's not personal. The day after his confrontation with Johnson, the governor points out that his office budget was cut nearly twice as much as that of the legislature and other state executive officers, like the attorney general and secretary of state. He complains they've even cut funding for the governor's Washington, D.C., office. "It's a battle for power," Ventura says on his next weekly radio show, this time broadcast from a school in Montevideo, Minnesota, a couple of hours west of the Twin Cities. "This is a way of eliminating an independent governor by hand-tying me, making it where we can't even function."

He also complains that he doesn't get nearly as much protection as other governors. "When Governor Gray Davis of California travels throughout the country, he has thirteen people with him to protect him. How many people here would know Governor Davis if he walked in the room right now?" he asks the audience listening to his broadcast at the school. No one raises a hand. "Nobody? Yet when Governor Ventura travels, he has two people. It's really embarrassing." For the record, I've been on trips where three or four Minnesota state troopers accompanied him. According to Department of Public Safety records, since Ventura took office, Minnesota taxpayers shelled out $2.3 million in overtime pay to state troopers protecting him. That's more than double the amount paid during the final term of Ventura's predecessor.

The squabbles over Ventura's security and the governor's mansion garner plenty of attention, but Minnesotans have resigned themselves to such disputes from the start. Don't forget, the ink was barely dry on the 1998 election returns when he started complaining that his wife wouldn't get paid a nickel to be Minnesota's First Lady. During his first legislative session he led the charge to repeal a $50 state-imposed surcharge on personal watercraft, primarily because *he* owns five of them. You'll also recall he wanted to lower auto license tab fees because the rate was so high for *his* Porsche. This kind of Ventura-centric governing style is the norm.

While many Minnesotans may take it in stride, legislators still seize on it whenever they can. On March 26 Ventura vetoed a bill that prohibits auto-glass companies from offering free steaks and cash rebates to customers. Lawmakers voted in favor of the bill because those incentives were contributing to higher auto-glass costs for insurance companies, who passed them on in higher premiums. Ventura vetoed it because he saw it as another government intrusion on private enterprise. But many lawmakers zero in on the fact he admitted on his weekly radio show that a friend in the auto-glass industry told him to veto it because it could hurt his business.

The House and Senate immediately and successfully move to override the veto. Senator James Metzen, one of the bill's authors, rises on the Senate floor and says he's not concerned about the governor's "buddy" or his auto-glass business. "I'm doing it for the consumers of Minnesota who are getting ripped off," Metzen says. In the House even members who don't normally engage in the Ventura-bashing rise to denounce his veto. "First of all it was the license plates, then it was the Jet Skis, then the bodyguards and the extracurricular activities," says a peeved Representative Luanne Koskinen of Coon Rapids, one of the northern Twin Cities suburbs where Ventura had strong support in 1998. "Every action the governor has supported has been specifically geared to his personal needs, and, frankly, I'm sick of it."

Legislators might be sick of it, but that doesn't necessarily mean most Minnesotans feel that way. Ventura was elected because many Minnesotans liked that he looked at things from the perspective of an "average" voter rather than of a politician in an ivory tower. Sure, he didn't like paying high license-tab fees on his Porsche, but most Minnesotans didn't like paying high fees for their Buicks and Chevrolets. Ventura did something about it. You would also be hard-pressed to find personal-watercraft owners who liked paying a $50 annual surcharge on each machine they owned. Ventura saw to it they wouldn't have to. High property taxes were another pet peeve of many Minnesota taxpayers. Ventura said he'd do something about it and he did. And I'd bet a lot of Minnesotans liked that free box of steaks with their auto-glass replacement and don't think eliminating that will reduce their insurance premiums one nickel.

April Fool

On April Fool's Day Ventura hastily calls a news conference. He doesn't inform anyone, even his staff, of the topic. For reporters, that means only one thing: don't even think about missing it! Newspaper, television, and radio newsrooms scramble crews through a snowstorm to get in position to cover whatever the governor is cooking up now. When the frazzled crews are in place, Ventura walks to the podium and promises to liven up a slow news day. "You've all been hounding me for months upon months, weeks upon weeks, years upon years of what I'm going to do. Am I going to run again? So I'm here to tell you this morning that yes, I will be seeking another term as governor of the state of Minnesota. That's all I have to say. Any questions?"

Everyone is momentarily stunned. Ventura continues, "Before I get to questions I'd like to maybe clarify one other thing. People have said I've gotten too serious at this job. People have said I've lost my sense of humor. Well, I want you to know I haven't lost it. APRIL FOOLS!" He quickly turns around and disappears into his office.

Ventura has plenty of time for pranks because the legislature continues to freeze him out of the second round of budget-balancing negotiations. With two key leaders in the House and Senate running for governor, Ventura claims it's nothing but an election-year power play. "It's very simply the Republicans and Democrats teaming up together to eliminate the third-party movement," he says.

By the end of April Ventura makes his own power play: he follows through on his threat to close the governor's mansion because the legislature won't restore $375,000 in funding for his security detail and operation of the mansion. On April 29, just three weeks before the end of what could be his final legislative session, workers from two museums begin removing artwork and antique furniture from the governor's official residence. Many of the art and furnishings are on loan to the state and will now be put into storage. The moving trucks backed up to the Minnesota governor's mansion are national news, demonstrating the state's severe financial woes.

Critics of the governor say he's using the mansion as an undignified political pawn. Ventura says he's just being prudent, cutting a luxury item rather than some vital state service from his budget. He blames the legislature for unfairly targeting his office for budget cuts. "I'll be blunt," he tells reporters. "This wouldn't be happening if there were a Democrat or Republican in this office. Their main goal is to get the big enchilada, which is my office."

Ventura makes one major miscalculation in deciding to close the mansion. He suddenly finds himself in the political ring with eighty-three-year-old Olivia Irvine Dodge, the only surviving member of the Horace Irvine family, who built the twenty-room mansion in 1910 and donated it to the state in 1965. She's outraged. "I am sure most Minnesotans feel betrayal, as I do, that the doors to 1006 Summit Avenue are going to be shut in our faces and locked," she says at a news conference on the front steps of her West St. Paul home. Ventura wanted this debate framed as him against the legislature. Instead, in the eyes of the public, it's now Jesse Ventura versus Mrs. Dodge—not exactly the macho matchup he wants in newspaper headlines. This genteel, soft-spoken woman isn't afraid to go toe-to-toe with Ventura, criticizing the use of her family home as a political football. "I have heard several people say to me that they are embarrassed by such unseemly behavior. I wholeheartedly concur. A residence that has been given with such love and pride should be treated with respect."

Despite her protests, Ventura and his family pack up their personal belongings and move out. Eight workers at the residence are laid off. The mansion closes as scheduled on April 30, even though attorney general Mike Hatch issues an unofficial legal opinion that the governor does not have the authority to close it. Hatch also renders a stinging personal opinion about the governor and the legislators, saying they're now running a "dysfunctional" government. "I could point the finger all over this place," Hatch says at a news conference in his office, directly across the hall from the governor's office. "The lack of civility. This 'gotcha' type of politics that's going on.... It is a great destruction to the integrity and the reputation of this state. We are making a mockery of ourselves."

Hatch's protestations don't stop legislators from taking another run at Ventura. Just one day after the mansion closing and Hatch's criticism, the House passes a bill that would require the governor to disclose the amount and sources of his outside income. The bill passes 94 to 30 with broad bipartisan support. Representative Matt Entenza, a Democrat, says the governor and the state's other constitutional officers should disclose the information because they oversee $53 billion of state investments. Entenza expresses his concern about possible conflicts of interest. He points out that another state law recently required the governor to reveal that the XFL paid $320,000 worth of expenses for

Ventura in 2001, mostly for private jets and limos. Ventura also had to reveal he holds World Wrestling Federation stock options. Apparently some legislators have convinced themselves the state might decide to invest all its money in WWF stock and create a "conflict of interest" for the governor.

Republican representative Mike Osskopp gets closer to the real reason for the legislation. "We have been insulted over the past three-and-a-half years by a governor who should have run for a part-time legislative position," he bellows during the House floor debate, taking aim at some legislators who are hesitant to vote for the bill. "And now we're playing all these Mickey Mouse games because a couple people are afraid to stand up to a bully. A bully who has gotten rich at the tax-payer's expense." Although the bill sails through the House, it never gets a vote in the Senate.

On May 15, just five days before the legislature is to adjourn, the House and Senate pass a $439 million budget-balancing bill with veto-proof majorities. Just as with the first phase of budget-balancing measures, legislators avoid raising taxes. They authorize more accounting shifts, like moving payments from one year to another, and use up what little is left of budget reserves. Ventura gets one small victory: the bill restores the $375,000 for his security and the mansion. Still, Ventura blasts the plan on his weekly radio show, calling it "Enron-omics" in honor of the infamous energy company that used shady accounting methods to mask its plunge into bankruptcy. He calls the two parties "Enronicans" and "Enronocrats."

The legislature convenes for a rare Saturday session on May 18 to await a budget veto from the governor so it can quickly override him again. The governor keeps the legislators guessing by playing golf all afternoon while they scurry to finish work on several major bills. He finally arrives at the State Capitol about 7 P.M. and immediately calls a news conference. "I said I would not be a part of a political solution that would put this state in fiscal jeopardy and therefore I have vetoed [the budget bill]," Ventura announces in his reception room. "I do not want my fingerprints on it in any way, shape, or form." Ventura claims the bill is just a short-term fix that leaves the state facing a $2.5 billion deficit for the next budget cycle.

The House and Senate override the veto with no debate and the budget is again balanced with no input from Ventura. It's the twelfth override of a Ventura veto, compared to four overrides for the previous twelve governors combined, dating back to 1939. But Ventura still has power. Two bills pass the House and Senate with overwhelming bipartisan support, including a bonding bill with $979 million worth of building projects around the state, and a Pledge of Allegiance bill that would require public school students to recite the pledge. Both pass with veto-proof majorities, but legislators waited so long to pass them that they will be forced to adjourn before they can override any vetoes.

Ventura has a gleam in his eye and his veto pen ready. He vetoes the Pledge of Allegiance bill, saying patriotism should be voluntary, not mandatory. He outrages some legislators when he states that forcing kids to recite the pledge is something the Taliban, the Nazis, and Fidel Castro would do. As for the bonding bill, even before it passed he threatened to be a "samurai governor" and chop the bill down to size. A few days after the session he line-item vetoes more than one hundred projects from the bill, totaling a whopping $357 million. Senate Majority Leader Roger Moe calls the vetoes nothing more than "petty, vindictive politics." Ventura simply says the state can't afford to borrow money for all those projects because the legislature passed an irresponsible budget bill. "If I don't keep an eye on the state's finances, who will? Certainly not legislators."

It's a fitting way to end Ventura's fourth legislative session, resembling the "cage matches" from his wrestling days: the governor and legislators locked in battle at the State Capitol, circling each other, taking the occasional cheap shot, and pouncing on one another whenever they sense a weakness.

On the final day of the session, May 20, 2002, Ventura finally admits what many of us have surmised from day one. He's on Minnesota Public Radio when a woman calls to say she agrees with many of Ventura's views but can't stand his governing style. "I think you need to improve your leadership skills and quit all this backstabbing and finger-pointing," she tells him.

Ventura answers bluntly and honestly. "People need to remember I was a villain in the world of pro wrestling for fifteen years, and as a villain your job was to offend people. Your job was to be outspoken, bombastic. And it's very difficult to get away from that persona when you did it for so many years. As a villain in wrestling you're forced to be confrontational. That's how you make your money."

That explains everything.

Less than one month later Governor Ventura marks the beginning of the end of his bumpy, gubernatorial thrill ride in the same venue where it began: talk radio. On June 17 he abruptly announces on Minnesota Public Radio that he will not seek reelection because he can no longer give his "heart and soul" to the job and he wants to restore his family's privacy. Not surprisingly, the announcement comes amid new controversy. Several former staff members fired from the governor's mansion claim that Ventura's twenty-two-year-old son, Tyrel, hosted a series of small parties in the governor's mansion over the previous three years. Some of the parties might have involved underage drinking, minor damage to antique furniture, and messes left behind for the mansion staff to clean up, including a "hat full of vomit" left on a night stand.

There is also a remarkable acknowledgment by State Patrol security guards that Tyrel Ventura allowed a man he barely knew to live at the mansion for a few weeks. This man turned out to be a con artist with a criminal record who convinced Tyrel he was the cousin of a Hollywood actor. According to the mansion staff, Governor Ventura and his wife instructed them to treat the twenty-two-year-old man like "family." And they did: the chef made his meals and the housekeepers did his laundry. He wasn't kicked out of the mansion until Tyrel became suspicious and had state troopers run a background check on him. The impostor was then thrown out.

During an interview in his office an hour after his announcement on talk radio, Ventura insisted to me he made the decision not to run again weeks ago, and the latest flap over the mansion was not a major factor. "I wanted to get it over with so the media would quit attacking my family," he emphasizes defiantly, noting that television stations devoted more time to the mansion story than to his recent trade mission to China. "That wasn't newsworthy enough, but reporting this garbage on my son, they all jump on board to do that." He says the allegations are coming from disgruntled former employees trying to settle a score. "They're taking two or three incidents that happened over a three-year period and they're trying to portray it that this happened every night. Yes, one kid, Tyrel's cousin, got sick one night and threw up. Big deal! Who hasn't had someone throw up in their house before?" Again, he leaves me speechless.

The first weeks and months after his election Ventura was treated like a rock star everywhere he went. He was so blindly popular for a time that he seemingly could do no wrong. He represented change and hope and unlimited possibilities because he was different, refreshing, and brutally honest.

These are the things Minnesotans like about Ventura. Where he loses a lot of support is in the abrasive way he goes about accomplishing things. Take education funding, for example. Ventura echoes many Minnesotans when he questions what taxpayers are getting for the *$8.7 billion* they'll spend on K–12 education over a two-year period. He has every right to demand accountability for how that money is spent. But bashing teachers, the media, and anyone else who questions his viewpoint that education finance is an "endless pit" results in people focusing too much on his antics and not enough on his message. The same can be said of nearly every time he has difficulty getting things his way, whether it's the budget or a unicameral legislature.

The Ventura administration can point to many innovative successes along the way, including historic property-tax reform and relief, across-the-board income-tax cuts, three straight tax-free rebates of surplus revenue, a dramatic lowering of automobile license-tab fees, final approval of a light-rail system, and even the framework of a public-financing deal for a new stadium to save the Minnesota Twins. The last accomplishment is no small feat when you consider that the controversial stadium issue bedeviled the previous governor and legislature for seven years. Not wanting any of these accomplishments to go unnoticed, Ventura launched www.bigplan.com to keep citizens informed of his good deeds.

But the governor also raised doubts among his supporters. Although his tax-increase plans weren't implemented, he did *propose* raising taxes over a three-year period by $1.7 billion, despite his "no new taxes" pledge being the centerpiece of his 1998 campaign. That prompted Minnesota's Republican Party to launch its own Web site, www.bigpromises.com, to alert voters to the governor's "broken" promises.

There have been failures as well. State spending has grown nearly 25 percent under Ventura's watch, despite a pledge to keep a lid on spending. He talks a good game on campaign-finance reform but hasn't used his bully pulpit as effectively as he could to force the legislature to make it happen. Legislative reforms like the unicameral idea went nowhere and probably took up a lot of time in the legislature that would have been better spent on other issues.

One pledge Ventura hasn't broken is his promise to always speak his mind, no matter how unpopular his opinion might be. Sure, he's apologized a few times, but reluctantly and only when persuaded by his political advisers. And nearly every time, he later recants his apology when the controversy-of-the-day subsides. There's no question he relishes the "bad guy" image he carried with him from the professional-wrestling ring to the political ring. On *Larry King Live*, Ventura once said he always liked the bad-guy role because "you don't have to be nice to anyone unless you want to."

In one-on-one situations, Governor Ventura *can* be a genuinely nice guy with an engaging, if not a bit self-centered, personality. His ability to get large segments of the population debating nerdy issues like unicameral government, campaign-finance reform, and per-pupil school-funding formulas is amazing. And yet, after observing Ventura up close for several years, I've come to believe he has a sincere interest in public service, but not a passion for it. That plays into one common thread through his years as governor: difficulty setting aside his self-interest to perform his job in the public interest. In 1999 and 2000 it was the World Wrestling Federation, cross-country book tours, and even *The Young and the Restless*. During the 2001 legislative session he spent nearly every weekend broadcasting XFL football games when he could have been focusing more on signals that the state and national economy were weakening. When the Minnesota Twins were threatened with contraction in November 2001, he jetted off to Hollywood to shoot a cameo role in *Master of Disguise*, a Dana Carvey movie, when he said he was too busy with state business to worry about the Twins. During the budget-slashing 2002 legislative session, Ventura spent time consulting with producers who paid him for the rights to a Broadway musical based on his life.

It's hard to say whether Jesse Ventura could have come from nowhere to win a governor's race if his campaign had been in the post–September 11 era rather than in 1998, during a time of unparalleled peace and prosperity. It seems that, post–September 11, voters would seek more experienced and serious leadership. Ventura does have the experience now and has proven to be capable, but his political gyroscope is so mercurial he isn't always taken seriously. On the other hand, some people say that's what makes him so refreshing.

Ventura shows no interest in playing down his celebrity in favor of a more cerebral approach to governing. In the midst of the 2002 session, while legislators haggle over details of how to balance the state's budget, he makes appearances on several national television talk shows, including Fox Sports Net's *Best Damn Sports Show Period.* Comedian Tom Arnold asks the governor via satellite how he's managed to stay married to the same woman for so many years. Without hesitation, Ventura blurts out, "Sex!"

You can't help but wonder how many people watching around the country sit there, shake their heads, and think, "I could never imagine *my* governor saying something like that." And there's probably an equal number out there wishing their governor *would* say something like that. Just once.

Index

campaign-finance reform, 112, 328, 335–36

campaign manager. *See* Friedline, Doug

Canterbury Park: election day at, 29–41

"Can't Touch This" debate, 300–302

capital bonding budget for 2000, 285

capital bonding projects, 367

"career politicians": campaign against, 25; Ventura as antidote to, xii

Carlson, Arne, 76, 130; criticism of Ventura and budget deficit, 387; election in 1994, 34; ethics law signed by, 70; fishing opener of, 164; on governor's security force, 170; at inauguration, 80; income-tax rebate plan, 68–69; supporting Coleman on election day, 35; testifying against Ventura, 346–47; trade missions of, 280; on University of Minnesota funding, 351; Ventura's meeting with, as governor-elect, 43, 44

Carlson, Barbara, 241, 246

Carlson, Jodi-Michaelle, 165

Carruthers, Phil, 34

Carter, Jimmy, 238, 263, 264, 310

Carter, Julien, 329, 331

Catholic League, 245

Cato Institute: luncheon at, 137

celebrity candidate: Ventura as, 7–8

Central Lakes College: debate at, 12–13

Chad and Barreiro talk show: Ventura's defense of Bosacker on, 325–26

Champlin Park High School: coaching at, 46, 49–50

Chicago: promoting Minnesota tourism in, 308–9

chief of staff. *See* Bosacker, Steven

chief political strategist. *See* Barkley, Dean

Children, Families, and Learning commissioner, 85

China: promoting admission to WTO of, 302–3, 310–11

Chirhirt, Nick, 24

Chyna, 199–200, 213, 224–25

Citizen Outreach office: *Playboy* interview and calls to, 258

Clark, Joe, 168

Clinton, Bill, xi, xii, 160, 267, 313; at governors dinner at White House, 107, 108; impeachment hearings, 74; invitation to stay in Lincoln Bedroom, 320–21; at National Governors Conference (1999), 211–12; promoting China's admission to WTO, 310–11; Ventura on behavior of, 52–53; Ventura's testimony before House Ways and Means and, 302–3

Clinton, Hillary Rodham: at governors dinner at White House, 107, 108; remarks during campaign, 23, 52

CNN: Internet poll about Ventura's election, 43; interview at National Governors Conference (1998), 57

Tom Hauser is the chief political reporter for KSTP-TV in Minneapolis–St. Paul, where his primary responsibilities are covering Governor Jesse Ventura, the Minnesota legislature, and the Minnesota congressional delegation. He has been a television journalist for eighteen years.